FLORIDA

GOLF GUIDE

YOUR PASSPORT TO GREAT GOLF!

ABOUT THE AUTHOR

Nobody knows Florida's great golf courses like Jimmy Shaclky, an avid golfer who's been playing Florida's golf courses for many years. In addition to FLORIDA GOLF GUIDE, Shacky is also the author of GOLF COURSES OF THE SOUTHWEST and GOLF COURSES OFNEW YORK/NEW JERSEY (Open Road Publishing). He lives in Coral Springs, Florida.

ACKNOWLEDGMENTS

I would like to the many people who have contributed their time and patience. These include the hundreds of owners, pro-shop staff, golfing pros, and management personnel who have generously cooperated in the writing of this book; Avery Cardoza and Jonathan Stein, and the rest of the staff at Open Road Publishing,for their helpful criticism and direction; William W. (Bill) Amick and Bill Love, for supplying me with a greater understanding of golf architecture; to David Fishman, Joe Traister, Rebel, and Kenny Wolf, who have collectively contributed to my computer knowledge and have always been there to answer my questions; and finally, to Julian and Lindy Silberstang, without whom this book would never have come to fruition.

Once again, I thank you all.

FLORIDA
GOLF GUIDE

YOUR PASSPORT TO GREAT GOLF!

JIMMY SHACKY

OPEN ROAD PUBLISHING

2nd Edition

Dedicated to my Date-A-Base partners:
Judy, Paul, Kenny, Laura, and Ilene ... I love you all!

Front and back cover photos courtesy of Bonaventure Resort & Country Club, Ft. Lauderdale.

CONTENTS

INDEX   217

MAPS

FOREWORD BY BILL AMICK

What pleasure and variety the more than 1,000 golf courses in Florida offer its hundreds of thousands of golfing residents and tens of millions of visitors! Whether you're a native Floridian, are planning to move here, or are coming down for a few refreshing days of great golf, **FLORIDA GOLF GUIDE** is the book for you.

This handy book gives you the vital statistics you'll need about each public and private course in Florida. Think of it as an encyclopedia of golf courses, covering the entire state, from the panhandle to the keys. This is your comprehensive guide to finding and playing the golf courses that will best suit your game.

As a golfer, I am extremely interested in this book. Because I have practiced golf course architecture in Florida for 35 years, I especially appreciate the details the book reveals about our state's golf courses. The Sunshine State is a special place for my profession. Nearly all of the great golf architects have designed courses in Florida. There's Donald Ross's classic *Seminole* course in Palm Beach County, Robert Trent Jones' *Inverrary* in Ft. Lauderdale, Dick Wilson's *Blue Monster* at Doral in Miami, and Pete Dye's *TPC Stadium Course* at Ponte Vedra, perhaps the most widely publicized course today, and more.

Nearly all Florida courses are beautifully landscaped works of art and golfing strategy. This book tells not only who designed each course, but also shows you how to get there, what to expect when you arrive, and gives a brief description of each course, from the first tee to the final green.

Golfers love new challenges. One of the exceptional appeals of golf is that each course is unique; each one has its own look, feel, and personality - like people! This book shows you the differences between courses so you can make an informed decision about where to play.

For your convenience and increased golfing enjoyment, Jimmy Shacky has gathered the most useful specifics about eahc course within the state. We golfers should make full use of the information contained in **FLORIDA GOLF GUIDE** to pick thebest courses to play.

So now you have no excuse for not finding a golf course that ideally suits you and your game. But you're strictly on your own when it comes to hitting fairways or water hazards, leaving it in or getting it close from sand bunkers, and one-putting, not three-putting, greens! No book is going to make those differences for you - only golfing more will help you with those.

This book can, however, help you find all those great Florida courses that you've always wanted to try - whether your aim is to improve that score or just enjoy a fun, sunny day on the links.

Happy golfing!

William W. "Bill" Amick, one of Florida's foremost golf course architects, has designed or remodeled 38 Florida golf courses. He resides in Daytona Beach, Florida, and is a member of the American Society of Golf Course Architects.

INTRODUCTION

Florida conjures up images of sunny skies, tall palm trees, and a never-ending oceanfront bordered by flat land. For the golfer, Florida is much more: it's beautiful ocean links courses with deep contours and natural bunkers, open to the windy and unpredictable winds off the Atlantic. It's inland courses hidden in deep forests and built on gently rolling terrain, set amidst mature pine trees and majestic oaks. It's playing in the middle of Mother Nature's playground: a mother fox watching her young play in the morning dew, a ground owl popping up to watch you take your swing, a family of spotted deer gracefully dashing across the fairway, an otter diving into a stream.

With more than 1,000 golf courses to choose from, you'll find no shortage of fun and exciting places to play. The weather is unbeatable year-round: picture yourself playing a round in the perfect December breeze of a Florida winter! That's one reason the PGA (Professional Golf Association), the LPGA (Ladies PGA), the Senior PGA, and many other prominent golf organizations and tournaments have made Florida their home.

This book offers comprehensive descriptions of every public and private course in Florida. It gives you a feel for how each course looks and plays, with all the important statistics you need to make an informed decision on where to play.

Every detail is covered: course type, year built, architect, local pro, amount of holes per locale, yardage, rating and slope, how many days in advance to place a tee time, price differences during peak and slow times, amenities, credit cards accepted, whether there's a driving range, practice greens, locker rooms, rental clubs, walkers, snack bars, restaurants, lounges, meeting rooms, and more!

Golfing in Florida can be one of the most exciting and memorable golf experiences you'll ever have, if you know what you're looking for. If you love the game of golf as much as I do, you'll find this book a complete reference guide to some of the world's greatest golf courses. From the most popular to the most remote, discover for yourself the fantastic diversity that Florida offers golfers of all skills.

Whether you're traveling to Florida for business or pleasure, whether you live in the Sunshine State or are visiting for the first time, the FLORIDA GOLF GUIDE is a unique, entertaining, and valuable resource. I'm certain you'll use this book again and again.

THE GROWTH OF GOLF

The game of golf as we know it today originated in the British Isles hundreds of years ago. Along the coast of Scotland where rivers like the Forth and Eden empty into the sea, the land many now refer to as "linksland" was formed by the forces of nature into a golfers' paradise. Nearby towns utilized the linksland mainly for agricultural purposes and grazing livestock, but because of its unique characteristics, linksland also afforded the townspeople a natural setting in which to create courses and play golf.

Early courses simply evolved from the linksland as a result of nature and become known by the names of the town nearby, such as Prestwick, Guillane, and Leith. The most notable of the early courses was St. Andrews, considered by many to be the "home" of golf. Records indicate a golf course existed in some form at St. Andrews as early as 1414. It was eventually designated "The Royal and Ancient Golf Club of St. Andrews." The rules of the game were first administered out of St. Andrews, and this course became the standard with which other courses were compared.

As the number of people interested in golf steadily increased, early courses were expanded and new ones "discovered" in the linksland. These golf courses served as a focal point around which towns grew, providing recreational activity and open space for the townspeople. For many of these small towns, golf became a part of everyday life; even people who did not play the game would stroll through the linksland and watch their neighbors pursue the sport.

By the mid-1800's, golf had spread throughout the British Isles along the coasts and inland, as well as in parts of Europe. Around the turn of the century, a great number of new golf courses were put into play due to the growing popularity of the game.

Golf was first introduced to the United States in the late 1700's, but it did not really become established until the late 1800's by Americans returning from vacationing in Great Britain. These golfers set about creating the first simple courses in order to continue playing the game they had enjoyed overseas. Before the turn of the century, many golf clubs had formed and the United States Golf Association was established to administer the game. In the 1900's, there were almost 1,000 golf courses in this country, more than the number in Britain.

Since then, golf has experienced periods of tremendous growth, especially in the late 1920's. This period is often referred to as the "golden age of golf." Popular golfers, such as Bobby Jones, competed for championships both at home and abroad, bringing national attention to the sport and generating more interest with the general public. As a result, there was a growing demand for new golf courses.

It has been estimated that approximately 500 new courses a year were being developed toward the end of the 1920's. Even at this rate the need for more courses continued as interest and the number of people playing golf increased during the Depression and World War II, the attention of the country was directed toward more pressing matters, and this slowed the growth of golf. At the beginning of the 1950's, there were an estimated three million golfers in the U.S. playing on 5,000 facilities. The popularity of major golf tournaments, professional golf tours, and the increased exposure from television coverage during this decade heightened the general public's interest in the game and refueled the growth of golf. By the 1960's, there were over four million people playing on almost 6,000 facilities. Golf was entering another "boom" period.

Heading into the 1970's, there were over nine million golfers and the demand for new courses accelerated. The number of new facilities however, had not kept pace, with only 10,000 courses.

The 1970's and 1980's experienced periods of economic recession and the fuel crisis. In spite of this, golf continued to grow by providing an affordable recreational activity that was conveniently located and accessible to many people. The demand for new golf courses was stronger than ever, with the number of golfers exceeding 17 million by the mid-1980's. These golfers played over 400 million rounds of golf on 12,000 facilities. This trend has continued, and today there are more than 27 million people playing the game at a rate of about 500 million times a year. Still, the number of golf courses has only reached 14,000.

Golf is now more popular in the US then it's ever been before. Based on current and projected participation rates, the number of rounds played in this country is expected to double by the end of the century. The demand for the development of new golf courses to meet the need of this growing golf population is expected to continue well into the future. Although golf may have had its beginning in the US among small select groups, now people of all ages and backgrounds are experiencing the pleasure and recreational benefits of this great game.

1. Cornish, Geoffrey S. and Whitton, Ronald E. The Golf Course (New York: Rutledge Press, Rev. 1987).
2. Golf Facilities in the United States (Jupiter, Florida: National Golf Foundation, 1991) and Golf Reference and Media Guide (Jupiter, Florida: National Golf Foundation, 1991).

THE DEVELOPMENT OF GOLF COURSES

The first golf courses of the British Isles came about in linksland areas because they were ideally suited to the game. Linksland is characterized by distinct features such as dunes or small hills and numerous hollows, covered with native grasses and few, if any trees. The soil in the linksland is typically sand-based with excellent drainage, and provides ideal conditions for growing grass. Recognizing these inherent characteristics, it was easy for the early golfers to walk among the dunes and select certain grassy hollows as the first golf holes. There were no standards to follow for laying out a golf course at this time, so a series of holes were simply selected with a routing that often ran along the coast and returned near to the starting point. The number of holes varied from course to course, and when it became desirable to enlarge the golf course, the players could simply venture farther into the linksland and discover more holes.

There was very little construction involved in these initial courses because of their advantageous settings and natural features. Even when the first man-made modifications occurred, they were done in concert with the existing land. As golf moved out of the linksland, new courses had to be constructed on sites that were not as well suited to golf as the seaside locations. Construction techniques were primitive at that time, relying on hand labor and equipment drawn by mules or oxen. The early architects were limited in what could be done to alter the landscape in building a new course. They worked carefully with the topography and existing features to avoid excessive disturbance as well as time and expense in construction.

Early courses in the U.S. often followed this tradition. Sites were selected for their inherent character and the ability to produce an outstanding test of golf. Some of the golf courses built in this country years ago, such as Pebble Beach and Cypress Point with their magnificent oceanside holes, Augusta National with tall Georgia pines lining holes that play over and around Rae's Creek, and Shinnecock Hills winding its way through the wind-blown landscape of Long Island, are still acknowledged as among the best in the game. These courses were carefully designed in response to their sites, and have since functioned compatibly as an integral part of their environments. The appeal of these golf courses can be attributed to the feeling that each course seems to belong in its setting.

Not all golf course development since the early years has been based solely on site selection. The growth of the game required that new facilities be more accessible to the public. During the "boom" periods, new golf courses tended to be located where the demand was the greatest. Since the 1950's, trends have been established in this country, producing golf courses in roles other than as private clubs. New residential developments contain courses as an amenity for enhancement, and vacation destinations include golf to serve as an added attraction. Perhaps the most significant trend, however, has been the increase in public golf courses which provide an affordable recreational activity for local communities. Prior to the 50's and 60's, private golf facilities outnumbered public. In 1990 the number of daily fee and municipal courses for public use was almost double that of private facilities.

Today sites are being selected for demographic and economic purposes as well as for their suitability as golf courses. Modern construction methods have made it possible to build golf courses in locations where there is a demand for new facilities Not all locations offer sites with an outstanding natural character. Often they contain no significant land forms, water features, trees or scenery. In some cases golf courses have been specifically developed to enhance the visual quality of feature-less sites and provide an attractive green, open space. Sites that have been mismanaged or abandoned after extensive use as agricultural fields, stone quarries, gravel pits, landfills, sludge disposal sites or other operations which degrade the land, can be reclaimed, improved and beautified through use as a golf course.

Bill Love is Chairman of the Environmental Committee
of the American Society Of Golf Course Architects.

HOW TO USE THIS BOOK

I've divided the State of Florida into seven regions. The following is a step-by-step breakdown of how each of these regions is represented. Each chapter begins with the regional name located at the top of the page.

NORTHWEST REGION

If an area is known by a secondary name (Panhandle in the example below), a forward slash is used to separate the primary name (Northwest) from the secondary.

NORTHWEST / PANHANDLE REGION

A regional map of the area is provided in the following manner:

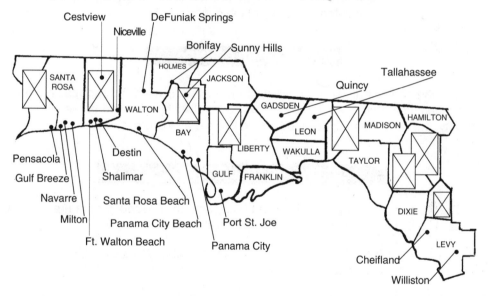

Each of the seven maps in this book clearly display the counties within a region followed by the cities within the counties. If you would take a look at the south-east corner of the map above, Levy County should easily come into view. The only cities

that are shown are the ones that feature golf courses for their county. They are attached by a straight line leading into a bullet-mark. The bullet-marks indicate the general location of each city within the county.

An aerial view of the region, within the context of the state, is provided to give you a general idea of its relation between the other six remaining regions. The black portion of this map identifies the Northwest / Panhandle Region.

Each regional page provides a **Top Ten** list of their finest courses along with their county names. These courses are consistently rewarded with the highest recommendations by both regional and national golf publications.

An opening description is provided to enhance your golfing knowledge of the region. Use it as a mood enhancer to influence your choice of play.

Average quarterly temperatures are provided on the bottom of each regional page.

FINDING THE RIGHT COURSE

Each course listing can be found in one of three ways.

1. Region: Regional names and their following page numbers are listed in the Table of Contents.

2. County: County names and their appropriate page numbers are listed in the Table of Contents. The names are written in white type on the title bar located at the top of every page:

BROWARD COUNTY

County names are listed in alphabetical order. Keep in mind that each page covers two independent courses. If the second course listing is located in the following county, both counties will be listed on the title bar as follows:

BROWARD / DADE COUNTIES

The title bar above indicates the county location of the two courses featured on the page. The first will be in Broward, the second in Dade.

3. Name: If you know the name of the course that you want to play, you can look it up in the Index .

COURSE LISTINGS

The following pages show the breakdown of the format used for each course listing.

Below the county title, you'll find the corresponding courses with their detailed information in alphabetical order. Look at the example below (Bonaventure Country Club). It is the first section that you will see directly below the title bar:

BONAVENTURE COUNTRY CLUB
200 Bonaventure Blvd., Ft. Lauderdale, FL 33326 / (305) 389-2100

The **BONAVENTURE COUNTRY CLUB** is the Name of the proper establishment and is followed by the course Address, City, State, Zip, Area Code and Phone Number.

The Phone Numbers listed are for the Pro Shop of each establishment. It is by far the quickest way to place your tee time or make an appointment with a golfing professional for a private lesson.

BASIC INFORMATION

Course Type: Semi-private
Year Built: 1969
Architect: J. Lee
Local Pro: Randy Webber

Course: East (18 / Par 72)
Holes: 36

Back: 7,011 yds. Rating: 74.2 Slope: 132
Middle: 6,557 yds. Rating: 72.5 Slope: 127
Ladies: 5,304 yds. Rating: 71.6 Slope: 122

Tee Time: 3 days in advance
Price: $35 - $65

Credit Cards: ■	Restaurant: ■	
Driving Range: ■	Lounge: ■	
Practice Green: ■	Meeting Rooms: ■	
Locker Room: ■	Tennis: ■	
Rental Clubs: ■	Swimming: ■	
Walkers:	Jogging Trails: ■	
Snack Bar: ■	Boating:	

This is the **BASIC INFORMATION** box that is included with every course description. Let's have a look at all of the individual sections.

Course Type: Most area golfers play on public courses, and this book's coverage of public courses is extensive. Many other types of courses allow non-members to play. Here is a listing and a definition for each title:

A **Municipal** course is one that is owned and operated by a local governing body. These courses are open to the general public without membership.

A **Public** course is one that is privately owned by a single owner or a corporation. Play is open to the general public. Many offer annual memberships at a discount rate.

A **Semi-private** course is one that is also owned privately or by a corporation. Like municipal and public courses, these courses are open to the general public. There is a slight difference between a semi-private course and a public or municipal course. The semi-private course members have priority in certain respects, especially as to reservations. Non-members should not feel out-of-place. Your business is the fuel that keeps these courses in prime condition.

A **Private** course is one that is reserved for membership play only. These courses are frequently called country clubs. You'll find them listed in the following manner at the end of each regional chapter:

TPC at Eagle Trace
(305) 753-7222
1111 Eagle Trace Blvd., Coral Springs
Local Pro: Scott Gray
Reciprocal Play: Yes

Private courses have a code of ethics that is strictly used throughout the United States. Please adhere to the following principles and practices.

If you happen to be a member of a private course, you may have the opportunity of playing other private courses too. The first thing you'll need to find out is whether the course you want to play will reciprocate with the course that you are a member of. Some courses will only reciprocate with courses in their immediate area and others will only reciprocate with courses out-of-state. There is no rule about reciprocal play. The proper method of communication is to have your golf professional set up an appointment with the pro at the course you want to play.

A **Resort** course is one that is owned and operated by the resort-hotel. These courses offer excellent vacation packages for people both in and out of the state of Florida. Some of these courses are privately run for the guests of the resort only. The great majority of them do allow public play.

Course Type: Semi-private
Year Built: 1969
Architect: J. Lee
Local Pro: Randy Webber
>This is the first section within the Basic Information box. Let's have a look at all of the individual sub-sections.

Course Type: Semi-Private
>The **Course Type** tells you about the type of play that each course allows.

Year Built: 1969 / 1993
>The **Year Built** corresponds to the year the course was opened. Over a certain period of time, courses lose their shape through the forces of nature. If any additional work has been done to the course by anyone after the original architect, a following date after a forward slash will indicate the year the change took place.

Architect: J. Lee / William W. Amick
>The original **Architect's** name will be the one listed primarily. If any additional work had been done to the course by anyone after the original architect, the secondary architect's name will be listed after the forward slash.

Local Pro: Randy Webber
>**Local Pro**: These are the people that you'll want to contact to book lessons. They often have the greatest knowledge of how the course should be played and the elements that you should watch out for.

Course: Champion
Holes: 18 / Par 72
>This is the second section in the Basic Information box. The following will explain both sub-headings.

Course: East (18 / Par 72)

Course: Some establishments have more than just one course for you to choose from. Each course is assigned a different name for easier identification. Many courses simply choose the location of each course from a certain starting point and end up calling their courses "East" and "West." Whenever this situation arose, I chose the course that was most sought after. In this particular example, the East was chosen. Following in parenthesis is the number of holes and the par.

Holes: 36

Holes: This item shows the number of holes for that particular course. if more than one course is featured, the hole number and par move into parenthesis under the sub-heading **Course**. The new number in the sub-heading **Holes** indicates the number of holes available to play.

Course: East (18 / Par 72)
Holes: 36

Looking at the top example to the left, we now know that the main body of the course description will be based on the East course. The numbers in the parenthesis tells us that it's an 18 hole / Par 72 layout. We also know that the establishment offers an additional course by the number 36 indicated in the sub-heading **Holes**.

Note: Some courses offer 27 holes of golf. In most instances they'll tie two courses together to get a total of three layouts for the public to choose from. Others may have as many as 99 holes. Resort establishments are usually the ones that feature the greatest variety of courses under a single location.

Back:	7,011 yds.	**Rating: 74.2**	**Slope: 132**
Middle:	6,557 yds.	**Rating: 72.5**	**Slope: 127**
Ladies:	5,304 yds.	**Rating: 71.6**	**Slope: 122**

As you work your way down the **Basic Information** box, you'll see a section like the one above. It is by far the most important section. The numbers here indicate the length and severity of the course from a number of different starting positions called **tee-markers**. The order of difficulty for these tee-markers are as follows: back tees, middle tees, and ladies tees. Knowing how to read and interpret the numbers in this section will help you choose the best course suited for your game.

Back:	7,011 yds.
Middle:	6,557 yds.
Ladies:	5,304 yds.

This sub-section indicates the total yardage from each of the individual tees. I chose to represent each course with these three sub-sections because it breaks down the entire playing-field to its simplest form. Many of the newer courses offer additional tees for a wider spectrum of players. Most courses color-code their tee-markers, from back to front, in the following way: **Blue** (Back tees), **White** (middle tees), and **Red** (ladies tees).

Rating: 74.2
Rating: 72.5
<u>**Rating: 71.6**</u>

RATING: Course ratings are an indication of how difficult a course is for a **scratch golfer** (a golfer who shoots par or better). This book includes the U.S.G.A. (United States Golf Association) ratings to the extent available. The best way to judge a course sight-unseen is to evaluate both the course rating and the slope rating. Each tee marker has a rating that indicates the difficulty of the distance to be played from that marker.

Here is an example that will help you understand the system. If course #1 and #2 are rated at 71.4, would it be safe to assume that these courses are equally difficult? Can a person judge the severity of play without ever seeing the courses in the first place?

Use this approach: When comparing two different courses, always look at the par rating for both courses. If course #1 is a par 72 at 6,624 yards, and course #2 is a par 70 at 6,515 yards, we now know that both of these courses are relatively the same. The biggest difference between the two is that course #1 is 109 yards longer than course #2 - a possible one stroke difference. The shorter course is harder to play because it is a Par 70 course rather than a Par 72. With a two-stroke difference minus the one-stroke given to the first course, the shorter course is still one stroke harder than the first.

You can also picture it this way. If you take that 109 yard difference and place it on any random hole on course #1, that hole will automatically change to a one-stroke par difference. Say we placed that 109 yard difference on a Par 4 hole that measures 408 yards. It can now be considered a Par 5 at 517 yards. Course #2 still has a one-stroke difference to make up despite its relative length. It is unquestionably the harder of the two.

Slope: 132
Slope: 127
Slope: 122

SLOPE: High handicap players (players that shoot well above par 72) can rely on this secondary system developed by the U.S.G.A.

When comparing two or more courses, the one with the highest slope rating will be the most difficult to play. The U.S.G.A. considers a slope rating of 113 to be of average difficulty. The only way you'll ever get a full understanding of how this number relates to your personal game would be to write down your final score along with the course ratings for the next 10 courses you play in the future.

When you look back at these numbers, pick the courses that you had posted similar numbers on. If their slope ratings are about even or closely related, the average number between them is the number best suited for your game. Always play from the tees that post the closest slope rating to the one you now consider your personal average. This will bring the course down to your playing style and will allow you to have the most amount of fun on a level that is challenging but not over-bearing. If your game has been improving, start playing from the back tees. If you find playing from the back tees too lengthy, search for a course that offers a higher slope rating from the middle tees.

Tee Time: 3 days in advance
Price: $35 - $65

This is the fourth section in the **Basic Information** box. The following will explain both sub-headings.

Tee Time: The numbers in this sub-heading indicate how many days the course will allow you to book a tee time (a reservation to play) in advance.

Note: The numbers used in this book are based on a walk-in scenario. Keep in mind that most of the Resort courses listed in this book will allow you to book a tee-time well in advance if you plan to stay at their establishment. It isn't unusual to post a tee time as far ahead as six months to a year.

Price: $35 - $65

Price: The numbers in this sub-heading indicate the price variance for the entire year based on the lowest to highest price. Prices are subject to change without notice. Please call to confirm.

Credit Cards:	■	Restaurant:	■
Driving Range:	■	Lounge:	■
Practice Green:	■	Meeting Rooms:	■
Locker Room:	■	Tennis:	■
Rental Clubs:	■	Swimming:	■
Walkers:		Jogging Trails:	■
Snack Bar:	■	Boating:	

This is the fifth and last section in the **Basic Information** box. Any listing with a black box next to it indicates that the course offers that item or amenity. A Black box by *Boating* indicates that the course is a half hour away from the ocean or any other body of water by automobile. Some courses only allow walking during certain hours of the day. If that happens to be an objective of yours, please call the course to confirm the proper time of the day.

COURSE DESCRIPTION

You'll find a concise course description for every listing with information that will help you choose the course that you'll want to play. The following is a sample piece:

"Both the East and the West course are exceptional in design and play. The holes are beautifully laid-out and meticulously kept.

The East course is a tremendous challenge, equally enjoyed by professionals and amateurs alike. One of the greatest aspects of this course is that each hole is designed with more than one option off the tee. This will allow you to play conservatively or aggressively depending on your style of play and ability. Water and wind play a big factor.

The 3rd hole, a par-3 that measures 163 yards in length, features a fantastic-looking waterfall that flows beneath a high elevated green."

Golf courses, or their particular holes, are often defined in one of three architectural terms: **Strategic**, **Penal,** and **Heroic**.

Strategic: Strategic holes allow a golfer two driving options off the tee. Think of a dog-leg left hole with water coming into play along the entire left side. Your first option would be to flirt with the water by playing your ball over the water, cutting off as much length from the hole as possible, and having the ball spin back and on to the fairway, leaving you with a simple short length shot to the green. If you're not successful and the ball ends up in the water, you'll be penalized two strokes. The next option would be to eliminate the water completely and play to the safest part of the fairway known as the **bailout** area. From this point you'll have a long and difficult approach shot.

Penal: Penal holes are the most demanding. You can only play the hole one way or you'll end up in a lot of trouble. An island par-3 hole with water dividing the teeing area from the green is a great example. You're forced to hit the ball over water and land it on the green to be successful.

Heroic: Heroic holes are a matter of taste. The basic premise is based on the nature of the terrain that the course was built on. Mountain courses with high elevation changes, desert courses secluded among hundreds of cacti, and oceanside courses with par-3's playing over ocean water fit into this category perfectly.

Some courses feature a healthy combination of all three types.

DIRECTIONS

The **directions** to each course are listed directly below its description. They start from a major highway en route to the course. If you're visiting an area for the first time, make sure you take along a good map.

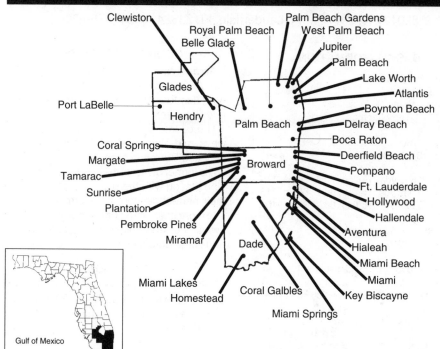

Clewiston
Royal Palm Beach
Belle Glade
Glades
Port LaBelle
Hendry
Coral Springs
Margate
Tamarac
Sunrise
Plantation
Pembroke Pines
Miramar
Miami Lakes
Homestead

Palm Beach Gardens
West Palm Beach
Jupiter
Palm Beach
Lake Worth
Atlantis
Boynton Beach
Palm Beach
Delray Beach
Boca Raton
Broward
Deerfield Beach
Pompano
Ft. Lauderdale
Hollywood
Hallendale
Aventura
Dade
Hialeah
Miami Beach
Miami
Coral Galbles
Key Biscayne
Miami Springs

Gulf of Mexico

TOP TEN

Bonaventure Country Club
(Broward County)

Breakers Ocean Golf Course
(Palm Beach County)

Carolina Club
(Broward County)

Colony West Country Club
(Broward County)

Doral Resort & Country Club
(Dade County)

Emerald Dunes Golf Club
(Palm Beach County)

Jacaranda Golf & C. C.
(Broward County)

Links at Key Biscayne
(Dade County)

PGA National Golf Club
(Broward County)

Turnberry Isle Country Club
(Dade County)

The **Southeast** region is unquestionably the most popular golfing destination in the world. Every year, millions of people from all over the globe come here to play the diverse courses that are available to the general public.

You'll find great historical and contemporary course designs. One of my personal favorites is the Breakers Ocean Golf Course. This course was designed by the late Donald Ross in 1897. It's a monumental tribute to his work. On the contemporary side, the Emerald Dunes Golf Club is one of the finest golf courses in the country. This Tom Fazio-designed course opened in 1990, making it the 1,000th golf course in Florida.

The Top Ten list on the left is simply a beginning. Some of the greatest golfing establishments ever built are described in detail in this chapter.

Average Temperatures (Fahrenheit)

Between **January** and **March** you'll find the low at **61** and the high up to **78**. Between **April** and **June** the low goes down to **69** and the high goes up to **87**. Between **July** and **September** the low goes down to **74** and the high goes up to **92**. And finally, between the months of **October** and **December**, the low goes down to **67** and the high goes up to **82**.

ARROWHEAD GOLF & SPORTS CLUB

8201 S.W. 24th St., Ft. Lauderdale, FL 33324 / (954) 475-8200

BASIC INFORMATION

Course Type: Public
Year Built: 1968
Architect: Watts / R.T. Jones
Local Pro: Terry Lanman

Course: N/A
Holes: 18 / Par 70

Back: 6,506 yds. Rating: 70.8 Slope: 115
Middle: 6,009 yds. Rating: 68.7 Slope: 113
Ladies: 5,025 yds. Rating: 68.7 Slope: 109

Tee Time: 3 days in advance
Price: $15 - $40

Credit Cards:	■	Restaurant:	■
Driving Range:	■	Lounge:	■
Practice Green:	■	Meeting Rooms:	■
Locker Room:		Tennis:	
Rental Clubs:	■	Swimming:	■
Walkers:		Jogging Trails:	
Snack Bar:	■	Boating:	

COURSE DESCRIPTION

Arrowhead has just recently been sold to the American Golf Co., which owns and operates four other courses between Dade and Broward counties.

The course is a nice layout with tight fairways, mid-high rough, and a good variety of elevated Bermuda greens.

The former owner of the course, Earl Morrall, who played with the Miami Dolphins during their perfect season, transformed this club into more than just a golf course. Bastketball; swimming, and volleyball are some of the additional attractions.

DIRECTIONS

Take I-95 to I-595. Go west to University Drive, south to Nova Dr. (24th St.), and west about half a mile to the course. It will be on your right.

BONAVENTURE COUNTRY CLUB

200 Bonaventure Blvd., Ft. Lauderdale, FL 33326 / (954) 389-2100

BASIC INFORMATION

Course Type: Semi-private
Year Built: 1969
Architect: J. Lee
Local Pro: Randy Webber

Course: East (18 / Par 72)
Holes: 36

Back: 7,011 yds. Rating: 74.2 Slope: 132
Middle: 6,557 yds. Rating: 72.5 Slope: 127
Ladies: 5,304 yds. Rating: 71.6 Slope: 122

Tee Time: 3 days in advance
Price: $35 - $65

Credit Cards:	■	Restaurant:	■
Driving Range:	■	Lounge:	■
Practice Green:	■	Meeting Rooms:	■
Locker Room:	■	Tennis:	■
Rental Clubs:	■	Swimming:	■
Walkers:		Jogging Trails:	■
Snack Bar:	■	Boating:	

COURSE DESCRIPTION

Both the East and the West course are exceptional in design and play. The holes are beautifully laid-out and meticulously kept.

The East course is a tremendous challenge, equally enjoyed by professionals and amateurs alike. One of the greatest features of this course is that each hole is designed with more than one option off the tee. This allows you to play conservatively or aggressively, depending on your style of play and ability.

Water and wind play a big factor.

The 3rd hole, a par-3 that measures 163 yards in length, features a lush waterfall that flows beneath a high elevated green.

DIRECTIONS

Take I-595 west to Exit 1. Continue west on Hwy. 84 and make a left at Bonaventure Blvd. The course will be on your left.

BROKEN WOODS COUNTRY CLUB

9001 W. Sample Rd., Coral Springs, FL 33071 / (954) 752-2140

BASIC INFORMATION

Course Type: Public
Year Built: N/A
Architect: N/A
Local Pro: Peter Vitale

Course: N/A
Holes: 18 / Par 71

Back: 6,281 yds. Rating: 66.0 Slope: 118
Middle: 5,695 yds. Rating: 64.0 Slope: 116
Ladies: 5,043 yds. Rating: 61.0 Slope: 113

Tee Time: 7 days in advance
Price: $10 - $25

Credit Cards:	■	Restaurant:	■
Driving Range:		Lounge:	■
Practice Green:	■	Meeting Rooms:	■
Locker Room:	■	Tennis:	
Rental Clubs:	■	Swimming:	■
Walkers:	■	Jogging Trails:	
Snack Bar:		Boating:	

COURSE DESCRIPTION

Although this course is not very long, it does demand a great deal of accuracy and patience. You'll find the fairways narrow with well-placed traps that lead to elevated Bermuda greens. Water comes into play on almost every single hole.

The 12th hole is a par-5 measuring 490 yards in length. A creek starts on your left, cuts across the fairway, and then comes back to the hole on the right side of the green. If that isn't enough, the following hole is also a challenging par-5. This is a very enjoyable course at an affordable price.

DIRECTIONS

Take I-95 to Sample Rd. Go west and the course will be a 1/4 mile ahead of University Dr.

CAROLINA CLUB

3011 Rock Island Rd., Margate, FL 33063 / (954) 753-4000

BASIC INFORMATION

Course Type: Semi-private
Year Built: 1972
Architect: Van Hagge / Devlin
Local Pro: Don Gillis

Course: N/A
Holes: 18 / Par 71

Back: 6,550 yds. Rating: 72.1 Slope: 135
Middle: 6,101 yds. Rating: 70.0 Slope: 131
Ladies: 4,978 yds. Rating: 69.2 Slope: 124

Tee Time: 2 days in advance
Price: $35 - $70

Credit Cards:	■	Restaurant:	■
Driving Range:	■	Lounge:	■
Practice Green:	■	Meeting Rooms:	■
Locker Room:	■	Tennis:	
Rental Clubs:	■	Swimming:	■
Walkers:		Jogging Trails:	
Snack Bar:	■	Boating:	

COURSE DESCRIPTION

The 18 holes here will put a smile on your face the moment you arrive. The huge Southern-style estate clubhouse is home to one of the greatest public courses in the country.

The *Carolina Club* has played host to the qualifying division of the Honda Classic, a PGA Tour event, on a number of occasions.

Oddly enough, the course is not as long as you would think the Tour would demand. The design is challenging; water often comes into play1.

The goal at the *Carolina Club* was to build a public golf course that would simulate some of the best private clubs in the country. An achievement well done!

DIRECTIONS

Take I-95 to Sample Rd. Go west six miles to Rock Island Rd. and make a left. The course will be 1/4 mile on your right.

COLONY WEST COUNTRY CLUB

6800 N.W. 88th Ave., Tamarac, FL 33021 / (954) 726-8430

BASIC INFORMATION

Course Type: Public
Year Built: 1970
Architect: Von Hagge / Devlin
Local Pro: Norm Rack

Course: Championship
Holes: 18 / Par 71

Back: 7,271 yds. Rating: 75.8 Slope: 138
Middle: 6,461 yds. Rating: 71.8 Slope: 130
Ladies: 5,422 yds. Rating: 71.6 Slope: 127

Tee Time: 3 days in advance
Price: $23 - $55

Credit Cards: ■   Restaurant: ■
Driving Range: Lounge: ■
Practice Green: ■   Meeting Rooms: ■
Locker Room: ■   Tennis:
Rental Clubs: ■   Swimming: ■
Walkers: Jogging Trails:
Snack Bar: ■   Boating:

COURSE DESCRIPTION

The prestigious Golf Digest magazine has named **Colony West** one of the 50 best public courses in the nation.

The course is an extremely hard challenge if you're up to it. The fairways are narrow, the bunkers are plenty, the rough is deep, and water comes into play often.

If you have always wanted to play a professional caliber course with fast greens and high rough, this is the course to be playing on. Playing well here is the most exciting feeling in the world for a golfer. If you can par this course, the PGA Tour will be waiting for you.

DIRECTIONS

Take I-95 to Commercial Blvd. and go seven miles west to Pine Island Rd. Go right and the course will be one mile on your right.

CRYSTAL LAKE COUNTRY CLUB

3800 Crystal Lake Dr., Pompano Beach, FL 33060 / (954) 943-2902

BASIC INFORMATION

Course Type: Semi-private
Year Built: 1965
Architect: R. Jones
Local Pro: Joe Pace

Course: N/A
Holes: 18 / Par 72

Back: 6,610 yds. Rating: 71.5 Slope: 120
Middle: 6,200 yds. Rating: 69.4 Slope: 116
Ladies: 5,458 yds. Rating: 71.5 Slope: 121

Tee Time: 2 days in advance
Price: $26 - $45

Credit Cards: ■   Restaurant: · ■
Driving Range: ■   Lounge: ■
Practice Green: ■   Meeting Rooms: ■
Locker Room: ■   Tennis: ■
Rental Clubs: ■   Swimming:
Walkers: Jogging Trails:
Snack Bar: ■   Boating:

COURSE DESCRIPTION

If you're looking for a course to boost your ego, **Crystal Lake Country Club** has been tailor-made for you.

Water only comes into play twice and the good majority of the holes run parallel to each other. In fact, most of the holes are straight with the exception of a few doglegs.

If you're a beginner, you might want to start your Florida golfing experience on this course so that you can build your confidence for the many harder courses that Broward County has to offer.

The course is a pretty straightforward design that is kept in excellent shape all year round.

DIRECTIONS

Take I-95 to Sample Rd. Go west until you get to Crystal Like Dr. Go left for three blocks and the course will be on your right.

DEER CREEK COUNTRY CLUB

2801 Deer Country Club Blvd., Deerfield Beach, FL 33442 / (954) 421-5550

BASIC INFORMATION

Course Type: Public
Year Built: 1971
Architect: B. Watts
Local Pro: Steve O'Hara

Course: N/A
Holes: 18 / Par 72

Back: 6,832 yds. Rating: 72.7 Slope: 121
Middle: 6,259 yds. Rating: 70.8 Slope: 118
Ladies: 5,611 yds. Rating: 69.6 Slope: 118

Tee Time: 2 days in advance
Price: $35 - $40

Credit Cards:	■	Restaurant:	■
Driving Range:	■	Lounge:	■
Practice Green:	■	Meeting Rooms:	■
Locker Room:	■	Tennis:	
Rental Clubs:	■	Swimming:	■
Walkers:		Jogging Trails:	
Snack Bar:	■	Boating:	

COURSE DESCRIPTION

Deer Creek Country Club is a prime public course with a real country club feel to it. You'll know you're in for something special as soon as you drive into the course and take in the view of the huge clubhouse. Inside you'll find a large pro-shop that is well stocked with the latest in golfing equipment.

The course plays fair to all types of golfers. The fairways are on the tight side and the rough can be troublesome. You won't find much water on this layout, except for the 13th hole, which features a big lake in the middle of the fairway.

DIRECTIONS

Take I-95 and go west on Hillsborough Blvd. Make a right on Deer Creek Blvd. and the course will only be about two miles further.

DIPLOMAT COUNTRY CLUB

501 Diplomat Parkway, Hallandale, FL 33009 / (954) 457-2082

BASIC INFORMATION

Course Type: Semi-private
Year Built: N/A
Architect: N/A
Local Pro: Nick Berson

Course: N/A
Holes: 18 / Par 72

Back: 6,624 yds. Rating: 70.6 Slope: N/A
Middle: 6,193 yds. Rating: 68.9 Slope: N/A
Ladies: 5,404 yds. Rating: 69.3 Slope: N/A

Tee Time: 3 days in advance
Price: $18 - $40

Credit Cards:	■	Restaurant:	
Driving Range:	■	Lounge:	
Practice Green:	■	Meeting Rooms:	
Locker Room:	■	Tennis:	■
Rental Clubs:	■	Swimming:	
Walkers:		Jogging Trails:	
Snack Bar:	■	Boating:	

COURSE DESCRIPTION

The *Diplomat Country Club* is a simple no-nonsense type of course.

You'll find the course open in design with very little water coming into play. This is an excellent course for beginners and senior citizens who prefer to play the easier types of courses for the sheer enjoyment of the game rather than the challenge of a harder course.

The clubhouse has become somewhat run-down and needs to be renovated inside and out. Other renovations need to be made as well if they are going to compete with some of the other courses in the area.

DIRECTIONS

Take I-95 to Hallandale Beach Blvd. and go east to the Diplomat Pkwy. Make a left and you'll find the course two miles further on your left.

EMERALD HILLS, THE CLUB AT

4100 N. Hills Dr., Hollywood, FL 33021 / (954) 961-4000

BASIC INFORMATION

Course Type: Semi-private
Year Built: 1989 (Redesigned)
Architect: C. Ankrom (Van Hagge / Devlin)
Local Pro: Dan Wilkins

Course: N/A
Holes: 18 / Par 72

Back: 7,003 yds. Rating: 74.1 Slope: 133
Middle: 6,583 yds. Rating: 72.2 Slope: 129
Ladies: 5,032 yds. Rating: 70.1 Slope: 112

Tee Time: 5 days in advance
Price: $40 - $70

Credit Cards:	■	Restaurant:	■
Driving Range:	■	Lounge:	■
Practice Green:	■	Meeting Rooms:	■
Locker Room:	■	Tennis:	
Rental Clubs:	■	Swimming:	■
Walkers:		Jogging Trails:	
Snack Bar:	■	Boating:	

COURSE DESCRIPTION

This course is a rare treat indeed. After its sale four years ago, over $2 million has been invested to make this course one of the best in Broward County.

You'll find an excellent combination of hole designs that are challenging for both the amateur and the professional. Really good golfing can be found here.

The course has been designed by Bruce Devlin and Robert Von Hagge, the phenomenal team that designed Colony West, one of the best public courses in the country.

DIRECTIONS

Take I-95 to Sterling Rd. and go west to N. 46th Ave. Left on N. Hills Dr. and another left on the following road. The course will be on your right.

FLAMINGO LAKES COUNTRY CLUB

701 Flamingo West Dr., Pembroke Pines, FL 33027 / (954) 435-6110

BASIC INFORMATION

Course Type: Semi-private
Year Built: 1984
Architect: K. Litton
Local Pro: John Corners

Course: N/A
Holes: 18 / Par 71

Back: 6,004 yds. Rating: 69.4 Slope: 127
Middle: 5,672 yds. Rating: 67.9 Slope: 124
Ladies: 5,082 yds. Rating: 69.7 Slope: 124

Tee Time: 2 days in advance
Price: $18 - $28

Credit Cards:	■	Restaurant:	■
Driving Range:		Lounge:	
Practice Green:	■	Meeting Rooms:	■
Locker Room:	■	Tennis:	■
Rental Clubs:	■	Swimming:	■
Walkers:		Jogging Trails:	
Snack Bar:		Boating:	

COURSE DESCRIPTION

This course is tailor-made for senior citizens and high-handicap players. Located in Century Village, an "infamous" South Florida retirement complex, the course plays wonderfully for these types of players.

The fairways are wide and open and the rough is cut low to allow a good amount of roll off the tee. Water comes into play on most of the course, most especially on the back nine holes.

The 17th hole, a par-4 that measures 352 yards from the back tees, is one of the best holes to play. The hole is a dogleg left that features water running along both the right and the left side of the fairway.

DIRECTIONS

Take I-95 to Hollywood Blvd. Go west 10 miles to 136th St. The course will be on your left two lights past Flamingo Rd.

GOLF CLUB OF PLANTATION, THE

7050 W. Broward Blvd., Plantation, FL 33317 / (954) 583-5341

BASIC INFORMATION

Course Type: Public
Year Built: 1953
Architect: N/A
Local Pro: N/A

Course: N/A
Holes: 18 / Par 72

Back: 6,900 yds. Rating: 73.6 Slope: 124
Middle: 6,252 yds. Rating: 70.5 Slope: 118
Ladies: 5,954 yds. Rating: 74.4 Slope: 124

Tee Time: 3 days in advance
Price: $17 - $40

Credit Cards:	■	Restaurant:	■
Driving Range:	■	Lounge:	■
Practice Green:	■	Meeting Rooms:	■
Locker Room:	■	Tennis:	
Rental Clubs:	■	Swimming:	
Walkers:		Jogging Trails:	
Snack Bar:	■	Boating:	

COURSE DESCRIPTION

The *Golf Club of Plantation* is an interesting layout that is both challenging and fun to play. You'll find many dogleg holes that lead to elevated Bermuda greens of all sizes.

Most of the fairways are nice and wide. You'll be tempted to bring out the driver on almost every par-4 and par-5 hole.

This strategically-styled course allows for many options off the tee. The wide fairways will give you the confidence to hit your drives long and the elevated tees will force you to be creative.

The course is kept in impeccable shape. More than $700,000 has been invested to maintain its great condition. A job well done!

DIRECTIONS

Take I-95 to Broward Blvd. The course will be about 10 miles west on your left side.

GRAND PALMS GOLF & COUNTRY CLUB

110 Grand Palms Dr., Pembroke Pines, FL 33027 / (954) 437-3334

BASIC INFORMATION

Course Type: Semi-private
Year Built: 1989
Architect: J. Ward
Local Pro: Jacky Grywazzbrito

Course: N/A
Holes: 18 / Par 72

Back: 6,057 yds. Rating: 71.6 Slope: 127
Middle: 6,551 yds. Rating: 68.0 Slope: 120
Ladies: 5,245 yds. Rating: 69.4 Slope: 119

Tee Time: 3 days in advance
Price: $25 - $40

Credit Cards:	■	Restaurant:	■
Driving Range:	■	Lounge:	■
Practice Green:	■	Meeting Rooms:	■
Locker Room:	■	Tennis:	■
Rental Clubs:	■	Swimming:	■
Walkers:		Jogging Trails:	■
Snack Bar:	■	Boating:	

COURSE DESCRIPTION

Grand Palms Golf and Country Club is a players' paradise. The course forces one to think about every shot before execution. Accuracy above distance is the golden rule.

Water comes into play on almost every hole. You'll also be confronted with plenty of bunkering on your way to the Bermuda greens. The rough is cut mid-high and can be very difficult to play out of.

Most of the doglegs will allow you a birdie opportuntiy if you place your tee shot in the right area. Good course management is the key element to playing well here.

DIRECTIONS

Take I-95 to I-595. Go to I-75 and head south to W. Pines Blvd. The course will be on the south side, less than a 1/4 mile from the exit.

HOLLYWOOD GOLF & COUNTRY CLUB

1600 Johnson St., Hollywood, FL 33020 / (954) 927-1751

BASIC INFORMATION

Course Type: Public
Year Built: 1924
Architect: Donald Ross
Local Pro: Joe Gerlak

Course: N/A
Holes: 18 / Par 70

Back: 6,500 yds. Rating: 70.0 Slope: N/A
Middle: 6,345 yds. Rating: 69.0 Slope: N/A
Ladies: 5,943 yds. Rating: 72.0 Slope: N/A

Tee Time: 1-7 days in advance
Price: $13 - $35

Credit Cards:	■	Restaurant:	■
Driving Range:		Lounge:	■
Practice Green:	■	Meeting Rooms:	■
Locker Room:		Tennis:	
Rental Clubs:	■	Swimming:	■
Walkers:		Jogging Trails:	■
Snack Bar:	■	Boating:	

COURSE DESCRIPTION

This is yet another example of a course design that invites a golfer to bring out the driver and let it rip on every hole.

"Don't worry, be happy"... the fairways are wide, the rough is cut short, water hardly ever comes into play... trust me, no matter how bad you hit your tee shot, you'll come out smelling like roses!

This is a great course to boost a golfer's ego. If you can't find a bird here, go back to the driving range!

The course holds no secrets and it is rarely crowded. Golfs Up!

DIRECTIONS

Take I-95 to Hollywood Beach Blvd. Go east to the first light and make a left on to 28th St. Go right on Johnson and the course will be about two miles down on the right side.

JACARANDA GOLF & COUNTRY CLUB

9200 W. Broward Blvd., Plantation, FL 33324 / (954) 472-5836

BASIC INFORMATION

Course Type: Semi-private
Year Built: 1971
Architect: M. Mahannah
Local Pro: Paul Scott

Course: East
Holes: 18 / Par 72

Back: 7,170 yds. Rating: 74.0 Slope: 130
Middle: 6,786 yds. Rating: 72.5 Slope: 127
Ladies: 5,668 yds. Rating: 72.3 Slope: 121

Tee Time: 7 days in advance
Price: $30 - $55

Credit Cards:	■	Restaurant:	■
Driving Range:	■	Lounge:	■
Practice Green:	■	Meeting Rooms:	■
Locker Room:	■	Tennis:	
Rental Clubs:	■	Swimming:	
Walkers:		Jogging Trails:	
Snack Bar:	■	Boating:	

COURSE DESCRIPTION

The greens at *Jacaranda Golf Club* are absolutely exceptional! The roll is so true and fast, you'll swear you're competing at the Masters!

Both the East and West courses are great designs that are kept in meticulous shape. The club alternates public play to only one course per month while the other is open to members only.

Both the East and the West course have water coming into play on 16 holes. Although the East course is slightly longer, both courses are equally difficult.

DIRECTIONS

Take I-95 to Broward Blvd. Go west to Central Park Dr. (Jacaranda Country Club Dr.) and make a left to the course. It will be about a quarter mile further. This road will take you straight to the clubhouse.

LAURELTON PARK GOLF & COUNTRY CLUB
3700 S. Douglas Rd., Miramar, FL 33024 / (954) 431-3800

BASIC INFORMATION

Course Type: Public
Year Built: 1963
Architect: N/A
Local Pro: J.C. Nadeau

Course: N/A
Holes: 18 / Par 72

Back: 6,650 yds. Rating: 71.4 Slope: 121
Middle: 6,011 yds. Rating: 68.8 Slope: 118
Ladies: 5,214 yds. Rating:70.1 Slope: 119

Tee Time: 1 day in advance
Price: $15 - $30

Credit Cards:	■	Restaurant:	■
Driving Range:	■	Lounge:	■
Practice Green:	■	Meeting Rooms:	■
Locker Room:		Tennis:	
Rental Clubs:	■	Swimming:	
Walkers:		Jogging Trails:	
Snack Bar:	■	Boating:	

COURSE DESCRIPTION
This course has gone through some major changes since it was sold recently. A lot of money has been spent to get it back in its present shape and it shows.

The course is set up to be played aggressively. With water mostly out of the way on the majority of the course, situations will come forth for you to shoot for the pin in the hope of a birdie.

The course is seldom crowded and allows a foursome the possibility of playing a round of golf in less than four hours.

DIRECTIONS
Take I-95 to Hallandale Beach Blvd. Go west to Douglas Rd. Make a left at Douglas and the course will be a block away.

OAK RIDGE COUNTRY CLUB
3490 Griffen Rd., Hollywood, FL 33312 / (954) 987-5552

BASIC INFORMATION

Course Type: Public
Year Built: 1961
Architect: N/A
Local Pro: Ron Dunn

Course: East
Holes: 18 / Par 72

Back: 6,517 yds. Rating: 69.1 Slope: 112
Middle: 6,264 yds. Rating: 68.1 Slope: 109
Ladies: 5,905 yds. Rating: 69.4 Slope: 112

Tee Time: 2 days in advance
Price: $15 - $25

Credit Cards:	■	Restaurant:	■
Driving Range:	■	Lounge:	■
Practice Green:	■	Meeting Rooms:	
Locker Room:	■	Tennis:	
Rental Clubs:	■	Swimming:	
Walkers:		Jogging Trails:	
Snack Bar:	■	Boating:	

COURSE DESCRIPTION
You can leave your driver at home! This is the perfect type of course to practice your mid-to-low iron shots.

The course is set on a flat terrain with very little water coming into play. Play it aggressively and never look back. If you've never shot par before, this may be the course that will change your life.

The club allows you to walk through the entire day. If you have never walked an eighteen hole course before, you really owe it to yourself to try.

DIRECTIONS
Take I-95 and exit west on to Griffin Rd. The course will be one mile away on your left side. Keep your eyes open for their sign. Many people pass the course without realizing it.

ORANGE BROOK GOLF COURSE
400 Entrada Dr., Hollywood, FL 33021 / (954) 987-9095

BASIC INFORMATION

Course Type: Municipal
Year Built: 1936
Architect: N/A
Local Pro: Jane Read

Course: East
Holes: 18 / Par 72

Back: 6,848 yds. Rating: 71.7 Slope: 118
Middle: 6,268 yds. Rating: 68.8 Slope: 114
Ladies: 5,645 yds. Rating: 70.6 Slope: 115

Tee Time: 1 day in advance
Price: $10 - $25

Credit Cards:		Restaurant:	■
Driving Range:	■	Lounge:	■
Practice Green:	■	Meeting Rooms:	■
Locker Room:	■	Tennis:	
Rental Clubs:	■	Swimming:	
Walkers:	■	Jogging Trails:	
Snack Bar:	■	Boating:	

COURSE DESCRIPTION

This Municipal course is inexpensive and allows walking anytime during the course of the week. The only set-back is the fact that it often gets quite crowded. In 1991, the City of Hollywood spent close to a quarter of a million dollars improving the course. PGA Tour professional Mike Donald grew up playing golf here.

The public (East) course measures 400 yards longer with a greater variety of dogleg holes. This course is more lushly landscaped and aesthetically appealing.

DIRECTIONS

Take I-95 to Hollywood Beach Blvd. Go west to the first light and head south on to Entrada St. The course will be less than half a mile away.

ORIOLE GOLF & TENNIS CLUB
8000 W. Margate Blvd., Margate, FL 33063 / (954) 972-8140

BASIC INFORMATION

Course Type: Semi-private
Year Built: N/A
Architect: N/A
Local Pro: Tom Hollinshead

Course: N/A
Holes: 18 / Par 72

Back: 6,418 yds. Rating: N/A Slope: 120
Middle: 6,070 yds. Rating: N/A Slope: 117
Ladies: 4,875 yds. Rating: N/A Slope: 111

Tee Time: 2 days in advance
Price: $16 - $32

Credit Cards:	■	Restaurant:	■
Driving Range:	■	Lounge:	■
Practice Green:	■	Meeting Rooms:	
Locker Room:	■	Tennis:	
Rental Clubs:	■	Swimming:	
Walkers:		Jogging Trails:	
Snack Bar:	■	Boating:	

COURSE DESCRIPTION

The *Oriole Golf & Tennis Club* is a modest establishment that will surprise you. You'll find many holes that will allow you a good chance at a par.

Some of the holes that have water coming into play have not been charted correctly on the course scorecard. Ask a golf professional if the cards have been updated since the writing of this book.

The 9th hole, which is a par-5 that measures 520 yards in length from the back tees is a challenging hole. Your tee shot must reach a landing area about 245 yards out. The approach shot is to a steep green with a lake in front of it. Much luck!

DIRECTIONS

Take I-95 to Atlantic Blvd. Go west to Rock Island Rd. Go north on Margate Blvd. west on Country Club Dr. and the course will be a little further up the road.

PEMBROKE LAKES GOLF & RACQUET CLUB
10500 Taft St., Pembroke Pines, FL 33026 / (954) 431-4144

BASIC INFORMATION

Course Type: Municipal
Year Built: 1974
Architect: T. Watson
Local Pro: Paul Perini

Course: N/A
Holes: 18 / Par 72

Back: 6,555 yds. Rating: 71.8 Slope: 124
Middle: 6,198 yds. Rating: 70.0 Slope: 119
Ladies: 5,577 yds. Rating: 72.1 Slope: 118

Tee Time: 5 days in advance
Price: $10 - $30

Credit Cards:		Restaurant:	■
Driving Range:	■	Lounge:	■
Practice Green:	■	Meeting Rooms:	■
Locker Room:	■	Tennis:	■
Rental Clubs:	■	Swimming:	■
Walkers:	■	Jogging Trails:	■
Snack Bar:	■	Boating:	

COURSE DESCRIPTION

Proper club selection is crucial to a good score at *Pembroke Lakes Golf & Racquet Club.*

If you're one to bring out the driver on every par-4 and par-5, don't. Many of the fairways are set up rather tight. If you can hit a straight you'll be doing fine, but if you're like the great majority of golfers you may be prone to hit a hook or a slice more often than not. The sand traps coupled with the rough will penalize shots left and right.

DIRECTIONS

Take I-95 to Shereton St. Go west until you get to Palm Ave. Go left at Palm Ave. and make a right on Taft St.

POMPANO BEACH GOLF COURSE
1101 N. Federal Hwy., Pompano Beach, FL 33062 / (954) 781-0426

BASIC INFORMATION

Course Type: Municipal
Year Built: 1957
Architect: Van Hagge / Devlin
Local Pro: Bob Mac.Millan

Course: Pines
Holes: 18 / Par 72

Back: 6,886 yds. Rating: 72.0 Slope: 117
Middle: 6,571 yds. Rating: 70.6 Slope: 114
Ladies: 5,980 yds. Rating: 73.4 Slope: 117

Tee Time: First come first served.
Price: $13 - $36

Credit Cards:		Restaurant:	■
Driving Range:	■	Lounge:	■
Practice Green:	■	Meeting Rooms:	■
Locker Room:	■	Tennis:	
Rental Clubs:	■	Swimming:	
Walkers:	■	Jogging Trails:	
Snack Bar:	■	Boating:	

COURSE DESCRIPTION

Pompano Beach Golf Course features two well-balanced municipal courses that are much in demand. Both courses are equally challenging, with the Palms course featuring more water than the Pines course. Another interesting fact about the Palms course is that it was designed and built inside the Pines course.

The Pines, which features fairways with mounds and holes that curve along wooded areas, is the more scenic of the two. It is also the course preferred by better players.

Both courses are fun to play and affordable.

DIRECTIONS

Take I-95 to Copens Rd. Head east until you get to US-1. Go right and the course will be one mile on your right side.

RAINTREE GOLF RESORT

3501 W. Rolling Hills Circle, Ft. Lauderdale, FL 33328 / (954) 475-3010

BASIC INFORMATION

Course Type: Semi-private
Year Built: 1968
Architect: Watts / R.T. Jones
Local Pro: Ron Baker

Course: N/A
Holes: 18 / Par 70

Back: 6,506 yds. Rating: 70.8 Slope: 115
Middle: 6,009 yds. Rating: 68.7 Slope: 113
Ladies: 5,025 yds. Rating: 68.7 Slope: 109

Tee Time: 3 days in advance
Price: $15 - $40

Credit Cards: ■	Restaurant: ■
Driving Range: ■	Lounge: ■
Practice Green: ■	Meeting Rooms: ■
Locker Room:	Tennis:
Rental Clubs: ■	Swimming: ■
Walkers:	Jogging Trails:
Snack Bar: ■	Boating:

COURSE DESCRIPTION

If you've never learned how to swim as a child, this course will give you many opportunities to learn. Needless to say, water is everywhere!

This is definitely not your everyday contemporary course. I'll let you in on something people rarely notice even while looking at the scorecard: this is the only course that I have ever played on that features six par-5's, six par-4's, and six par-3's. Every par-72 or par-71 course that I have played or written about features more par-4's than par-5's and par-3's. Although I don't have the facts at hand, I'm willing to guess that this is the first course of its kind.

DIRECTIONS

Take I-75 and exit on to Pines Blvd. Go east to Hiatus and south to the course. Look for the entrance sign.

ROLLING HILLS GOLF RESORT

3501 W. Rolling Hills Cr., Ft. Lauderdale, FL 33328 / (954) 475- 3010

BASIC INFORMATION

Course Type: Public
Year Built: 1959
Architect: W. Mitchell
Local Pro: Jacky Grywazzbrito

Course: The Oaks
Holes: 18 / Par 72

Back: 6,906 yds. Rating: 72.7 Slope: 124
Middle: 6,306 yds. Rating: 69.8 Slope: 120
Ladies: 5,630 yds. Rating: 71.7 Slope: 121

Tee Time: 3 days in advance
Price: $17 - $48

Credit Cards: ■	Restaurant: ■
Driving Range: ■	Lounge: ■
Practice Green: ■	Meeting Rooms: ■
Locker Room: ■	Tennis: ■
Rental Clubs: ■	Swimming: ■
Walkers:	Jogging Trails:
Snack Bar: ■	Boating:

COURSE DESCRIPTION

Without a "palm tree" in sight, this course looks and feels very much like a northern type course. The fairways are tight and the rough can be devastating. You'll find plenty of water and sand and the majority of the holes are of the dogleg variety.

The additional 9 hole "University" course features more water and less trees.

Rolling Hills is a fine example of what can be achieved when an architect gets all of the elements perfectly right.

Trivia: Which movies were filmed here?
Answer: Caddyshack I and II.

DIRECTIONS

Take I-95 to I-595 and go west to University Dr. Go south on University and the course will be one mile on the right.

SABAL PALMS GOLF COURSE

5101 W. Commercial Blvd., Tamarac, FL 33328 / (954) 731-2600

BASIC INFORMATION

Course Type: Public
Year Built: 1968
Architect: F. Murray
Local Pro: Fred Robinson

Course: N/A
Holes: 18 / Par 71

Back: 6,410 yds. Rating: 66.1 Slope: 112
Middle: 5,975 yds. Rating: 64.4 Slope: 109
Ladies: 5,559 yds. Rating: 67.5 Slope: 117

Tee Time: 7 days in advance
Price: $14 - $29

Credit Cards:	■	Restaurant:	■
Driving Range:		Lounge:	■
Practice Green:	■	Meeting Rooms:	
Locker Room:		Tennis:	
Rental Clubs:	■	Swimming:	
Walkers:		Jogging Trails:	
Snack Bar:	■	Boating:	

COURSE DESCRIPTION

Sabal Palms Golf Course is a straight-forward, understated golf course with many dogleg holes.

The fairways are mostly wide and allow a good amount of roll. You'll find the rough cut low to allow the average golfer a chance to get the ball up high and out of trouble.

One of the interesting holes on this course is the par-5, 13th hole that measures in at 540 yards from the back tees. This dogleg right features a creek that runs along the entire length of the hole on its right side.

If you hold a handicap of 18 or lower, birdie opportunities will be knocking on your door.

DIRECTIONS

Take I-95 to Commercial Blvd. Go west on Commercial until you get to Rock Island Rd. You'll see the clubhouse on the corner.

SUNRISE COUNTRY CLUB

7400 N.W. 24th Pl., Sunrise, FL 33313 / (954) 742-4333

BASIC INFORMATION

Course Type: Semi-private
Year Built: 1960
Architect: B. Watts
Local Pro: Mary Daegart

Course: N/A
Holes: 18 / Par 72

Back: 6,668 yds. Rating: 70.8 Slope: 114
Middle: 6,362 yds. Rating: 79.4 Slope: 111
Ladies: 5,311 yds. Rating: 79.1 Slope: 113

Tee Time: 7 days in advance
Price: $20 - $40

Credit Cards:	■	Restaurant:	■
Driving Range:	■	Lounge:	■
Practice Green:	■	Meeting Rooms:	
Locker Room:	■	Tennis:	■
Rental Clubs:	■	Swimming:	■
Walkers:		Jogging Trails:	
Snack Bar:		Boating:	

COURSE DESCRIPTION

Sunrise Country Club is an incredibly fun course to play if you can place yourself in the "John Daly" zone.

Most of the fairways are open nice and wide for you to bring out the driver. The rough is cut low and is easy to get out of.

Water doesn't come into play often, but when it does, it is rather interesting, like the 13th hole, a par-5 dogleg left that features a creek running through the fairway just after the dogleg turn. If you can't place your second shot over the creek, you'll be forced to lay up and go for your par rather than birdie. Trees are abundant!

DIRECTIONS

Take I-95 to Sunrise Blvd. Go west on Sunrise until you get to Sunset Strip. Go north and follow the green and white signs.

BAYSHORE GOLF CLUB

2301 Alton Rd., Miami, FL 33140 / (305) 532-3350

BASIC INFORMATION

Course Type: Public
Year Built: N/A
Architect: R. Von Hagge / B. Devlin
Local Pro: N/A

Course: N/A
Holes: 18 / Par 72

Back: 6,903 yds. Rating: 73.0 Slope: 127
Middle: 6,203 yds. Rating: 69.8 Slope: 119
Ladies: 5,538 yds. Rating: 71.6 Slope: 120

Tee Time: 1 day in advance
Price: $25 - $50

Credit Cards:	■	Restaurant:	■
Driving Range:	■	Lounge:	■
Practice Green:	■	Meeting Rooms:	
Locker Room:	■	Tennis:	
Rental Clubs:	■	Swimming:	
Walkers:	■	Jogging Trails:	
Snack Bar:		Boating:	

COURSE DESCRIPTION

Bayshore is a well-balanced design that will challenge the accomplished golfer and compliment the amateur. When you first play this course, you automatically think that the design is handcrafted exclusively for long hitters. Don't be alarmed. Most of the holes are dogleg designs that allow you to bite off a good portion of the distance with good tee shots.

Walking is allowed on certain occasions during the course of the year. Please call to confirm.

DIRECTIONS

Take the I-95 Miami Beach exit to Alton Rd. (1st Exit). Go south directly to the course.

BILTMORE GOLF COURSE

1210 Anastasia Ave., Coral Gables, FL 33134 / (305) 460-5364

BASIC INFORMATION

Course Type: Municipal
Year Built: 1926
Architect: D. Ross
Local Pro: N/A

Course: N/A
Holes: 18 / Par 71

Back: 6,652 yds. Rating: 71.9 Slope: 127
Middle: 6,259 yds. Rating: 70.1 Slope: 123
Ladies: 5,697 yds. Rating: 72.6 Slope: 125

Tee Time: 3 days in advance
Price: $25 - $50

Credit Cards:	■	Restaurant:	■
Driving Range:	■	Lounge:	
Practice Green:	■	Meeting Rooms:	
Locker Room:	■	Tennis:	
Rental Clubs:	■	Swimming:	
Walkers:		Jogging Trails:	
Snack Bar:	■	Boating:	

COURSE DESCRIPTION

In 1926, the legendary golfing architect, Donald Ross, designed this course and it quickly became one of the best courses in the area. In the 1930's, it played host to the Biltmore Open (later renamed the Coral Gables Open) attracting the greatest names of that era.

The *Biltmore* has been redesigned to more closely resemble the original layout. It is an excellent design that allows many opportunities for low scores. Many of the holes have nice openings in front of the greens, allowing golfers the option to pitch-and-run their shots - a Donald Ross trademark.

DIRECTIONS

Take the Palmetto Expressway and exit onto Bird Rd East. Go north on Granada, then west on Anastasia. You can't miss it!

CALUSA COUNTRY CLUB
9400 S.W. 130th Ave., Miami, FL 33179 / (305) 386-5533

BASIC INFORMATION

Course Type: Semi-private
Year Built: 1968
Architect: M. Mahannah
Local Pro: Martin Mangels

Course: North
Holes: 18 / Par 72

Back: 7,185 yds. Rating: 73.1 Slope: 118
Middle: 6,749 yds. Rating: 71.8 Slope: 116
Ladies: 5,638 yds. Rating: 70.7 Slope: 114

Tee Time: 2 days in advance
Price: N/A

Credit Cards:	■	Restaurant:	■
Driving Range:	■	Lounge:	■
Practice Green:	■	Meeting Rooms:	■
Locker Room:	■	Tennis:	■
Rental Clubs:	■	Swimming:	
Walkers:		Jogging Trails:	
Snack Bar:	■	Boating:	

COURSE DESCRIPTION

With wide fairways on practically every hole, this unbelievable monster of a course can be brought to its knees with good drives on a dry Floridian day.

You'll have many opportunities to test your long game off the tee and on your approach shots. It makes for an interesting day of golf.

The #1 handicap hole is the par-5, 2nd hole, measuring 569 yards. It's a straight hole with bunkers coming into play on the left and right side of the fairway. The green has bunkers right, left, and front. Good luck!

DIRECTIONS

Take the Turnpike exit to Kendell Dr. west. Go left on 133rd Ave. and left again at the upcoming fork, which will take you to 130th Ave.

DORAL PARK SILVER GOLF COURSE
4825 N.W. 104th Ave., Miami, FL 33178 / (305) 594-0954

BASIC INFORMATION

Course Type: Semi-private
Year Built: 1983
Architect: Von Hagge / Devlin
Local Pro: Artie McNickle

Course:N/A
Holes: 18 / Par 72

Back: 6,614 yds. Rating: 72.0 Slope: 129
Middle: 6,315 yds. Rating: 70.5 Slope: 122
Ladies: 4,661 yds. Rating: 66.6 Slope: 113

Tee Time: 3 days in advance
Price: $25 - $50

Credit Cards:	■	Restaurant:	■
Driving Range:	■	Lounge:	■
Practice Green:	■	Meeting Rooms:	■
Locker Room:	■	Tennis:	■
Rental Clubs:	■	Swimming:	■
Walkers:		Jogging Trails:	
Snack Bar:	■	Boating:	

COURSE DESCRIPTION

This course is one of the area's finest. You'll find water on every hole with an abundance of sand traps. The course can be brutal at times, with lots of mounds in the fairway and fast Bermuda greens.

The island green on the 14th hole was used for an American Express television commercial. You see a golfer putting in and the American Express card serving as a bridge to the island green.

This course is kept in perfect shape all year round. For this reason and more, it has attracted a strong membership.

You'll love the golfing experience here. It truly is a special course.

DIRECTIONS

Take the Palmetto Expressway and exit on N.W. 36th St. Go west for two miles until you reach the end of the road.

DORAL RESORT & COUNTRY CLUB
440 N.W. 104th Ave., Miami, FL 33178 / (305) 592-2000

BASIC INFORMATION

Course Type: Resort
Year Built: 1962
Architect: D. Wilson
Local Pro: A. McNickle

Course: Blue (18 / Par 72)
Holes: 90

Back: 6,939 yds. Rating: 72.0 Slope: 127
Middle: 6,597 yds. Rating: 70.4 Slope: 122
Ladies: 5,786 yds. Rating: 71.8 Slope: 124

Tee Time: 1 day in advance
Price: $50 - $125

Credit Cards:	■	Restaurant:	■
Driving Range:	■	Lounge:	■
Practice Green:	■	Meeting Rooms:	■
Locker Room:	■	Tennis:	■
Rental Clubs:	■	Swimming:	■
Walkers:		Jogging Trails:	■
Snack Bar:	■	Boating:	

COURSE DESCRIPTION
Doral offers 81 holes of pure golf pleasure. Every year the resort plays host to the PGA Tour with the Doral Ryder Open, one of the most exciting tournaments of the year.

The "Blue Monster" course, as it is known around the world, is the hardest of the four 18 hole courses. The finishing hole on this course is one of the greatest in the world.

The Gold course plays tough, with water on every hole. The Red course is another challenging course with lots of sand and water. The White course, with its wide fairways, is the easiest of the four. The 9-hole executive course is both fun and challenging too.

DIRECTIONS
Take the Palmetto Expressway and exit onto N.W. 36th St. Go west two miles to 87th Ave.

FOUNTAINEBLEU GOLF COURSE
9603 Fountainebleu Blvd., Miami, FL 33172 / (305) 221-5181

BASIC INFORMATION

Course Type: Public
Year Built: 1961
Architect: M. Mahannah
Local Pro: Ken Juhn

Course: West
Holes: 18 / Par 72

Back: 6,465 yds. Rating: 71.0 Slope: 113
Middle: 6,107 yds. Rating: 71.0 Slope: 121
Ladies: 5,378 yds. Rating: 69.0 Slope: 113

Tee Time: 5 days in advance
Price: $25 - $50

Credit Cards:	■	Restaurant:	■
Driving Range:	■	Lounge:	
Practice Green:	■	Meeting Rooms:	■
Locker Room:		Tennis:	
Rental Clubs:	■	Swimming:	
Walkers:		Jogging Trails:	
Snack Bar:	■	Boating:	

COURSE DESCRIPTION
Both the West and the East course at the *Fountainebleu* allow golfers many opportunities to score well.

The average-sized fairways, coupled with a good assortment of bunkers leading to the Bermuda greens, makes this course fun to play. You'll find the fairways firm, the rough minimal, and the greens in great shape.

The 13th is a 605-yard, dogleg-left, par-5 hole, and is the number one handicap hole. From the tee, the out-of-bounds line and water come into play along the left side of the hole. Your second shot is similar with the addition of sand and water on your right. Your approach shot will be to a big-green with 2-bunkers: front-center and back-left.

DIRECTIONS
Take the Palmetto Expressway, exit west on Flagler St., north on 97th and east at the dead end.

GOLF CLUB OF MIAMI

6801 N.W. Miami Gardens Dr., Hialeah, FL 33015 / (305) 829-8449

BASIC INFORMATION

Course Type: Semi-private
Year Built: N/A
Architect: N/A
Local Pro: John Norton

Course: West
Holes: 18 / Par 72

Back: 7,017 yds. Rating: 73.5 Slope: 130
Middle: 6,139 yds. Rating: 69.4 Slope: 124
Ladies: 5,298 yds. Rating: 70.1 Slope: 123

Tee Time: 3 days in advance
Price: $20 - $45

Credit Cards:	■	Restaurant:	■
Driving Range:	■	Lounge:	■
Practice Green:	■	Meeting Rooms:	■
Locker Room:	■	Tennis:	
Rental Clubs:	■	Swimming:	
Walkers:		Jogging Trails:	
Snack Bar:	■	Boating:	

COURSE DESCRIPTION

All three of the courses at this facility are exceptional. Major reconstruction has raised the level of golf to the days when the West course played host to a major PGA tournament.

The greens on the two championship courses, the West and the East, are by far an exception from the norm. Your ball will always roll true to the line of your putt.

The West is the harder of the two with difficult starting holes. The East, a shorter course, puts an emphasis on accuracy. The par-62 South course is a pleasure to play and well maintained.

DIRECTIONS

Take I-75 to the Miami Gardens east exit. Go north on 68th Ave. straight to the course. You can't miss it.

KENDALE LAKES GOLF & COUNTRY CLUB

6401 Kendale Lakes Dr., Miami, FL 33183 / (305) 382-3935

BASIC INFORMATION

Course Type: Semi-private
Year Built: 1962
Architect: D. Wilson
Local Pro: Robert Brand

Course: Emerald / Ruby
Holes: 18 / Par 72

Back: 6,815 yds. Rating: 70.8 Slope: 123
Middle: 6,335 yds. Rating: 68.7 Slope: 120
Ladies: 5,670 yds. Rating: 69.6 Slope: 119

Tee Time: 1 day in advance
Price: $25 - $50

Credit Cards:	■	Restaurant:	■
Driving Range:	■	Lounge:	■
Practice Green:	■	Meeting Rooms:	■
Locker Room:		Tennis:	■
Rental Clubs:	■	Swimming:	■
Walkers:		Jogging Trails:	
Snack Bar:	■	Boating:	

COURSE DESCRIPTION

With water coming into play on virtually every hole, this is a challenging course:

The good news is that the fairways are nice and wide and allow a generous amount of space for your tee-shot landing area. The bad news is the rough; it almost doesn't exist. If you slice or pull your drives, the odds will be against your ball staying dry.

The most exciting news is the Bermuda greens. They are all large enough for a 2 to 3 club length variance. All three nine-hole courses are a fun adventure to play. The most popular is the Emerald / Ruby combination. The Jade course is the longest of the three.

DIRECTIONS

Take the Fl. Turnpike to 88th St. (Kendall Dr.) and go west for two miles. Go north on 142nd Ave. to the dead end.

KENDALL GOLF CLUB
9980 S.W. 104th St., Miami, FL 33183 / (305) 271-0917

BASIC INFORMATION

Course Type: Semi-private
Year Built: 1965
Architect: N/A
Local Pro: Chuck Hart

Course:N/A
Holes: 18 / Par 72

Back: 6,400 yds. Rating: N/A Slope: N/A
Middle: 6,011 yds. Rating: N/A Slope: N/A
Ladies: 5,319 yds. Rating: N/A Slope: N/A

Tee Time: 2 days in advance
Price: $20 - $30

Credit Cards: ■	Restaurant: ■
Driving Range: ■	Lounge: ■
Practice Green: ■	Meeting Rooms:
Locker Room:	Tennis: ■
Rental Clubs: ■	Swimming: ■
Walkers: ■	Jogging Trails:
Snack Bar: ■	Boating:

COURSE DESCRIPTION
This course was originally called Crooked Creek Country Club, when it was owned by an NFL pro named Ted Hendricks.

A lot of money has been put back into this wonderful course making it better than ever before. With its new name, the course is reaching out to new customers by offering unbelievable golf memberships and packages. The golf is always terrific and the course is kept in great shape.

It may be a short course, but beware, there are moments when you have to settle your ego down and play the hole as a par rather than a birdie, like the 334 yard, par-4 hole that has a creek running across the fairway. A truly challenging hole.

DIRECTIONS
Take the Palmetto Expressway south and go west on S.W. 88th St. Go south on S.W. 147th Ave. and east on 104th St.

KEYS GATE GOLF CLUB
2300 Palm Dr., Homestead, FL 33035 / (305) 230-0362

BASIC INFORMATION

Course Type: Public
Year Built: 1990
Architect: R. I. Lightstone
Local Pro: N/A

Course: N/A
Holes: 18 / Par 71

Back: 6,397 yds. Rating: 69.3 Slope: 116
Middle: 5,996 yds. Rating: 67.9 Slope: 114
Ladies: 5,641 yds. Rating: 71.2 Slope: 112

Tee Time: 7 days in advance
Price: $15 - $25

Credit Cards: ■	Restaurant:
Driving Range: ■	Lounge:
Practice Green: ■	Meeting Rooms:
Locker Room: ■	Tennis:
Rental Clubs: ■	Swimming:
Walkers: ■	Jogging Trails:
Snack Bar: ■	Boating:

COURSE DESCRIPTION
This course is a great place to play aggressive golf. The fairways are nice and open and firm enough to let your drives roll that extra 10-15 yards on a windy day.

The course has a good amount of water and not too many trees, thanks to Hurricane Andrew.

Just recently, the course completed its new clubhouse (in light pastel colors) and an aquatic driving range.

The price is always right, even during the winter season when Florida opens its arms and embraces golfers from all over the world.

DIRECTIONS
Take the Fl. Turnpike to Hwy. 1, go east on Palm Dr. and the course will be three miles down on the right hand side.

LINKS AT KEY BISCAYNE

6400 Crandon Blvd., Key Biscayne, FL 33149 / (305) 361-9129

BASIC INFORMATION

Course Type: Public
Year Built: 1972
Architect: Von Hagge / Devlin
Local Pro: Jerry Castigaliano

Course:West
Holes: 18 / Par 72

Back: 7,070 yds. Rating: 74.0 Slope: 138
Middle: 6,389 yds. Rating: 71.0 Slope: 129
Ladies: 5,690 yds. Rating: 72.7 Slope: 125

Tee Time: 1 day in advance
Price: $15 - $30

Credit Cards:	■	Restaurant:	■
Driving Range:	■	Lounge:	
Practice Green:	■	Meeting Rooms:	■
Locker Room:		Tennis:	
Rental Clubs:	■	Swimming:	
Walkers:		Jogging Trails:	
Snack Bar:	■	Boating:	

COURSE DESCRIPTION

The *Links at Key Biscayne* is considered by many to be the best public course in the US. Every year the Senior PGA Tour comes here to compete in the Royal Caribbean Classic which takes place in February.

The course is in immaculate shape. The staff did an excellent job of restoring the course after Hurricane Andrew. Many professionals gave the course commendable reviews after playing in the 1993 tournament.

With lots of water and sand coupled with random winds from the nearby Atlantic, the drama never ends! You'll have many stories to talk about after a round at Key Biscayne.

DIRECTIONS

Take I-95 to the Key Biscayne exit. Hop on to the Rickenbackher Causeway and that will take you directly to the course.

MELREESE GOLF COURSE

1802 N.W. 37th Ave., Miami, FL 33125 / (305) 633-4583

BASIC INFORMATION

Course Type: Municipal
Year Built: 1969
Architect: N/A
Local Pro: Charles Pifer

Course: N/A
Holes: 18 / Par 72

Back: 6,785 yds. Rating: 72.0 Slope: N/A
Middle: 6,452 yds. Rating: 70.5 Slope: N/A
Ladies: 5,645 yds. Rating: 71.5 Slope: N/A

Tee Time: First come first served!
Price: $25 - $35

Credit Cards:	■	Restaurant:	■
Driving Range:	■	Lounge:	■
Practice Green:	■	Meeting Rooms:	■
Locker Room:		Tennis:	
Rental Clubs:	■	Swimming:	
Walkers:		Jogging Trails:	
Snack Bar:	■	Boating:	

COURSE DESCRIPTION

After Hurricane Andrew came through these fairways no one knew what to think. What happened to the course? Was it still in good shape or will it need some major work?

The truth of the matter is that Hurricane Andrew actually improved the layout of the course by knocking down trees that came into play more often than needed.

It took one month to clean up the mess, which allowed the greens to grow out and become the best that they have ever been.

You'll find this course to be a great challenge at 6,785 yards from the back tees.

DIRECTIONS

Take Hwy. 386 to the end of the Miami International Airport until you get to Douglas Rd. This road will take you to the course which you'll find on 18th St.

MIAMI SHORES COUNTRY CLUB
10000 Biscayne Blvd., Miami FL 33134 / (305) 795-2366

BASIC INFORMATION

Course Type: Semi-private
Year Built: 1939
Architect: R. Lawrence
Local Pro: Mike Walsh

Course: N/A
Holes: 18 / Par 71

Back: 6,400 yds. Rating: 71.1 Slope: 120
Middle: 6,200 yds. Rating: 60.9 Slope: 116
Ladies: 5,400 yds. Rating: 71.3 Slope: 121

Tee Time: 1 day in advance
Price: $21 - $50

Credit Cards:	■	Restaurant:	■
Driving Range:	■	Lounge:	■
Practice Green:	■	Meeting Rooms:	■
Locker Room:	■	Tennis:	■
Rental Clubs:	■	Swimming:	■
Walkers:		Jogging Trails:	
Snack Bar:	■	Boating:	

COURSE DESCRIPTION
This former private course has just recently opened its doors to non-members. The main challenge here is accuracy. You won't find a lot of water, but you will have to contend with the many sand traps.

The Bermuda greens are mostly of average size. Not many of them allow a bump-& run type of approach and thus will force you to keep the ball in the air. A soft landing high fade is the shot to develop before playing this course.

The Professional Course Management Team has done an excellent job of raising the quality of play. They and the course staff are to be highly commended.

DIRECTIONS
Take I-95 south and Exit onto N.W. 125th St. Go east to US-1 (Biscayne Blvd.) and make a right. Course will be on right.

MIAMI SPRINGS GOLF COURSE
650 Curtis Pkwy., Miami Springs, FL 33166 / (305) 888-2377

BASIC INFORMATION

Course Type: Semi-private
Year Built: 1939
Architect: N/A
Local Pro: Mike Walsh

Course: N/A
Holes: 18 / Par 72

Back: 6,403 yds. Rating: N/A Slope: N/A
Middle: 6,086 yds. Rating: N/A Slope: N/A
Ladies: 5,742 yds. Rating: N/A Slope: N/A

Tee Time: 1 day in advance
Price: $20 - $40

Credit Cards:		Restaurant:	■
Driving Range:	■	Lounge:	■
Practice Green:	■	Meeting Rooms:	■
Locker Room:		Tennis:	
Rental Clubs:	■	Swimming:	
Walkers:		Jogging Trails:	
Snack Bar:	■	Boating:	

COURSE DESCRIPTION
This course has taken on new life after the devastation of Hurricane Andrew. It has been beautifully rebuilt and the greens have never been better.

The layout is easily understood by studying the scorecard. You'll find many interesting holes that will test your golfing abilities from tee to green. If you can find your playing zone, play the course aggressively for the best results.

The holes are long and the doglegs are many. In particular, the 3rd hole, a par-3 that measures 250 yards long, is the longest par-3 in Dade County.

DIRECTIONS
Take I-95 to Exit 112 and go straight onto N.W. 36th St. Keep right towards 57th Ave. and make a right. The course will be five blocks further down.

NORMANDY SHORES GOLF COURSE
2401 Biarritz Dr., Miami Beach, FL 33141 / (305) 868-6502

BASIC INFORMATION

Course Type: Municipal
Year Built: 1940
Architect: N/A
Local Pro: Dan Breslin

Course: N/A
Holes: 18 / Par 71

Back: 6,402 yds. Rating: 70.5 Slope: 120
Middle: 6,055 yds. Rating: 68.9 Slope: 116
Ladies: 5,527 yds. Rating: 71.0 Slope: 119

Tee Time: 1 day in advance
Price: $10 - $35

Credit Cards:	■	Restaurant:	■
Driving Range:	■	Lounge:	■
Practice Green:	■	Meeting Rooms:	■
Locker Room:	■	Tennis:	
Rental Clubs:	■	Swimming:	
Walkers:		Jogging Trails:	
Snack Bar:	■	Boating:	

COURSE DESCRIPTION
I can't think of a better place for a golfer to experiment and grow as a player. With wide fairways and water coming into play on only one hole, you'll find yourself in situations that will allow you to take a chance without having to worry about the outcome of the shot.

For many people, this will be a good course to practice and experiment, and in the process build your confidence for more demanding courses.

DIRECTIONS
Take I-95 south to the East 79th St. Exit. Make a left on Biarritz and that will take you to the course.

PALMETTO GOLF COURSE
9300 S.W. 152nd, Miami, FL 33157 / (305) 238-2922

BASIC INFORMATION

Course Type: Municipal
Year Built: 1961
Architect: D. Wilson
Local Pro: Ron Frazier

Course:N/A
Holes: 18 / Par 70

Back: 6,798 yds. Rating: 71.3 Slope:
Middle: 6,360 yds. Rating: 69.3 Slope:
Ladies: 5,733 yds. Rating: 71.2 Slope:

Tee Time: 5 days in advance
Price: $10 - $25

Credit Cards:	■	Restaurant:	■
Driving Range:	■	Lounge:	
Practice Green:	■	Meeting Rooms:	
Locker Room:		Tennis:	
Rental Clubs:	■	Swimming:	
Walkers:	■	Jogging Trails:	
Snack Bar:	■	Boating:	

COURSE DESCRIPTION
The *Palmetto golf Course* was one of the hardest hit by Hurricane Andrew.

New construction is in progress to double the size of the driving range. The 10th hole has been shortened from a par-5 (494 yards) to a par-4 (419 yards) to accommodate the extra space needed. Further talk suggests that the 18th hole will be changed from a par-4 to a par-5 to make up the distance that has been lost.

This is a wonderful course with many exciting holes. Five of the eighteen holes have water cutting across the fairway forcing a golfer to choose between laying-up short or going-for-the-pin.

DIRECTIONS
Take Hwy. 1 south of Miami and go west on 152nd St.

PRESIDENTIAL GOLF COURSE

19650 S.W. 152nd St., N. Miami Beach, FL 33179 / (305) 933-5266

BASIC INFORMATION

Course Type: Public
Year Built: 1962
Architect: M. Mahannah
Local Pro: Frank LaBella

Course: N/A
Holes: 18 / Par 72

Back: 6,964 yds. Rating: 72.2 Slope: 131
Middle: 6,406 yds. Rating: 69.9 Slope: 126
Ladies: 5,794 yds. Rating: 72.1 Slope: 127

Tee Time: 3 days in advance
Price: $25 - $50

Credit Cards:	■	Restaurant:	
Driving Range:	■	Lounge:	■
Practice Green:	■	Meeting Rooms:	
Locker Room:	■	Tennis:	
Rental Clubs:	■	Swimming:	
Walkers:		Jogging Trails:	
Snack Bar:	■	Boating:	

COURSE DESCRIPTION

The *Presidential* stirs up a special feeling from the moment you enter it. The huge clubhouse is both beautiful and grand and the lush landscaping is meticulously kept.

The good majority of the holes on this course reward accuracy over length. You'll also find a healthy amount of dogleg holes that will allow you a good chance to bite off a considerable amount of yardage with well-placed tee shots.

This course is like an addiction; once you play it, you'll always want to come back. It is an aesthetically beautiful course with many challenging holes that are fun to play.

DIRECTIONS

Take I-95 and go east on Ives Dairy Rd. Make a right on Highland Lakes and the course will be on your right.

REDLAND COUNTRY CLUB

24451 S.W. 177th Ave., Homestead, FL 33090 / (305) 247-8503

BASIC INFORMATION

Course Type: Semi-private
Year Built: 1963
Architect: N/A
Local Pro: Jimmie Brothers

Course:N/A
Holes: 18 / Par 72

Back: 6,796 yds. Rating: 70.5 Slope: 118
Middle: 6,306 yds. Rating: 69.2 Slope: 117
Ladies: 5,854 yds. Rating: 71.0 Slope: 123

Tee Time: 2 days in advance
Price: $20 - $40

Credit Cards:	■	Restaurant:	■
Driving Range:	■	Lounge:	■
Practice Green:	■	Meeting Rooms:	■
Locker Room:		Tennis:	
Rental Clubs:	■	Swimming:	
Walkers:		Jogging Trails:	
Snack Bar:	■	Boating:	

COURSE DESCRIPTION

After the passing of Hurricane Andrew, the board of directors decided to invest a generous amount of money to bring this course back to life. With an excellent new staff, the course is in better shape then it has ever been.

It is a straightforward design with few doglegs and no water. Birdies can be plentiful. Placing your drives on the proper side of the fairway is the key to setting up a good approach shot to the green, especially on the Bermuda greens, which are mostly small.

The price of admission is well worth the time and enjoyment you'll get from playing golf here.

DIRECTIONS

Take Hwy. 1 south to Coconut Palm Dr. (248th St.) and go west to Krome Ave. Turn south to the course.

SHULA'S HOTEL & GOLF CLUB
15400 N.W. 77th Ave., Miami Lakes, FL 331 / (305) 821-1150

BASIC INFORMATION

Course Type: Resort
Year Built: 1962
Architect: D. Wilson
Local Pro: Frankie Jones

Course: Blue
Holes: 18 / Par 72

Back: 7,055 yds. Rating: 73.0 Slope: 124
Middle: 6,512 yds. Rating: 70.5 Slope: 120
Ladies: 5,639 yds. Rating: 70.5 Slope: 120

Tee Time: 5 days in advance
Price: $27 - $75

Credit Cards:	■	Restaurant:	■
Driving Range:	■	Lounge:	■
Practice Green:	■	Meeting Rooms:	■
Locker Room:	■	Tennis:	■
Rental Clubs:	■	Swimming:	■
Walkers:	■	Jogging Trails:	■
Snack Bar:	■	Boating:	

COURSE DESCRIPTION
For those of you curious about the name, this course *is* owned and operated by the Miami Dolphins coach Don Shula.

The course is a demanding layout with plenty of water, trees, and elevated greens. It is a solid golf course with a good combination of hole designs.

The 18th hole is a good indication of what you will be up against. This dogleg left hole is a par-4 measuring 463 yards in length. If you want to make a birdie on this hole, you need to hit your drive at least 235 yards over the edge of the dogleg to beat the water that surrounds it.

DIRECTIONS
Take I-95 south to the 826 (Palmetto Expwy.) Exit onto Miami Lakes Dr. and go east to the course.

TURNBERRY ISLE YACHT & COUNTRY CLUB
19999 W. Country Club Dr., Aventura, FL 33180 / (305) 932-6200

BASIC INFORMATION

Course Type: Resort
Year Built: 1970
Architect: R.T. Jones Sr.
Local Pro: Dan Fournier

Course: South
Holes: 18 / Par 72

Back: 7,003 yds. Rating: 73.9 Slope: 140
Middle: 6,458 yds. Rating: 71.1 Slope: 122
Ladies: 6,581 yds. Rating: 71.9 Slope: 121

Tee Time: 2 days in advance
Price: N/A

Credit Cards:	■	Restaurant:	■
Driving Range:	■	Lounge:	■
Practice Green:	■	Meeting Rooms:	■
Locker Room:	■	Tennis:	■
Rental Clubs:	■	Swimming:	■
Walkers:		Jogging Trails:	■
Snack Bar:	■	Boating:	■

COURSE DESCRIPTION
Both of the courses on this wonderful resort are exceptional designs. The North course is shorter and has less water. The South course is the more difficult of the two with water hugging 12 of the holes. Holes number 2, 6, 15, and 18 all have additional water in front of the green.

Raymond Floyd, the great PGA and Senior PGA Tour player, is a local resident. Other celebrities that have been spotted on these courses include Jack Nicholson and Sophia Loren.

Turnberry is the kind of place that offers golf and pampered relaxation. You're going to love playing here!

DIRECTIONS
Take I-95 south to Ives Dairy Rd. Go east to Biscayne Blvd. and south to Aventura Blvd. Go east on Aventura Blvd. and south on Country Road Dr. to the course.

44

CLEWISTON GOLF COURSE
1200 San Luiz, Clewiston, FL 33440 / (813) 983-7064

BASIC INFORMATION

Course Type: Municipal
Year Built: 1929
Architect: N/A
Local Pro: Bob Rush

Course: N/A
Holes: 18 / Par 72

Back: 6,500 yds. Rating: 69.3 Slope: 115
Middle: 6,306 yds. Rating: 69.3 Slope: 109
Ladies: 5,294 yds. Rating: 69.2 Slope: 109

Tee Time: 4 days in advance
Price: $9 - $15

Credit Cards:		Restaurant:	■
Driving Range:	■	Lounge:	■
Practice Green:	■	Meeting Rooms:	
Locker Room:	■	Tennis:	
Rental Clubs:	■	Swimming:	
Walkers:	■	Jogging Trails:	
Snack Bar:	■	Boating:	

COURSE DESCRIPTION
For a course that only plays 6,500 yards from the back tee, this is a good solid test of golf that is challenging despite the 115 slope rating.

Clewiston Golf Course is a fair shotmakers' course. I say that because the course favors neither a fade nor a draw. You'll end up playing every club in your bag by the end of the game. If you can play a good game from about 170-150 yards out, you'll end up scoring some really good numbers.

Get your birdies as early as possible. The back nine is the harder of the two off the tee and around the greens.

The course features wide fairways and small greens.

DIRECTIONS
Take Hwy. 27 east of Clewiston. The course is close to the airport.

OXBOW GOLF CLUB AT PORT LABELLE
1 Oxbow Dr., Port Labelle, FL 33935 / (813) 675-4411

BASIC INFORMATION

Course Type: Resort
Year Built: 1970
Architect: A. Phillips / A. Hills
Local Pro: Gary Keating

Course: N/A
Holes: 18 / Par 72

Back: 6,862 yds. Rating: 72.7 Slope: 129
Middle: 6,348 yds. Rating: 70.3 Slope: 125
Ladies: 5,005 yds. Rating: 68.5 Slope: 116

Tee Time: 3 days in advance
Price: $24 - $40

Credit Cards:	■	Restaurant:	■
Driving Range:	■	Lounge:	■
Practice Green:	■	Meeting Rooms:	■
Locker Room:	■	Tennis:	■
Rental Clubs:	■	Swimming:	■
Walkers:		Jogging Trails:	
Snack Bar:	■	Boating:	

COURSE DESCRIPTION
This is an exciting course that plays like two different challenges in one. The front nine is set up strategically, allowing you many options to play aggressive golf. This is where you'll want to score your low numbers.

You'll find the back nine much more challenging with narrow fairways and many more trees coming into the play of action. You'll often end up having to play your ball around a tree for good position. "How many trees?" you might ask. After completing a ather difficult round, a gentleman swore that he would cut down every tree on the course. You've got to be a real shotmaker here.

Water comes into play on 15 holes.

DIRECTIONS
Take Hwy. 80 west of LaBelle and follow the signs to the course.

ATLANTIS COUNTRY CLUB & INN

301 Orange Tree Dr., Atlantis, FL 33462 / (561) 968-1300

BASIC INFORMATION

Course Type: Resort
Year Built: 1973
Architect: R. Simmons
Local Pro: Jim Simon

Course: N/A
Holes: 18 / Par 72

Back: 6,477 yds. Rating: 71.1 Slope: 126
Middle: 6,060 yds. Rating: 69.1 Slope: 122
Ladies: 5,258 yds. Rating: 70.9 Slope: 123

Tee Time: 2 days in advance
Price: $35 - $65

Credit Cards:	■	Restaurant:	■
Driving Range:	■	Lounge:	■
Practice Green:	■	Meeting Rooms:	■
Locker Room:	■	Tennis:	■
Rental Clubs:	■	Swimming:	■
Walkers:		Jogging Trails:	■
Snack Bar:	■	Boating:	■

COURSE DESCRIPTION

This course plays increasingly well with each hole. It's not a long course, but the strategic design will force you to play the good majority of your clubs by the time you finish your round.

Despite the short yardage, many people seem to have a hard time scoring well here. Half of the course features water that comes into play. Thousands of trees can be found throughout the course and are often in the way of an errant shot. The greens are on the small side. At times it feels as though the entire course is set up to challenge the 8th hole at Royal Troon (Postage Stamp).

If you do well from the proper tees, you're going to want to come back.

DIRECTIONS

Exit 6th Ave off I-95 and go west to Congress. Make a left at JFK Circle and the course will be on your right.

BELLE GLADE GOLF & COUNTRY CLUB

110 S.W. Ave. E., Belle Glade, FL 33430 / (561) 996-6605

BASIC INFORMATION

Course Type: Public
Year Built: 1987
Architect: N/A
Local Pro: Mike Underwood

Course: N/S
Holes: 18 / Par 72

Back: 6,558 yds. Rating: 70.0 Slope: 116
Middle: 6,044 yds. Rating: 67.7 Slope: 112
Ladies: 5,182 yds. Rating: 65.5 Slope: 112

Tee Time: First come basis
Price: $20.67 - $28.09

Credit Cards:		Restaurant:	■
Driving Range:	■	Lounge:	■
Practice Green:	■	Meeting Rooms:	■
Locker Room:		Tennis:	■
Rental Clubs:		Swimming:	
Walkers:	■	Jogging Trails:	
Snack Bar:	■	Boating:	■

COURSE DESCRIPTION

Belle Glade Golf & Country Club is a competitive design with many challenging holes. The course is set up to be a shotmakers' run at par. Every shot needs to be thought about carefully before execution.

The fairways are narrow and feature lots of mature palm trees leading up to small greens. You'll need to hit your drives long and straight to get into position for a proper shot to the green. The loftier the club, the better your chances of keeping the ball on the small putting surfaces.

Consistency is everything here. A strong short game is the key to making pars and birdies.

DIRECTIONS

Take Hwy. 17 from St. Rd. 7 (441) and turn right at the second light. Proceed straight to the course.

BOCA GOLF & TENNIS CLUB

17751 Boca Club Blvd., Boca Raton, FL 33487 / (561) 997-8463

BASIC INFORMATION

Course Type: Resort
Year Built: 1986
Architect: J. Lee
Local Pro: Daryl Hollins

Course: N/A
Holes: 18 / Par 72

Back: 6,564 yds. Rating: 71.1 Slope: 129
Middle: 6,175 yds. Rating: 69.1 Slope: 123
Ladies: 5,565 yds. Rating: 71.2 Slope: 124

Tee Time: 1 day in advance
Price: $69 - $92

Credit Cards:	■	Restaurant:	■
Driving Range:	■	Lounge:	■
Practice Green:	■	Meeting Rooms:	■
Locker Room:	■	Tennis:	■
Rental Clubs:	■	Swimming:	■
Walkers:		Jogging Trails:	
Snack Bar:	■	Boating:	■

COURSE DESCRIPTION

Joe Lee has a way of designing a course with subtle surprises that will creep up on you. This par-72 course is only 6,564 yards in length from tee to finishing green. Yet it has a slope rating of 129. Like I said, it'll creep up on you.

Take, for example, the 10th hole (par-4 / 399 yards). This dogleg right hole is one of the most demanding holes on the course. You'll have to hit your drive through a narrow shoot onto a small defined landing area. Two lakes come into play on the right. Your approach shot will have to land softly on the small, well-bunkered green.

This is a shot-makers' dream.

DIRECTIONS

Exit Yamato Rd. west off I-95 and go north on Congress. Follow that road and the course will be on your left.

BOCA RATON MUNICIPAL GOLF COURSE

8111 S. 205th St., Boca Raton, FL 33428 / (561) 483-6100

BASIC INFORMATION

Course Type: Municipal
Year Built: 1982
Architect: C. Ankrom
Local Pro: Bob Imbaglia

Course: Champion (18 / Par 72)
Holes: 27

Back: 6,593 yds. Rating: 71.0 Slope: 120
Middle: 6,167 yds. Rating: 69.0 Slope: 116
Ladies: 5,306 yds. Rating: 69.4 Slope: 116

Tee Time: 3 days in advance
Price: $17 - $30

Credit Cards:		Restaurant:	■
Driving Range:	■	Lounge:	■
Practice Green:	■	Meeting Rooms:	■
Locker Room:	■	Tennis:	
Rental Clubs:	■	Swimming:	
Walkers:	■	Jogging Trails:	
Snack Bar:		Boating:	■

COURSE DESCRIPTION

This is a surprisingly well-kept course for a Municipal. The challenge will become evident right from the first tee. Although the fairways are wide, many of their bunkers will come into play to devour your drives.

Try to play your ball for position rather than sheer length. This is not a very long course so you might as well set yourself up for good approach shots to the greens.

If you can play a solid game from inside of 150 yards, you should post good numbers.

All of the greens and bunkers have recently been redone. Your putts should roll smooth and true.

DIRECTIONS

Exit Yamato Rd. off I-95 and go east to the first light. Go north on N.W. 2nd and the course will be on your left.

BOCA RATON RESORT & CLUB

501 E. Camino Real, Boca Raton, FL 33432 / (561) 338-2418

BASIC INFORMATION

Course Type: Resort
Year Built: 1926
Architect: W. Flynn
Local Pro: Ray Metz

Course: Boca Country Club (18 / Par 71)
Holes: 36

Back: 6,564 yds. Rating: 71.1 Slope: 126
Middle: 6,175 yds. Rating: 69.1 Slope: 123
Ladies: 5,565 yds. Rating: 71.2 Slope: 124

Tee Time: 5 days in advance
Price: $56 - $91

Credit Cards:	■	Restaurant:	■
Driving Range:	■	Lounge:	■
Practice Green:	■	Meeting Rooms:	■
Locker Room:	■	Tennis:	■
Rental Clubs:	■	Swimming:	■
Walkers:		Jogging Trails:	■
Snack Bar:	■	Boating:	■

COURSE DESCRIPTION

The **Boca Raton Resort and Golf**, is a smart layout that is forgiving for the occasional player. It has wide fairways and only four holes that feature water. However, from the Blue tees, it plays a long 6,770 yards long at par-71.

The course is most challenging when the prevailing winds make their way onto it via the Atlantic. The Resort features beautiful tropical foliage dating back to the 1920's. Noted golf designer Joe Lee redesigned the course in 1988 with all the best playable grasses. The club has only had three golf professionals since it first opened: Sam Snead, Tommy Armour and, presently, Ron Polane.

DIRECTIONS

Exit Palmetto Pk. Rd. from I-95 and go east to Federal Hwy, south to Camino Real, and east to the course.

BOYNTON BEACH MUNICIPAL GOLF COURSE

8020 Jog Rd., Boynton Beach, FL 33437 / (561) 655-6611

BASIC INFORMATION

Course Type: Municipal
Year Built: 1984
Architect: Von Hagge / Devlin
Local Pro: Daniel Hager

Course: Championship (18 / Par 72)
Holes: 27

Back: 6,305 yds. Rating: 70.1 Slope: 120
Middle: 5,975 yds. Rating: 68.5 Slope: 117
Ladies: 5,083 yds. Rating: 65.2 Slope: 109

Tee Time: 2 days in advance
Price: $15.50 - $33

Credit Cards:		Restaurant:	
Driving Range:	■	Lounge:	
Practice Green:	■	Meeting Rooms:	
Locker Room:	■	Tennis:	
Rental Clubs:	■	Swimming:	
Walkers:	■	Jogging Trails:	
Snack Bar:	■	Boating:	

COURSE DESCRIPTION

Boynton Beach Municipal Golf Course has two Championship nines (Red and White courses) and an Executive nine (Blue course). All 27 holes wind through nine lakes, Florida slash pines, and other native species of trees. The many sets of tees allow golfers of all levels a good chance to score well. The natural wildlife on the course is spectacular.

The staff is comprised of PGA Professionals who take the time to make sure you'll have a great day. All rounds are closely monitored to run not more than four-and-a-half hours.

DIRECTIONS

Take I-95 to Boynton Beach Blvd. Go west to Jog Rd. and north to the course, which will be on your right.

BREAKERS OCEAN GOLF COURSE

North 1 South Country Rd., Palm Beach, FL 33418 / (561) 655-6611

BASIC INFORMATION

Course Type: Resort
Year Built: 1897
Architect: D. Ross
Local Pro: Mike Rusinko

Course: N/A
Holes: 18 / Par 70

Back: N/A   Rating: N/A Slope: N/A
Middle: 6,015 yds. Rating: 68.0 Slope: 121
Ladies: 5,677 yds. Rating: 71,o Slope: 119

Tee Time: 2 days in advance
Price: $75

Credit Cards: ■	Restaurant: ■
Driving Range: ■	Lounge: ■
Practice Green: ■	Meeting Rooms: ■
Locker Room: ■	Tennis: ■
Rental Clubs: ■	Swimming: ■
Walkers:	Jogging Trails:
Snack Bar: ■	Boating: ■

COURSE DESCRIPTION

This course is the oldest 18-hole layout in the state of Florida, and is listed on the National Register of Historic Places.

Donald Ross designed this course on a hundred acre lot on the Atlantic Ocean. Like most of the courses built at the turn of the century, you'll find many small greens that are strategically bunkered with an undulating surface.

Donald Ross left his stamp on this course. The greens are open in front for bump-and-run shots, strategically placed hazards appear to be closer than they really are, and so much more. This course is extremely well thought out. You'll love it!

DIRECTIONS

Take I-95 to Okeechobee Blvd. and go east over the bridge to Palm Beach. Make a left onto S. Country Rd. and the course will be on your right.

BREAKERS WEST GOLF CLUB

1550 Flager Pkwy., Boca Raton, FL 33411 / (561) 790-7020

BASIC INFORMATION

Course Type: Resort
Year Built: 1968
Architect: W. Byrd
Local Pro: Gary Soul

Course: N/A
Holes: 18 / Par 72

Back: 7,101 yds. Rating: 73.7 Slope: 133
Middle: 6,388 yds. Rating: 70.1 Slope: 127
Ladies: 5,616 yds. Rating: 71.3 Slope: 127

Tee Time: 2 days in advance
Price: $75

Credit Cards: ■	Restaurant: ■
Driving Range: ■	Lounge: ■
Practice Green: ■	Meeting Rooms: ■
Locker Room: ■	Tennis: ■
Rental Clubs: ■	Swimming: ■
Walkers:	Jogging Trails:
Snack Bar: ■	Boating: ■

COURSE DESCRIPTION

The back nine on this course has just recently been redone and the overall condition is perfect.

This course is the harder of the two courses that the Breakers has to offer. You'll find many challenging holes with good solid designs that allow more than just a single option when you finally take your stance.

This finely tuned golf course can play as tough or as easy as you want. The multiple tees attest to that. You'll have to decide which set is best for your style and play.

Play the course with imagination. Choose the option that is best for your game. With a little luck, you'll do great!

DIRECTIONS

The course is three miles west of the Fl. Tpke. on Okeechobee Blvd.

CAMINO DEL MAR COUNTRY CLUB

22689 Camino Del Mar Dr., Boca Raton, FL 33433 / (561) 392-7992

BASIC INFORMATION

Course Type: Semi-private
Year Built: 1975
Architect: J. Lee
Local Pro: Ron Tapper

Course: N/A
Holes: 18 / Par 72

Back: 6,668 yds. Rating: 71.2 Slope: 120
Middle: 6,318 yds. Rating: 69.5 Slope: 117
Ladies: 5,225 yds. Rating: 69.0 Slope: 115

Tee Time: 2 days in advance
Price: $15 - $47

Credit Cards:	■	Restaurant:	■
Driving Range:	■	Lounge:	■
Practice Green:	■	Meeting Rooms:	■
Locker Room:	■	Tennis:	■
Rental Clubs:	■	Swimming:	■
Walkers:		Jogging Trails:	■
Snack Bar:	■	Boating:	■

COURSE DESCRIPTION

Camino Del Mar Country Club is a semi-private championship course that offers you an opportunity to test your strength, skill, and ingenuity on 18 holes of varying difficultly and complexity. Some holes are relatively simple, while others will serve as a barometer of your ability to deal with dogleg holes, water, and embankments.

All of Joe Lee's courses feature excitement for both the average and professional golfer. This is one course that will thrill you from tee to green no matter what your handicap may be. All of the holes are competitively designed and fun to play.

DIRECTIONS

Take I-95 to Palmetto Park Rd. and go west to Military Trail and south to Camino Real. Go west to your third left (Camino Del Mar) and south to the Club. It will be on your right.

CYPRESS CREEK COUNTRY CLUB

9400 N. Military Trail, Boynton Beach, FL 33436 / (561) 732-4203

BASIC INFORMATION

Course Type: Semi-private
Year Built: 1963
Architect: R. Von Hagge
Local Pro: Rick Durham (P.G.A.)

Course: N/A
Holes: 18 / Par 72

Back: 6,808 yds. Rating: 72.0 Slope: 114
Middle: 6,369 yds. Rating: 70.0 Slope: 110
Ladies: 5,530 yds. Rating: 71.0 Slope: 109

Tee Time: 1 day in advance
Price: $20 - $40

Credit Cards:	■	Restaurant:	■
Driving Range:	■	Lounge:	■
Practice Green:	■	Meeting Rooms:	■
Locker Room:	■	Tennis:	
Rental Clubs:	■	Swimming:	■
Walkers:		Jogging Trails:	
Snack Bar:	■	Boating:	

COURSE DESCRIPTION

This course is beautifully laid out for both the novice and the professional. It is the type of layout that will have you thinking about every shot you make.

Although the slope rating is only 114, the course does add a lot more pressure than you may think. From the tee, most of the fairways are of average size with a low cut rough. The pressure builds up as you get closer to the pin. Water comes into play on 14 holes, five of which force you to play your approach shot over water to reach the green.

The open and flat terrain of the course is easily susceptible to high winds from time to time. You'll have to keep your shots low.

DIRECTIONS

Take I-95 to Boynton Beach Blvd. and west to Military Trail. The course will be a mile further on your right.

DELRAY BEACH MUNICIPAL GOLF COURSE

2200 Highland Ave., Delray Beach, FL. 33445 / (561) 278-0315

BASIC INFORMATION

Course Type: Municipal
Year Built: 1923
Architect: D. Ross
Local Pro: Sandra Friksson

Course: N/A
Holes: 18 / Par 72

Back: 6,657 yds. Rating: 71.5 Slope: 119
Middle: 6,201 yds. Rating: 69.2 Slope: 114
Ladies: 5,265 yds. Rating: 69.5 Slope: 115

Tee Time: 2 days in advance
Price: $14 - $33

Credit Cards:	■	Restaurant:	■
Driving Range:	■	Lounge:	■
Practice Green:	■	Meeting Rooms:	■
Locker Room:	■	Tennis:	
Rental Clubs:	■	Swimming:	
Walkers:	■	Jogging Trails:	
Snack Bar:	■	Boating:	

COURSE DESCRIPTION

Any time you get a chance to play a course designed by Donald Ross, do it! He was one of the most influential designers of all time.

The *Delray Beach Municipal Golf Club* is a wonderful course that plays long and challenging. It was designed during the 1920's, when strategy was the rule over distance. This beautifully maintained course is great for golfers of all levels. It is a fair course built on flat terrain with many hazards and very little water coming into play.

You'll love playing golf the way it was meant to be played: no homes and only nature between you and your target. This is a golf course to remember.

DIRECTIONS

Take I-95 to Atlantic and go west to Homewood Blvd. Make a left at Highland Ave. and another left to the clubhouse.

DOUG FORD'S LACUNA GOLF CLUB

6400 Grand Lacuna Blvd., Lake Worth, FL 33467 / (561) 433-3006

BASIC INFORMATION

Course Type: Semi-private
Year Built: 1985
Architect: J. Lee
Local Pro: Mike Ford

Course: N/A
Holes: 18 / Par 72

Back: 6,800 yds. Rating: 70.4 Slope: 121
Middle: 6,400 yds. Rating: 69.7 Slope: 118
Ladies: 5,200 yds. Rating: 67.5 Slope: 111

Tee Time: 4 days in advance
Price: $20 - $40

Credit Cards:	■	Restaurant:	■
Driving Range:	■	Lounge:	■
Practice Green:	■	Meeting Rooms:	■
Locker Room:	■	Tennis:	■
Rental Clubs:	■	Swimming:	■
Walkers:		Jogging Trails:	
Snack Bar:	■	Boating:	■

COURSE DESCRIPTION

Doug Ford's Lacana Golf Club is an interesting layout that will bring you pleasure on every shot. You'll have many moments to hit your best drives onto the wide and generous fairways. The course is a straightforward strategic design that mostly features non-dogleg holes.

The back nine is the harder half of the course with two really tough finishing holes. Golfer beware! Get your birdies while you can on the front half. If you're above a 10 handicap, play the course from the middle tees. It's 400 yards shorter and much more manageable. You should be able to set yourself up nicely off the tee.

DIRECTIONS

Take I-95 to Lantana Rd. and go west for about eight miles. The course will be on your right side.

EMERALD DUNES GOLF CLUB
2100 Emerald Dunes Dr., West Palm Beach, FL 33411 / (561) 784-4653

BASIC INFORMATION

Course Type: Public
Year Built: 1990
Architect: T. Fazio
Local Pro: Rob Young

Course: N/A
Holes: 18 / Par 72

Back: 7,006 yds. Rating: 73.8 Slope: 133
Middle: 6,120 yds. Rating: 69.7 Slope: 125
Ladies: 4,676 yds. Rating: 67.1 Slope: 115

Tee Time: 7 days in advance
Price: $65 - $120

Credit Cards:	■	Restaurant:	■
Driving Range:	■	Lounge:	■
Practice Green:	■	Meeting Rooms:	■
Locker Room:	■	Tennis:	
Rental Clubs:	■	Swimming:	
Walkers:		Jogging Trails:	
Snack Bar:	■	Boating:	

COURSE DESCRIPTION

Even though the course was only completed in 1990, it has quickly become legendary for being the 1,000th course built in Florida. But that's only the beginning.

Golf Digest magazine has named this course the best new course of the year in 1991. It's an incredible challenge and another wonderful tribute to Tom Fazio's work. You'll enjoy the structure of the holes as they magically fuse elements of both a Scottish links course and a touch of the Carolina's. The hallmark of this outstanding golf course is the 50 foot high super dune tee.

DIRECTIONS

At the intersection of Okeechobee Blvd., and the Fl. Tpke. Less than ten minutes from the Palm Beach International Airport.

EXECUTIVE GOLF COURSE
6561 Flanders Way, Delray Beach, FL 33484 / (561) 499-7840

BASIC INFORMATION

Course Type: Resort
Year Built: 1967
Architect: B. Amick
Local Pro: Keven Gabard

Course: South & East (18 / Par 72)
Holes: 27

Back: 7,025 yds. Rating: 73.9 Slope: 133
Middle: 6,412 yds. Rating: 71.0 Slope: 126
Ladies: 5,661 yds. Rating: 73.0 Slope: 123

Tee Time: 7 days in advance
Price: $30 - $35

Credit Cards:	■	Restaurant:	■
Driving Range:	■	Lounge:	■
Practice Green:	■	Meeting Rooms:	■
Locker Room:	■	Tennis:	■
Rental Clubs:	■	Swimming:	■
Walkers:	■	Jogging Trails:	■
Snack Bar:	■	Boating:	■

COURSE DESCRIPTION

The Sprint Classic, one of the most exciting tournaments on the PGA Tour, is played here each year. The back tees are an awesome challenge at 7,025 yards. Play from the white tees if you're above a single digit handicapper. You'll need the reduced yardage to place your drives in good position for the approach shots to the greens.

This scenic course features some of the most beautiful holes you'll ever encounter. It's a layout that needs to be studied in advance to play well on. The total make-up of the course will bring out the best within you: It's a special place to experience the game.

DIRECTIONS

Exit Hwy. 319 off I-10 and go north to Killearney Way and east to Shamrock. Go west on Shamrock and follow the road to the course.

INDIAN CREEK GOLF CLUB
1800 Central Blvd., Jupiter, FL 33458 / (561) 747-6262

BASIC INFORMATION
Course Type: Public
Year Built: 1982
Architect: L. Smith
Local Pro: Bobby Dodson

Course: N/A
Holes: 18 / Par 72

Back: 6,155 yds. Rating: 69.9 Slope: 117
Middle: 5,668 yds. Rating: 67.4 Slope: 114
Ladies: 5,150 yds. Rating: 69.5 Slope: 118

Tee Time: 4 days in advance
Price: $25 - $42

Credit Cards: ■   Restaurant: ■
Driving Range: ■   Lounge: ■
Practice Green: ■   Meeting Rooms:
Locker Room: ■   Tennis:
Rental Clubs: ■   Swimming:
Walkers: Jogging Trails:
Snack Bar: ■   Boating:

COURSE DESCRIPTION
Indian Creek Golf Club is a delightful place to play a relaxing game of golf. The course is a relatively easy one in which most players should post a good score.

Golfers who are looking to practice their short games will love this course. It favors straight shots over draws and fades. Keep your drives down the middle of the fairway and you'll usually end up only a 7-iron away from the green.

The course is surrounded by trees and very little water. You'll find the back nine to be the tougher half of the course. The friendly atmosphere adds to the enjoyment.

DIRECTIONS
From I-95 or the Fl. Tpke. take Jupiter Exit (Indiantown Road) east to Central Blvd. (first traffic light). Go right one mile from East Jupiter (beaches) and take Indiantown Road west to Central Blvd.

LAKE WORTH GOLF CLUB
7th Ave. North & Lakeside, Lake Worth, FL 33460 / (561) 582-9713

BASIC INFORMATION
Course Type: Municipal
Year Built: 1925 / 1991
Architect: D. Wilson
Local Pro: Merrill Hubbard

Course: N/A
Holes: 18 / Par 70

Back: 6,113 yds. Rating: 68.6 Slope: 116
Middle: 5,744 yds. Rating: 67.1 Slope: 112
Ladies: 5,423 yds. Rating: 69.6 Slope: 113

Tee Time: 1 day in advance
Price: $10 - $23

Credit Cards: Restaurant:
Driving Range: Lounge:
Practice Green: ■   Meeting Rooms:
Locker Room: ■   Tennis:
Rental Clubs: ■   Swimming:
Walkers: ■   Jogging Trails:
Snack Bar: ■   Boating: ■

COURSE DESCRIPTION
Lake Worth Golf Club is a fine course with thoughtful hole designs that are both fun and challenging to play. The course is situated beside the Intracoastal Waterway and is prone to the winds that come off the Atlantic ocean. The regular players here call Lake Worth the *Air Conditioned Golf Course.*

This isn't a very difficult place to play. If you're looking for a fair challenge that emphasizes the short game in particular, this may be your course. With the prevailing winds, you'll need to come up with a swing that will keep the ball below the wind. This is when the course is most challenging and fun to play.

DIRECTIONS
Exit I-95 to 10th Ave. and go east to Federal Hwy. Go south to 7th Ave. and east to the course.

LUCERNE LAKES GOLF COURSE

144 Lucerne Lakes Blvd., Lake Worth, FL 33467 / (561) 967-6810

BASIC INFORMATION

Course Type: Public
Year Built: 1971
Architect: N/A
Local Pro: Karl Schmidt

Course: N/A
Holes: 18 / Par 72

Back: 5,583 yds. Rating: 67.9 Slope: 118
Middle:5,212 yds. Rating: 65.8 Slope: 116
Ladies: 4,661 yds. Rating: 67.4 Slope: 115

Tee Time: First come basis
Price: $15 - $28

Credit Cards:		Restaurant:	
Driving Range:		Lounge:	
Practice Green:	■	Meeting Rooms:	
Locker Room:		Tennis:	
Rental Clubs:	■	Swimming:	
Walkers:	■	Jogging Trails:	
Snack Bar:	■	Boating:	■

COURSE DESCRIPTION

Don't be discouraged by the short distance of the course. This is a demanding layout for golfers of all abilities.

The fairways here are pencil thin and only the most accurate shots will make it onto the proper landing areas. Combined with the many trees surrounding the course, you'll quickly come to realize that this is a very serious golf course.

Put your driver away and play the course for what it was meant to be: a tremendous challenge directed at a golfer's short iron ability.

This is a well-conditioned course that favors a fade over a draw.

DIRECTIONS

Take the Fl. Tpke. to Lake Worth Rd. and go east to Lucerne Lakes Blvd. Go south and watch for the course.

NORTH PALM BEACH COUNTRY CLUB

951 U.S. Hwy. 1, North Palm Beach, FL 33408 / (561) 626-4344

BASIC INFORMATION

Course Type: Public
Year Built: 1946 / 1989
Architect: M. McCumber
Local Pro: John Scott

Course: N/A
Holes: 18 / Par 72

Back: 6,275 yds. Rating: 70.0 Slope: 117
Middle: 5,769 yds. Rating: 67.6 Slope: 113
Ladies: 5,055 yds. Rating: 68.7 Slope: 113

Tee Time: 1 day in advance
Price: $19 - $42

Credit Cards:	■	Restaurant:	■
Driving Range:	■	Lounge:	■
Practice Green:	■	Meeting Rooms:	■
Locker Room:	■	Tennis:	■
Rental Clubs:	■	Swimming:	■
Walkers:	■	Jogging Trails:	
Snack Bar:	■	Boating:	■

COURSE DESCRIPTION

This course is a great achievement for one that is only 6,275 yards from the back tees. It's a strategically designed course that features water coming into play on every hole. The wide fairways give you a good chance to set up your approach shots from the tee. If you can keep your ball in play and on the right part of the fairway, you'll usually have a good chance to place your ball on the green for a two putt par.

The front nine is the harder half of the course. Play a steady game and go for your birdies on the second half. This is a real shotmakers' course which favors a draw. Get on the range early and practice your right to left shots.

DIRECTIONS

Exit PGA Blvd. off I-95 and go east to to Hwy. 1. Go south to the course and look for the sign.

PALM BEACH LAKES GOLF CLUB

1100 N. Congress Ave., West Palm Beach, FL 33401 / (561) 683-2710

BASIC INFORMATION

Course Type: Public
Year Built: 1963
Architect: W. Mitchell
Local Pro:Bill Arnold

Course: N/A
Holes: 18 / Par 72

Back: 5,400 yds. Rating: 65.2 Slope: 110
Middle: 5,187 yds. Rating: 64.3 Slope: 108
Ladies: 4,924 yds. Rating: 67.0 Slope: 111

Tee Time: 2 days in advance
Price: $8 - $20

Credit Cards:	■	Restaurant:	■
Driving Range:	■	Lounge:	■
Practice Green:	■	Meeting Rooms:	■
Locker Room:		Tennis:	
Rental Clubs:	■	Swimming:	■
Walkers:	■	Jogging Trails:	■
Snack Bar:	■	Boating:	■

COURSE DESCRIPTION

This honest and mature golf course plays longer than it measures when the winds start twirling around from the ocean.

It's an exceptional course to practice your short game. Senior citizens love the fact that the course only plays 5,400 yards from the back tees. This is also one of the only courses in the county that allows walking during the entire day.

You'll find a nice variety of tropical foliage and wildlife that will add to your golfing enjoyment. *Palm Beach Lakes* offers a lot of fun for those of you who prefer to play shorter courses.

DIRECTIONS

Take I-95 to Exit 53 to Palm Beach Lakes Blvd. Go east on Palm Beach Lakes Blvd. to N. Congress Ave. and make a right at WPB Auditorium to course.

PALM BEACH POLO & COUNTRY CLUB

11830 Polo Club Dr., West Palm Beach , FL 33414 / (561) 798-7401

BASIC INFORMATION

Course Type: Resort
Year Built: 1978 / 1984
Architect: P. Dye / P.B.Dye
Local Pro: Kyle Kolls

Course: Cypress (18 / Par 72)
Holes: 45

Back: 7,116 yds. Rating: 74.4 Slope: 138
Middle: 6,678 yds. Rating: 72.2 Slope: 135
Ladies: 5,157 yds. Rating: 69.8 Slope: 121

Tee Time: 2 days in advance
Price: $75

Credit Cards:	■	Restaurant:	■
Driving Range:	■	Lounge:	■
Practice Green:	■	Meeting Rooms:	■
Locker Room:	■	Tennis:	■
Rental Clubs:	■	Swimming:	■
Walkers:		Jogging Trails:	■
Snack Bar:	■	Boating:	■

COURSE DESCRIPTION

Every one of the 45 holes throughout this establishment are great. G. Fazio, R. Garl, and J. Pate have all put their signatures on some of the finest holes in the country. The Cypress course, designed by Pete Dye and his son P.B. Dye, is no exception. Like many of his other courses, Pete Dye enjoys the fine elements that make a professional shine above everyone else. This course is undulating with many changes in elevation and 13 holes that feature water. The course has a links feel to it and plays into big bunkers and mounds.

It's an exceptional challenge, innovative and beautiful.

DIRECTIONS

Take I-95 and exit on to Forest Hills Blvd. The course will be about eight miles west.

PGA NATIONAL GOLF CLUB

1000 Ave. of the Champions, Palm Beach Gardens, FL 33418 / (561) 627-1800

BASIC INFORMATION

Course Type: Resort
Year Built: 1981 / 1990
Architect: T. Fazio / Jack Nicklaus
Local Pro: Bob Coleman

Course: Champion (18 / Par 72)
Holes: 90

Back: 7,022 yds. Rating: 74.7 Slope: 142
Middle: 6,742 yds. Rating: 71.1 Slope: 129
Ladies: 5,377 yds. Rating: 71.1 Slope: 123

Tee Time: Call to confirm.
Price: $70 - $120

Credit Cards:	■	Restaurant:	■
Driving Range:	■	Lounge:	■
Practice Green:	■	Meeting Rooms:	■
Locker Room:	■	Tennis:	■
Rental Clubs:	■	Swimming:	■
Walkers:		Jogging Trails:	■
Snack Bar:	■	Boating:	■

COURSE DESCRIPTION

This is one of the most important establishments in the golfing world today. With 90 holes of golf to choose from, no one gets left behind.

Imagine having Tom Fazio design your golf course for you. Nine years later, you decide that your course needs to be updated a bit. Who do you call? The PGA called Jack Nicklaus and the final outcome was sensational. The course is a typical Nicklaus design with outrageous mounds and graceful bunkers. The 15th, 16th, and 17th holes are known on the Senior PGA Tour as the "Bear Trap." Many of the pros consider them to be the hardest holes on their tour.

DIRECTIONS

Take the Fl. Tpke. to PGA Blvd. (Palm Beach Gardens). Go west and follow the signs.

ROYAL PALM BEACH GOLF COURSE

900 Royal Palm Beach Blvd., Royal Palm Beach, FL 33411 / (561) 798-6430

BASIC INFORMATION

Course Type: Public
Year Built: 1961
Architect: M. Mahannah
Local Pro: Theresa Farino

Course: N/A
Holes: 18 / Par 72

Back: 7,067 yds. Rating: 72.5 Slope: 122
Middle: 6,547 yds. Rating: 70.7 Slope: 116
Ladies: 5,711 yds. Rating: 65.9 Slope: 105

Tee Time: 3 days in advance
Price: $14 - $35

Credit Cards:	■	Restaurant:	
Driving Range:	■	Lounge:	■
Practice Green:	■	Meeting Rooms:	
Locker Room:		Tennis:	
Rental Clubs:	■	Swimming:	
Walkers:		Jogging Trails:	
Snack Bar:		Boating:	

COURSE DESCRIPTION

Royal Palm Beach Golf Course is so challenging that it never plays the same two days in a row. Signature holes are 11 and 15 and feature double-greens and Royal Palms. Both holes are bunkered.

This old-styled Florida course is known for its Banyan tree-bordered fairways. There's a generous number of well-placed bunkers just hungry for your ball. The front nine features more water than the back, yet the back nine, which favors a draw, is more challenging off the tee with its narrow fairways.

Ask about the local tournaments that are held each Wednesday and Saturday.

DIRECTIONS

From the Fl. Tpke. exit onto Okeechobee Blvd. and go west to Royal Palm Beach Blvd. Make a left here and the course will be on your left side one mile away.

SANDALFOOT COUNTRY CLUB
1400 Country Club Dr., Boca Raton, FL 33428 / (561) 893-2186

BASIC INFORMATION

Course Type: Semi-private
Year Built: 1969
Architect: Devlin / Von Hagge
Local Pro: Bob Crissy

Course: N/A
Holes: 18 / Par 72

Back: 6,625 yds. Rating: 72.2 Slope: 124
Middle: 6,127 yds. Rating: 70.0 Slope: 119
Ladies: 5,325 yds. Rating: 71.0 Slope: 119

Tee Time: 3 days in advance
Price: $18 - $45

Credit Cards:	■	Restaurant:	■
Driving Range:	■	Lounge:	■
Practice Green:	■	Meeting Rooms:	■
Locker Room:	■	Tennis:	
Rental Clubs:	■	Swimming:	■
Walkers:		Jogging Trails:	
Snack Bar:	■	Boating:	

COURSE DESCRIPTION
The great architectural team of Devlin and Von Hagge did a superb job of designing this course.

The fairways are narrow and contoured to perfection with distinctive outlines on every hole. All greens are very large, elevated, and well-trapped. You'll also find large berms and sand-traps strategically located throughout the course. The rough is lined with over 400 Sabal Palms and close to 800 blooming Oleanders.

Water comes into play on seven holes. The course represents a tough challenge to the best player and offers a pleasurable experience for the high handicap golfer.

DIRECTIONS
Take I-95 to Plametto Park Rd. exit and go west to Lyons Rd. Make a left to S.W. 8th St. and turn right. Go west to the clubhouse.

SOUTHWINDS GOLF COURSE
19557 Lyons Rd., Boca Raton, FL 33434 / (561) 483-1305

BASIC INFORMATION

Course Type: Public
Year Built: 1987
Architect: C. Lifton
Local Pro: Frank Wyant

Course: N/A
Holes: 18 / Par 71

Back: 6,000 yds. Rating: 67.7 Slope: 120
Middle: 5,200 yds. Rating: 65.1 Slope: 114
Ladies: 4,200 yds. Rating: 69.8 Slope: 120

Tee Time: 3 days in advance
Price: $15.50 - $27.50

Credit Cards:		Restaurant:	■
Driving Range:	■	Lounge:	■
Practice Green:	■	Meeting Rooms:	■
Locker Room:	■	Tennis:	
Rental Clubs:	■	Swimming:	
Walkers:	■	Jogging Trails:	
Snack Bar:	■	Boating:	■

COURSE DESCRIPTION
This interesting course has a number of inventive holes that make it both challenging and fun to play.

Don't get fooled into thinking that you'll drive each hole with ease. Water comes into play on 16 holes. There is a great premium placed on your tee shots; play them to your favorite approach distance to the green. Try hitting your 3-wood or 4-wood for accuracy and just the right amount of distance.

This is a tight course that will demand your best. If you play an intelligent game, you'll do terrific!

DIRECTIONS
Take the Fl. Tpke. to Glades Rd. and go west. Go north on Lyons and watch for the signs to the course.

VILLA DELRAY GOLF COURSE

6200 Via Delray Dr., Delray Beach, FL 33484 / (561) 498-1444

BASIC INFORMATION

Course Type: Semi-private
Year Built: 1973
Architect: F. Batto
Local Pro: Debbie Hall

Course: N/A
Holes: 18 / Par 71

Back: 6,150 yds. Rating: 69.0 Slope: 116
Middle: 5,843 yds. Rating: 67.3 Slope: 116
Ladies: 5442 yds. Rating: 70.3 Slope: 116

Tee Time: 2 days in advance
Price: $12 - $40

Credit Cards:	■	Restaurant:	■
Driving Range:	■	Lounge:	■
Practice Green:	■	Meeting Rooms:	
Locker Room:	■	Tennis:	
Rental Clubs:	■	Swimming:	
Walkers:	■	Jogging Trails:	
Snack Bar:	■	Boating:	■

COURSE DESCRIPTION

This is another interesting example of a short course design that is both challenging and fun to play.

Accuracy above distance is the golden rule here. The fairways are narrow and hitting into the rough will usually cause you to score a bogey. Only the best finesse shots will produce pars on the six holes that feature water coming into play.

One of the hardest holes on the course is the 11th (Par-3 / 188 yards). You'll be hitting out of a narrow teeing area towards an elevated "postage-stamp" green.

The back nine is the harder half of the course. Get your birdies early!

DIRECTIONS

Exit onto Atlantic Ave. from I-95 and go west to Military Trail. Drive north to Via Del Ray and the course will be on your right.

VILLAGE GOLF CLUB, THE

122 Country Club Dr., Royal Palm Beach, FL 33411 / (561) 793-1400

BASIC INFORMATION

Course Type: Public
Year Built: 1969
Architect: M. Mahannah
Local Pro: Jim Cassia

Course: N/A
Holes: 18 / Par 72

Back: 6,880 yds. Rating: 73.3 Slope: 134
Middle: 6,079 yds. Rating: 69.0 Slope: 123
Ladies: 5,455 yds. Rating: 71.7 Slope: 126

Tee Time: 2 days in advance
Price: $19 - $42

Credit Cards:	■	Restaurant:	
Driving Range:	■	Lounge:	■
Practice Green:	■	Meeting Rooms:	■
Locker Room:	■	Tennis:	■
Rental Clubs:	■	Swimming:	■
Walkers:	■	Jogging Trails:	
Snack Bar:	■	Boating:	

COURSE DESCRIPTION

The *Village Golf Club* in Royal Palm Beach is ranked one of the most difficult golf courses in South Florida. Four sets of tee markers give the option of playing between 5,400 yards to nearly 7,000 yards. The course is lined with flowering shrubbery adding to a bright and upbeat experience.

Architect Mark Mahannah's version of an Island green is the 5th hole (par-3). This signature hole is guarded by water semi-circling from front and around the right side. It plays 194 yards from the back tees.

There are numerous scenic lakes that all come into play. It is one of the favorite courses for many visiting golf professionals.

DIRECTIONS

Take the Fl. Tpke. to Okeechobe Blvd. five miles west to Royal Palm Beach Blvd. Go north 1/4 mile to Country Club Mile. The course wil be on your right.

WESTCHESTER GOLF & COUNTRY CLUB

12250 Westchester Club Dr., Boynton Beach, FL 33437 / (561) 734-6300

BASIC INFORMATION

Course Type: Semi-private
Year Built: 1988
Architect: K. Litten
Local Pro: Dan Robinson

Course: Championship (18 / Par 72)
Holes: 36

Back: 6,760 yds. Rating: 72.0 Slope: 128
Middle: 6,297 yds. Rating: 69.0 Slope: 121
Ladies: 4,886 yds. Rating: 67.5 Slope: 111

Tee Time: 2 days in advance
Price: $17 - $47

Credit Cards:	■	Restaurant:	■
Driving Range:	■	Lounge:	■
Practice Green:	■	Meeting Rooms:	
Locker Room:	■	Tennis:	
Rental Clubs:	■	Swimming:	
Walkers:		Jogging Trails:	
Snack Bar:	■	Boating:	

COURSE DESCRIPTION

Westchester Golf & Country Club is an interesting design with numerous doglegs and multiple tees.

This links-styled course features an open playing field with strategically placed bunkers that come into play often. It is both a fun and challenging course, especially when you have to play it against the wind. If your natural shot sails on a low trajectory, the course will compliment your playing style.

Many of the greens are open enough to allow bump-and-run approach shots from the fairway.

DIRECTIONS

Take I-95 to Exit 43. and go west to Military Trail. Go south on Military Trail and the course will be one mile on your left.

BROWARD COUNTY

Adios Country Club
(954) 429-0990
7740 N.W. 39th Ave., Coconut Creek
Local Pro: Tom Stewart
Reciprocal Play: No

Coral Ridge Country Club
(954) 566-4746
3801 Bayview Dr., Ft. Lauderdale
Local Pro: Ron Sharp
Reciprocal Play: Yes

Country Club at Coral Springs
(954) 753-2930
10800 W. Sample Rd., Coral Springs
Local Pro: Michael Brian
Reciprocal Play: No

Deerfield Country Club
(954) 427-4400
50 Fairway Dr., Pembroke Pines
Local Pro: Tim Evans
Reciprocal Play: No

Ft. Lauderdale Golf Club
(954) 587-4700
415 Country Club Dr., Plantation
Local Pro: David Carter
Reciprocal Play: Yes (Local)

Hillcrest Country Club
(954) 987-5000
4600 Hillcrest Dr., Hollywood
Local Pro: Wes Smith
Reciprocal Play: No

Hollybrook Golf & Tennis Club
(954) 431-4545
900 Hollybrook Dr., Pembroke Pines
Local Pro: Joel Hyman
Reciprocal Play: No

Inverrary Country Club
(954) 733-7550
3840 Inverrary Blvd., Lauderhill
Local Pro: John Nelson
Reciprocal Play: Yes (Out-of-town-only)

Largo Mar Country Club
(954) 472-7047
500 N.W. 127th Ave., Plantation
Local Pro: John Francis
Reciprocal Play: Yes (Local)

Oak Tree Country Club
(954) 733-8616
2400 W. Prospect Blvd.
Local Pro: Michael Brod
Reciprocal Play: No

Palm Air
(954) 968-2775
2501 Palm-Aire Dr. N., Pompano Beach
Local Pro: Tom Malone
Reciprocal Play: Yes (Summer)

TPC at Eagle Trace
(954) 753-7222
1111 Eagle Trace Blvd., Coral Springs
Local Pro: Scott Gray
Reciprocal Play: Yes

Weston Hills Country Club
(954) 384-4600
2600 Country Club Way, Ft. Lauderdale
Local Pro: Bob Bourne
Reciprocal Play: Yes (Out-of-state)

Woodlands Country Club
(954) 731-2500
4600 Woodlands Blvd., Tamarac
Local Pro: Gary Axelrod
Reciprocal Play: Yes (Local)

Woodmont Country Club
(954) 722-4300
7801 N.W. 80th Ave., Tamarac
Local Pro: Steve Downey
Reciprocal Play: No

DADE COUNTY

PALM BEACH

Deering Bay Country Club
(305) 256-2500
13605 Old Cutler Rd., Miami
Local Pro: Mike Nedrow
Reciprocal Play: Yes

Indian Creek Country Club
(305) 866-1263
Indian Creek Village, Miami Beach
Local Pro: Tony Morosco
Reciprocal Play: No

La Gorce Country Club
(305) 866-4421
5685 Alton Rd., Miami Beach
Local Pro: J.R. Congdon
Reciprocal Play: Yes (Fisher Island)

Links at Fisher Island, The
(305) 535-6016
One Fisher Island Dr., Fisher Island
Local Pro: Pam Elders
Reciprocal Play: Yes

Riviera Country Club
(305) 661-4653
1155 Blue Road, Coral Gables
Local Pro: Ted Antononpoulos
Reciprocal Play: Yes (Local)

Westview Country Club
(305) 685-2411
2601 N.W. 119th St., Miami
Local Pro: Nick Fortunato
Reciprocal Play: No

Williams Island Country Club
(305) 652-4741
750 N.E. 195th St., North Miami
Local Pro: Nick Fortunato
Reciprocal Play: No

Atlantis Golf Course
(954) 967-7056
301 Orange Tree Dr., Atlantis
Local Pro: Jim Simon
Reciprocal Play: Yes

Ballen Isles Country Club
(954) 622-0220
100 Ballen Isle Circle, Palm Beach Gardens
Local Pro: Mike Hattman
Reciprocal Play: No

Banyan Golf Course
(954) 793-0177
9059 Ranch Rd., West Palm Beach
Local Pro: Bill Simmons
Reciprocal Play: Yes (Local)

Bear Lakes Country Club
(954) 478-0001
1901 Village Blvd., West Palm Beach
Local Pro: Ken Murphy
Reciprocal Play: Yes

Binks Forest Golf Course
(954) 795-0595
400 Binks Forest Dr., Wellington
Local Pro: Shannon Getty
Reciprocal Play: Yes

Boca Country Club
(954) 997-8463
Boca Club Blvd., Boca Raton
Local Pro: Darral Hollinstad
Reciprocal Play: Yes (Local)

Boca Del Mar Country Club
(954) 392-7990
6200 Boca Del Mar Dr., Boca Raton
Local Pro: Tom Laraia
Reciprocal Play: No

Boca Greens Country Club
(954) 852-8800
19642 Trophy Dr., Boca Raton
Local Pro: Bill Bogenhard
Reciprocal Play: Yes (Local)

PALM BEACH

Boca Grove Plantation Golf Course
(954) 487-5300
21351 Whitaker Dr., Boca Raton
Local Pro: Butch Bryant
Reciprocal Play: Yes

Boca Largo Golf Course
(954) 482-7765
8665 Juego Way, Boca Raton
Local Pro: Mile McLellan
Reciprocal Play: Yes

Boca Pointe Country Club
(954) 391-5100
7144 Boca Pointe Dr., Boca Raton
Local Pro: Buck Diebal
Reciprocal Play: Yes

Boca Rio Golf Course
(954) 482-3300
11041 Boca Rio Rd., Boca Raton
Local Pro: Jay Bechtold
Reciprocal Play: Yes

Boca Teeca Country Club
(954) 994-0400
5800 N.W. 2nd Ave., Boca Raton
Local Pro: Wanda Krolikowski
Reciprocal Play: No

Boca West Golf Course
(954) 488-6924
20583 Boca West Dr., Boca Raton
Local Pro: Brad Luken
Reciprocal Play: No

Boca Woods Country Club
(954) 482-6011
10471 Boca Woods Lane, Boca Raton
Local Pro: Dave Selerno
Reciprocal Play: Yes

Bocaire Country Club
(954) 997-6556
4989 Bocaire Blvd., Boca Raton
Local Pro: Gordy Powell
Reciprocal Play: No

Broken Sound Club
(954) 241-6860
2401 Willow Springs Dr., Boca Raton
Local Pro: Donny Green
Reciprocal Play: Yes

Country Club of Florida
(954) 734-1341
Box 755 Golf Rd., Village of Golf 33436
Local Pro: John Fleming
Reciprocal Play: No

Del Aire Country Club
(954) 499-0770
4645 White Cedar Lane, Delray Beach
Local Pro: Joe Jones
Reciprocal Play: Yes

Delray Dunes Golf & Country Club
(954) 732-1600
12005 Dunes Rd., Boynton Beach
Local Pro: Laurie Hammer
Reciprocal Play: Yes (Local)

Eastpointe Country Club
(954) 626-6863
13535 Eastpointe Blvd., Palm Bch. Gardens
Local Pro: Frank Nastri
Reciprocal Play: Yes

Everglades Golf Course
(954) 655-4189
356 Worth Ave., Palm Beach
Local Pro: Dick Wilson
Reciprocal Play: No

Falls Country Club, The
(954) 964-5700
6455 Jog Rd., Lake Worth
Local Pro: Dave Alvarez
Reciprocal Play: No

Fountains Country Club
(954) 965-8400
4476 Fountain Dr., Lake Worth
Local Pro: Ray Yacobellis
Reciprocal Play: No

PALM BEACH

Frenchman's Creek Golf Course
(954) 622-1620
13495 Tournament Dr., P. Bch. Gardens
Local Pro: Tim O'Neal
Reciprocal Play: Yes (Local)

Gleneagles Country Club
(954) 496-1333
7667 Victory Lane, Delray Beach
Local Pro: Dave Rossi
Reciprocal Play: No

Golf & Racquet Club at Eastpointe
(954) 627-5502
13462 Crosspointe Dr., P. Bch. Gardens
Local Pro: Rich LeConche
Reciprocal Play: No

Greenview Cove Golf Course
(954) 798-2660
2470 Greenview Cove Dr., Wellington
Local Pro: Jerry Wiegold
Reciprocal Play: Yes

Gulf Stream Golf Course
(954) 272-4421
2401 N. Ocean Blvd., Gulf Stream
Local Pro: N/A
Reciprocal Play: No

Hamlet Golf Course
(954) 498-8198
3600 Hamlet Dr., Delray Beach
Local Pro: Bob Gordon
Reciprocal Play: Yes

High Ridge Country Club
(954) 586-3333
2400 Hypoloxo Rd. Lantana
Local Pro: Marshall Carpenter
Reciprocal Play: Yes

Hunter's Run Golf Course
(954) 737-0410
3500 Club House Lane, Boynton Beach
Local Pro: Patrick Leahy
Reciprocal Play: No

Ibis Golf & Country Club
(954) 624-8900
100 Ryder Cup Blvd., Palm Beach Gardens
Local Pro: Bill Whary
Reciprocal Play: Yes

Indian Spring Country Club
(954) 737-5510
11501 Indian Spring Trail, Boynton Beach
Local Pro: John Orsino
Reciprocal Play: No

Jonathan's Landing
(954) 747-7600
17290 Jonathan Dr., Jupiter
Local Pro: Fred Harkness
Reciprocal Play: No

Leisureville Golf Course
(954) 732-0593
2004 Ocean Ave., Boynton Beach
Local Pro: N/A
Reciprocal Play: No

Little Club
(954) 746-1869
9601 S.E. Little Clubway N., Tequesta
Local Pro: N/A
Reciprocal Play: No

Little Club, The
(954) 278-5830
100 Little Club Rd., Delray Beach
Local Pro: N/A
Reciprocal Play: No

Lost Tree Club
(954) 626-1400
Lost Tree Village, North Palm Beach
Local Pro: Larry Dornish
Reciprocal Play: No

Loxahatchee Club, The
(954) 744-5533
1350 Echo Dr., Jupiter
Local Pro: Jack Druga
Reciprocal Play: No

PALM BEACH

Mayacoo Lakes Country Club
(954) 793-1700
9697 Mayacoo Club Dr., W. Palm Beach
Local Pro: Cary McGaughey
Reciprocal Play: No

Old Marsh Golf Course
(954) 694-9267
7500 Old Marsh Rd., N. Palm Beach
Local Pro: Buddy Antanopolis
Reciprocal Play: Yes

Palm Beach Country Club
(954) 844-3501
760 N. Ocean Blvd., Palm Beach
Local Pro: Bobby Benson
Reciprocal Play: No

Palm Beach Polo & Country Club
(954) 798-7000
3600 Hamlet Dr., Delray Beach
Local Pro: Kyle Cove
Reciprocal Play: Yes

PGA National Estates Golf Course
(954) 627-1614
8581 Marlmoor Lane, Lake Park
Local Pro: Benjamin Franklin
Reciprocal Play: No

Pine Tree Golf Course
(954) 732-6404
10600 Pine Tree Terrace, Boynton Beach
Local Pro: Mark Alwin
Reciprocal Play: No

Poinciana Country Club
(954) 439-4721
3536 Poinciana Dr., Lake Worth
Local Pro: Gary Rogers
Reciprocal Play: Yes

Polo Club Boca Raton, The
(954) 997-5544
5400 Champion Blvd., Boca Raton
Local Pro: Mary Beth
Reciprocal Play: No

Polo Trace West Course
(954) 495-5301
13397 Hagen Ranch Rd., Delray Beach
Local Pro: Bob Foster
Reciprocal Play: Yes

President Country Club
(954) 686-4700
2300 Presidential Way, West Palm Beach
Local Pro: Scott Mailloux
Reciprocal Play: No

Quail Ridge Country Club
(954) 734-8307
3715 Golf Road, Boynton Beach
Local Pro: Charlie Bowie
Reciprocal Play: Yes (Local)

Royal Palm Yacht & Country Club
(954) 395-2202
199 Royal Palm Way, Boca Raton
Local Pro: Paul Ryz
Reciprocal Play: No

Seminole Golf Course
(954) 626-0280
901 Seminole Blvd., North Palm Beach
Local Pro: N/A
Reciprocal Play: No

Sherbrooke Golf & Country Club
(954) 964-6014
6151 Lyons Rd., Lake Worth
Local Pro: Tom Fisher
Reciprocal Play: No

St. Andrews Country Club
(954) 487-2205
17557 Claridge Oval W., Boca Raton
Local Pro: John Lubin
Reciprocal Play: No

St. Andrews Club Inc., The
(954) 272-5050
4475 N. Ocean Blvd., Delray Beach
Local Pro: N/A
Reciprocal Play: No

PALM BEACH

Stonebridge Golf & Country Club
(954) 488-0808
17501 N. St. Rd. 7, Boca Raton
Local Pro: Rick McGee
Reciprocal Play: Yes

Tequesta Country Club
(954) 746-4620
201 Country Club Dr.
Local Pro: Ed Fisher
Reciprocal Play: Yes (Local)

Wellington Club Golf Course
(954) 793-3366
Aero Club Dr., Wellington
Local Pro: Donna White
Reciprocal Play: Yes

Woodfield Country Club
(954) 994-1000
3650 Club Place, Boca Raton
Local Pro: Russ Holden
Reciprocal Play: Yes

Wycliffe Golf & Country Club
(954) 641-2000
4650 Wycliffe Country Club Rd., Lk. Worth
Local Pro: Andy Anderson
Reciprocal Play: Yes

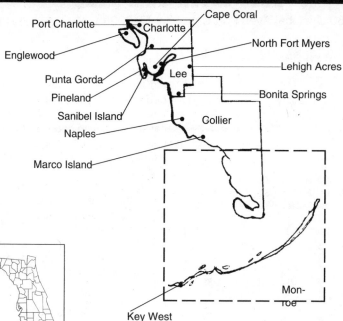

Port Charlotte — Charlotte
Cape Coral
Englewood
North Fort Myers
Punta Gorda
Lehigh Acres
Lee
Pineland
Bonita Springs
Sanibel Island
Collier
Naples
Marco Island
Mon-roe
Key West

Gulf of Mexico

TOP TEN

Bonita Springs Golf & C.C.
(Lee County)

Cape Coral Golf & T. Resort
(Lee County)

Eastwood Golf Club
(Lee County)

Lely Flamingo Island Golf C.
(Collier County)

Gateway Golf Club
(Lee County)

Marco Shores Country Club
(Collier County)

Lochmoor Country Club
(Lee County)

Naples Beach Hotel Golf C.
(Collier County)

Palm River Country Club
(Collier County)

Pelican's Nest
(Lee County)

The **Southwest** is a region filled with subtle beauty and understated elegance. As you read through this section of the book, you'll find courses that are innovative, challenging, and most importantly ... fun to play.

Once in Collier county, consider playing the Lely Flamingo Island Golf Club. This Robert Trent Jones Sr. design is a fabulous course with many challenging holes.

The Gateway Golf Club and Pelican's Nest are two Tom Fazio Courses situated in Lee County that you won't want to miss. They are both excellent examples of why Mr. Fazio is considered to be one of the best architects in the game today. Both courses are tremendously challenging and aesthetically beautiful.

If you prefer playing golf on an ocean view course or perhaps a secluded nature preserve, discover the game amongst the serenity and natural beauty of the southwest.

Average Temperatures (Fahrenheit)

Between **January** and **March** you'll find the low at **54** and the high up to **78**. Between **April** and **June** the low goes down to **64** and the high goes up to **81**. Between **July** and **September** the low goes down to **74** and the high goes up to **93**. And finally, between the months of **October** and **December**, the low goes down to **59** and the high goes up to **78**.

DEEP CREEK GOLF CLUB

1260 Cristobal Ave., Port Charlotte, FL 33983 / (941) 625-6911

BASIC INFORMATION

Course Type: Semi-private
Year Built: 1985
Architect: M. McCumber
Local Pro: Bruce Harris

Course: N/A
Holes: 18 / Par 70

Back: 6,005 yds. Rating: 67.5 Slope: 112
Middle: 5,630 yds. Rating: 66.0 Slope: 118
Ladies: 4,860 yds. Rating: 68.0 Slope: 110

Tee Time: 2 days in advance
Price: $15 - $30

Credit Cards:	■	Restaurant:	■
Driving Range:	■	Lounge:	■
Practice Green:	■	Meeting Rooms:	
Locker Room:		Tennis:	
Rental Clubs:	■	Swimming:	
Walkers:	■	Jogging Trails:	
Snack Bar:	■	Boating:	■

COURSE DESCRIPTION

I wasn't aware of the fact that Mark McCumber (PGA Tour Professional) has been designing courses for such a long time. It really is a pleasure to see someone of his caliber designing courses that are fun and challenging for all types of players. That is exactly what you will find here at **Deep Creek Golf Club**.

This course has a wonderful layout with holes that make their way in and around woods and water. In fact, water comes into play on 12 holes. You'll find the fairways a little on the tight side, but most of the holes will allow you a good shot at par or birdie.

It is next to impossible not to have fun on this course.

DIRECTIONS

Take I-75 to Exit 30 and go east to Rio De Janero. Follow the signs to the course.

LEMON BAY GOLF CLUB

9600 Eagle Preserve Dr., Englewood, FL 34224 / (941) 697-4190

BASIC INFORMATION

Course Type: Semi-private
Year Built: 1989
Architect: N/A
Local Pro: Bob Ridge

Course: N/A
Holes: 18 / Par 72

Back: 6,170 yds. Rating: 68.9 Slope: 116
Middle: 5,811 yds. Rating: 67.4 Slope: 113
Ladies: 4,955 yds. Rating: 67.6 Slope: 112

Tee Time: 2 days in advance
Price: Call to verify

Credit Cards:	■	Restaurant:	■
Driving Range:	■	Lounge:	■
Practice Green:	■	Meeting Rooms:	
Locker Room:	■	Tennis:	
Rental Clubs:	■	Swimming:	
Walkers:	■	Jogging Trails:	
Snack Bar:	■	Boating:	■

COURSE DESCRIPTION

The length on this course makes it quite appealing to the average golfer. At 6,170 yards from the back tees, anyone with a 10 handicap and below should have no problem scoring very close to par. Birdies should be plentiful.

For those of you who can hit the ball straight, but lack the distance needed for longer courses, this challenge will serve your particular style of play beautifully.

Most of the fairways are of average width and water comes into play on every single hole. Try hitting your 3-wood for added spin and accuracy off the tee. The small amount of distance you'll be giving up for accuracy will be well worth it.

DIRECTIONS

Take Hwy. 775 (Placida Rd.) south of Englewood. Look for the entrance sign.

PORT CHARLOTTE GOLF CLUB

22400 Gleneagles Terr. / Port Charlotte, FL. 33952 / (941) 625-4109

BASIC INFORMATION

Course Type: Semi-private
Year Built: 1950
Architect: N/A
Local Pro: N/A

Course: N/A
Holes: 18 / Par 72

Back: 6,699 yds. Rating: 71.8 Slope: 125
Middle: 6,339 yds. Rating: 70.4 Slope: 122
Ladies: 5,810 yds. Rating: 72.6 Slope: 125

Tee Time: 2 days in advance
Price: $10 - $35

Credit Cards:	■	Restaurant:	
Driving Range:	■	Lounge:	■
Practice Green:	■	Meeting Rooms:	
Locker Room:	■	Tennis:	■
Rental Clubs:	■	Swimming:	
Walkers:	■	Jogging Trails:	
Snack Bar:	■	Boating:	■

COURSE DESCRIPTION

The *Port Charlotte Golf Club* is a nice, understated course with many exciting hole designs. You have to play an accurate game of golf to do well here, especially in the summertime when the rough is kept at its highest. Study the course on the scorecard and ask a knowledgeable player about the layout. Good course management will make a big difference in producing a low score.

One of the most exciting holes is the 12th (Par-4 / 438 yards). You'll have to hit your tee shot up a hill to a landing area approximately 200 yards out. The approach is played downhill to an average size green with two bunkers front-right and back-right. Have fun!

DIRECTIONS

Take Hwy. 41 to Conway and go east. Look for the course on your right.

PUNTA GORDA COUNTRY CLUB

6100 Duncan Rd. / Punta Gorda , FL. 33951 / (941) 639-1494

BASIC INFORMATION

Course Type: Semi-private
Year Built: 1927
Architect: D. Ross
Local Pro: Dennis Palmer

Course: N/A
Holes: 18 / Par 72

Back: 6,117 yds. Rating: 68.9 Slope: 115
Middle: N/A   Rating: N/A Slope: N/A
Ladies: 5,613 yds. Rating: 72.2 Slope: 125

Tee Time: 1 day in advance
Price: $11 - $30

Credit Cards:		Restaurant:	■
Driving Range:	■	Lounge:	■
Practice Green:	■	Meeting Rooms:	■
Locker Room:	■	Tennis:	
Rental Clubs:	■	Swimming:	■
Walkers:	■	Jogging Trails:	
Snack Bar:	■	Boating:	■

COURSE DESCRIPTION

This interesting course hosted the Charlotte Harbor Invitational in the 1950's. One of the major players back then was Patty Berg, one of the few women who have made it into the coveted LPGA Hall of Fame - an honor bestowed only on those who have won either 30 tour events and two majors, 35 events and one major, or 40 LPGA tournaments.

The course is mostly flat and open. At times it can get difficult because of its vulnerability to the wind. You'll have to keep your shots on a low trajectory to keep your line straight.

DIRECTIONS

Take I-75 to Exit 29. Go east and look for the signs to the course.

68

COUNTRYSIDE GOLF & COUNTRY CLUB
500 Countryside Dr., Naples, FL 33942 / (941) 455-0001

BASIC INFORMATION

Course Type: Semi-private
Year Built: 1988
Architect: A. Hills
Local Pro: Stu Raymond

Course: N/A
Holes: 18 / Par 70

Back: 5,511 yds. Rating: 68.8 Slope: 124
Middle: 5,052 yds. Rating: 67.1 Slope: 117
Ladies: 4,363 yds. Rating: 64.9 Slope: 113

Tee Time: 2 days in advance
Price: $15 - $22

Credit Cards: ■   Restaurant: ■
Driving Range: ■   Lounge: ■
Practice Green: ■   Meeting Rooms: ■
Locker Room: ■   Tennis: ■
Rental Clubs: ■   Swimming: ■
Walkers: ■   Jogging Trails:
Snack Bar: ■   Boating: ■

COURSE DESCRIPTION

If you play golf below a 15 handicap, this course will be like a walk in the park. But, if you're above a 15 handicap and are looking for some place to experiment, this course will serve your purpose perfectly.

If you want to play an all-out aggressive "Greg Norman" type of game, the course can certainly be played that way. Keep in mind that a lot of the fairways are on the narrow side and you may want to bring out the 3-wood for accuracy. The short yardage on most of the holes will leave you with an easy approach shot to the green.

This course will also be enjoyed by senior citizens who may be short on distance, and for beginning golfers.

DIRECTIONS

Take Hwy. 41 south to Hwy. 84 and go east for about four miles to the course.

FLAMINGO ISLAND CLUB
8002 Lely Resort Blvd., Naples, FL 33962 / (941) 793-2223

BASIC INFORMATION

Course Type: Resort
Year Built: 1990
Architect: R. Trent Jones, Sr.
Local Pro: Pat Cattanach

Course: N/A
Holes: 18 / Par 72

Back: 7,171 yds. Rating: 73.9 Slope: 135
Middle: 6,527 yds. Rating: 70.9 Slope: 129
Ladies: 5,377 yds. Rating: 70.6 Slope: 126

Tee Time: 3 days in advance
Price: $25 - $82

Credit Cards: ■   Restaurant: ■
Driving Range: ■   Lounge: ■
Practice Green: ■   Meeting Rooms:
Locker Room: ■   Tennis:
Rental Clubs: ■   Swimming:
Walkers: Jogging Trails:
Snack Bar: ■   Boating: ■

COURSE DESCRIPTION

The *Flamingo Island Club* is a good challenge from all of the tees and offers something special for many different types of players. This course is the last course designed by Robert Trent Jones, Sr., and one of his all-time best.

If you play golf below a 15 handicap you'll absolutely fall in love with this course. If you're above a 15 handicap, play from the middle tees for the most amount of enjoyment. This is a very demanding layout that will eat you alive from the back tees.

Many of the greens are both undulating and elevated. The fairways go from narrow to wide and bunkers can be found everywhere. Water comes into play on 14 holes.

DIRECTIONS

Take Hwy. 41 south from Naples and exit north on Lely Resort Blvd. to the course.

HIBISCUS GOLF CLUB
175 Doral Circle, Naples, FL 33962 / (941) 774-0088

BASIC INFORMATION

Course Type: Pulic
Year Built: 1969
Architect: N/A
Local Pro: Jeff Raimer

Course: N/A
Holes: 18 / Par 72

Back: 6,540 yds. Rating: 70.3 Slope: 121
Middle: 6,242 yds. Rating: 69.3 Slope: 117
Ladies: 5,294 yds. Rating: 68.2 Slope: 112

Tee Time: 3 days in advance
Price: $26 - $45

Credit Cards:		Restaurant:	■
Driving Range:	■	Lounge:	■
Practice Green:	■	Meeting Rooms:	
Locker Room:	■	Tennis:	
Rental Clubs:	■	Swimming:	
Walkers:	■	Jogging Trails:	
Snack Bar:	■	Boating:	■

COURSE DESCRIPTION

The *Hibiscus Golf Club* is a well-conditioned scenic course that is priced well and fun to play.

In the early 1970's, this course played host to the Lely Hibiscus Open, a favorite spot for the LPGA Tour. The course is still as challenging as ever with many interesting holes that will have you thinking about your options. On most occasions, the shape of the holes combined with the average width of the fairways makes it safe for you to use your driver. Although the rough is kept a little higher than most courses, with a little more effort your ball will come out of it. Water comes into play on 12 holes.

DIRECTIONS

Take Hwy. 41 south from Naples and make a left at Rattlesnake Hammock Rd. to Doral Circle.

MARCO SHORES COUNTRY CLUB
P.O. Box 1057, Marco Island, FL 33969 / (941) 394-2581

BASIC INFORMATION

Course Type: Public
Year Built: 1975
Architect: R. Von Hagge / B. Devlin
Local Pro: Bill Hobbs

Course: N/A
Holes: 18 / Par 72

Back: 6,879 yds. Rating: 73.0 Slope: 125
Middle: 6,368 yds. Rating: 70.7 Slope: 120
Ladies: 5,634 yds. Rating: 72.3 Slope: 121

Tee Time: 4 days in advance
Price: $22 - $65

Credit Cards:	■	Restaurant:	■
Driving Range:	■	Lounge:	■
Practice Green:	■	Meeting Rooms:	
Locker Room:	■	Tennis:	
Rental Clubs:	■	Swimming:	
Walkers:		Jogging Trails:	
Snack Bar:	■	Boating:	■

COURSE DESCRIPTION

Marco Shores Country Club is the closet golf course to the beach on Marco Island and one of the most challenging, too. Robert Von Hagge and Bruce Devlin did an incredible job designing this course to be very competitive from all of the tees. Choose the right tee for your game and you'll be that much closer to golfing paradise.

The course is actually built on a mangrove swamp by a natural waterway. The fairways are nice and wide, the rough is about average height, and hungry bunkers seem to pop up everywhere. You'll find a good combination of hole designs that are evenly distributed for both a fade and a draw. This is a great place to play golf!

DIRECTIONS

Take Hwy. 41 south to Hwy. 951 and go south again to Mainsail Drive. Go left to the course.

NAPLES BEACH HOTEL & GOLF CLUB

851 Golf Shore Blvd. N., Naples, FL 33940 / (941) 261-2222

BASIC INFORMATION

Course Type: Resort
Year Built: 1940's
Architect: R. Garl
Local Pro: Dan Brace

Course: N/A
Holes: 18 / Par 72

Back: 6,462 yds. Rating: 70.6 Slope: 120
Middle: 6,101 yds. Rating: 68.8 Slope: 116
Ladies: 5,315 yds. Rating: 70.1 Slope: 115

Tee Time: 2 days in advance
Price: $28 - $70

Credit Cards:	■	Restaurant:	■
Driving Range:	■	Lounge:	■
Practice Green:	■	Meeting Rooms:	■
Locker Room:	■	Tennis:	■
Rental Clubs:	■	Swimming:	■
Walkers:	■	Jogging Trails:	■
Snack Bar:	■	Boating:	■

COURSE DESCRIPTION

This course offers many inviting holes to satisfy the golfer lacking the distance needed on so many of today's larger golf courses.

The course is very tight off the tee and will force you to play to a well-defined landing area for a good approach shot to the green.

The number 7 hole is undoubtedly one of the hardest holes on the course. It's a par-3 that measures 166 yards from tee to "island" green. The 18th hole (par-4 / 398 yards) is another fine example of what this course has in store for you. You'll have to carry your drive over water and hit your approach shot to a heavily bunkered green.

DIRECTIONS

Take Hwy. 41 and stay on the right lane until you get to 7th Ave. Go north to Golf Shore Blvd. and turn right to the course.,

PALM RIVER COUNTRY CLUB

Palm River Blvd., Naples, FL 33942 / (941) 597-6002

BASIC INFORMATION

Course Type: Semi-private
Year Built: 1960
Architect: E. Smith
Local Pro: Sam Zeiteiders

Course: N/A
Holes: 18 / Par 72

Back: 6,718 yds. Rating: 72.3 Slope: 128
Middle: 6,426 yds. Rating: 70.7 Slope: 120
Ladies: 5,716 yds. Rating: 71.5 Slope: 124

Tee Time: 2 days in advance
Price: $25 - $45

Credit Cards:	■	Restaurant:	■
Driving Range:	■	Lounge:	■
Practice Green:	■	Meeting Rooms:	■
Locker Room:	■	Tennis:	
Rental Clubs:	■	Swimming:	
Walkers:	■	Jogging Trails:	
Snack Bar:	■	Boating:	■

COURSE DESCRIPTION

This beautiful course offers good opportunities for all types of players. At 6,718 yards from the back tees, you'll need to drive the ball well to get into good position for your approach shots to the greens. The front nine plays a little bit harder than the back. If you can keep your game intact for these serious holes, the back nine should be the place for you to pick up your birdies.

The course also favors a fade. Try to get to the course early enough to hit a bucket of balls. Work the ball from left to right. It will help you feel comfortable throughout the day and prepare you for the first tee.

DIRECTIONS

Take I-75 to Exit 17 and go west on Immokalle Rd. Watch for Palm River Blvd. and make a right to the clubhouse.

QUALITY INN GOLF AND COUNTRY CLUB

4100 Golden Gate Pkwy., Naples, FL 33999 / (941) 455-1010

BASIC INFORMATION

Course Type: Resort
Year Built: 1964
Architect: D. Wilson / J. Lee
Local Pro: Tim Fredeen

Course: N/A
Holes: 18 / Par 72

Back: 6,570 yds. Rating: 71.2 Slope: 125
Middle: 6,210 yds. Rating: 69.4 Slope: 121
Ladies: 5,374 yds. Rating: 72.1 Slope: 124

Tee Time: 2 days in advance
Price: $29 - $49

Credit Cards:	■	Restaurant:	■
Driving Range:	■	Lounge:	■
Practice Green:	■	Meeting Rooms:	■
Locker Room:	■	Tennis:	■
Rental Clubs:	■	Swimming:	■
Walkers:	■	Jogging Trails:	
Snack Bar:	■	Boating:	■

COURSE DESCRIPTION

This is an excellent challenge of golf with thought provoking holes.

Study the scorecard and learn where to place your tee shots for position. Don't be fooled by the wide fairways. Many times you'll have to keep your ball back to stay away from trouble.

The course features many undulating greens that can be difficult to two-putt on if you place your approach shots on the wrong side of the holes. Take a look at the slope of the hole from the fairway and play your shots to the highest point. On most occasions the ball will roll towards the hole.

DIRECTIONS

Take I-75 to Exit 15 and turn north on Rt. 951, approximately two miles from the first traffic light (Golden Gate Pkwy), and turn left. The resort will be on your left.

ALDEN PINES COUNTRY CLUB

14027 Club House Dr., Pineland, FL 33945 / (941) 283-2179

BASIC INFORMATION

Course Type: Semi-private
Year Built: 1981
Architect: B. Maddox
Local Pro: Tom Robertson

Course: N/A
Holes: 18 / Par 71

Back: 5,600 yds. Rating: 68.0 Slope: 118
Middle: 5,471 yds. Rating: N/A Slope: N/A
Ladies: 4,333 yds. Rating: 65 Slope: 111

Tee Time: 2 days in advance
Price: $12 - $25

Credit Cards:		Restaurant:	■
Driving Range:		Lounge:	■
Practice Green:	■	Meeting Rooms:	
Locker Room:		Tennis:	■
Rental Clubs:	■	Swimming:	
Walkers:		Jogging Trails:	
Snack Bar:	■	Boating:	■

COURSE DESCRIPTION

Alden Pines Country Club should be exhibited in Walt Disney World as the "Aquatic Underwater World of Golf."

Is it possible to pistolwhip a golfer with only 5,600 yards of course to play on? Absolutely! This is how you do it. Build your fairways as wide as a new born Walkingstick, keep the rough low, and if by chance the golfer hits a bad shot from the tee, make sure none of the fairways feature bunkers to stop the ball.

In a nutshell... KEEP YOUR WOODS IN YOUR GOLF-BAG! This is really an unforgettable course. Don't forget to purchase an extra box of balls; water comes into play on 17 holes.

DIRECTIONS

Take Hwy. 41 north to Hwy. 78. Go west to Hwy. 767 and north to Pineland. Look for the course sign.

BEACHVIEW GOLF CLUB
1100 Parview Dr., Sanibel Island, FL 33957 / (941) 472-2626

BASIC INFORMATION

Course Type: Semi-private
Year Built: 1978
Architect: N/A
Local Pro: Robby Wilson

Course: N/A
Holes: 18 / Par 71

Back: 6,250 yds. Rating: 69.9 Slope: 124
Middle: 5,781 yds. Rating: 68.0 Slope: 118
Ladies: 4,737 yds. Rating: 66.9 Slope: 110

Tee Time: 1 day in advance
Price: $36 - $55

Credit Cards:	■	Restaurant:	■
Driving Range:		Lounge:	■
Practice Green:	■	Meeting Rooms:	
Locker Room:		Tennis:	■
Rental Clubs:	■	Swimming:	
Walkers:	■	Jogging Trails:	
Snack Bar:	■	Boating:	■

COURSE DESCRIPTION
I like the way this course is set up. The doglegs are well balanced with the straight holes and the course is set up for low numbers. The layout is not very long with a total yardage of 6,250 from the back tees, so if you can hit your drives straight, you'll have many chances at par or better. Play smart and manage your game accordingly.

The 14th hole (Par-4 / 384 yards) is the hardest on the course. You'll be hitting your drive to a narrow fairway with a river running along the left side. Your approach shot will be to a green with water left and right. Water comes into play on 12 holes.

DIRECTIONS
Take Hwy. 41 south to Gladiolus and go west to McGregor Blvd. Go southwest and cross the toll causeway. Go west on Periwinkle Way and follow the signs.

BONITA SPRINGS GOLF & COUNTRY CLUB
10200 Maddox Ln., Bonita Springs, FL 33923 / (941) 992-2800

BASIC INFORMATION

Course Type: Semi-private
Year Built: 1977
Architect: W. Maddox
Local Pro: Dale Warner

Course: N/A
Holes: 18 / Par 72

Back: 6,761 yds. Rating: 73.3 Slope: 126
Middle: 6,135 yds. Rating: 70.3 Slope: 121
Ladies: 5,308 yds. Rating: 71.1 Slope: 122

Tee Time: 2 days in advance
Price: $20 - $40

Credit Cards:	■	Restaurant:	■
Driving Range:		Lounge:	■
Practice Green:	■	Meeting Rooms:	
Locker Room:		Tennis:	
Rental Clubs:	■	Swimming:	
Walkers:	■	Jogging Trails:	
Snack Bar:	■	Boating:	

COURSE DESCRIPTION
Bonita Springs Golf & Country Club is a long and challenging course that is beautifully laid out with tree-lined fairways. Both the front and back nine are an equally inviting and comparable test of golf.

You're bound to run into some sort of trouble on some of the tougher holes, but avoid the urge to let loose with a Babe Ruth swing. The original biting edge of the holes will have you using every club in your bag. For me, this is what golf is all about. Having the ability to work the ball as a draw or a fade will help you out tremendously in conquering this course.

The price of admission is well worth the enjoyment.

DIRECTIONS
The course is two miles north of the Dogtrack off of Old US 41 (Country RD 887).

CAPE CORAL GOLF & TENNIS RESORT
4003 Palm Tree Blvd., Cape Coral, FL 33904 / (941) 542-7879

BASIC INFORMATION

Course Type: Resort
Year Built: 1965
Architect: D. Wilson
Local Pro: Todd Strane

Course: N/A
Holes: 18 / Par 72

Back: 6,649 yds. Rating: 71.6 Slope: 122
Middle: 6,250 yds. Rating: 69.8 Slope: 118
Ladies: 5,464 yds. Rating: 71.2 Slope: 119

Tee Time: 3 days in advance
Price: $25 - $50

Credit Cards:	■	Restaurant:	■
Driving Range:	■	Lounge:	■
Practice Green:	■	Meeting Rooms:	■
Locker Room:		Tennis:	■
Rental Clubs:	■	Swimming:	■
Walkers:		Jogging Trails:	
Snack Bar:	■	Boating:	■

COURSE DESCRIPTION
The *Cape Coral Golf & Tennis Resort* is a good test of golf, with a solid design that is set up to be complimentary to many types of players. The back tees might be a little too hard for players with a handicap above 15.

The course winds its way around mature oaks, pines, and palm trees. It's a scenic course with a good variety of straight and dogleg holes. The fairways are of average width and the rough is kept relatively low. You'll find 114 sand traps strategically waiting for your ball. Water comes into play on seven holes.

DIRECTIONS
Take Hwy. 41 north to Hwy. 78 and go west to Santa Barbara. Go south to Cape Coral Pkwy., east to Palm Tree Blvd., and north to the course.

CORAL OAKS GOLF COURSE
P.O. Box 150027, Cape Coral, FL 33915 / (941) 283-4100

BASIC INFORMATION

Course Type: Municipal
Year Built: 1988
Architect: A. Hills
Local Pro: Jerry Wood

Course: N/A
Holes: 18 / Par 72

Back: 6,623 yds. Rating: 71.7 Slope: 123
Middle: 6,078 yds. Rating: 69.2 Slope: 118
Ladies: 4,803 yds. Rating: 68.9 Slope: 117

Tee Time: 2 days in advance
Price: $17 - $41

Credit Cards:	■	Restaurant:	■
Driving Range:	■	Lounge:	
Practice Green:	■	Meeting Rooms:	
Locker Room:		Tennis:	
Rental Clubs:	■	Swimming:	
Walkers:	■	Jogging Trails:	
Snack Bar:	■	Boating:	

COURSE DESCRIPTION
The *Coral Oaks Golf Course* was rated among the top 50 in the state by the Florida Golf Reporter magazine. It is a difficult course that demands good shot placements to score well.

The course is a good challenge from all of the tees. If your handicap is above 10, consider playing the middle tees for the most amount of fun. The back tees can be brutal at times and that may take you away from the excitement that this course has to offer. The 17th (Par-3 / 208 yards) hole will kill you. You'll be hitting your ball to a green that slopes toward water and is surrounded by bunkers. Much luck!

DIRECTIONS
Take Hwy. 41 north to Hwy. 78 and west to Burnt Store Rd. Go south to Van Buran and west to N.W. 28th Ave.

CYPRESS PINES COUNTRY CLUB
11750 Homestead Rd. S., Lehigh Acres, FL 33936 / (941) 369-8216

BASIC INFORMATION

Course Type: Semi-public
Year Built: 1982
Architect: R. Petrucka
Local Pro: Jeann Rubado

Course: N/A
Holes: 18 / Par 72

Back: 6,682 yds. Rating: 73.2 Slope: 126
Middle: 6,438 yds. Rating: 71.3 Slope: 123
Ladies: 5,603 yds. Rating: 72.2 Slope: 122

Tee Time: 3 days in advance
Price: $17 - $40

Credit Cards: ■	Restaurant:
Driving Range: ■	Lounge: ■
Practice Green: ■	Meeting Rooms:
Locker Room: ■	Tennis:
Rental Clubs: ■	Swimming: ■
Walkers: ■	Jogging Trails:
Snack Bar: ■	Boating:

COURSE DESCRIPTION
Cypress Pines Country Club is a nice test for golfers interested in a challenging course that is both fair and fun to play.

Golfing amidst 5,000 trees gives you a special feeling of isolation from the rest of the world. It makes the game more enjoyable by allowing you to think about your next shot without any disturbances.

The fairways are of average size and the rough is kept low in the winter and high in the summer. Good course management will get you a long way on this course. Try to study the score-card ahead of time and work out a plan of action that you can stick by.

DIRECTIONS
Take Exit 23 (Immokalee Rd.) to Hwy. 82 and go east to Lee Blvd. Make a left to Homestead Rd. and a right to the course.

DUNES GOLF & TENNIS CLUB
949 Sand Castle Rd., Sanibel Island, FL 33957 / (941) 472-2535

BASIC INFORMATION

Course Type: Semi-private
Year Built: 1983
Architect: M. McCumber
Local Pro: Catherine Ransavage

Course: N/A
Holes: 18 / Par 70

Back: 5,800 yds. Rating: 68.4 Slope: 124
Middle: 5,500 yds. Rating: 67.0 Slope: 121
Ladies: 4,100 yds. Rating: 64.9 Slope: 113

Tee Time: 1 day in advance
Price: $40 - $71

Credit Cards: ■	Restaurant: ■
Driving Range: ■	Lounge: ■
Practice Green: ■	Meeting Rooms:
Locker Room:	Tennis: ■
Rental Clubs: ■	Swimming: ■
Walkers: ■	Jogging Trails:
Snack Bar: ■	Boating: ■

COURSE DESCRIPTION
The *Dunes Golf & Tennis Club* will soothe your mind from the moment you arrive. The atmosphere is one of peace and quiet throughout the entire day. If you enjoy the part of golf that takes you out of your element and into a new environment, this course perfectly serves that purpose.

What you need to accomplish on this course is the ability to hit your mid-to-low irons consistently well. The course is filled with interesting holes that bring out your short game.

Keep you eye open for the 13th and 14th holes. The locals have named them *Amen Corner!*

DIRECTIONS
Take Hwy. 41 and go south to Gladiolus, west to McGregor, south-west to Bailey and make a right. Watch for the signs.

EASTWOOD GOLF COURSE

4600 Bruce Herd Ln., Ft. Myers, FL 33905 / (941) 275-4848

BASIC INFORMATION

Course Type: Public
Year Built: 1977
Architect: Von Hagge / Devlin
Local Pro: Tom Wallace & Richard Lamb

Course: N/A
Holes: 18 / Par 72

Back: 6,770 yds. Rating: 73.3 Slope: 130
Middle: 6,234 yds. Rating: 70.7 Slope: 125
Ladies: 5,116 yds. Rating: 68.4 Slope: 116

Tee Time: 1 day in advance
Price: $29.15 - $39.75

Credit Cards:		Restaurant:	
Driving Range:	■	Lounge:	
Practice Green:	■	Meeting Rooms:	
Locker Room:	■	Tennis:	
Rental Clubs:	■	Swimming:	
Walkers:		Jogging Trails:	
Snack Bar:	■	Boating:	

COURSE DESCRIPTION

This is an exceptional course surrounded by the beauty of nature. The enthralling feeling of being isolated from the world with only the golf course awaiting your next swing can never be beaten.

The fairways are wide and open, inviting you to hit your longest drives on the majority of the holes. The subtle topographical changes combined with the expert placement of the sand traps makes this course a very serious challenge to contend with. You'll have to know when to stand back and bring out your 3-wood for good position.

This course offers exciting possibilities.

DIRECTIONS

Take the East-West exit from I-4 and go east to Alafaya Trail. The course will be three miles further south.

FT. MYERS COUNTRY CLUB

1445 Hill Ave., Ft. Myers, FL 33901 / (941) 936-2457

BASIC INFORMATION

Course Type: Public
Year Built: 1917
Architect: D. Ross
Local Pro: Mark Haluska

Course: N/A
Holes: 18 / Par 71

Back: 6,414 yds. Rating: 70.5 Slope: 119
Middle: 6,066 yds. Rating: 68.7 Slope: 115
Ladies: 5,396 yds. Rating: 70.6 Slope: 119

Tee Time: 1 day in advance
Price: $29.15 - $39.75

Credit Cards:		Restaurant:	■
Driving Range:	■	Lounge:	■
Practice Green:	■	Meeting Rooms:	
Locker Room:	■	Tennis:	
Rental Clubs:	■	Swimming:	
Walkers:		Jogging Trails:	
Snack Bar:		Boating:	

COURSE DESCRIPTION

Every Donald Ross course is a tribute to the man who designed some of the most memorable holes in golf.

This course is no exception. All of the Ross Trademarks are evident here: generous fairways allowing a good variety of shaped shots to the proper landing area, bunkers set 100 yards from the green making them appear closer than they actually are from an approach shot of about 150 yards, and beautifully contoured bunkers with concave lips that are designed to allow the ball to roll back into a fair position without severely punishing a player. The greens will allow you to play a bump-and-run approach down the middle or keep the ball high in the air. You'll love it!

DIRECTIONS

Take Hwy. 41 into Fort Meyers and go west on Hill Ave. to the end.

GATEWAY GOLF CLUB
11360 Championship Dr., Ft. Myers, FL 33913 / (941) 561-1010

BASIC INFORMATION

Course Type: Semi-private
Year Built: 1988
Architect: Tom Fazio
Local Pro: Greg Wetzel

Course: N/A
Holes: 18 / Par 72

Back: 6,974 yds. Rating: 73.7 Slope: 130
Middle: 6,204 yds. Rating: 69.9 Slope: 122
Ladies: 5,323 yds. Rating: 70.6 Slope: 120

Tee Time: 2 days in advance
Price: $21.20 - $85.00

Credit Cards:	■	Restaurant:	■
Driving Range:	■	Lounge:	■
Practice Green:	■	Meeting Rooms:	
Locker Room:	■	Tennis:	■
Rental Clubs:	■	Swimming:	
Walkers:		Jogging Trails:	
Snack Bar:		Boating:	

COURSE DESCRIPTION

This course is a fair test of golf for all levels of players. It's in excellent shape and always well-manicured. The front nine is a links-styled course, designed in a figure eight pattern around native marshland. The rolling fairways are scattered with grass bunkers.

The course is relatively wide for tee shots. Most of its' character is a result of many large fairway and green-side bunkers. The putting greens here are spectacular. You'll have to take your time and walk around the hole carefully. The subtle undulations will sometimes divert your attention from the proper line to the hole. Pick your line and putt aggressively.

DIRECTIONS

Take I-75 to Exit 21 and head east towards the airport. Follow the signs to the club.

HUNTER'S RIDGE COUNTRY CLUB
12500 Hunter's Ridge Dr., Bonita Springs, FL. 33923 / (941) 992-7667

BASIC INFORMATION

Course Type: Semi-private
Year Built: 1988
Architect: G. Lewis
Local Pro: Geoff Hunter

Course: N/A
Holes: 18 / Par 72

Back: 6,337 yds. Rating: 71.4 Slope: 129
Middle: 5,796 yds. Rating: 68.7 Slope: 119
Ladies: 4,740 yds. Rating: 68.3 Slope: 121

Tee Time: 2 days in advance
Price: $20 - $60

Credit Cards:	■	Restaurant:	■
Driving Range:	■	Lounge:	■
Practice Green:	■	Meeting Rooms:	
Locker Room:	■	Tennis:	■
Rental Clubs:	■	Swimming:	■
Walkers:		Jogging Trails:	
Snack Bar:	■	Boating:	■

COURSE DESCRIPTION

Hunter's Ridge Country Club is more than just a short test of golf. It's an intelligently designed course that will bring out your best.

With water coming into play on 17 holes, you'll need to factor your drives accurately and swing through the ball smoothly to get the ball to the small landing areas. If you can work the ball into the green from about 140 yards away, you'll come in with a respectable number. Hunter's Ridge is unquestionably a shotmakers' golf course.

This scenic course is home to many interesting animals. Look for exotic birds and alligators.

DIRECTIONS

Take I-75 to Exit 18 and go west on Bonita Beach Rd. Make a right on Old Hwy. 41 and follow the sign.

LOCHMOOR COUNTRY CLUB

3911 Orange Grove Blvd., North Ft. Myers, FL 33903 / (941) 995-0501

BASIC INFORMATION

Course Type: Semi-private
Year Built: 1972
Architect: B. Mitchell
Local Pro: Todd Goodhue

Course: N/A
Holes: 18 / Par 72

Back: 6,908 yds. Rating: 71.3 Slope: 128
Middle: 6,514 yds. Rating: 70.7 Slope: 123
Ladies: 5,152 yds. Rating: 69.1 Slope: 116

Tee Time: 2 days in advance
Price: $12 - $40

Credit Cards:	■	Restaurant:	■
Driving Range:	■	Lounge:	■
Practice Green:	■	Meeting Rooms:	■
Locker Room:	■	Tennis:	■
Rental Clubs:	■	Swimming:	■
Walkers:		Jogging Trails:	
Snack Bar:	■	Boating:	■

COURSE DESCRIPTION

Lochmoor Country Club is a fair venue for all types of players. This strategically-styled course features lush, wide fairways, moderate rough, and a good variety of sand bunkers that come into play often.

You'll have to be on your game to play well here. Make it a point to get to the course early and study one of the scorecards. Plan each hole to your particular style of play and manage your game accordingly. If 6,908 yards is too much course for you, play from the next set of tees and you won't be disappointed.

Many of the holes are quite beautiful and will add to your golfing experience.

DIRECTIONS

Take Hwy. 41 north to Hancock Bridge Rd. and go west to Orange Grove Blvd. and south to the course.

PELICAN'S NEST GOLF CLUB

4450 Bay Creek Dr., Bonita Springs, FL 33923 / (941) 947-4600

BASIC INFORMATION

Course Type: Resort
Year Built: 1985
Architect: T. Fazio
Local Pro: Bill Ciaffoletti

Course: Hurricane / Gator (18 / Par 72)
Holes: 36

Back: 6,950 yds. Rating: 74.2 Slope: 138
Middle: 6,549 yds. Rating: 72.4 Slope: 135
Ladies: 5,259 yds. Rating: 70.9 Slope: 126

Tee Time: 2 days in advance
Price: $35 - $99

Credit Cards:	■	Restaurant:	■
Driving Range:	■	Lounge:	■
Practice Green:	■	Meeting Rooms:	
Locker Room:	■	Tennis:	■
Rental Clubs:	■	Swimming:	
Walkers:		Jogging Trails:	
Snack Bar:	■	Boating:	

COURSE DESCRIPTION

Pelican's Nest Golf Club is one of the most sought-after courses in the nation. It hosts numerous golf outings for Fortune 500 companies year round. The course has been ranked the 5th best public golf course in the United States by the Golf Course Architects Association, in the Top Ten for golf courses in the State of Florida by Florida Golfer magazine, and ranked in the top 25 Public Golf Courses in the United States by Golf Digest magazine.

The incredible landscaping throughout features rolling fairways, mangroves, natural vegetation, and lakes. This is another brilliant design by Tom Fazio.

DIRECTIONS

Take I-75 to Exit 18 and go west three miles to US 44. Go north for about four miles on US 44 to the course.

SAN CARLOS GOLF & COUNTRY CLUB

7470 Constitution Circle, Ft. Myers, FL 33912 / (941) 267-3131

BASIC INFORMATION

Course Type: Semi-private
Year Built: 1972
Architect: N/A
Local Pro: N/A

Course: N/A
Holes: 18 / Par 71

Back: 6,446 yds. Rating: 70.0 Slope: 123
Middle: 6,058 yds. Rating: 68.3 Slope: 119
Ladies: 5,588 yds. Rating: 71.2 Slope: 122

Tee Time: 2 days in advance
Price: $18 - $40

Credit Cards: ■	Restaurant:	
Driving Range: ■	Lounge:	
Practice Green: ■	Meeting Rooms: ■	
Locker Room: ■	Tennis:	
Rental Clubs: ■	Swimming:	
Walkers: ■	Jogging Trails:	
Snack Bar: ■	Boating: ■	

COURSE DESCRIPTION

For a course that only plays 6,446 yards from the back tees, the *San Carlos Golf & Country Club* is a facinating golf course with many cleverly designed holes.

If you can keep the ball in position off the tee and set yourself up for your approach shots, you shouldn't have much trouble getting the ball close to the hole.

Aggresive play is favored on the front nine. The back nine is the harder of the two sides with narrow fairways that are much more demanding off the tees.

Water comes into the play of action on three holes. Play them conservatively and go for your pars.

DIRECTIONS

Head south on Hwy. 41 to Constitution Blvd. and go east to the course. It will be on your left.

WORTHINGTON COUNTRY CLUB

13500 Worthington Way, Bonita Springs, FL 33923 / (941) 495-1750

BASIC INFORMATION

Course Type: Semi-private
Year Built: 1991
Architect: G. Lewis
Local Pro: Jim Wolf

Course: N/A
Holes: 18 / Par 72

Back: 6,851 yds. Rating: 72.7 Slope: 126
Middle: 6,169 yds. Rating: 69.6 Slope: 120
Ladies: 4,570 yds. Rating: 65.9 Slope: 112

Tee Time: 2 days in advance
Price: $25 - $65

Credit Cards: ■	Restaurant: ■	
Driving Range: ■	Lounge: ■	
Practice Green: ■	Meeting Rooms: ■	
Locker Room: ■	Tennis: ■	
Rental Clubs: ■	Swimming: ■	
Walkers: ■	Jogging Trails:	
Snack Bar: ■	Boating: ■	

COURSE DESCRIPTION

Worthington Country Club is nicely designed with many strategically-styled holes. The layout is straightforward without any surprises waiting in the wings. Take a good look at each approach and choose the best approach to the hole.

The route that seems to be the easiest and the most logical may set you back too far to make par so you'll have to take some chances off the tee. Many of the fairways offer contoured mounds and crests. The greens are designed to accept both a bump-and-run approach to the pin or a high flying, soft landing fade.

This course will keep you alert from the very first tee.

DIRECTIONS

Take I-75 to Exit 18 and go east on Bonita Beach Rd. The course will be on your left.

KEY WEST RESORT GOLF COURSE

6450 E. Junior College Rd., Key West, FL 33040 / (305) 294-5232

BASIC INFORMATION

Course Type: Public
Year Built: 1984
Architect: R. Jones
Local Pro: Betsy Barritt

Course: N/A
Holes: 18 / Par 70

Back: 6,526 yds. Rating: 68.4 Slope: 122
Middle: 5,843 yds. Rating: 71.6 Slope: 118
Ladies: 5,183 yds. Rating: 70.0 Slope: 115

Tee Time: 7 days in advance
Price: $35 - $40

Credit Cards:	■	Restaurant:	■
Driving Range:	■	Lounge:	■
Practice Green:	■	Meeting Rooms:	
Locker Room:	■	Tennis:	
Rental Clubs:	■	Swimming:	
Walkers:	■	Jogging Trails:	
Snack Bar:	■	Boating:	■

COURSE DESCRIPTION

Key West Resort Golf Course is a fun challenge for players of all skill levels. It's an aesthetically beautiful course located in one of the most attractive parts of Florida.

The overall design is short and tight, demanding accuracy above distance throughout. You'll have to play a smart game here to set yourself up well on approach shots to the greens.

The dogleg 14th hole is one of the hardest holes on the course. You'll have to hit a demanding drive to a landing area, just past the beginning of the dogleg, while flirting with neighboring trees.

Key West is only minutes away from the course.

DIRECTIONS

Take Hwy. 1 to College Rd. and make a right. You'll find the course one mile ahead of Key West.

CHARLOTTE

Burnt Store Village Resort
(941) 637-1577
301 Madrid Blvd., Punta Gorda
Local Pro: David Proctor
Reciprocal Play: Yes

Lemon Bay Golf Club
(941) 697-3729
9600 Eagle Preserve Dr., Englewood
Local Pro: Bob Ridge
Reciprocal Play: Yes

St. Andrews South Golf Course
(941) 639-8353
1901 Debrah Dr., Punta Gorda
Local Pro: Keven Bessonen
Reciprocal Play: No

COLLIER

Audubon Country Club
(941) 566-9800
625 Audubon Blvd., Naples
Local Pro: Ben Steele
Reciprocal Play: Yes

Bears Paw Country Club
(941) 262-1836
2500 Golden Gate Parkway, Naples
Local Pro: Bill Shaw
Reciprocal Play: Yes

Bentley Village Golf Club
(941) 597-4249
704 Village Circle, Naples
Local Pro: Bill Cook
Reciprocal Play: No

Country Club of Naples
(941) 261-1267
185 Burning Tree Dr., Naples
Local Pro: Mike Arthur
Reciprocal Play: Yes (Local)

Club at Pelican Bay, The
(941) 597-2105
707 Gulf Park Dr., Naples
Local Pro: John Carroll
Reciprocal Play: Yes

Eagle Creek Country Club
(941) 793-0500
1 Eagle Creek Dr., Naples
Local Pro: N/A
Reciprocal Play: No

Glades Country Club
(941) 774-1443
210 Teryl Rd., Naples
Local Pro: Bill Gramener
Reciprocal Play: Yes

Hideaway Beach Sports Center
(941) 642-6300
1 Hideaway Circle, Marco Island
Local Pro: Lou Thibeault
Reciprocal Play: Yes (Local)

Hole In The Wall Golf Course
(941) 261-0756
Goodlett Rd., Naples
Local Pro: John Ebert
Reciprocal Play: No

Imperial Golf Course
(941) 597-7186
1808 Imperial Golf Course Blvd., Naples
Local Pro: Jack MeKelvey
Reciprocal Play: Yes

Island Country Club
(941) 394-3151
500 Nassau Blvd., Marco Island
Local Pro: Dennis Farrell
Reciprocal Play: Yes (Local)

Lakewood Country Club
(941) 864-1595
4235 Lakewood Blvd.
Local Pro: Eric Adams
Reciprocal Play: No

COLLIER

Moorings Country Club, The
(941) 261-1033
2500 Crayton Rd., Naples
Local Pro: Harold Kneece
Reciprocal Play: Yes

Quail Creek Country Club
(941) 597-2900
Indian Creek Village, Miami Beach
Local Pro: A.J. Duncan
Reciprocal Play: Yes

Quail Run Golf Course
(941) 261-3308
Forest Lakes Dr., Naples
Local Pro: N/A
Reciprocal Play: No

Quail Village Golf Course
(941) 598-9922
11719 Quail Village Way, Naples
Local Pro: Gary Craft
Reciprocal Play: Yes

Royal Palm Country Club
(941) 775-1150
400 Forest Hills Blvd., Naples
Local Pro: Rick Neet
Reciprocal Play: Yes (Local)

Royal Poinciana Golf Course
(941) 261-3968
P.O. Box 1387, Naples
Local Pro: Rick Werner
Reciprocal Play: Yes (Local)

Vineyards of Naples
(941) 353-1500
400 Vineyards Blvd., Naples
Local Pro: Paul Thomas
Reciprocal Play: Yes (Local)

Wilderness Country Club
(941) 261-5505
101 Clubhouse Dr., Naples
Local Pro: Jay Staton
Reciprocal Play: Yes (Local)

Windstar on Naples Bay
(941) 775-3500
1700 Windstar Blvd., Naples
Local Pro: Matt Bricker
Reciprocal Play: Yes (Local)

Wyndemere Country Club
(941) 263-1700
700 Wyndemere Way, Naples
Local Pro: Roby Armstrong
Reciprocal Play: Yes

LEE

Bonita Bay Club
(941) 495-0200
26660 Country Club Dr., Bonita Springs
Local Pro: Tom McCarthy
Reciprocal Play: Yes

Cypress Lake Country Club
(941) 481-3222
6767 Winkler Rd., Ft. Myers
Local Pro: Ron Leatherwood
Reciprocal Play: Yes (Local)

Eagle Ridge Golf & Tennis Club
(941) 768-1888
14589 Eagle Ridge Dr., Ft. Myers
Local Pro: N/A
Reciprocal Play: Yes

Estero Woods Village Golf Course
(941) 992-1141
R.R. #2, Box 740, Estero
Local Pro: N/A
Reciprocal Play: No

Fiddlesticks Country Club
(941) 768-4111
15391 Canongate Dr., Ft. Myers
Local Pro: Ron Hall
Reciprocal Play: Yes

PRIVATE COURSES / SOUTHWEST REGION

LEE

Forest Country Club, The
(941) 481-5700
6100 Club Blvd., Ft. Myers
Local Pro: James Butler
Reciprocal Play: Yes

Kelly Greens Golf & Country Club
(941) 466-9570
12300 Kelly Green Blvd. S.W., Ft. Myers
Local Pro: Joe Donnelly
Reciprocal Play: Yes

Hideaway Country Club
(941) 275-5581
5670 Trailwinds Dr., Ft. Myers
Local Pro: Josh Meredith
Reciprocal Play: Yes (Local)

Landings Yacht, Golf, & Ten. Club, The
(941) 482-0242
4420 Flagship Dr., Ft. Myers
Local Pro: Scott Yates
Reciprocal Play: Yes (Local)

Myerlee Country Club
(941) 481-1440
1380 Myerlee C. Club Blvd., Ft Myers
Local Pro: Vaughn Clay
Reciprocal Play: Yes

Palmetto / Pine Country Club
(941) 574-2141
S.W. 9th Court, Cape Coral
Local Pro: Alan Magneson
Reciprocal Play: Yes (Local)

Six Lakes Country Club, Inc.
(941) 995-5434
9151 Little Tin Rd. N. Ft. Myers
Local Pro: Mike Hayes
Reciprocal Play: No

Spanish Wells Country Club
(941) 992-5100
9838 Treasure Cay Lane, Bonita Springs
Local Pro: Tal Buchannon
Reciprocal Play: Yes (Local)

Vines Country Club
(941) 267-7003
19501 Vintage Trace Cr., Ft. Myers
Local Pro: Brian Kautz
Reciprocal Play: Yes

Whiskey Creek Country Club
(941) 481-3021
1449 Whiskey Creek Dr., Ft. Myers
Local Pro: N/A
Reciprocal Play: Yes (Local)

Wildcat Run Country Club
(941) 495-3031
20300 County Club Dr., Estero
Local Pro: Peter Beringer
Reciprocal Play: Yes

MONROE

Card Sound Golf Course
(941) 367-2433
100 Country Club Rd., Key Largo
Local Pro: N/A
Reciprocal Play: Yes

Ocean Reef Club
(941) 367-2311
1 Harbor Course Dr., Key Largo
Local Pro: Danny Miller
Reciprocal Play: Yes

Sombrero Country Club
(941) 743-3433
4000 N. Sombrero Blvd., Marathon
Local Pro: Bob Williams
Reciprocal Play: Yes

CENTRAL-EAST REGION

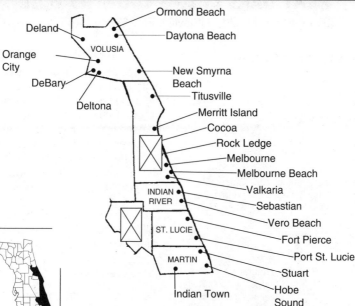

Gulf of Mexico

TOP TEN

Bent Oaks Golf & C. C.
(Brevard County)

Daytona Beach Golf & C.C.
(Volusia County)

DeBary Plantation Golf Club
(Volusia County)

Habitat Golf Course
(Brevard County)

Indigo Lakes Resort &
Conference Center
(Volusia County)

River Bend Golf Club
(Volusia County)

Sandridge Golf Club
(Indian River County)

Spruce Creek Golf Club
(Volusia County)

St. Lucie West Country Club
(St. Lucie County)

Sugar Mill Country Club
(Volusia County)

The **Central-East** features many fine oceanfront courses, offering natural beauty and demanding play.

Volusia County is a great starting point. One of the most popular courses here is the <u>DeBary Plantation Golf Club</u>. This notable establishment has been used as a qualifying location for the U.S. Open, the State Open and the PGA Qualifying School. Players have to compete in a one day pre-tournament and place in the top categories, listed by the PGA and the Tournament directors, to qualify for the official tournament to be played from Thursday-to-Sunday of each given week.

Another interesting course in Volusia County is the <u>Indigo Lakes Resort & Conference Center</u>. This course has been used as a qualifying venue for the LPGA Tour. It's really quite remarkable!

As you make you're way south into Brevard County, try to play a round at the <u>Habitat Golf Course</u>, another clear winner.

Average Temperatures (Fahrenheit)

Between **January** and **March** you'll find the low at **51** and the high up to **74.** Between **April** and **June** the low goes down to **62** and the high goes up to **83.** Between **July** and **September** the low goes down to **69** and the high goes up to **90.** And finally, between the months of **October** and **December**, the low goes down to **57** and the high goes up to **77.**

84

BENT OAKS GOLF & COUNTRY CLUB
4335 Londentown Rd., Titusville, FL 32796 / (407) 269-4653

BASIC INFORMATION

Course Type: Public
Year Built: 1967
Architect: B. Amick
Local Pro: Bob Carson

Course: N/A
Holes: 18 / Par 71

Back: 6,517 yds. Rating: 70.3 Slope: 124
Middle: 6,161 yds. Rating: 68.4 Slope: 120
Ladies: 5,611 yds. Rating: 69.3 Slope: 121

Tee Time: 1 day in advance
Price: $16 - $32

Credit Cards:	■	Restaurant:	■
Driving Range:	■	Lounge:	■
Practice Green:	■	Meeting Rooms:	■
Locker Room:	■	Tennis:	■
Rental Clubs:	■	Swimming:	
Walkers:	■	Jogging Trails:	■
Snack Bar:	■	Boating:	■

COURSE DESCRIPTION

Bent Oaks Golf & Country Club is a well-produced facility with many attractive holes. From the back tees you'll be facing a good series of holes that measure 6,517 yards from the first tee to the last green.

Each hole blends beautifully in a challenging manner. Choose the tees that are right for you and you'll clearly have a good time with just the right amount of yardage to play on.

That, above all else, is the key factor to a William A. "Bill" Amick design. Each course caters to the wide assortment of talent in the golfing world, ultimately bringing the joy of golf to everyone.

DIRECTIONS

Take I-95 to Exit 81. Go west on Hwy. 46, turn South on Carpenter Rd., proceed two miles and turn on Londentown.

COCOA BEACH COUNTRY CLUB
P.O. Box 320280, Cocoa, FL 32937 / (407) 868-3351

BASIC INFORMATION

Course Type: Public
Year Built: 1968 / 1992
Architect: M. Mahannah / C. Ankrom
Local Pro: Keven Gabard

Course: River / Dolphin (18 / Par 71)
Holes: 27

Back: 6,363 yds. Rating: 69.9 Slope: 116
Middle: 5,459 yds. Rating: 65.7 Slope: 106
Ladies: 4,903 yds. Rating: 66.6 Slope: 110

Tee Time: 4 days in advance
Price: $17 - $25

Credit Cards:	■	Restaurant:	■
Driving Range:	■	Lounge:	■
Practice Green:	■	Meeting Rooms:	■
Locker Room:	■	Tennis:	■
Rental Clubs:	■	Swimming:	■
Walkers:	■	Jogging Trails:	
Snack Bar:	■	Boating:	■

COURSE DESCRIPTION

There is a lot of character to this astounding golfing facility. If you enjoy the beauty of nature combined with a good round of golf, this is the place you want to be.

This scenic course features 1.7 miles of fairways that run along three sides of the Banana River. The River is part of a Bird Sanctuary that has recorded 42 species of water fowls.

The course is an open design with many striking holes from both the strategic and penal schools of architecture. The winds that ride off of the Atlantic and swirl their way around the course can often instigate dramatic outcomes. Keep the ball low!

DIRECTIONS

On A1A go South of Hwy. 520 and turn west on Minute Man Causeway. Watch for the signs to the course.

GREAT OUTDOORS RV/GOLF RESORT, THE

4505 West Cheney Hwy., Titusville, FL 32780 / (407) 269-5004

BASIC INFORMATION

Course Type: Semi-private
Year Built: 1988
Architect: R. Garl
Local Pro: Bryan Silwanicz

Course: N/A
Holes: 18 / Par 72

Back: 6,627 yds. Rating: 71.2 Slope: 125
Middle: 6,011 yds. Rating: 68.4 Slope: 120
Ladies: 4,892 yds. Rating: 67.5 Slope: 106

Tee Time: 3 days in advance
Price: Call to confirm

Credit Cards:	■	Restaurant:	■
Driving Range:	■	Lounge:	■
Practice Green:	■	Meeting Rooms:	
Locker Room:		Tennis:	
Rental Clubs:	■	Swimming:	
Walkers:		Jogging Trails:	
Snack Bar:	■	Boating:	■

COURSE DESCRIPTION

The *Great Outdoors RV/Golf Resort* blends beautifully with its surroundings. The course is a fine challenge to the many levels of golfers that play it each year. It's tight and challenging, and that will force you to think about every shot.

Play the front nine a little more conservatively than the back. Feel your way through it and try to figure out the common denominator. By the time you place your feet on the 10th tee, you'll have the knowledge to manage your game well enough to soak up some birdies.

The open design of this course has been built over dramatic marshlands. A good shotmaker will score respectably.

DIRECTIONS

Go 1/2 mile west of I-95 on SR 50, Exit 79 off I-95.

HABITAT GOLF COURSE

3591 Fairgreen, Valkaria, FL 32905 / (407) 952-6312

BASIC INFORMATION

Course Type: Municipal
Year Built: 1991
Architect: C. Ankrom
Local Pro: Alex Romanoff

Course:N/A
Holes: 18 / Par 72

Back: 6,836 yds. Rating: 72.9 Slope: 129
Middle: 6,468 yds. Rating: 71.2 Slope: 126
Ladies: 4,969 yds. Rating: 69.2 Slope: 115

Tee Time: 3 days in advance
Price: $13 - $31

Credit Cards:	■	Restaurant:	
Driving Range:	■	Lounge:	
Practice Green:	■	Meeting Rooms:	
Locker Room:	■	Tennis:	
Rental Clubs:	■	Swimming:	
Walkers:		Jogging Trails:	
Snack Bar:	■	Boating:	■

COURSE DESCRIPTION

The *Habitat Golf Course* is an imaginative layout with good solid hole designs.

This strategic-styled course can be very difficult from the back tees if you're not careful. The fairways are tight and feature many mounds that come into play. You'll have to hit your tee shots accurately to score well.

The hardest hole on this course is the 12th (par-4 / 392 yards). From the tips, you'll have to hit your drive 200 yards over wetlands and onto the middle part of the fairway to open up the dogleg left. Anything less won't do. You'll find 58 sand bunkers and 13 holes that feature water coming into play.

DIRECTIONS

Take I-95 to Palm Bay / Port Malabar (Exit 70B) and go east to Bobcock Rd. South three miles to Valkaria Rd. and east to the course.

HARBOR CITY MUNICIPAL GOLF COURSE

2750 Lake Washington Rd., Melbourne, FL 32935 / (407) 255-4606

BASIC INFORMATION

Course Type: Public
Year Built: 1969
Architect: Bill Amick
Local Pro: Adolph Pop

Course: N/A
Holes: 18 / Par 72

Back: 6,955 yds. Rating: 72.8 Slope: 119
Middle: 6,304 yds. Rating: 69.2 Slope: 114
Ladies: 5,399 yds. Rating: 70.6 Slope: 117

Tee Time: 2 days in advance
Price: $11.61 - $16.16

Credit Cards:		Restaurant:	
Driving Range:	■	Lounge:	■
Practice Green:	■	Meeting Rooms:	
Locker Room:	■	Tennis:	
Rental Clubs:	■	Swimming:	
Walkers:	■	Jogging Trails:	
Snack Bar:	■	Boating:	■

COURSE DESCRIPTION

This is another fine example of a Bill Amick designed course. All of his courses play beautifully for the amateur and professional alike.

The fairways on this course are attractive and generous in size. This gives you the option of playing a fade or a draw to the proper landing area on the tee. Always play this course for position. If you favor a 7-iron over a 6-iron or 8-iron, try to set yourself up for that 7-iron off the tee. At times you'll have to club down to achieve this. If you must play a 3-wood, do so. Always keep the particular hole in mind when choosing your club.

Water comes into play on 8 holes.

DIRECTIONS

Take I-95 and Exit off Hwy. 192 east. Turn north on Wickham Rd., east on Lake Washington Rd. Watch for the sign.

MELBOURNE MUNICIPAL GOLF COURSE

475 W. New Haven Ave., Melbourne, FL 32901 / (407) 722-6016

BASIC INFORMATION

Course Type: Municipal
Year Built: 1978
Architect: B. Amick
Local Pro: Steve Operman

Course: N/A
Holes: 18 / Par 71

Back: 5,886 yds. Rating: 67.6 Slope: 114
Middle: 5,344 yds. Rating: 65.6 Slope: 110
Ladies: 4,656 yds. Rating: 67.2 Slope: 107

Tee Time: 2 days in advance
Price: $9 - $15

Credit Cards:		Restaurant:	
Driving Range:	■	Lounge:	■
Practice Green:	■	Meeting Rooms:	
Locker Room:	■	Tennis:	
Rental Clubs:	■	Swimming:	
Walkers:	■	Jogging Trails:	
Snack Bar:	■	Boating:	■

COURSE DESCRIPTION

Good course management is the key to scoring well here. Although the course only measures 5,886 yards from the back tees, you will find some surprisingly long holes. The 5th hole is a good example. It's a par-3 that measures 191 yards from the tips. You'll have to hit your ball solidly and straight onto an elevated tee guarded by a bunker on the center-right. If that isn't difficult enough, you'll often have to play this hole against a left-to-right prevailing wind factor.

You'll be playing every club in your bag by the time 18 holes are under your belt.

DIRECTIONS

I-95 to Hwy. 192. Head east and watch for signs on the south side.

ROYAL OAK RESORT AND GOLF CLUB
2150 Country Club Dr., Titusville, FL 32780 / (407) 268-1550

BASIC INFORMATION

Course Type: Resort
Year Built: 1963
Architect: Von Hagge / D. Wilson
Local Pro: Steven Hill

Course: N/A
Holes: 18 / Par 71

Back: 6,609 yds. Rating: 72.3 Slope: 126
Middle: 6,257 yds. Rating: 70.1 Slope: 122
Ladies: 5,471 yds. Rating: 71.5 Slope: 120

Tee Time: 2 days in advance
Price: $16 - $30

Credit Cards:	■	Restaurant:	■
Driving Range:	■	Lounge:	
Practice Green:	■	Meeting Rooms:	■
Locker Room:	■	Tennis:	■
Rental Clubs:	■	Swimming:	■
Walkers:		Jogging Trails:	
Snack Bar:	■	Boating:	■

COURSE DESCRIPTION

The *Royal Oak Resort & Golf Club* will please golfers of all abilities. It's an open design with wide enough fairways to work the ball as a draw or a fade off the tees.

The challenge of each hole builds as you get closer to the green. The fairways start to narrow inwards with strategically placed sand-traps coming into play. You'll often be in a situation that will have you wondering whether to send your ball over a sand trap to position yourself in front of the pin. If you want to bail out, most of the greens are large enough to allow you that option. Yet most of the time you'll have a long two putt for par. Strategy is everything!

DIRECTIONS

Take I-95 and exit off of 79 east, turn north on Hwy. 405, turn east on Park Ave., and watch for Country Club Dr.

SAVANNAHS AT SYKES CREEK GOLF COURSE, THE
3915 Savannahs Tr., Merritt Island, FL 32953 / (407) 455-1375

BASIC INFORMATION

Course Type: Public
Year Built: 1990
Architect: G. Lewis
Local Pro: Dave Pemberton

Course: N/A
Holes: 18 / Par 72

Back: 6,636 yds. Rating: 70.6 Slope: 118
Middle: 6,116 yds. Rating: 67.5 Slope: 113
Ladies: 4,795 yds. Rating: 65.2 Slope: 110

Tee Time: 3 days in advance
Price: $25 - $31

Credit Cards:	■	Restaurant:	■
Driving Range:	■	Lounge:	■
Practice Green:	■	Meeting Rooms:	
Locker Room:	■	Tennis:	■
Rental Clubs:	■	Swimming:	
Walkers:	■	Jogging Trails:	
Snack Bar:	■	Boating:	■

COURSE DESCRIPTION

The *Savannahs At Sykes Creek Golf Course* plays through hardwoods and wet-lands.

This strategically designed course offers many creative holes of varying difficulty. You'll have to hit your drives accurately, with the right amount of distance, to place your ball in good postion for your approach shots to the greens.

Many of the holes can be won with thought-ful play. You don't need to be a long hitter to win. Knowing where to place your following shot is the key to making par or better.

DIRECTIONS

Exit 528 off I-95. Go east and turn north on Hwy. 3. Then go east on Halls Rd. to Savannahs Tr.

SPESSARD HOLLAND GOLF CLUB

2374 Oaks St., Melbourne Beach, FL 32951 / (407) 952-4529

BASIC INFORMATION

Course Type: Public
Year Built: 1977
Architect: A. Palmer
Local Pro: Mike Skovran

Course: N/A
Holes: 18 / 67

Back: 5,211 yds. Rating: 63.8 Slope: 101
Middle: 4,821 yds. Rating: 62.1 Slope: 98
Ladies: 3,946 yds. Rating: 61.5 Slope: 95

Tee Time: 3 days in advance
Price: $12 - $20

Credit Cards:	Restaurant:	
Driving Range: ■	Lounge:	
Practice Green: ■	Meeting Rooms:	
Locker Room:	Tennis:	
Rental Clubs: ■	Swimming:	
Walkers: ■	Jogging Trails:	
Snack Bar: ■	Boating:	

COURSE DESCRIPTION

This course provides a formidable challenge for your game. It is open in design and features six acres of water.

This scenic course is mostly flat and easy to walk. Arnold Palmer did a great job of creating a small course with many interesting holes. It forces you to think about which club to hit off the tee for best position.

You'll know what John Daly goes through when you play here. You'll often have to club down at the tee to keep your ball in play. If you take too much club, you'll end up sending your ball into trouble.

If you're looking for a course to practice your short game, play *Spessard Holland*.

DIRECTIONS

From US 1 go east on 192 to Hwy. A1A. Go south for about three miles and look for the course on your right.

TURTLE CREEK GOLF CLUB

1278 Admiralty Blvd., Rock Ledge, FL 32955 / (407) 632-2520

BASIC INFORMATION

Course Type: Public
Year Built: 1973
Architect: S. Rinaud
Local Pro: David Scull

Course: N/A
Holes: 18 / Par 72

Back: 6,700 yds. Rating: 70.1 Slope: 129
Middle: 6,195 yds. Rating: 68.8 Slope: 126
Ladies: 4,880 yds. Rating: 68.8 Slope: 121

Tee Time: 7 days in advance
Price: $15 - $35

Credit Cards: ■	Restaurant: ■	
Driving Range: ■	Lounge: ■	
Practice Green: ■	Meeting Rooms: ■	
Locker Room:	Tennis:	
Rental Clubs: ■	Swimming:	
Walkers:	Jogging Trails:	
Snack Bar: ■	Boating: ■	

COURSE DESCRIPTION

Turtle Creek Golf Club is a penal designed golf course that will have you praying for mercy if you're not careful. Every hole is a new challenge.

With water coming into play on the entire course, a conservative approach will gain you the most ground. Keep chipping away at the course at a slow pace until you can finally open up an opportunity for a birdie. A lot of pressure will be placed on your ability to keep the ball straight. Get to the driving range early and work on keeping the ball on a controlled flight path.

If you can't seem to get a par from the back tees, play the course from the middle.

DIRECTIONS

Take I-95 and exit at Friske Blvd. at Rockledge. Turn east on Barnes and watch for the signs to the course.

DODGER PINES COUNTRY CLUB
4600 26th St., Vero Beach, FL 32960 / (407) 569-4400

BASIC INFORMATION

Course Type: Semi-private
Year Built: 1971
Architect: M. Luke
Local Pro: Roger Boot

Course: N/A
Holes: 18 / Par 73

Back: 6,692 yds. Rating: 71.2 Slope: 122
Middle: 6,288 yds. Rating: 69.4 Slope: 118
Ladies: 5,776 yds. Rating: 72.3 Slope: 124

Tee Time: 2 days in advance
Price: $15 - $40

Credit Cards:	■	Restaurant:	■
Driving Range:	■	Lounge:	■
Practice Green:	■	Meeting Rooms:	
Locker Room:	■	Tennis:	
Rental Clubs:	■	Swimming:	
Walkers:	■	Jogging Trails:	
Snack Bar:	■	Boating:	■

COURSE DESCRIPTION

Dodger Pines Country Club is a well-designed golf course with interesting holes that follow each other in a well-balanced form. No matter what your handicap may be, you'll surely find a set of tees that are right for your game.

The course features narrow fairways with average height rough. You'll have to play each hole cautiously. It's a course that dictates the necessity to hit accurate drives to precise landing areas. If you can achieve the test at hand, you'll have a terrific time at *Dodger Pines*.

The course is primarily made up of strategically designed holes with water coming into play on six. Keeping the ball straight off the tee is the key to posting a low score.

DIRECTIONS

Take I-95 and exit off Hwy. 60. Head east and turn north on 43rd., then west onto 26th.

SANDRIDGE GOLF CLUB
5300 73rd St., Vero Beach, FL 32967 / (407) 770-5000

BASIC INFORMATION

Course Type: Public
Year Built: 1986
Architect: R. Garl
Local Pro: Bob Komarinetz

Course: Ola / Dunes (18 / Par 72)
Holes: 36

Back: 6,817 yds. Rating: 72.2 Slope: 123
Middle: 6,079 yds. Rating: 68.7 Slope: 116
Ladies: 4,944 yds. Rating: 68.8 Slope: 109

Tee Time: 2 days in advance
Price: $15 - $32

Credit Cards:		Restaurant:	
Driving Range:	■	Lounge:	
Practice Green:	■	Meeting Rooms:	
Locker Room:		Tennis:	
Rental Clubs:	■	Swimming:	
Walkers:	■	Jogging Trails:	
Snack Bar:	■	Boating:	■

COURSE DESCRIPTION

The game of golf here is a little different than what you may be used to. The front nine is a more traditional course with lush fairways and a good assortment of bunkers with elevated greens. Like many other American courses, the shot to play here is the high flying fade that lands softly on the green with a minimum of roll. It has been the bread and butter shot that has made Jack Nicklaus the greatest player to ever hit the fairways.

The back nine is set up like a traditional Scottish Links course. It's an open venue that is susceptible to the wind. Try to keep the ball on a low trajectory for maximum gain. Many of the greens will allow you to play a bump-and-run shot approach.

DIRECTIONS

Take Hwy. 1 and turn west on Hwy. 510. Go south on Hwy. 613 and watch for the signs to the course.

SEBASTIAN MUNICIPAL GOLF COURSE
101 E. Airport Dr., Sebastian, FL 32958 / (407) 589-6880

BASIC INFORMATION

Course Type: Municipal
Year Built: 1982
Architect: C. Ankrom
Local Pro: Joe O'Rourke

Course: N/A
Holes: 18 / Par 72

Back: 6,800 yds. Rating: 71.0 Slope: 112
Middle: 6,200 yds. Rating: 68.6 Slope: 107
Ladies: 5,500 yds. Rating: 69.5 Slope: 111

Tee Time: 7 days in advance
Price: $10 - $32

Credit Cards:	■	Restaurant:	■
Driving Range:	■	Lounge:	
Practice Green:	■	Meeting Rooms:	
Locker Room:		Tennis:	
Rental Clubs:	■	Swimming:	
Walkers:	■	Jogging Trails:	
Snack Bar:	■	Boating:	■

COURSE DESCRIPTION

The beauty of this course shines through from hole to hole. It's nestled around a bird sanctuary and the wildlife around the perimeter is phenomenal. You'll have bluejays eating from your hand as alligators bask in the sun.

The most demanding moment on this golf course is when you finally take your stance on the 11th tee. It is a par-3 hole that measures 245 yards from the back tees. A strong prevailing wind is usually present to make the hole play even longer.

Nothing can really compare to playing golf in the middle of a forest without a house in sight to disturb your thoughts. If you're looking for a serene golf course with a northern feel to it, you'll want to play **Sebastian**.

DIRECTIONS

Between Vero Beach and Melbourne off US 1.

HERITAGE RIDGE GOLF CLUB
6510 S.E. Heritage Blvd., Hobe Sound, FL 33455 / (407) 546-2800

BASIC INFORMATION

Course Type: Semi-private
Year Built: 1980
Architect: T. Fazio/D. Le Conte
Local Pro:Mike Dero

Course: N/A
Holes: 18 / Par 69

Back: 5,800 yds. Rating: 67.2 Slope: 118
Middle: 5,200 yds. Rating: 65.6 Slope: 113
Ladies: 4,500 yds. Rating: 66.2 Slope: 110

Tee Time: 2 days in advance
Price: $26.38

Credit Cards:	■	Restaurant:	■
Driving Range:	■	Lounge:	■
Practice Green:	■	Meeting Rooms:	■
Locker Room:	■	Tennis:	
Rental Clubs:	■	Swimming:	
Walkers:		Jogging Trails:	
Snack Bar:	■	Boating:	■

COURSE DESCRIPTION

The course may not be long, but the test is calibrated on par with many larger venues. The quality of the design will have you playing every club in your bag.

It's a good solid strategic design with innovative ideas. One of the hardest holes on the course is the 8th hole. It's a par-5 that measures 550 yards from the tips. You'll have to carry water three times before you hit the green. First from the tee, and twice on the following two approach shots to the green.

Water comes into play on 14 holes and each one of them count. Play a little more conservatively. Hold back on the driver and play a club that will give you more spin and accuracy.

DIRECTIONS

South of Stuart on US 1. Follow the signs to the course and it will be on your left.

INDIAN WOOD GOLF & COUNTRY CLUB
14057 S.W. Golf Club Dr., Indian Town, FL 34956 / (407) 597-3794

BASIC INFORMATION

Course Type: Semi-Private
Year Built: 1984
Architect: T. Mc Alis
Local Pro: N/A

Course: N/A
Holes: 18 / Par 70

Back: 6,008 yds. Rating: 68.7 Slope: 118
Middle: 5,616 yds. Rating: 66.9 Slope: 114
Ladies: 4,750 yds. Rating: 66.5 Slope: 110

Tee Time: 2 days in advance
Price: $20 - $35

Credit Cards:	■	Restaurant:	■
Driving Range:	■	Lounge:	■
Practice Green:	■	Meeting Rooms:	■
Locker Room:		Tennis:	■
Rental Clubs:	■	Swimming:	■
Walkers:		Jogging Trails:	
Snack Bar:	■	Boating:	

COURSE DESCRIPTION

The hardest hole to play on this course is the 9th. It is a par-4 that measures 394 yards from the tips. As you stand on the tee, you'll be facing twin lakes that come into play in front of the green. Don't worry about them on your drive, they're too far away. Rather, keep the ball straight to avoid hitting the trees that come into play by the fairway. Block out the water on your approach shot to the green and you should do fine.

Strive to get your low numbers on the front nine. It's the easier half of the course with wider fairways.

You'll find water coming into play on 15 holes.

DIRECTIONS

Take Hwy. 714 off I-95 and go west to Hwy. 609. Head south and watch for the entrance sign.

MARTIN COUNTY GOLF & COUNTRY CLUB
2000 S.E. St. Luice Blvd., Stuart, FL 33494 / (407) 287-3747

BASIC INFORMATION

Course Type: Public
Year Built: 1989
Architect: R. Garl
Local Pro: Lynn Stellman

Course: Gold / Blue (18 / Par 72)
Holes: 36

Back: 6,117 yds. Rating: 69.6 Slope: 120
Middle: 5,636 yds. Rating: 67.4 Slope: 116
Ladies: 5,054 yds. Rating: 69.1 Slope: 117

Tee Time: 2 days in advance
Price: $29.68

Credit Cards:		Restaurant:	■
Driving Range:	■	Lounge:	■
Practice Green:	■	Meeting Rooms:	
Locker Room:	■	Tennis:	
Rental Clubs:	■	Swimming:	
Walkers:		Jogging Trails:	
Snack Bar:	■	Boating:	■

COURSE DESCRIPTION

Martin County Golf & Country Club is the second busiest course in the nation. Many people enjoy this course because it gives the average golfer a chance to perform well.

The course has a special North Carolina feel to it. It plays through a wonderful playing field that truly compliments the surrounding area. You'll find lots of beautiful trees and 16 holes that feature water.

I love playing golf when there isn't a piece of real-estate blocking my view. If you're thinking about playing golf in an enclosed environment that is serene and attractive, this is the place to be.

DIRECTIONS

Exit Hwy. 76 off I-95, go east to Indian St. and south to the end of the road. Turn left to the course.

CLUB MED AT SANDPIPER BAY

3500 Morningside Dr., Port St. Lucie, FL 34952 / (407) 337-6638

BASIC INFORMATION

Course Type: Resort
Year Built: 1960's
Architect: C. Ankrom
Local Pro: Chuck Johnson Jr.

Course: Sinners (18 / Par 72)
Holes: 36

Back: 6,896 yds. Rating: 72.2 Slope: 121
Middle: 6,577 yds. Rating: 70.6 Slope: 120
Ladies: 5,793 yds. Rating: 72.0 Slope: 116

Tee Time: 1 day in advance
Price: $32 - $47

Credit Cards:	■	Restaurant:	■
Driving Range:	■	Lounge:	■
Practice Green:	■	Meeting Rooms:	■
Locker Room:	■	Tennis:	■
Rental Clubs:	■	Swimming:	■
Walkers:		Jogging Trails:	■
Snack Bar:	■	Boating:	■

COURSE DESCRIPTION

This course has all the attributes that make playing the game fun. Most of the fairways are wide enough to let you work the ball to the proper landing area. Whether you draw the ball or fade it, you'll need to know where to place the ball for position. On many holes, if you're not careful, you'll end up putting yourself out of par range.

It's a fair course that will have you reaching for every club in your bag by the time your round is over. This high quality course is kept in great shape all year long - it makes for a great place to play golf.

Water comes into play on 13 holes.

DIRECTIONS

The course is located south of Port St. Lucie. Take Hwy. 1 to Westmorland and go west to Pine Valley. Watch for the signs to the course.

GATOR TRACE GOLF & COUNTRY CLUB

3302 Gator Trace Dr., Ft. Pierce, FL 34982 / (407) 464-0407

BASIC INFORMATION

Course Type: Semi-private
Year Built: 1986
Architect: A. Hills
Local Pro: Lantie Hughes

Course: N/A
Holes: 18 / Par 70

Back: 6,079 yds. Rating: 68.9 Slope: 123
Middle: 5,530 yds. Rating: 66.9 Slope: 116
Ladies: 4,573 yds. Rating: 67.1 Slope: 122

Tee Time: 2 days in advance
Price: $16 - $38

Credit Cards:	■	Restaurant:	■
Driving Range:		Lounge:	■
Practice Green:	■	Meeting Rooms:	■
Locker Room:	■	Tennis:	■
Rental Clubs:	■	Swimming:	■
Walkers:	■	Jogging Trails:	
Snack Bar:	■	Boating:	■

COURSE DESCRIPTION

Gator Trace Golf & Country Club plays short, tight, and demanding.

This strategic-styled course is very difficult despite its yardage. You'll have to play every shot with accurate precision to score well. This shotmakers' course features a nice rolling terrain that will often place your ball on an uneven lie. If you're going to score well here, you'll have to learn how to hit the ball from beneath and above your stance.

Most of the bunkers have flat bottoms and grassy lips. Every hole on this course features water coming into play. The course is kept in great shape all year long. Watch for out-of-bounds throughout the course.

DIRECTIONS

Take I-95 and take the Midway Rd. E. Go to Hwy. 1 and go north to Weatherby and east to the course.

INDIAN HILLS GOLF & COUNTRY CLUB
1600 S. 3rd St., Ft. Pierce, FL 34950 / (407) 461-9620

BASIC INFORMATION

Course Type: Semi-private
Year Built: 1938
Architect: N/A
Local Pro: Gary Griffith

Course: N/A
Holes: 18 / Par 72

Back: 6,049 yds. Rating: 68.3 Slope: 114
Middle: 5.798 yds. Rating: 66.9 Slope: 110
Ladies: 5,232 yds. Rating: 70.0 Slope: 116

Tee Time: 2 days in advance
Price: $10 - $28

Credit Cards:		Restaurant:	■
Driving Range:		Lounge:	■
Practice Green:	■	Meeting Rooms:	
Locker Room:	■	Tennis:	
Rental Clubs:	■	Swimming:	
Walkers:		Jogging Trails:	
Snack Bar:	■	Boating:	■

COURSE DESCRIPTION

The old design norms of small tees and greens are evident throughout this course.

The open structure of the fairways make it easy to place your ball in good position. The competitive edge of the course comes to fruition at the 150 yard marker. If you can consistently hit accurate shots from this distance to the small greens, you'll have scored a good number by the time you come into the clubhouse.

One of the most important factors in a golfers' growth is the ability to play well in short distances. It's this part of the game that this particular course gravitates to. The nature of the course will have you pitching and chipping from every angle.

DIRECTIONS

Take Hwy. 1 and turn east on Ohio Ave. and look for the signs.

INDIAN PINES GOLF CLUB
5700 Indian Pines Blvd., Ft. Pierce, FL 34951 / (407) 464-7018

BASIC INFORMATION

Course Type: Semi-private
Year Built: 1972
Architect: A. Young
Local Pro: Jeff Hower

Course: N/A
Holes: 18 / Par 71

Back: 6,440 yds. Rating: 71.2 Slope: 122
Middle: 6,030 yds. Rating: 69.6 Slope: 116
Ladies: 5,180 yds. Rating: 69.3 Slope: 113

Tee Time: 2 days in advance
Price: $11 - $20

Credit Cards:		Restaurant:	
Driving Range:	■	Lounge:	■
Practice Green:	■	Meeting Rooms:	■
Locker Room:	■	Tennis:	
Rental Clubs:	■	Swimming:	
Walkers:	■	Jogging Trails:	
Snack Bar:	■	Boating:	■

COURSE DESCRIPTION

This very demanding course features narrow fairways and an abundance of oak, pine, and rosewood trees.

Precision means everything. Each hole is neighbored by a canal running beside it or sometimes across it.

The course favors neither a fade nor a draw. You'll need to play a consistently straight game without much error. The short distance of every hole should work to your advantage in keeping the ball in play. Put your driver in the bag and club down to a more accurate club. Set yourself up for each approach shot with confidence and take control of the situation.

DIRECTIONS

The course is located north of Ft. Pierce. To get there, you'll need to take Hwy. 1 to Hwy. 713 and go west. Watch for the course.

ST. LUCIE WEST COUNTRY CLUB

951 Southwest Coutry Club Dr., Port St. Lucie, FL 34986 / (407) 340-1911

BASIC INFORMATION

Course Type: Semi-private
Year Built: 1989
Architect: J. Fazio
Local Pro: Ramsey Williams

Course: N/A
Holes: 18 / Par 72

Back: 6,801 yds. Rating: 72.7 Slope: 130
Middle: 6,272 yds. Rating: 70.7 Slope: 127
Ladies: 5,054 yds. Rating: 69.8 Slope: 121

Tee Time: 2 days in advance
Price: $18 - $50

Credit Cards:	■	Restaurant:	■
Driving Range:	■	Lounge:	■
Practice Green:	■	Meeting Rooms:	■
Locker Room:	■	Tennis:	■
Rental Clubs:	■	Swimming:	■
Walkers:		Jogging Trails:	
Snack Bar:	■	Boating:	■

COURSE DESCRIPTION

You won't forget your round of golf at the Jim Fazio-designed *St. Lucie West Country Club*. Perhaps you will carry memories of the striking beauty, with towering pines and dense wetlands framing the fairways. When Jim Fazio planned the course, he worked with the natural terrain, not against it. But perhaps your memories will center on the course's challenge. It is anything but a boring course; in fact it has been noted for having the best five finishing holes in South Florida.

Fazio designed rolling fairways and 11 holes that feature water. The greens are superb. They're true and they hold. Four sets of tees make it fun for all!

DIRECTIONS

Exit St. Lucie Blvd. W. (63C) off I-95 and go east to Country Club Dr. Turn right to the course. The course will be on your right.

DAYTONA BEACH GOLF & COUNTRY CLUB

600 Wilder Blvd., Daytona Beach, FL 32014 / (904) 258-3119

BASIC INFORMATION

Course Type: Public
Year Built: 1921
Architect: D. Ross
Local Pro: Dick Medford

Course: North (18 / Par 72)
Holes: 36

Back: 6,567 yds. Rating: 71.0 Slope: 115
Middle: 6,059 yds. Rating: 69.0 Slope: 111
Ladies: 5,247 yds. Rating: 69.1 Slope: 122

Tee Time: 1 day in advance
Price: $11 - $22.76

Credit Cards:	■	Restaurant:	■
Driving Range:	■	Lounge:	■
Practice Green:	■	Meeting Rooms:	
Locker Room:	■	Tennis:	■
Rental Clubs:		Swimming:	
Walkers:	■	Jogging Trails:	
Snack Bar:	■	Boating:	■

COURSE DESCRIPTION

Daytona Beach Golf & Country Club is the busiest golf course in the country. During the winter months, over 750 rounds of golf are played here each day. Under these circumstances, the staff should be truly complemented for keeping the course in such good condition.

The slight dogleg left 11th hole is one of the hardest on the course. You'll have to drive your ball accurately to get good position on the fairway. You'll find water coming into play in front of the green. You'll have to play your shot over it to get close to the pin.

A 10-20 handicapper will get the most amount of fun from this layout.

DIRECTIONS

Take Hwy.1 to Wilder Blvd. Turn west and watch for signs.

DEBARY PLANTATION GOLF CLUB
300 Plantation Club Dr., DeBary, FL 32713 / (407) 668-2061

BASIC INFORMATION

Course Type: Semi-private
Year Built: 1990
Architect: L. Clifton
Local Pro: Jim Muszak

Course: N/A
Holes: 18 / Par 72

Back: 6,776 yds. Rating: 72.3 Slope: 128
Middle: 6,234 yds. Rating: 69.8 Slope: 123
Ladies: 5,060 yds. Rating: 68.8 Slope: 122

Tee Time: 3 days in advance
Price: $28 - $46

Credit Cards:	■	Restaurant:	■
Driving Range:	■	Lounge:	■
Practice Green:	■	Meeting Rooms:	
Locker Room:	■	Tennis:	
Rental Clubs:	■	Swimming:	
Walkers:		Jogging Trails:	
Snack Bar:	■	Boating:	■

COURSE DESCRIPTION
This wonderful Lloyd Clifton design will bring out the best you have to offer. The course has hosted the PGA Tour Qualifying School, the US Open, and the State Open Qualifiers.

All 18 holes are tree lined on both sides. The elevation changes run up to 45 feet. That is something quite rare in most of the courses you will play in Florida.

This is a well-designed golf course that has proven its integrity to the best players in the world. Choose the right set of tees for your game and I'll guarantee that you'll want to come back here for another 18 holes.

DIRECTIONS
Take I-4 east to Exit 53 and turn right at Dirkson Rd. to 17-92. Turn right and follow the road to the course. It'll be on your left.

DELTONA HILLS GOLF & COUNTRY CLUB
1120 Elkcam Blvd., Deltona, FL 32725 / (904) 789-4911

BASIC INFORMATION

Course Type: Public
Year Built: 1965
Architect: D. Wallace
Local Pro: Rick Hughes

Course: N/A
Holes: 18 / Par 72

Back: 6,841 yds. Rating: 72.6 Slope: 125
Middle: 6,483 yds. Rating: 70.7 Slope: 121
Ladies: 5,882 yds. Rating: 74.2 Slope: 132

Tee Time: 2 days in advance
Price: $21 - $32

Credit Cards:	■	Restaurant:	■
Driving Range:	■	Lounge:	■
Practice Green:	■	Meeting Rooms:	■
Locker Room:	■	Tennis:	■
Rental Clubs:	■	Swimming:	■
Walkers:		Jogging Trails:	
Snack Bar:	■	Boating:	■

COURSE DESCRIPTION
Deltona Hills Golf & Country Club is a special course with many exciting holes to make your game exciting and challenging.

This links-styled course takes good advantage of the natural contours of the land. The course is like a hybrid of two different courses in one. It has all of the best attributes of a true Scottish links course with an added twist. Rather than being completely open and highly susceptible to the wind, it throws a curve ball on tradition by the very nature of its location. Trees are abundant everywhere. If you can imagine placing St. Andrews inside of Pinehurst #2, and ... don't even think about it!

DIRECTIONS
Exit Hwy. 53 off I-4 and go east to Deltona and north until the road comes to an end. Left to Normandy and right on Elkcam.

INDIGO LAKES RESORT & CONFERENCE CENTER
312 Indigo Dr., Daytona Beach, FL 32120 / (904) 254-3607

BASIC INFORMATION

Course Type: Resort
Year Built: 1976
Architect: L. Clifton
Local Pro: Tom Ferguson

Course: N/A
Holes: 18 / Par 72

Back: 7,131 yds. Rating: 73.5 Slope: 128
Middle: 6,171 yds. Rating: 69.0 Slope: 122
Ladies: 5,159 yds. Rating: 69.1 Slope: 123

Tee Time: 1 day in advance
Price: $25 - $42

Credit Cards:	■	Restaurant:	■
Driving Range:	■	Lounge:	■
Practice Green:	■	Meeting Rooms:	■
Locker Room:	■	Tennis:	■
Rental Clubs:	■	Swimming:	■
Walkers:		Jogging Trails:	
Snack Bar:	■	Boating:	■

COURSE DESCRIPTION

The beauty of *Indigo Lakes Resort & Conference Center* shines through from the moment you arrive at the front doors. This wonderful destination is extreemly well-maintained. There's some modern history also: this Championship course has hosted the Qualifying School for the Ladies Professional Golf Association (LPGA).

The course is a dynamite test of golf built with many great attributes. If you're looking for a design with an underlying belief that every hole should offer more than one route to the cup, this is the place for you. The strategic concept to course design is evident everywhere.

Water comes into play on eight holes.

DIRECTIONS
Exit 87 off I-95. Go east and watch for the signs.

MONASTERY GOLF & COUNTRY CLUB
1717 Monestery Rd., Orange City, FL 32763 / (904) 774-2714

BASIC INFORMATION

Course Type: Semi-private
Year Built: 1985
Architect: P. Craig
Local Pro: Chuck Scherbarth

Course: N/A
Holes: 72

Back: 6,500 yds. Rating: 71.3 Slope: 121
Middle: 6,096 yds. Rating: 69.1 Slope: 116
Ladies: 5,158 yds. Rating: 69.7 Slope: 125

Tee Time: 5 days in advance
Price: $22 - $30

Credit Cards:	■	Restaurant:	■
Driving Range:	■	Lounge:	■
Practice Green:	■	Meeting Rooms:	■
Locker Room:		Tennis:	
Rental Clubs:	■	Swimming:	
Walkers:		Jogging Trails:	
Snack Bar:	■	Boating:	■

COURSE DESCRIPTION

This is how golf should be played throughout the country. Not too long, allowing the golfer to work the ball into position, and not too short, allowing the golfer to hit the ball as hard as possible with control.

You will need to play this course intelligently. The fairways are tight all around and you'll have to figure out how much distance you can afford to give back to the course for the sake of accuracy. It makes for an admirable challenge. The winner, as it should be for every competition, will be the player with the best all-around game.

DIRECTIONS
Exit 54 and make a left at the first light. That will take you straight to the course.

NEW SMYRNA BEACH MUNICIPAL GOLF COURSE

1000 Wayne Ave., New Smyrna Beach, FL 32168 / (904) 424-2192

BASIC INFORMATION

Course Type: Municipal
Year Built: 1952
Architect: D. Ross
Local Pro: Bill Berl

Course: N/A
Holes: 18 / Par 72

Back: 6,400 yds. Rating: 70.2 Slope: 113
Middle: 6,008 yds. Rating: 68.2 Slope: 110
Ladies: 5,500 yds. Rating: 71.6 Slope: 126

Tee Time: 2 days in advance
Price: $15.5. - $23.50

Credit Cards:	■	Restaurant:	■
Driving Range:	■	Lounge:	■
Practice Green:	■	Meeting Rooms:	
Locker Room:	■	Tennis:	
Rental Clubs:	■	Swimming:	
Walkers:	■	Jogging Trails:	
Snack Bar:	■	Boating:	■

COURSE DESCRIPTION

If you're serious about golf and want to learn as much as possible about it, you'll inevitably end up reading about how courses are designed and the famous architects that built them. It will give you an understanding of why golf holes are built and designed a certain way, and thus, a greater understanding of how to play them more precisely.

Perhaps no one in America's history has had such an impact on course design than the late, great Donald Ross.

This course is yet another great gift from one of the most important designers of our decade. Relatively easy but interesting!

DIRECTIONS

Take Hwy. 1 and turn west on Wayne Ave. Watch for the course.

RIVER BEND GOLF CLUB

730 Airport Rd., Ormond Beach, FL 32174 / (904) 673-6000

BASIC INFORMATION

Course Type: Public
Year Built: 1990
Architect: L. Clifton
Local Pro: Lawson Mitchell

Course: N/A
Holes: 18 / Par 72

Back: 6,821 yds. Rating: 72.3 Slope: 126
Middle: 6,347 yds. Rating: 70.1 Slope: 122
Ladies: 5,112 yds. Rating: 69.6 Slope: 120

Tee Time: 4 days in advance
Price: $25 - $32

Credit Cards:	■	Restaurant:	
Driving Range:	■	Lounge:	■
Practice Green:	■	Meeting Rooms:	
Locker Room:	■	Tennis:	
Rental Clubs:	■	Swimming:	
Walkers:		Jogging Trails:	
Snack Bar:	■	Boating:	■

COURSE DESCRIPTION

River Bend Golf Club is an aesthetically beautiful golf course. It subtly blends into its environment; you won't find any homes on this golf course. The fairways have many mounds that come into play to redirect your ball and it isn't uncommon to find your ball sitting on an uneven lie because of them. The best players will be the ones who can manufacture a stance and a swing to complement contours of this course.

Learn to hit the ball from above and below your stance. It will give you the edge that you'll need to play well on this demanding course.

DIRECTIONS

Take US 1 to Airport Rd., and watch for the signs.

SOUTH RIDGE GOLF COURSE
800 Euclid Ave., Deland, FL 32720 / (904) 736-0733

BASIC INFORMATION

Course Type: Public
Year Built: 1968
Architect: D. Wallace
Local Pro: Bill Morgan

Course: N/A
Holes: 18 / Par 72

Back: 6,234 yds. Rating: N/A Slope: N/A
Middle: 6,013 yds. Rating: N/A Slope: N/A
Ladies: 5,628 yds. Rating: N/A Slope: N/A

Tee Time: 2 days in advance
Price: $17 - $24

Credit Cards:		Restaurant:	
Driving Range:	■	Lounge:	
Practice Green:	■	Meeting Rooms:	
Locker Room:	■	Tennis:	
Rental Clubs:		Swimming:	
Walkers:	■	Jogging Trails:	
Snack Bar:	■	Boating:	

COURSE DESCRIPTION

Most of the holes play to a short distance. Make that work to your advantage by playing a calculated and conservative approach on every hole.

Capitalize on this good fortune by keeping your driver mostly in your bag. Choose the club that will give you the best amount of spin for control and just the right amount of yardage. The fairways are narrow and can be demanding. Hitting the proper landing area will take skill and confidence. If you can control this part of your game throughout the course, you'll do well at the end of the 18th hole.

No homes, no water, and a healthy dose of beautiful scenery. Welcome to *South Ridge Golf Course*.

DIRECTIONS

Exit Deland Rd. from I-4. Go west and turn left onto Hill St. and make a right on Euclid.

SPRUCE CREEK GOLF CLUB
1900 Country Club Dr., Daytona Beach, FL 32124 / (904) 756-6114

BASIC INFORMATION

Course Type: Semi-private
Year Built: 1974
Architect: B. Amick
Local Pro: Chip Harris

Course: N/A
Holes: 18 / Par 72

Back: 6,717 yds. Rating: 72.2 Slope: 125
Middle: 6,243 yds. Rating: 69.9 Slope: 120
Ladies: 5,157 yds. Rating: 70.3 Slope: 121

Tee Time: 2 days in advance
Price: $26 - $40

Credit Cards:	■	Restaurant:	■
Driving Range:	■	Lounge:	■
Practice Green:	■	Meeting Rooms:	■
Locker Room:	■	Tennis:	
Rental Clubs:	■	Swimming:	
Walkers:		Jogging Trails:	
Snack Bar:	■	Boating:	■

COURSE DESCRIPTION

This course offers all the luxuries a golfer can ask for in a challenging design that is not overwhelmingly difficult. It features generous tee boxes, big enough to allow you an undisturbed part of land with a level lie to set up your ball and take your stance. You'll be driving the ball to large landing areas with subtle undulations that may redirect your ball.

The front side features trees that are abundant on both sides of the undulated fairways. The back side, which is much more open and susceptible to the wind, features seven holes that play into water. The course is a wonderful challenge for all types of golfers.

DIRECTIONS

Exit 85 from I-95. Go west on Taylor Road and look for the signs.

SUGAR MILL COUNTRY CLUB
150 Clubhouse Dr., New Smyrna Beach, FL 32168 / (904) 426-5211

BASIC INFORMATION

Course Type: Semi-private
Year Built: 1970 / 1983
Architect: J. Lee
Local Pro: Ted Carlson

Course: White / Red
Holes: 27

Back: 6,766 yds. Rating: 72.1 Slope: 125
Middle: 6,449 yds. Rating: 70.5 Slope: 120
Ladies: 5,425 yds. Rating: 71.0 Slope: 122

Tee Time: 2 days in advance
Price: $29 - $53

Credit Cards:	■	Restaurant:	■
Driving Range:	■	Lounge:	■
Practice Green:	■	Meeting Rooms:	
Locker Room:	■	Tennis:	■
Rental Clubs:	■	Swimming:	■
Walkers:		Jogging Trails:	
Snack Bar:	■	Boating:	■

COURSE DESCRIPTION

All golfers, regardless of their individual abilities, will have a good time at *Sugar Mill Country Club*. Architect Joe Lee did a splendid job of building this course to suit the needs and whims of different-style golfers.

The course plays long and tough with many interesting and colorful holes. The 8th hole is a good example. It is a dogleg-right that plays exceptionally well.

To avoid the water that is off to your right and the fairway bunkers that come into play on the left requires an accurate tee shot. The hole is a par 4 that measures 409 yards from tee to green.

DIRECTIONS

Exit 84 from I-95 and go east on Hwy. 44. The course will be on your left.

TOMOKA OAKS GOLF & COUNTRY CLUB
20 Tomoka Blvd., Ormond Beach, FL 32074 / (904) 677-7117

BASIC INFORMATION

Course Type: Semi-private
Year Built: N/A
Architect: N/A
Local Pro: Bill Breen

Course: N/A
Holes: 18 / Par 72

Back: 6,856 yds. Rating: 72.0 Slope: 144
Middle: 6,448 yds. Rating: 71.0 Slope: 120
Ladies: 5,538 yds. Rating: 71.0 Slope: 118

Tee Time: 2 days in advance
Price: $12 - $25

Credit Cards:	■	Restaurant:	■
Driving Range:	■	Lounge:	■
Practice Green:	■	Meeting Rooms:	■
Locker Room:	■	Tennis:	■
Rental Clubs:	■	Swimming:	■
Walkers:	■	Jogging Trails:	■
Snack Bar:	■	Boating:	■

COURSE DESCRIPTION

Tomoka Oaks Golf & Country Club is a course that has earned the respect of both pros and beginners alike.

The course design is strategic through and through. Taking control of the situation can sometimes be difficult and may require you to come up with a quick solution. That is what a good golf course is all about and that is exactly what you will find here.

Water comes into the play of action on two holes. Play conservatively and you'll score well. The course is an excellent test of golf for all types of players.

DIRECTIONS

Hwy.1 turn west on Nova Dr., watch for the signs.

BREVARD

Barefoot Bay Golf & Country Club
(407) 664-3174
1125 Barefoot Blvd., Barefoot Bay
Local Pro: James Kormondy
Reciprocal Play: No

Indian River Colony Club
(407) 255-6050
6205 Murrel Rd., Melbourne
Local Pro: Jim Kuhfeld
Reciprocal Play: Yes

Lacita Golf & Country Club
(407) 267-2955
777 Country Club Dr., Titusville
Green Cove Springs
Local Pro: Sott Frazer
Reciprocal Play: Yes

Port Malabar Country Club
(407) 729-6533
1300 Country Club Dr., Palm Bay
Local Pro: Chip Fair
Reciprocal Play: Yes

Rockledge Country Club
(407) 636-3160
1591 S. Fiske Blvd., Rockledge
Local Pro: Ed Buckey
Reciprocal Play: Yes

Suntree Country Club
(407) 242-6230
1 Country Club Dr., Melbourne
Local Pro:
Reciprocal Play:

INDIAN RIVER

Bent Pine Golf Course
(407) 567-6838
6001 Clubhouse Dr., Vero Beach
Local Pro: Pat Gorman
Reciprocal Play: Yes

Grand Harbor Golf & Beach Club
(407) 562-9000
2121 Grand Harbor Blvd., Vero Beach
Local Pro: John Joseph
Reciprocal Play: Yes

Hawk's Nest Golf Course
(407) 569-9400
6005 Old Dixie, Vero Beach
Local Pro: Brian Paquette
Reciprocal Play: Yes (Local)

John's Islands Club
(407) 231-2522
350 Beach Road, Vero Beach
Local Pro: David Marrad
Reciprocal Play: No

Moorings Club, The
(407) 231-5990
400 Harbour Dr., Vero Beach
Local Pro: Tom Thorton
Reciprocal Play: Yes (Local)

Rio Mar Country Club
(407) 231-6888
2100 Club Dr., Vero Beach
Local Pro: Brian Glasco
Reciprocal Play: Yes (Local)

River Club at Grand Harbor, The
(407) 778-8999
5400 Via Marbella, Vero Beach
Local Pro: John Joseph
Reciprocal Play: Yes

Vero Beach Country Club
(407) 562-2775
800 30th St., Vero Beach
Local Pro: Bill Girard
Reciprocal Play: Yes (Local)

MARTIN

Cobblestone Country Club
(407) 597-4501
13903 Clubhouse Dr., Tampa
Local Pro: Larry Laoretti
Reciprocal Play: Yes (Local clubs).

Cypress Links
(407) 575-7891
1808 Colony Way, Jupiter
Local Pro: Brian Peaper
Reciprocal Play: Yes

Eaglewood Golf Course
(407) 546-3656
8500 S.E. Eaglewood Way, Hobe Sound
Local Pro: N/A
Reciprocal Play: Yes (Local)

Evergreen Club, The
(407) 286-2111
4225 S.W. Bimini Cr. S., Palm City
Local Pro: Roger Maas
Reciprocal Play: Yes (Local)

Hobe Sound Golf Course
(407) 546-4600
11671 S.E. Plandome Dr., Hobe Sound
Local Pro: Steve Watson
Reciprocal Play: No

Jupiter Hills Club
(407) 746-5228
17800 S.E. Federal Hwy., Tequesta
Local Pro: Bill Davis
Reciprocal Play: No

Jupiter Island Club
(407) 546-2617
Estrada Rd., Hobe Sound
Local Pro:
Reciprocal Play:

Loblolly Pines Golf Course
(407) 546-8705
7407 S.E. Hill Terr., Hobe Sound
Local Pro: Rick Whitfeild
Reciprocal Play: No

Martin Downs Country Club
(407) 286-6828
3801 Greenwood Way, Palm City
Local Pro: Carter Murchison
Reciprocal Play: Yes (Local)

Miles Grant Country Club
(407) 283-6011
5105 S.E. Miles Grant Rd., Stuart
Local Pro: Dan Maselli
Reciprocal Play: No

Monarch Country Club
(407) 286-8447
1801 S.W. Monarch G.C. Dr., Palm City
Local Pro: Mike Ellis
Reciprocal Play: Yes (Local)

Monterey Yacht & Country Club
(407) 283-7600
1900 Palm City Rd., Stuart
Local Pro: N/A
Reciprocal Play: No

Piper's Landing Country Club
(407) 283-7000
6160 S.W. Thistle Terr., Palm City
Local Pro: Ed McConnell
Reciprocal Play: Yes (Local)

River Bend Golf Course
(407) 746-1619
18600 Country Club Dr., Tequesta
Local Pro: N/A
Reciprocal Play: No

Sailfish Point Golf & Country Club
(407) 225-1500
2203 Sailfish Point Blvd. S.E., Stuart
Local Pro: Victor Tortorici
Reciprocal Play: No

Turtle Creek Club
(407) 746-8884
2 Club Circle Dr., Tequesta
Local Pro: Tom Minnehan
Reciprocal Play: Yes (Local)

MARTIN

Willoughby Golf Course
(407) 220-6000
3001 S.E. Doublton, Stuart
Local Pro: Jerry Knebbles
Reciprocal Play: Yes (Local)

Yacht & Country Club, The
(407) 283-1966
3885 S.E. Fairway E., Stuart
Local Pro: Mike McNeal
Reciprocal Play: Yes (Local)

ST. LUCIE

Golf Village Country Club
(407) 335-4510
100 W. Caribbean, Port St. Lucie
Local Pro: None available
Reciprocal Play: No

Harbour Ridge Yacht & Country Club
(407) 336-8900
12600 Harbour Ridge Blvd., Palm City
Local Pro: Bob Reynes
Reciprocal Play: Yes (Local)

Island Dunes Country Club
(407) 229-2739
8735 S. Ocean Dr., Jensen Beach
Local Pro: Michael Martino
Reciprocal Play: Yes

Meadowood
(407) 464-4466
9425 Meadowood Ft. Pierce
Local Pro: John Volz
Reciprocal Play: Yes (Local)

Reserve Golf & Tennis, The
(407) 466-7895
9000 Country Club Dr., Port St. Lucie
Local Pro: Jim Wagner
Reciprocal Play: Yes

St. Lucie W. Country Club
(407) 340-1911
951 S.W. Country Club Dr., Port St. Lucie
Local Pro: Ramsey Williams
Reciprocal Play: No

VOLUSIA

Club De Bonmont Plantation Bay
(904) 437-4776
300 Plantation Dr, Ormond Beach
Local Pro: Jerry Raymond
Reciprocal Play: No

Deland Country Club
(904) 734-3161
2289 Country Club Dr., Deland
Local Pro: Rick Hendershot
Reciprocal Play: No

Glen Abbey Golf Course
(407) 668-4209
391 N. Pine Meadow Dr., DeBary
Local Pro: Don Koerner
Reciprocal Play: Yes

Oceanside Golf & Country Club
(904) 672-1991
75 N. Halifax Dr., Ormond Beach
Local Pro: Bob Greenhalgh
Reciprocal Play: No

Pelican Bay Golf & Country Club
(904) 756-0040
350 Pelican Bay Dr., Daytona Beach
Local Pro: Bob Kendra
Reciprocal Play: Yes (Local)

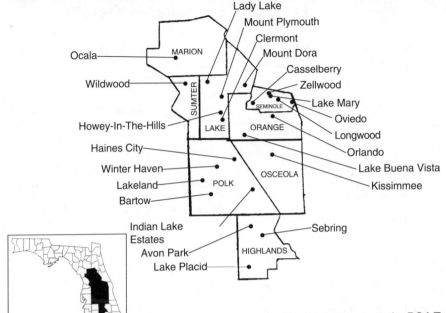

Lady Lake
Mount Plymouth
Clermont
Mount Dora
Casselberry
Zellwood
Lake Mary
Oviedo
Longwood
Orlando
Lake Buena Vista
Kissimmee
Sebring

Ocala — MARION
Wildwood
SUMTER
Howey-In-The-Hills
SEMINOLE
LAKE   ORANGE
Haines City
Winter Haven
Lakeland   POLK
Bartow
OSCEOLA
Indian Lake Estates
Avon Park   HIGHLANDS
Lake Placid

Gulf of Mexico

TOP TEN

Bay Hill Club & Lodge
(Orange County)

Golden Ocala Golf & C. C.
(Marion County)

Grand Cypress G.C.
(Orange County)

Grenelefe Club
(Polk County)

Mission Inn Golf & T. Resort
(Lake County)

Palisades Country Club
(Lake County)

Silver Springs Shores C. C.
(Marion County)

Timacuen Golf & C. C.
(Seminole County)

Walt Disney World Resort
(Orange County)

Willowbrook Golf Club
(Polk County)

Some of the most exciting tournaments on the PGA Tour are held in Central Florida annually. The 18th hole at the Bay Hill Club & Lodge is a notorious challenge that has gained fame on the PGA Tour. Yet this is just the beginning.

When you leaf through the pages of this section, you'll be entering some of the most inventive landscapes ever created by man. For example: the 99 holes of golf that can be found in the Walt Disney World Resort are prime examples of architectural masterpieces that stretch imaginatively around thousands of acres of land. If that isn't enough, try the Grand Cypress Golf Course. It features a spectacular layout and one of the finest golfing schools in the country.

Another interesting course to consider is the Golden Ocala Golf & Country Club. It features replica holes from Royal Troon, Muirfeild, Augusta, St. Andrew and Baltusrol. This is the only place in the world where you can experience first-hand these cherished holes ... all in one place!

Average Temperatures (Fahrenheit)

Between **January** and **March** you'll find the low at **50** and the high up to **76**. Between **April** and **June** the low goes down to **62** and the high goes up to **90**. Between **July** and **September** the low goes down to **69** and the high goes up to **92**. And finally, between the months of **October** and **December**, the low goes down to **57** and the high goes up to **81**.

GOLF HAMMOCK COUNTRY CLUB

2222 Golf Hammock Dr., Sebring, FL 33872 / (813) 382-2151

BASIC INFORMATION

Course Type: Semi-private
Year Built: 1976
Architect: R. Garl
Local Pro: John Donahue

Course: N/A
Holes: 18 / Par 72

Back: 6,357 yds. Rating: 70.7 Slope: 118
Middle: 5,911 yds. Rating: 69.5 Slope: 116
Ladies: 5,260 yds. Rating: 69.7 Slope: 112

Tee Time: 2 days in advance
Price: $11 - $28

Credit Cards:	■	Restaurant:	■
Driving Range:	■	Lounge:	■
Practice Green:	■	Meeting Rooms:	■
Locker Room:	■	Tennis:	■
Rental Clubs:	■	Swimming:	■
Walkers:		Jogging Trails:	
Snack Bar:	■	Boating:	

COURSE DESCRIPTION

If you're looking for an enjoyable day of golf without the harshness of a penal design, this strategically-designed course serves a nice blend of enjoyable golf with just the right amount of challenge. The fairways are narrow and you'll be forced to hit a straight ball off the the tee. Since the course is only 6,357 yards from the back tees, you'll gain the accuracy that you'll need with a 3-wood or 4-wood. Distance lost won't really matter because you'll still land close enough to the green to play a high-lofted club on your approach.

The course features many mature oak trees. Water comes into play on five of the eighteen holes.

DIRECTIONS

Take Hwy. 27 to Gulf Hammock Dr. and go west for several miles to the course. Look for it on your right.

HARDER HALL COUNTRY CLUB

3600 Golf View Rd., Sebring, FL 33870 / (813) 382-0500

BASIC INFORMATION

Course Type: Semi-private
Year Built: 1928 (9-holes) / 1950's (18-holes)
Architect: D. Ross
Local Pro: Bill Krug

Course: Ross (18 / Par 72)
Holes: 36

Back: 6,300 yds. Rating: 70.0 Slope: 116
Middle: 6,022 yds. Rating: 78.8 Slope: 113
Ladies: 5,003 yds. Rating: 68.4 Slope: 112

Tee Time: 2 days in advance
Price: $10 - $30

Credit Cards:	■	Restaurant:	
Driving Range:	■	Lounge:	■
Practice Green:	■	Meeting Rooms:	
Locker Room:		Tennis:	
Rental Clubs:	■	Swimming:	
Walkers:		Jogging Trails:	
Snack Bar:	■	Boating:	

COURSE DESCRIPTION

This historical course has played host to some of the most celebrated golfers in the game today, people like Sam Snead, Jim Turnesa, Mason Rudolph, Gardener Dickenson, Mickie Wright, Kathy Whitworth and Pete Dye.

The course is a fair challenge with a good combination of rewarding holes. You'll have to finesse many of your approach shots to be successful around the small greens. Most of the bunkers have been placed on the sides of the greens allowing you the option of playing a bump-and-run shot on your approach.

Water comes into play on two holes.

DIRECTIONS

Take Hwy. 27 to the Harder Hall Hotel and go west to Golfview Dr. Harder Hall will take you right there.

HIGHLANDS RIDGE GOLF CLUB

3455 E. Fairway Vista Dr., Avon Park, FL 33825 / (813) 471-2299

BASIC INFORMATION

Course Type: Semi-private
Year Built: 1990
Architect: S. Smyers
Local Pro: Gordon Jeffries

Course: N/A
Holes: 18 / Par 72

Back: 6,297 yds. Rating: 70.4 Slope: 120
Middle: 5,775 yds. Rating: 68.1 Slope: 115
Ladies: 4,625 yds. Rating: 66.9 Slope: 110

Tee Time: 3 days in advance
Price: $14 - $28

Credit Cards: ■	Restaurant:	
Driving Range: ■	Lounge:	
Practice Green: ■	Meeting Rooms:	
Locker Room:	Tennis:	
Rental Clubs:	Swimming:	
Walkers: ■	Jogging Trails:	
Snack Bar: ■	Boating:	

COURSE DESCRIPTION

The total yardage of this 1990 course is rather small in relation to the majority of newly constructed golf courses throughout Florida. The course design is solid and was obviously constructed for the masses. The course is of a caliber best attuned to the average golfer.

You'll have to hit your drives straight to get into good position on the narrow fairways which feature rolling terrain and mature oak trees. If you're going to make an aggressive move to pick up a birdie or two, you'll want to do it on the front side. The back nine is both longer and much more demanding.

Water comes into play on five holes.

DIRECTIONS

Take Hwy. 17 to Powerline Rd. and go east to the course. Look for the sign.

PINECREST GOLF CLUB

2250 S. Little Lake Bonnnet Rd., Avon Park, FL 33825 / (813) 453-7555

BASIC INFORMATION

Course Type: Semi-private
Year Built: 1926
Architect: D. Ross
Local Pro: Dan O'Neil

Course: N/A
Holes: 18 / Par 72

Back: 6,449 yds. Rating: 70.3 Slope: 119
Middle: 6,247 yds. Rating: 69.4 Slope: 117
Ladies: 5,350 yds. Rating: 69.8 Slope: 114

Tee Time: 2 days in advance
Price: $15 - $30

Credit Cards:	Restaurant: ■	
Driving Range: ■	Lounge: ■	
Practice Green: ■	Meeting Rooms: ■	
Locker Room: ■	Tennis:	
Rental Clubs:	Swimming:	
Walkers:	Jogging Trails:	
Snack Bar: ■	Boating:	

COURSE DESCRIPTION

Pinehurst Golf Club is a splendid example of Donald Ross's genius as an architect. It isn't the hardest course that you will find, but it does post a formidable challenge that goes way beyond the typical 7,000 + layouts of modern design. This strategic layout is spread among orange groves, oak trees, and pine. The front side is the most demanding half of the course. Don't trust the tee markers for your alignment. Most of them are aimed at the wrong direction to fool you before you even take your stance. The course favors a draw for the most part. Birdies can be made easily on the short par-5's. The par-3's are very demanding.

DIRECTIONS

Take Hwy 27. to Hwy. 64 and go east to Hwy. 17. Go south for about three miles to the course.

PLACID LAKES INN & COUNTRY CLUB

3601 Jefferson Ave., Lake Placid, FL 33852 / (813) 465-4333

BASIC INFORMATION

Course Type: Resort
Year Built: 1967
Architect: N/A
Local Pro: Jeff Moorman

Course: N/A
Holes: 18 / Par 72

Back: 6,727 yds. Rating: 70.9 Slope: 118
Middle: 6,190 yds. Rating: 68.4 Slope: 112
Ladies: 5,486 yds. Rating: 70.8 Slope: 117

Tee Time: 2 days in advance
Price: $20 - $25

Credit Cards:	■	Restaurant:	■
Driving Range:	■	Lounge:	■
Practice Green:	■	Meeting Rooms:	
Locker Room:	■	Tennis:	■
Rental Clubs:		Swimming:	■
Walkers:	■	Jogging Trails:	
Snack Bar:	■	Boating:	

COURSE DESCRIPTION

You'll find lots of water here. The course features average size fairways with many elevation changes. All of the holes feature a good variety of bunkers that come into play often. Your approach shots need to be accurate.

This is a real shotmakers' course. If you can only move the ball one way, don't despair; most of the holes will leave you enough room to play your natural line. The player who can work the ball both ways will have an advantage by playing the ball away from the green-side bunker and on to the putting surface.

At one time, this course was rated 7th in the state. Get your birds on the short par-5's.

DIRECTIONS

Take Hwy. 27 to Interlake Blvd. and go west for about seven miles to the course. Look for the sign.

RIVER GREENS GOLF COURSE

47 Lake Amon Dr., Avon Park, FL 33825 / (813) 453-5210

BASIC INFORMATION

Course Type: Semi-private
Year Built: 1969
Architect: J. Kidwell
Local Pro: Lisa Davis (Director of Golf)

Course: N/A
Holes: 18 / Par 72

Back: 5,798 yds. Rating: 67.8 Slope: 114
Middle: 5,583 yds. Rating: 66.7 Slope: 111
Ladies: 4,950 yds. Rating: 68.0 Slope: 109

Tee Time: 2 days in advance
Price: $12 - $32

Credit Cards:	■	Restaurant:	■
Driving Range:	■	Lounge:	■
Practice Green:	■	Meeting Rooms:	■
Locker Room:		Tennis:	
Rental Clubs:	■	Swimming:	
Walkers:	■	Jogging Trails:	
Snack Bar:	■	Boating:	

COURSE DESCRIPTION

This is an interesting design that benefits short hitters, senior citizens, new players, and advanced players looking for a course to practice their short games.

The configuration of the course is set up rather tight with narrow fairways that mostly favor straight shooters. Play a little more cautiously on the front. It's the harder and more demanding half of the course. Most of your approach shots will have to sail high and land soft to get into any position on the small greens.

River Greens is a genuine penal target golf layout. Every shot needs to be placed or you may often end up out-of-bounds. Water comes into play on seven holes.

DIRECTIONS

Take Hwy. 27 to Lake Damon Dr. and that will lead you to the course. You'll see Walker Memorial Hospital from Damon Dr.

SEBRING GOLF CLUB

3129 Golfview Rd., Sebring, FL 33870 / (813) 385-0889

BASIC INFORMATION

Course Type: Municipal
Year Built: 1940
Architect: N/A
Local Pro: T. Mc.Clurg

Course: N/A
Holes: 18 / Par 72

Back: 6,062 yds. Rating: 68.7 Slope: 115
Middle: N/A Rating: N/A Slope: N/A
Ladies: 5,512 yds. Rating: 70.6 Slope: 116

Tee Time: 7 days in advance
Price: $10 - $30

Credit Cards:	■	Restaurant:	■
Driving Range:	■	Lounge:	■
Practice Green:	■	Meeting Rooms:	■
Locker Room:		Tennis:	
Rental Clubs:	■	Swimming:	
Walkers:	■	Jogging Trails:	
Snack Bar:	■	Boating:	

COURSE DESCRIPTION

The Sebring Golf Club is a nonchalant type of course that is laid back and easy to play. If you're a Senior or a beginner looking for a course that won't destroy you, this is it.

The course plays friendly to all. The open fairways will give you a chance to drive the ball a long distance. Many of your approach shots will have to be played accurately. It's from here that the true challenge of the course comes in. You'll have to play a sharply tuned short game to score well.

The course features many smartly designed dogleg holes that play from both the left and the right.

DIRECTIONS

Take Hwy. 27 and go north of Sebring and west on Golf View. The course will be on your right.

SPRING LAKE GOLF & TENNIS RESORT

100 Clubhouse Ln., Sebring, FL 33870 / (813) 655-0276

BASIC INFORMATION

Course Type: Public
Year Built: 1979
Architect: B. Solomon / M. Telshaw
Local Pro: Tim Melooh

Course: N/A
Holes: 18 / Par 72

Back: 6,621 yds. Rating: 72.1 Slope: 127
Middle: 5,818 yds. Rating: 68.0 Slope: 116
Ladies: 5,362 yds. Rating: 70.0 Slope: 117

Tee Time: 2 days in advance
Price: $18 - $30

Credit Cards:	■	Restaurant:	■
Driving Range:	■	Lounge:	■
Practice Green:	■	Meeting Rooms:	■
Locker Room:	■	Tennis:	■
Rental Clubs:	■	Swimming:	■
Walkers:		Jogging Trails:	■
Snack Bar:	■	Boating:	■

COURSE DESCRIPTION

This course measures 6,621 yards from the back tees. The design will be best appreciated by all golfers regardless of their individual handicaps. The course is mostly flat and straightforward. Most people find the front nine the harder half of the course. Once you feel your way around the first three holes, you'll have another three quarters of play to be aggressive and shoot for those birdies.

The course favors neither a fade nor a draw, making the straight the most workable. The fairways are nice and wide and will allow you to play your best drives throughout the day.

DIRECTIONS

Take Hwy. 27 to Hwy. 98 and go east to Spring Lake.

SUN 'N' LAKES GOLF & COUNTRY CLUB

5200 Columbus Circle, Sebring, FL 33872 / (813) 385-4830

BASIC INFORMATION

Course Type: Resort
Year Built: 1975
Architect: D. Dyer
Local Pro: Don Barie

Course: 1 & 2 (18 / Par 72)
Holes: 27

Back: 6,931 yds. Rating: 72.0 Slope: 121
Middle: 6,430 yds. Rating: 70.5 Slope: 117
Ladies: 5,349 yds. Rating: 70.3 Slope: 120

Tee Time: 6 days in advance
Price: $17 - $32

Credit Cards:	■	Restaurant:	■
Driving Range:	■	Lounge:	■
Practice Green:	■	Meeting Rooms:	■
Locker Room:	■	Tennis:	■
Rental Clubs:	■	Swimming:	■
Walkers:		Jogging Trails:	
Snack Bar:	■	Boating:	

COURSE DESCRIPTION

Nothing is worse than stepping up to a tee and not finding a comfortable place to take your stance. The tees at the **Sun 'N' Lakes Golf & Country Club** are built larger than average with lots of room for perfect ball placement.

Don't be deceived by the open architecture of the fairways. Many of the holes feature sand traps that are hard to spot from the tee and others that are difficult to play around the greens.

The course demands both distance and accuracy to play well. Good course management is critical.

Water comes into play on 10 holes.

DIRECTIONS

Take Hwy. 27 to Sun "N" Lake Blvd. Head west and watch for the signs to the course.

BELLA VISTA GOLF & YACHT CLUB

Hwy. 48, Box 66, Howey In The Hills, FL 34737 / (904) 324-3233

BASIC INFORMATION

Course Type: Semi-private
Year Built: 1989
Architect: L. Clifton
Local Pro: Ric Quinn

Course: N/A
Holes: 18 / Par 72

Back: 6,321 yds. Rating: 68.4 Slope: 119
Middle: 6,072 yds. Rating: 67.1 Slope: 116
Ladies: 5,386 yds. Rating: 71.9 Slope: 123

Tee Time: 7 days in advance
Price: $16.50 - $38.00

Credit Cards:	■	Restaurant:	■
Driving Range:	■	Lounge:	■
Practice Green:	■	Meeting Rooms:	
Locker Room:	■	Tennis:	■
Rental Clubs:	■	Swimming:	■
Walkers:		Jogging Trails:	■
Snack Bar:	■	Boating:	■

COURSE DESCRIPTION

This exemplary golf course features outstanding views of Lake Harris. You'll be excited by the natural beauty and challenge that this course has to offer.

Bella Vista (Beautiful Views) lives up to its Spanish name. The course runs through a gorgeous forested shoreline that sweeps the eastern horizon. You'll find cypress, fragrant magnolias, and oak trees throughout. This course features up to 50 feet of elevation changes. You'll find a lake or a stream on every hole. A long and sleek creek works its way through the back nine.

Practice your best fade shot. This is the type of course you'll always want to come back to.

DIRECTIONS

Take Hwy. 27 north or south to Leesburg and go east to the course. Follow the signs.

COUNTRY CLUB OF MOUNT DORA

1900 Country Club Blvd., Mount Dora, FL 32757 / (904) 735-0115

BASIC INFORMATION

Course Type: Semi-private
Year Built: 1991
Architect: L. Clifton
Local Pro: Jeff Cothran

Course: N/A
Holes: 18 / Par 72

Back: 6,612 yds. Rating: 71.5 Slope: 121
Middle: 6,056 yds. Rating: 68.9 Slope: 116
Ladies: 5,705 yds. Rating: 67.3 Slope: 115

Tee Time: 3 days in advance
Price: $23 - $37

Credit Cards:	■	Restaurant:	■
Driving Range:	■	Lounge:	■
Practice Green:	■	Meeting Rooms:	
Locker Room:		Tennis:	■
Rental Clubs:	■	Swimming:	■
Walkers:		Jogging Trails:	
Snack Bar:	■	Boating:	

COURSE DESCRIPTION

The *Country Club of Mount Dora* is an inviting layout designed by one of the areas most celebrated architects, Lloyd Clifton. This challenging course is playable for many different types of golfers and the natural beauty of the location makes it an inviting place to play.

This isn't a course for the weak. It measures 6,612 yards from the back tees, but feels more like 7,000 and above because of the narrow fairways. You'll have to hit your shots straight to gain good position. This shotmakers' course will demand all the shots in your bag of tricks.

Water comes into play on 16 holes.

DIRECTIONS

Take Hwy. 441 into Mount Dora and watch for the signs. The course is southeast of Hwy. 441.

GREEN VALLEY COUNTRY CLUB

SR 50 West, Clermont, FL 32711 / (904) 394-2133

BASIC INFORMATION

Course Type: Semi-private
Year Built: 1963 / 1990
Architect: J. Lee / L. Clifton
Local Pro: Bill Westburg

Course: N/A
Holes: 18 / Par 72

Back: 6,655 yds. Rating: 71.6 Slope: 118
Middle: 6,095 yds. Rating: 68.8 Slope: 114
Ladies: 5,160 yds. Rating: 69.4 Slope: 116

Tee Time: 3 days in advance
Price: $14 - $30

Credit Cards:	■	Restaurant:	■
Driving Range:	■	Lounge:	■
Practice Green:	■	Meeting Rooms:	■
Locker Room:		Tennis:	
Rental Clubs:	■	Swimming:	
Walkers:	■	Jogging Trails:	
Snack Bar:	■	Boating:	

COURSE DESCRIPTION

This is a great course for long hitters. The fairways are wide and only five holes play into water. Most of the demanding bunkers that come into play do so around the greens.

The course is remarkably hilly and demanding on the fairway. You'll often find your ball on an uneven lie. If you've never experienced the game of golf on this type of surface, get to the driving range early and hit a bucket of balls. Make sure you hit the balls above and below your feet.

You should be ready to make your birds by the time you get onto the easier half of the course on the 10th tee. Much luck!

DIRECTIONS

Get onto Hwy. 27 off the Turnpike on Exit 285. Go south to Clermount and west on Hwy. 50 to the course.

HACIENDA HILLS & COUNTRY CLUB

1200 Avenida Central, Lady Lake, FL 32159 / (904) 753-5155

BASIC INFORMATION

Course Type: Semi-private
Year Built: 1991
Architect: L. Clifton
Local Pro: Steve Wresh

Course: N/A
Holes: 18 / Par 72

Back: 6,417 yds. Rating: 70.4 Slope: 122
Middle: 6,005 yds. Rating: 68.4 Slope: 115
Ladies: 5,150 yds. Rating: 67.6 Slope: 110

Tee Time: 1 day in advance
Price: $15 - $32

Credit Cards: ■	Restaurant:
Driving Range: ■	Lounge: ■
Practice Green: ■	Meeting Rooms:
Locker Room:	Tennis:
Rental Clubs: ■	Swimming:
Walkers: ■	Jogging Trails:
Snack Bar: ■	Boating:

COURSE DESCRIPTION

The *Hacienda Hills & Country Club* has gentle mounds that come into play on the well-manicured fairways. The course is heavily trapped with strategically-placed bunkers that come into play often.

The course is presently being re-evaluated and the ratings listed will change. Both the #1 and #10 holes are being restructured. Chi Chi Rodriguez has endorsed them as "two of my favorite holes" of the future.

Two features will stay with you for some time after you play this course: the double-horseshoe tee and the huge double green.

This is a course with character and many challenging holes.

DIRECTIONS

Go two miles north of Lady Lake just west of Hwy. 441/27. Make a left on Avenida Central. The course will be on your right.

MISSION INN GOLF & TENNIS RESORT

SR 19 & 48, Howey In The Hills, FL 32737 / (904) 324-3885

BASIC INFORMATION

Course Type: Resort
Year Built: 1926
Architect: C. Clarke
Local Pro: Jack Hoogewind

Course: El Campeon (18 / Par 72)
Holes: 36

Back: 6,842 yds. Rating: 73.5 Slope: 134
Middle: 6,292 yds. Rating: 70.9 Slope: 129
Ladies: 5,038 yds. Rating: 68.0 Slope: 122

Tee Time: 3 days in advance
Price: $35 - $75

Credit Cards: ■	Restaurant: ■
Driving Range: ■	Lounge: ■
Practice Green: ■	Meeting Rooms: ■
Locker Room: ■	Tennis: ■
Rental Clubs: ■	Swimming: ■
Walkers:	Jogging Trails: ■
Snack Bar: ■	Boating:

COURSE DESCRIPTION

This is truly a professional caliber course with spectacular hole designs. The hilly design makes its way through rolling fairways and elevation changes ranging up to 85 feet. *Are we in Florida?* You bet!

You'll find beautiful trees lining the fairways and only one home can be seen on the entire course. It really feels like a mountain course on the tip of North Carolina. It's a scenic delight with protected wildlife that live in the immediate area. If you're lucky, you may end up seeing one of the following: bears, otters, deers, panthers, gators or exotic birds.

Play from the middle tees if you're not a scratch golfer. Water comes into play on 17 holes.

DIRECTIONS

Take Hwy. 27 to Hwy. 48 and go south to the course. Look for the signs.

MOUNT DORA GOLF CLUB

1100 S. Highland, Mount Dora, FL 32757 / (904) 383-3954

BASIC INFORMATION

Course Type: Semi-private
Year Built: 1945
Architect: C. Demming
Local Pro: Mark Windram

Course: N/A
Holes: 18 / Par 70

Back: 5,719 yds. Rating: 66.9 Slope: 114
Middle: 5,470 yds. Rating: 66.8 Slope: 111
Ladies: 5,238 yds. Rating: 70.8 Slope: 118

Tee Time: 3 days in advance
Price: $17.50 - $25

Credit Cards:		Restaurant:	
Driving Range:		Lounge:	
Practice Green:	■	Meeting Rooms:	■
Locker Room:	■	Tennis:	■
Rental Clubs:	■	Swimming:	
Walkers:	■	Jogging Trails:	
Snack Bar:	■	Boating:	

COURSE DESCRIPTION

When you play the *Mount Dora Golf Club,* you'll feel as though you're in a different era. The course is a short distance when you accumulate the total yardage from the back tees. As it stands, it's a great challenge for people who lack distance and golfers searching for a place to practice their short-games.

The course features a hilly terrain with many oak trees and pines making their presence known. Strategically-placed bunkers can destroy you around the greens. You'll want to get your birds on the easier front half of the course.

Water comes into play on three holes.

DIRECTIONS

Go west on Hwy. 46 off Hwy. 441 and make a left at the first intersection. The course will be on your left.

MOUNT PLYMOUTH GOLF CLUB

25843 Pine Valley Dr., Mount Plymouth, FL 32776 / (904) 383-4821

BASIC INFORMATION

Course Type: Semi-private
Year Built: 1926
Architect: N/A
Local Pro: Tom Hampton

Course: N/A
Holes: 18 / Par 70 (Ladies: Par 71)

Back: 6,457 yds. Rating: 71.4 Slope: 111
Middle: 6,003 yds. Rating: 68.2 Slope: 109
Ladies: 5,445 yds. Rating: 70.7 Slope: 114

Tee Time: 3 days in advance
Price: $13 - $25

Credit Cards:	■	Restaurant:	■
Driving Range:	■	Lounge:	■
Practice Green:	■	Meeting Rooms:	
Locker Room:		Tennis:	
Rental Clubs:	■	Swimming:	
Walkers:	■	Jogging Trails:	
Snack Bar:	■	Boating:	

COURSE DESCRIPTION

This course holds nothing back. Everything is wide open and straightforward. It's an old design with surprisingly wide fairways (you can certainly spray some shots here) and very demanding greens. It goes through some wonderful elevation changes (40' - 50') that will often place your ball on an uneven lie.

You'll have to keep your ball on the fairway and off of the rough. At times, especially in the summer, the rough can be very tough to play out of. The course is most pleasurable for long and straight hitters. Many of your approach shots will have to be accurately played to stay on the small greens.

DIRECTIONS

Take Hwy. 441 to Hwy. 46 and go east to Hwy. 435. The course will be one mile further on your left side.

ORANGE BLOSSOM HILLS GOLF & COUNTRY CLUB

1 Water Tower Cr., Lady Lake, FL 32195 / (904) 753-5200

BASIC INFORMATION

Course Type: Semi-private
Year Built: 1985
Architect: N/A
Local Pro: Steve Wresh

Course: Orange Blossom Hills (18 / Par 72)
Holes: 45

Back: 6,100 yds. Rating: 69.1 Slope: 117
Middle: 5,680 yds. Rating: 67.3 Slope: 112
Ladies: 4,970 yds. Rating: 68.9 Slope: 117

Tee Time: 1 day in advance
Price: $32

Credit Cards:	■	Restaurant:	■
Driving Range:	■	Lounge:	■
Practice Green:	■	Meeting Rooms:	■
Locker Room:	■	Tennis:	■
Rental Clubs:	■	Swimming:	■
Walkers:	■	Jogging Trails:	
Snack Bar:	■	Boating:	

COURSE DESCRIPTION

The locals will have you believing in no time that this is the hardest challenge in Lady Lake for a course that only measures 6,100 yards from the back tees.

Its' hilly design features out-of-bounds on practically every hole. Let's look at the toughest hole. From the tee, the number 12 hole (par-5 / 480 yards) features trees both left and right that run along the entire length of this double-dogleg hole. Hit your drive with accuracy, your first approach with finesse. Don't let the bunker on the right side of the green fool you. It's 10-15 yards away from the green.

Water comes into play on 3 holes.

DIRECTIONS

Take Hwy. 27 right to the course. It will be two miles north of Lady Luck in your right side. Look for the sign.

PALISADES COUNTRY CLUB

16510 Palisades Blvd., Clermont, FL 34711 / (904) 394-0085

BASIC INFORMATION

Course Type: Semi-private
Year Built: 1991
Architect: J. Lee
Local Pro: Warron Stanchina

Course: N/A
Holes: 18 / Par 72

Back: 7,002 yds. Rating: 73.8 Slope: 127
Middle: 6,430 yds. Rating: 71.2 Slope: 123
Ladies: 5,541 yds. Rating: 72.1 Slope: 122

Tee Time: 7 days in advance
Price: $15 - $45

Credit Cards:	■	Restaurant:	
Driving Range:	■	Lounge:	
Practice Green:	■	Meeting Rooms:	
Locker Room:	■	Tennis:	
Rental Clubs:		Swimming:	
Walkers:		Jogging Trails:	
Snack Bar:	■	Boating:	■

COURSE DESCRIPTION

Joe Lee, renowned for designing the *Palisades Country Club*, felt that this course was sitting on the most spectacular piece of land in Central Florida.

The golf course was designed around many acres of rolling hills and natural lake fronts. One of the most spectacular features on the course is the 80-foot high green that provides panoramic views from atop one of the highest points overlooking Lake Minneola.

This course will provide you with a challenging and enjoyable game that you'll surely remember for a long time.

DIRECTIONS

From Orlando take Hwy. 50 or the East-West Expressway west to US 27 and turn north to SR 561/A.

URICO GOLF & COUNTRY CLUB
37700 Rolling Acres Rd., Lady Lake, FL 32159 / (904) 753-4848

BASIC INFORMATION

Course Type: Semi-private
Year Built: 1987
Architect: Han Yoo
Local Pro: Glen Koomble

Course: N/A
Holes: 18 / Par 72

Back: 6,367 yds. Rating: 70.9 Slope: 120
Middle: 6,162 yds. Rating: 69.9 Slope: 117
Ladies: 5,459 yds. Rating: 75.4 Slope: 126

Tee Time: 1 day in advance
Price: $13

Credit Cards:		Restaurant:	■
Driving Range:	■	Lounge:	■
Practice Green:	■	Meeting Rooms:	
Locker Room:	■	Tennis:	
Rental Clubs:	■	Swimming:	
Walkers:	■	Jogging Trails:	
Snack Bar:	■	Boating:	

COURSE DESCRIPTION

This is a very well-crafted golf course designed to be challenging for all types of golfers. The layout has an interesting twist when you analyze it. The front nine is the wider half with less trees and a better chance of reaching par than the back. If you're feeling confident, this is the half to play aggressively.

The second half is the more challenging side with tighter fairways and more trees that come into the play of action. You'll have to hold back your drives for the sake of accuracy to place the ball on the fairway.

The greens are challenging and well designed.

DIRECTIONS

Take Hwy. 27 north to Hwy. 466 and south on Landfill Rd. to the course.

WATER OAK GOLF COURSE
106 Evergreen Lane, Lady Lake, FL 32159 / (904) 753-3905

BASIC INFORMATION

Course Type: Semi-private
Year Built: 1982
Architect: M. Bishop
Local Pro: Tim Allen

Course: N/A
Holes: 18 / Par 72

Back: 5,758 yds. Rating: 67.4 Slope: 109
Middle: N/A yds. Rating: N/A Slope: N/A
Ladies: 4,767 yds. Rating: 67.9 Slope: 113

Tee Time: 2 days in advance
Price: $16 - $25

Credit Cards:		Restaurant:	■
Driving Range:	■	Lounge:	■
Practice Green:	■	Meeting Rooms:	■
Locker Room:		Tennis:	
Rental Clubs:	■	Swimming:	
Walkers:	■	Jogging Trails:	
Snack Bar:	■	Boating:	

COURSE DESCRIPTION

Every course has a character all its own. The *Water Oak Golf Course* may not be the most extravagant course in Lady Lake, but it surely is a fun place to play a light game of golf without having to hit a perfect shot every single time.

The layout is simple without holding anything away from the golfer. Big oak trees stand by the fairway lining up the shape of the holes from afar.

You'll need to hit your drives accurately to stay on the narrow rolling fairways. Approach shots should be hit crisp with a lot of backspin to hold on to the small greens.

Water comes into play on six holes.

DIRECTIONS

The course is seven miles north of Leesburg on Hwy. 27/441. Look for the sign.

GOLDEN OCALA GOLF & COUNTRY CLUB

7300 U.S. Hwy. 27, Ocala, FL 34482 / (904) 629-6229

BASIC INFORMATION

Course Type: Public
Year Built: 1986
Architect: R. Garl
Local Pro: Jeff Austin

Course: N/A
Holes: 18 / Par 72

Back: 6,735 yds. Rating: 72.2 Slope: 132
Middle: 6,197 yds. Rating: 69.5 Slope: 124
Ladies: 5,595 yds. Rating: 72.2 Slope: 124

Tee Time: 7 days in advance
Price: $25 - $40

Credit Cards:		Restaurant:	
Driving Range:	■	Lounge:	
Practice Green:	■	Meeting Rooms:	
Locker Room:		Tennis:	
Rental Clubs:	■	Swimming:	
Walkers:		Jogging Trails:	
Snack Bar:		Boating:	

COURSE DESCRIPTION

The *Golden Ocala Golf & Country Club* features eight replica holes from the most famous golfing venues around the world. It was voted in the top 75 public golf courses in the US by Golf Digest magazine.

The eight replica holes are from the following courses: Augusta National (#12, #13, and #16), Royal Troon (#8), Murfield (#9), St. Andrews (#1 and #17), and Baltusrol (#4). The attention to detail that has gone into the construction of these holes is astounding. Even if you've seen them photographed in a major golfing publication, or seen them featured on television, you're still going to be amazed when you view these holes in person.

DIRECTIONS

Take Exit 70 off I-75 and go 3 miles west, on US 27, to the course.

MARION OAKS COUNTRY CLUB

4260 S.W. 162nd St., Ocala, FL 34473 / (904) 347-1271

BASIC INFORMATION

Course Type: Semi-private
Year Built: 1974
Architect: N/A
Local Pro: Randy Scott

Course: N/A
Holes: 18 / Par 72

Back: 7,100 yds. Rating: 72.9 Slope: 130
Middle: 6,500 yds. Rating: 70.6 Slope: 126
Ladies: 5,300 yds. Rating: 69.5 Slope: 110

Tee Time: 5 days in advance
Price: $21 - $23

Credit Cards:	■	Restaurant:	■
Driving Range:	■	Lounge:	■
Practice Green:	■	Meeting Rooms:	
Locker Room:	■	Tennis:	
Rental Clubs:	■	Swimming:	
Walkers:		Jogging Trails:	
Snack Bar:	■	Boating:	

COURSE DESCRIPTION

If you need a place that will take you out of your everyday routine and into a world filled with extraordinary fairways, wide and generous, just looking at you and daring you to hit your best possible drive... welcome to *Marion Oaks*. This tremendous course will have you reaching for every club in your bag by the time your game is over.

It's all here, folks: long par-5's, penal par-3's, strategic par-4's, all combined in a menagerie of fine doglegs and straight holes.

If you want a course that offers peace of mind along with terrific golf, this is the place you'll want to play. Anyone above a 10 handicap should play from the middle tees.

DIRECTIONS

Exit Hwy. 484 from I-75 and go west to the course. Look for the signs.

OCALA MUNICIPAL GOLF COURSE

3130 E. Silver Springs Blvd., Ocala, FL 32670 / (904) 622-8681

BASIC INFORMATION

Course Type: Municipal
Year Built: 1930 / 1989
Architect: N/A / L. Clifton
Local Pro: Jim Yancey

Course: N/A
Holes: 18

Back: 6,367 yds. Rating: 71.1 Slope: 129
Middle: 5,966 yds. Rating: 69.5 Slope: 125
Ladies: 5,738 yds. Rating: 70.6 Slope: 120

Tee Time: 2 days in advance
Price: $13 - $15

Credit Cards: ■	Restaurant:
Driving Range: ■	Lounge:
Practice Green: ■	Meeting Rooms:
Locker Room: ■	Tennis:
Rental Clubs: ■	Swimming:
Walkers: ■	Jogging Trails:
Snack Bar: ■	Boating:

COURSE DESCRIPTION

This Municipal course is a marvellous layout with many interesting holes.

To play well here, you'll have to hit your drives down the middle of the narrow fairways to keep your ball away from trouble.

Most of the greens are undulating and slope from back-to-front. If you can calculate the slope of the greens from the fairways, the odds will favor you to play your ball to the highest level and have it roll back towards the hole.

The course also features many subtle contours around the greens. Making par usually means having to putt aggressively to minimize the breaks on the putting surface.

DIRECTIONS

Take Hwy. 40 straight to the course. It will be east of the downtown area.

PINE OAKS GOLF COURSE

2201 N.W. 21 Street, Ocala, FL 32675 / (904) 622-8558

BASIC INFORMATION

Course Type: Municipal
Year Built: 1986
Architect: R. Garl
Local Pro: Joe Lopez

Course: North / South (18 / Par 72)
Holes: 27

Back: 6,403 yds. Rating: 70.4 Slope: 128
Middle: 5,872 yds. Rating: 69.0 Slope: 124
Ladies: 4,957 yds. Rating: 68.5 Slope: 113

Tee Time: 2 days in advance
Price: $7.42 - $15.90

Credit Cards: ■	Restaurant: ■
Driving Range: ■	Lounge: ■
Practice Green: ■	Meeting Rooms: ■
Locker Room: ■	Tennis:
Rental Clubs: ■	Swimming:
Walkers: ■	Jogging Trails:
Snack Bar: ■	Boating:

COURSE DESCRIPTION

You'll find a nice series of hole designs at the *Pine Oaks Golf Course*.

This venue features many wide fairways which makes it a great place to play aggressive golf. Yet, it isn't as simple as you may think. The rolling terrain of these fairways will often place your ball on an uneven lie.

If you're not used to this type of situation, you'll have a hard time gaining good position on your approach shots. That is why the slope ratings are so much higher than they would normally be in relation to the total yardage of the course. Don't be deceived by the wide fairways. This course will rip you apart if you don't keep your shots straight and accurate.

DIRECTIONS

Exit Hwy. 27 from I-75 and go east for a mile and north on 27th Ave. Make a right on 21St. to the course.

SILVER SPRINGS SHORE COUNTRY CLUB
565 Silver Rd., Ocala, FL 32672 / (904) 687-2828

BASIC INFORMATION

Course Type: Semi-private
Year Built: 1972
Architect: D. Muirhead
Local Pro: Tim Eckstein

Course: N/A
Holes: 18 / Par 72

Back: 6,857 yds. Rating: 73.7 Slope: 131
Middle: 6,131 yds. Rating: 69.5 Slope: 122
Ladies: 5,188 yds. Rating: 70.2 Slope: 120

Tee Time: 7 days in advance
Price: $18 - $32

Credit Cards:	■	Restaurant:	■
Driving Range:	■	Lounge:	■
Practice Green:	■	Meeting Rooms:	■
Locker Room:	■	Tennis:	
Rental Clubs:	■	Swimming:	
Walkers:		Jogging Trails:	
Snack Bar:	■	Boating:	

COURSE DESCRIPTION

This is the type of challenge golf pros are faced with everyday on the PGA Tour. If you're going to go for the full challenge at 6,857 yards from the back tees, you better be prepared to hit many long approach shots to highly demanding greens.

If you're an average golfer who normally shoots somewhere in the 90's, be prepared to play your 3-wood off the fairway on most of your approach shots. I highly recommend that you play the course from the middle tees for maximum enjoyment.

Single handicap players will end up using every club in their bag by the time they finish their rounds.

DIRECTIONS

Exit Silver Springs Blvd. (Hwy. 40) and go east to Hwy. 441/301 and south to 17th St. Go east to Hwy. 646 (Maricamp Rd.) and southeast to the course.

BAY HILL CLUB & LODGE
9000 Bay Hill Blvd., Orlando, FL 32819 / (407) 876-2429

BASIC INFORMATION

Course Type: Resort
Year Built: 1961
Architect: D. Wilson
Local Pro: Jim Deaton

Course: Challenger / Champion (18 / Par 72)
Holes: 27

Back: 7,114 yds. Rating: 74.6 Slope: 141
Middle: 6,586 yds. Rating: 71.8 Slope: 127
Ladies: 5,192 yds. Rating: 72.3 Slope: 133

Tee Time: 7 days in advance
Price: $125 - $125

Credit Cards:	■	Restaurant:	■
Driving Range:	■	Lounge:	■
Practice Green:	■	Meeting Rooms:	■
Locker Room:	■	Tennis:	■
Rental Clubs:	■	Swimming:	■
Walkers:		Jogging Trails:	
Snack Bar:	■	Boating:	■

COURSE DESCRIPTION

This spectacular course is home to one of the most exciting tournaments on the PGA Tour: The Nestle Invitational. Some of the notable winners are Payne Stewart, Paul Azinger, Tom Kite, Fuzzy Zoeller and Robert Gamez, who in 1990 defied the odds by holing in an Eagle on the 18th hole.

Bay Hill is a beautiful challenge of golf for all caliber players. The course is meticulously well-maintained and the greens are always true to the roll. If you get lucky, you may even get in on a pick-up round with Arnold Palmer, Payne Stewart, Scott Hoch, Mark O'Meara, Corey Pavin, Steve Lowery ... or me!

DIRECTIONS

Take I-4 to Exit 29 (Sand Lake Rd.) west to Apopka Vineland Rd. Turn right and go straight to Bay Hill Blvd.

CYPRESS CREEK COUNTRY CLUB

5353 Vinelake Rd., Orlando, FL 32811 / (407) 351-2187

BASIC INFORMATION

Course Type: Semi-private
Year Built: 1969
Architect: L. Clifton
Local Pro: David Graulan

Course: N/A
Holes: 18 / Par 72

Back: 7,000 yds. Rating: 73.6 Slope: 126
Middle: 6,500 yds. Rating: 70.6 Slope: 120
Ladies: 5,700 yds. Rating: 72.2 Slope: 121

Tee Time: 7 days in advance
Price: $17 - $35

Credit Cards:	■	Restaurant:	■
Driving Range:	■	Lounge:	■
Practice Green:	■	Meeting Rooms:	■
Locker Room:	■	Tennis:	■
Rental Clubs:	■	Swimming:	■
Walkers:		Jogging Trails:	
Snack Bar:	■	Boating:	

COURSE DESCRIPTION

This challenging course is a very tough layout to take control of. With over 7,000 yards of real estate from the back tees, you better have your long game down to a science. The course is filled with hungry obstacles that can magically funnel your ball into the land of the unknown.

Here is an example of what you'll be up against: the 16th hole (383 yards) is a challenging 90% dogleg-right. You'll have to hit a scorching drive at least 260 yards to get into good position for your approach shot to the green.

You'll save yourself a great amount of yardage if you can hit your drives straight and accurate. Play from the middle tees if you're not a single-digit-handicapper.

DIRECTIONS

Take Exit 435 from I-4 and go north to Vineland Rd. Go east to the course.

DUBSDRED GOLF COURSE

549 W. Par, Orlando, FL 32804 / (407) 246-2551

BASIC INFORMATION

Course Type: Municipal
Year Built: 1922
Architect: C. Dann Sr.
Local Pro: Dave Johnson Sr.

Course: N/A
Holes: 18 / Par 70

Back: 6,055 yds. Rating: 69.0 Slope: 115
Middle: 5,865 yds. Rating: 68.0 Slope: 113
Ladies: 5,565 yds. Rating: 70.8 Slope: 112

Tee Time: 2 days in advance
Price: $17 - $28

Credit Cards:	■	Restaurant:	■
Driving Range:	■	Lounge:	■
Practice Green:	■	Meeting Rooms:	■
Locker Room:	■	Tennis:	
Rental Clubs:	■	Swimming:	
Walkers:	■	Jogging Trails:	
Snack Bar:	■	Boating:	

COURSE DESCRIPTION

If you love old courses that haven't been tampered with, this is one you'll remember for a long time. Like many older courses, it features tree-lined fairways that are wide with few traps and highly cut rough.

You'll have to hit your tee-shots accurately to take advantage of the layout. The greens are small and always demanding. If your natural shot is a fade, keeping the ball on a high trajectory will improve your chances of stopping the ball quickly on your approach shots to the greens.

If that isn't one of your better shots, you'll often end up chipping onto the putting surface with a single putt left for par.

DIRECTIONS

Take I-4 to directly to Par Ave. and the course will be west about two miles on your left.

EASTWOOD GOLF & COUNTRY CLUB

13950 Golfway Blvd., Orlando, FL 32828 / (407) 281-9207

BASIC INFORMATION

Course Type: Public
Year Built: 1990
Architect: L. Clifton
Local Pro: N/A

Course: N/A
Holes: 18 / Par 72

Back: 7,176 yds. Rating: 73.9 Slope: 124
Middle: 6,503 yds. Rating: 70.7 Slope: 118
Ladies: 5,393 yds. Rating: 70.5 Slope: 117

Tee Time: 7 days in advance
Price: $20 - $45

Credit Cards: ■	Restaurant:
Driving Range: ■	Lounge:
Practice Green: ■	Meeting Rooms:
Locker Room:	Tennis:
Rental Clubs: ■	Swimming:
Walkers:	Jogging Trails:
Snack Bar: ■	Boating:

COURSE DESCRIPTION

This is an exceptional place to play golf for players of all skill levels. No matter what your handicap may be, you'll surely find a place for your game from one of the multiple tees. The course is filled with imaginative holes that feature wide fairways and well- groomed greens.

The course also features 17 lakes that often come into the play of action. You can shorten the layout quite considerably by playing your approach shots over water on most of the dogleg-holes.

The 4th hole, a 90% dogleg, is one of the finest in Orlando.

DIRECTIONS

From the East-West Expressway go to Alafaya Trail and turn south approximately one mile to Eastwood Entrance. From there, turn left on Golfway Blvd. and drive one mile to the course. It will be on your right.

GRAND CYPRESS GOLF CLUB

1 N. Jacaranda, Orlando, FL 32819 / (407) 239-3620

BASIC INFORMATION

Course Type: Resort
Year Built: 1967
Architect: B. Amick
Local Pro: Keven Gabard

Course: South & East (18 / Par 72)
Holes: 27

Back: 7,025 yds. Rating: 73.9 Slope: 133
Middle: 6,412 yds. Rating: 71.0 Slope: 126
Ladies: 5,661 yds. Rating: 73.0 Slope: 123

Tee Time: 7 days in advance
Price: $30 - $35

Credit Cards: ■	Restaurant: ■
Driving Range: ■	Lounge: ■
Practice Green: ■	Meeting Rooms: ■
Locker Room: ■	Tennis: ■
Rental Clubs: ■	Swimming: ■
Walkers: ■	Jogging Trails: ■
Snack Bar: ■	Boating: ■

COURSE DESCRIPTION

This is a wonderful 4-star resort with enough activity for the most demanding of golfers. Jack Nicklaus did a splendid job of designing this course with many excellent features. The course plays long and challenging from the back-tees at over 7,000 yards. You'll need to hit your tee-shots solidly throughout the day to post a good score. This is the type of course that will force you to use your entire collection of clubs by the time you reach the 18th green.

The most dramatic hole on the course is the 5th. This beautiful par-3 hole measures 153 yards and plays to a very demanding island green.

DIRECTIONS

Take I-4 to Lake Buena Vista. Go Northbound to the 2nd traffic light and West to the course. It will be on your right.

HUNTER'S CREEK GOLF COURSE

14401 Sports Club Way, Orlando, FL 32837 / (407) 240-4653

BASIC INFORMATION

Course Type: Public
Year Built: 1986
Architect: L. Clifton
Local Pro: Danny Boswell

Course: N/A
Holes: 18 / Par 72

Back: 7,432 yds. Rating: 75.2 Slope: 127
Middle: 6,521 yds. Rating: 71.0 Slope: 118
Ladies: 5,755 yds. Rating: 72.5 Slope: 120

Tee Time: 3 days in advance
Price: $30 - $50

Credit Cards: ■	Restaurant:	
Driving Range: ■	Lounge:	■
Practice Green: ■	Meeting Rooms:	
Locker Room:	Tennis:	
Rental Clubs: ■	Swimming:	
Walkers:	Jogging Trails:	
Snack Bar: ■	Boating:	

COURSE DESCRIPTION

Hunters Creek Golf Course offers the avid golfer the opportunity of matching par-72 around some of the most exquisitely maintained 18 holes of golf. Each one offers no less than three tee boxes allowing golfers of all levels to enjoy the course to its maximum. For water lovers, 13 of Hunter Creek's picturesque fairways are complemented by sparkling lakes.

If you're a long hitter looking for the ultimate challenge, try playing the back tees which measure an unbelievable 7,432 yards. Golf Digest magazine ranked the course in their top 50 public course list. You won't be disappointed.

DIRECTIONS

From I-4 go eight miles south on St. Rd. 441 and the course will be on your right.

INTERNATIONAL GOLF CLUB

6351 International Golf Club, Orlando, FL 32821 / (407) 239-6909

BASIC INFORMATION

Course Type: Public
Year Built: 1988
Architect: J. Lee
Local Pro: Gary Riby

Course: N/A
Holes: 18

Back: 6,776 yds. Rating: 71.7 Slope: 119
Middle: 6,190 yds. Rating: 69.0 Slope: 115
Ladies: 5,078 yds. Rating: N/A   Slope: 107

Tee Time: 4 days in advance
Price: $59

Credit Cards: ■	Restaurant:	■
Driving Range:	Lounge:	■
Practice Green: ■	Meeting Rooms:	
Locker Room: ■	Tennis:	
Rental Clubs: ■	Swimming:	
Walkers:	Jogging Trails:	
Snack Bar: ■	Boating:	

COURSE DESCRIPTION

This is a very playable layout with many fascinating approaches to the putting green. The fairways are tight and will only accept the most accurate drives. Knowing where to place the ball on the many undulating putting greens is the key to playing well here.

The 11th hole (par-5 / 566 yards) is one of the most demanding on the course. This dramatic double-dogleg will have you driving your ball down a tight fairway with out-of-bounds on the left and tall trees both left and right. You'll find a pond on the left front portion of the green. The green itself slopes sharply from left to right. Play a knock-down to the right fringe and roll the ball to the hole.

DIRECTIONS

Exit onto Hwy. 528 from 1-4 and go southwest on International Dr. to the course.

LAKE BUENA VISTA CLUB

7500 Exchange Dr., Orlando, FL 32830 / (407) 828-3741

BASIC INFORMATION

Course Type: Public
Year Built: 1972
Architect: J. Lee
Local Pro: Dave Bolton

Course: N/A
Holes: 18 / Par 72

Back: 6,829 yds. Rating: 72.7 Slope: 128
Middle: 6,268 yds. Rating: 70.1 Slope: 123
Ladies: 5,917 yds. Rating: 68.2 Slope: 120

Tee Time: 7 days in advance
Price: $35 - $75

Credit Cards:	■	Restaurant:	■
Driving Range:	■	Lounge:	■
Practice Green:	■	Meeting Rooms:	■
Locker Room:	■	Tennis:	■
Rental Clubs:	■	Swimming:	■
Walkers:	■	Jogging Trails:	■
Snack Bar:	■	Boating:	

COURSE DESCRIPTION

This course is evenly set up for golfers who play their natural shots from both the left and right. It's a good layout with many exciting holes that will challenge you to think about what you want to do rather than dictate a single path. It makes for interesting golf because now you have the option of playing your game, rather than conforming to a game with which you're not familiar.

The course is severe from the back tees and should only be played by single digit handicap players.

Water comes into play on nine holes.

DIRECTIONS

Exit onto Lake Buena Vista from I-4 and you'll see a sign for the *WDW Complex*. The signs will lead you to the course.

MARRIOT'S ORLANDO WORLD

One World Center Dr., Orlando, FL 32821 / (407) 239-5659

BASIC INFORMATION

Course Type: Public
Year Built: 1986
Architect: J. Lee
Local Pro: Tony Austin (Director of Golf)

Course: N/A
Holes: 18 / Par 71

Back: 6,307 yds. Rating: 69.8 Slope: 121
Middle: 5,956 yds. Rating: 68.3 Slope: 117
Ladies: 5,048 yds. Rating: 68.5 Slope: 115

Tee Time: 7 days in advance
Price: $55 - $85

Credit Cards:	■	Restaurant:	■
Driving Range:	■	Lounge:	■
Practice Green:	■	Meeting Rooms:	■
Locker Room:	■	Tennis:	■
Rental Clubs:	■	Swimming:	■
Walkers:		Jogging Trails:	
Snack Bar:	■	Boating:	

COURSE DESCRIPTION

This is a quite dramatic layout for a course that only measures 6,307 yards from the back tees. Try to keep yourself one stroke in front by consistently setting yourself up for each following shot towards the green.

When standing on the tee, consider playing a low iron instead of a wood. It will increase your chances of keeping the ball on the fairway and should be long enough to set yourself up for a good approach shot to the green.

The greens are small and demanding. You'll often find yourself having to chip on and one putt for par. Water comes into play on 15 holes.

DIRECTIONS

Exit onto Hwy. 536 (26A) from I-4 and go east to the course. You can't miss it.

MEADOW WOODS GOLF CLUB
13001 Landstar Blvd., Orlando, FL 32824 / (407) 859-9778

BASIC INFORMATION

Course Type: Public
Year Built: 1985
Architect: B. Blanford
Local Pro: Richard Stroes

Course: N/A
Holes: 18 / Par 70 (Ladies: Par 69)

Back: 6,065 yds. Rating: 68.9 Slope: N/A
Middle: 5,570 yds. Rating: 67.0 Slope: N/A
Ladies: 4,355 yds. Rating: 59.6 Slope: N/A

Tee Time: 2 days in advance
Price: $15.90 - $30

Credit Cards:	■	Restaurant:	
Driving Range:	■	Lounge:	■
Practice Green:	■	Meeting Rooms:	
Locker Room:		Tennis:	■
Rental Clubs:	■	Swimming:	■
Walkers:		Jogging Trails:	
Snack Bar:	■	Boating:	■

COURSE DESCRIPTION

Meadow Woods Golf Club is under new ownership and they are doing everything they can to make this course an even better test of golf. The rating/slope numbers are being reevaluated as I write this description.

You'll find many pleasurable and exciting moments on this golf course. It makes for a great place to practice your short game if you're an accomplished player and an even better challenge for the golfer in need of distance off the tee.

This is one of the very few courses in Florida that will use "Bent" grass rather than Bermuda on their winter greens.

This shotmakers' course features water coming into play on 16 holes.

DIRECTIONS
Take Hwy. 527 south of Hwy. 528 to the course. Look for the entrance sign.

METRO WEST COUNTRY CLUB
2100 S. Hiawassee Rd., Orlando, FL 32811 / (407) 299-1099

BASIC INFORMATION

Course Type: Semi-private
Year Built: 1987
Architect: R. Trent Jones, Sr.
Local Pro: Brad Houer

Course: N/A
Holes: 18 / Par 72

Back: 7,051yds. Rating: 73.1 Slope: 126
Middle: 6,467 yds. Rating: 70.4 Slope: 120
Ladies: 5,325 yds. Rating: 69.6 Slope: 117

Tee Time: 7 days in advance
Price: $42 - $62

Credit Cards:	■	Restaurant:	■
Driving Range:	■	Lounge:	■
Practice Green:	■	Meeting Rooms:	■
Locker Room:	■	Tennis:	■
Rental Clubs:	■	Swimming:	■
Walkers:		Jogging Trails:	
Snack Bar:	■	Boating:	

COURSE DESCRIPTION

Metro West Country Club features beautiful holes that flow throughout in an imaginative design. No matter what your handicap may be, you'll be assured of an incredible challenge of golf from one of the numerous tees.

On a clear day, hole numbers 13 and 14 serve as a looking glass into the downtown portion of Orlando. You'll find the course to be fairly wide open with many strategically-placed bunkers around its hilly terrain.

The Arnold Palmer Course Management Company has been doing a brilliant job of keeping the place in top shape throughout the year. This is a great place to enjoy the game of golf to its fullest.

DIRECTIONS
From I-4, Exit. 30B and take Rt. 435 north. The main entrance will be three miles on your left.

ROSEMONT GOLF & COUNTRY CLUB

4224 Clubhouse Rd., Orlando, FL 32801 / (407) 298-1230

BASIC INFORMATION

Course Type: Semi-private
Year Built: 1972
Architect: L. Clifton
Local Pro: Lyle Beaver

Course: N/A
Holes: 18 / Par 72

Back: 6,803 yds. Rating: 72.3 Slope: 130
Middle: 6,271 yds. Rating: 69.6 Slope: 122
Ladies: 5,498 yds. Rating: 70.3 Slope: 114

Tee Time: 7 days in advance
Price: $16 - $40

Credit Cards:	■	Restaurant:	■
Driving Range:	■	Lounge:	■
Practice Green:	■	Meeting Rooms:	■
Locker Room:	■	Tennis:	■
Rental Clubs:	■	Swimming:	■
Walkers:		Jogging Trails:	
Snack Bar:	■	Boating:	

COURSE DESCRIPTION

Welcome to aqua heaven. This is a course that features water coming into play on every hole. You'll have to play more than once to really appreciate the design.

Good course management is essential to scoring well. Take a look at the scorecard and work out an approach that you feel comfortable with. Play to the bail out spots if you need to. Any player above a 15 handicap should play from the middle tees.

The front nine is the harder. half. Play it conservatively until you get a feel for the course. The course seems to open up a little more on the back nine allowing for more aggressive play.

DIRECTIONS

Exit onto Hwy. 483 (Lee Rd.) from I-4 and go west to Lake Breeze Dr. Make a left at the dead end.

VENTURA COUNTRY CLUB

3201 Woodgate Blvd., Orlando, FL 32822 / (407) 277-2640

BASIC INFORMATION

Course Type: Semi-private
Year Built: 1980
Architect: M. Mahannah
Local Pro: Gene Smith

Course: N/A
Holes: 18 / Par 70

Back: 5,467 yds. Rating: 66.1 Slope: 112
Middle: 5,041 yds. Rating: 64.0 Slope: 108
Ladies: 4,392 yds. Rating: 64.4 Slope: 106

Tee Time: 2 days in advance
Price: $25 - $37

Credit Cards:	■	Restaurant:	■
Driving Range:	■	Lounge:	■
Practice Green:	■	Meeting Rooms:	
Locker Room:		Tennis:	■
Rental Clubs:	■	Swimming:	■
Walkers:	■	Jogging Trails:	
Snack Bar:	■	Boating:	

COURSE DESCRIPTION

The *Ventura Country Club* is a fun course that is short and easy to play. If you're looking for an ego booster, this may be the course that will make you the new Mr. 59.

The course is a good start for a golfer that hasn't played in a while and needs to warm up for the season. If you're an accomplished golfer, you can certainly get a good work-out on your short game. If you're a senior citizen, the course was manufactured especially for you.

You'll have to play an accurate game of golf to put the ball on the narrow fairways. Water comes into play on 15 holes and the course favors a fade. Have fun!

DIRECTIONS

Take Somoran Blvd. (Hwy. 436) to Curry Ford Rd. Proceed east and straight to the course.

WALT DISNEY WORLD RESORT

P.O. Box 10,000, Lake Buena Vista , FL 32830 / (407) 824-2288

BASIC INFORMATION

Course Type: Public
Year Built: 1992
Architect: T. Fazio
Local Pro: Keven Weieckel

Course: Bonnet Creek (18 / Par 72)
Holes: 99

Back: 7,101 yds. Rating: 73.9 Slope: 135
Middle: 6,680 yds. Rating: 71.8 Slope: 128
Ladies: 5,402 yds. Rating: 70.4 Slope: 124

Tee Time: 7 days in advance
Price: $70

Credit Cards:	■	Restaurant:	■
Driving Range:	■	Lounge:	■
Practice Green:	■	Meeting Rooms:	■
Locker Room:	■	Tennis:	■
Rental Clubs:	■	Swimming:	■
Walkers:		Jogging Trails:	■
Snack Bar:	■	Boating:	■

COURSE DESCRIPTION

This is without question one of the best locations in the world to play the game of golf. There are 99 holes designed by the finest architects of our time. Every course is a thrill to play on and quite an adventure.

Bonnet Creek, which was designed by Tom Fazio, is the most popular attraction at present. This incredible layout offers everything you would want in a course. Long par 5's, strategic par- 4's, heroic par-3's, all built in a very serene and private expanse of property.

You'll surely find your brand of golf on one of the four tee markers. Choose the right one for your game and you'll be one step closer to heaven.

DIRECTIONS

Take I-4 to the Magic Kingdom Exit and the signs will lead you to all of the courses.

WEDGEFIELD GOLF & COUNTRY CLUB

20550 Maxim Parkway, Orlando, FL 32833 / (407) 568-2116

BASIC INFORMATION

Course Type: Semi-private
Year Built: 1970
Architect: N/A
Local Pro: Warren Stanchina

Course: N/A
Holes: 18 / Par 72

Back: 6,738 yds. Rating: 72.8 Slope: 124
Middle: 6,231 yds. Rating: 70.1 Slope: 120
Ladies: 5,327 yds. Rating: 72.8 Slope: 119

Tee Time: 3 days in advance
Price: $14 - $31

Credit Cards:	■	Restaurant:	■
Driving Range:	■	Lounge:	■
Practice Green:	■	Meeting Rooms:	■
Locker Room:	■	Tennis:	■
Rental Clubs:	■	Swimming:	■
Walkers:		Jogging Trails:	
Snack Bar:	■	Boating:	

COURSE DESCRIPTION

Wedgefield Golf & Country Club is an interesting design with many wonderful holes that golfers of all abilities will enjoy.

The wide fairways allow you a good margin of error without penalizing you severely. This makes for aggressive competition, and for an enjoyable day of golf.

The course features five dogleg-left and six dogleg-right holes. You'll need to have the ability to work the ball both ways if you're going to score a really low number. The back is the harder half, so try to get your birdies on the front.

Water comes into play on seven holes.

DIRECTIONS

Take I-95 to SR 520. Take SR 520 towards Orlando and the course will be 16 miles on your left.

BUENAVENTURA LAKES COUNTRY CLUB WEST

290 Competition Dr., Kissimmee, FL 34743 / (407) 348-4915

BASIC INFORMATION

Course Type: Public
Year Built: 1983
Architect: N/A
Local Pro: Richard Stroes

Course: N/A
Holes: 18 / Par 70

Back: 6,000 yds. Rating: 68.7 Slope: 117
Middle: 5,800 yds. Rating: 66.4 Slope: 112
Ladies: 5,500 yds. Rating: 67.5 Slope: 114

Tee Time: 7 days in advance
Price: $15 - $35

Credit Cards:	■	Restaurant:	■
Driving Range:	■	Lounge:	■
Practice Green:	■	Meeting Rooms:	■
Locker Room:		Tennis:	
Rental Clubs:	■	Swimming:	■
Walkers:		Jogging Trails:	
Snack Bar:	■	Boating:	■

COURSE DESCRIPTION

This terrific course has many great holes that will challenge the best of golfers while thrilling the beginner. A tight layout makes it mandatory to hit solid drives straight down the middle of the fairways for proper position. You'll need to bring out a less powerful club than a driver.

You really don't have to worry about distance on this course. It is only 6,000 yards from the back tees.

The back nine is the harder half and should be played more strategically.

The course is quite scenic with a nice variety of wildlife. You'll find 13 holes that feature water coming into the action.

DIRECTIONS

Get onto south Orange Blossom Tr. from Hwy. 441 and go south to Dart Blvd. Head an east to Buenaventura Blvd. The course will be south.

KISSIMMEE BAY COUNTRY CLUB

2801 Kissimmee Bay Blvd., Kissimmee, FL 34744 / (407) 348-4653

BASIC INFORMATION

Course Type: Semi-private
Year Built: 1990
Architect: L. Clifton
Local Pro: Chris Eichstedt

Course: N/A
Holes: 18 / Par 72

Back: 6,846 yds. Rating: 72.2 Slope: 125
Middle: 6,383 yds. Rating: 70.1 Slope: 119
Ladies: 5,171 yds. Rating: 71.0 Slope: 122

Tee Time: 7 days in advance
Price: $35 - $50.60

Credit Cards:	■	Restaurant:	■
Driving Range:	■	Lounge:	■
Practice Green:	■	Meeting Rooms:	
Locker Room:	■	Tennis:	
Rental Clubs:	■	Swimming:	
Walkers:		Jogging Trails:	
Snack Bar:	■	Boating:	

COURSE DESCRIPTION

Here's a scenic and great layout that will challenge all types of golfers.

Most people get excited over the natural beauty of the course and the overall good conditioning of the fairways and greens. Many of these wonderful holes feature grass mounds strategically-placed to redirect your approaching shots. Water is another calculating factor that you'll have to watch out for.

You really have to play a well-managed game to score well here. Your drives have to be long and accurate, long iron-play will often be the case on your approach shots, and you'll have to putt aggressively for par. The course is mostly flat.

DIRECTIONS

From Orlando take the Fl. Tpke. south to Exit 244. Make a right at the first, second, and third traffic lights.

KISSIMMEE GOLF CLUB
3101 Florida Coach Rd., Kissimmee, FL 32741 / (407) 847-2816

BASIC INFORMATION

Course Type: Semi-private
Year Built: 1950's (9-holes) / 1982 (9-holes)
Architect: N/A / Bill Bulmer
Local Pro: Rick Sargent

Course: N/A
Holes: 18 / Par 72

Back: 6,537 yds. Rating: 71.4 Slope: 119
Middle: 5,980 yds. Rating: 69.1 Slope: 114
Ladies: 5,083 yds. Rating: 68.6 Slope: 109

Tee Time: 4 days in advance
Price: $28 - $40

Credit Cards: ■	Restaurant: ■
Driving Range: ■	Lounge: ■
Practice Green: ■	Meeting Rooms:
Locker Room:	Tennis:
Rental Clubs: ■	Swimming:
Walkers: ■	Jogging Trails:
Snack Bar: ■	Boating:

COURSE DESCRIPTION

This charismatic course is both fun and challenging for all golfers.

This is not a long course compared to the average, but it can play sneaky long because of the tight fairways. A successful round here means having to hit many of the fairways without letting the ball fall into the rough or out-of-bounds. You'll often need to hold back your drives for the sake of accuracy. The course plays well to both a fade and a draw.

Every once in awhile, if you look up in the sky, you'll more than likely see an old fighting plane from the near-by War Bird Museum.

Water comes into play on 12 holes.

DIRECTIONS

Take Hwy. 192 from I-4 and go east to Hoagland Blvd. You'll see the course from here. Go two miles south to the sign.

ORANGE LAKES COUNTRY CLUB
8505 W. Irla Bronson Mem. Hwy., Kissimmee, FL 34746 / (407) 239-0000

BASIC INFORMATION

Course Type: Resort
Year Built: 1981
Architect: J. Lee
Local Pro: Rick McCord

Course: Oragnge / Cypress (18 / Par 72)
Holes: 27

Back: 6,654 yds. Rating: 72.6 Slope: 131
Middle: 6,279 yds. Rating: 70.8 Slope: 128
Ladies: 5,525 yds. Rating: 70.5 Slope: 128

Tee Time: 7 days in advance
Price: $30 - $60

Credit Cards: ■	Restaurant: ■
Driving Range: ■	Lounge: ■
Practice Green: ■	Meeting Rooms: ■
Locker Room: ■	Tennis: ■
Rental Clubs: ■	Swimming: ■
Walkers:	Jogging Trails: ■
Snack Bar: ■	Boating: ■

COURSE DESCRIPTION

Orange Lakes Country Club offers a dramatic layout that is challenging from tee to green on all 18 holes.

Golfweek magazine has ranked it one of the top 50 courses in the state, and rightly so! It's beautifully maintained all year round.

You don't have to hit your driver for distance on every hole. If you want to score well here you'll have to bring out your 3-wood for accuracy above distance. Most of the holes will still allow you a nice short iron on your approach shots to the greens.

This is a real thinking player's golf course that will have you questioning your actions as you play. Thus, confidence is the key to playing well.

DIRECTIONS

Take I-4 west to Exit 25B (Disney Rt. 192). Take 192 west for four miles and the course will be on your right side.

OVEROAKS COUNTRY CLUB

3232 S. Bermuda Ave., Kissimmee, FL 32741 / (407) 847-3773

BASIC INFORMATION

Course Type: Semi-private
Year Built: 1985
Architect: K. Litten
Local Pro: David Anderson

Course: N/A
Holes: 18 / Par 72

Back: 6,942 yds. Rating: 71.9 Slope: 128
Middle: 6,550 yds. Rating: 69.3 Slope: 122
Ladies: 5,021 yds. Rating: 63.6 Slope: 110

Tee Time: 3 days in advance
Price: $32 - $50

Credit Cards:	■	Restaurant:	■
Driving Range:	■	Lounge:	■
Practice Green:	■	Meeting Rooms:	
Locker Room:	■	Tennis:	■
Rental Clubs:	■	Swimming:	
Walkers:		Jogging Trails:	
Snack Bar:	■	Boating:	

COURSE DESCRIPTION

This course offers an interesting layout that will challenge all who choose to play it.

It's located in a scenic area of Kissimmee with no homes in sight. The atmosphere is serene and tranquil.

You'll have to hit your drives accurately and straight to get into good position for your approach shots to the greens. Some holes will have you hitting your drives over oak trees. Is that how the course was named?

Putting is one of the most demanding attributes of playing well here. Many of the greens are both undulating and multi-tiered.

Water comes into play on 14 holes.

DIRECTIONS

Take Hwy. 17/92 to Bermuda Ave. and turn left towards the course. You can't miss it.

POINCIANA GOLF & RACQUET RESORT

500 Cypress Pkwy., Kissimmee, FL 32758 / (407) 933-4426

BASIC INFORMATION

Course Type: Resort
Year Built: 1972
Architect: Von Hagge / Devlin
Local Pro: Tim Giger

Course: N/A
Holes: 18 / Par 72

Back: 6,700 yds. Rating: 72.2 Slope: 125
Middle: 6,030 yds. Rating: 69.1 Slope: 118
Ladies: 4,988 yds. Rating: 68.4 Slope: 118

Tee Time: 3 days in advance
Price: Please call to confirm.

Credit Cards:	■	Restaurant:	■
Driving Range:	■	Lounge:	■
Practice Green:	■	Meeting Rooms:	■
Locker Room:	■	Tennis:	■
Rental Clubs:	■	Swimming:	■
Walkers:		Jogging Trails:	■
Snack Bar:	■	Boating:	

COURSE DESCRIPTION

This is an exceptional course that is carved through a rich cypress forest.

The challenge here is to keep the ball straight and accurate from tee to green on every single hole. You really have to stay focused on what you are doing. Many of the fairway bunkers are set up as an illusion by playing much farther than they appear. Try to talk to one of the PGA Professionals before you play the course and ask them for a few hints on the ins and outs of the course.

If you can set a plan of action and stick to your plan, you'll have a good chance of coming in with a low score.

DIRECTIONS

Take Hwy. 17 south to Poinciana Blvd and make a right on Pleasant Hill Rd. to Cypress Pkwy.

BARTOW GOLF COURSE

150 Edlewood Ave., Bartow, FL 33839 /(961) 533-9183

BASIC INFORMATION

Course Type: Public
Year Built: 1915
Architect: N/A
Local Pro: Lee Pearson

Course: N/A
Holes: 18 / Par 72

Back: 6,289 yds. Rating: N/A Slope: 118
Middle: 6,024 yds. Rating: 68.9 Slope: 113
Ladies: 5,300 yds. Rating: 70.3 Slope: 120

Tee Time: 2 days in advance
Price: $8 - $12

Credit Cards:		Restaurant:	■
Driving Range:	■	Lounge:	■
Practice Green:	■	Meeting Rooms:	■
Locker Room:		Tennis:	
Rental Clubs:	■	Swimming:	
Walkers:	■	Jogging Trails:	
Snack Bar:	■	Boating:	

COURSE DESCRIPTION

Here's a golf course that has brought joy to golfers for over 73 years. The original design still works charmingly for both the senior citizens and the golfer who is new to the game. If you're a better than average golfer, you may want to play here to strengthen your short game.

The fairways are wide enough to let you work the ball from both the left and the right, and it is forgiving off the short rough in the wintertime. The front is the tougher half of the course and you ought to play it conservatively. You'll have plenty of opportunities to get your birdies on the back. Bring your best draw!

DIRECTIONS

Take Hwy. 17 north to Bartow. Once you cross the county line, make a right at the fourth set of lights to Main St. Look for the course on your right.

BIG CYPRESS GOLF COURSE

10000 N. U.S. Hwy. 98, Lakeland, FL 33809 /(961) 859-6871

BASIC INFORMATION

Course Type: Semi-private
Year Built: 1987
Architect: R. Garl
Local Pro: Jeff O'Malley

Course: N/A
Holes: 18 / Par 72

Back: 6,650 yds. Rating: 71.7 Slope: 124
Middle: 5,607 yds. Rating: 66.8 Slope: 114
Ladies: 4,862 yds. Rating: 67.0 Slope: 112

Tee Time: 3 days in advance
Price: $15 - $25

Credit Cards:	■	Restaurant:	
Driving Range:	■	Lounge:	
Practice Green:	■	Meeting Rooms:	
Locker Room:		Tennis:	■
Rental Clubs:	■	Swimming:	■
Walkers:		Jogging Trails:	
Snack Bar:	■	Boating:	

COURSE DESCRIPTION

Another fine design by Ron Garl, this superb course, with its rolling fairways and large greens, winds among Florida's tall, beautiful cypress trees and tropical foliage. The rich landscaping and strategically-placed bunkers produce an exceptional playing field to test golfers of all abilities.

You'll have a lot of fun playing golf here. It isn't a very long course from the back tees at all. If you can consistently hit your drives between 220 and 230 yards to the proper landing areas, you'll have many opportunities to score birdies.

Try to practice your short game before you play here. That is by far the most challenging part of this course.

DIRECTIONS

Take I-4 to Exit 18. Travel Hwy. 98 north for about eight miles. The course will be on your left.

BRAMBLE RIDGE GOLF COURSE
2925 San Lan Ranch, Lakeland, FL 33813 / (961) 667-1988

BASIC INFORMATION

Course Type: Public
Year Built: 1990
Architect: E. Holloway
Local Pro: J. Roxboro

Course: N/A
Holes: 18 / Par 72

Back: 5,859 yds. Rating: 68.3 Slope: 125
Middle: 5,482 yds. Rating: 66.6 Slope: 121
Ladies: 4,833 yds. Rating: N/A   Slope: N/A

Tee Time: 7 days in advance
Price: $12 - $16

Credit Cards:	■	Restaurant:	
Driving Range:	■	Lounge:	
Practice Green:	■	Meeting Rooms:	
Locker Room:		Tennis:	
Rental Clubs:	■	Swimming:	
Walkers:	■	Jogging Trails:	
Snack Bar:		Boating:	

COURSE DESCRIPTION

The **Bramble Ridge Golf Course** is a pleasurable, scenic course. Most everyone can have a fun day here. The forgiving layout give you many opportunities to score low.

The key to playing well here is to simply hit your drives on the fairway, keeping your ball away from trouble. If you hit too far left or right, you'll often be searching for your ball inside of the tall trees or out-of-bounds.

The wildlife on this course is terrific. Many people enjoy both the golf and the spectacular scenery.

DIRECTIONS

Take Hwy. 98 south and go west on Edgewood Ave. Go south on Lakeland Highland Rd. for about three miles to the course.

CLEVELAND HEIGHTS GOLF & COUNTRY CLUB
2900 Buckingham Ave., Lakeland, FL 33803 / (961) 682-3277

BASIC INFORMATION

Course Type: Public
Year Built: 1924 / 1981
Architect: Finn / Toomey / R. Garl
Local Pro: Lee Fireson

Course: A & B (18 / Par 72)
Holes: 27

Back: 6,359 yds. Rating: N/A Slope: 118
Middle: 6,016 yds. Rating: N/A Slope: 115
Ladies: 5,394 yds. Rating: N/A Slope: 116

Tee Time: N/A
Price: $10 - $20

Credit Cards:		Restaurant:	■
Driving Range:		Lounge:	■
Practice Green:	■	Meeting Rooms:	■
Locker Room:		Tennis:	
Rental Clubs:	■	Swimming:	
Walkers:	■	Jogging Trails:	
Snack Bar:	■	Boating:	

COURSE DESCRIPTION

This course features a variety of challenging hole designs.

The fairways are wide and inviting, and you shouldn't have much trouble placing your ball on the proper landing area. The course does favor a draw.

You'll find beautiful trees surrounding the entire course with no homes in sight. It has that grand North Carolina mountain course feel to it. You'll find undulating fairways with small natural rolling hills.

The wildlife around the course is spectacular. One of the most surprising of all the animals is the peacock. Someone must have brought them here years ago. Water comes into play on nine holes.

DIRECTIONS

Take Exit 18 from I-4 and go south on Hwy. 98. Go east on Edgewood to Buckingham.

GRENELEFE GOLF & RACQUET CLUB
33200 SR 544, Hains City, FL 33844 / (961) 422-7511

BASIC INFORMATION

Course Type: Resort
Year Built: 1972 / 1978 / 1983
Architect: R. Jones / E. Seay / R. Garl
Local Pro: Randy Cahall

Course: West (18 / Par 72)
Holes: 54

Back: 7,325 yds. Rating: 75.0 Slope: 130
Middle: 6,199 yds. Rating: 70.5 Slope: 122
Ladies: 5,398 yds. Rating: 70.9 Slope: 118

Tee Time: 1 day in advance
Price: $25 - $100

Credit Cards: ■   Restaurant: ■
Driving Range: ■   Lounge: ■
Practice Green: ■   Meeting Rooms: ■
Locker Room: Tennis: ■
Rental Clubs: ■   Swimming: ■
Walkers: Jogging Trails: ■
Snack Bar: ■   Boating: ■

COURSE DESCRIPTION

This is an awesome challenge of golf and only the best single handicapped players should try to attempt it from the back tees. Anyone above a 9 handicap should play the course from the middle tees. It is the only way to be competitive on such a demanding layout.

The difficult par-3's are long and strategically-designed. The number 4 hole is 230 yards, number 7 is 206 yards, number 13 is 204 yards, and number 16 is 210 yards.

You'll have a lot of challenging golf to look forward to in each one of the three available golf courses featured here.

DIRECTIONS

Take I-4 west to US 27. Go south to SR 544 and turn left. Go six miles to the Grenelefe entrance and the course will be on your right.

INDIAN LAKE ESTATES GOLF & COUNTRY CLUB
Desota Ave., Indian Lake Estates, FL 33855 / (961) 692-1514

BASIC INFORMATION

Course Type: Semi-private
Year Built: 1974
Architect: N/A
Local Pro: Boyd Tong

Course: N/A
Holes: 18 / Par 72

Back: 6,413 yds. Rating: 70.2 Slope: N/A
Middle: 6,228 yds. Rating: 69.5 Slope: 115
Ladies: 5,157 yds. Rating: 70.1 Slope: 116

Tee Time: 3 days in advance
Price: $12 - $24

Credit Cards: ■   Restaurant: ■
Driving Range: ■   Lounge: ■
Practice Green: ■   Meeting Rooms:
Locker Room: ■   Tennis:
Rental Clubs: Swimming:
Walkers: ■   Jogging Trails:
Snack Bar: ■   Boating:

COURSE DESCRIPTION

This is another splendid course in the Indian Lake Estates area. It's not difficult, but it does have some interesting holes to make your golfing day a fun one, especially if you're an average-to-beginning golfer.

The fairways are neither tight nor wide and demand accuracy off the tee. Because of the relative width of the fairway, the better player will have enough room to play the ball as a fade or a draw for the best possible position to the hole.

The course has a lot of trees lining the fairways and greens. Water comes into the play of action on five holes.

DIRECTIONS

Take Hwy. 60 about 15 miles east of Lake Wales. Look for the sign to the course.

SANDPIPER GOLF & COUNTRY CLUB
6001 Sandpiper Dr., Lakeland, FL 33809 / (961) 859-5461

BASIC INFORMATION

Course Type: Public
Year Built: 1974
Architect: E. Packard
Local Pro: Bill Zimmer

Course: N/A
Holes: 18 / Par 72

Back: 6,364 yds. Rating: 70.1 Slope: 121
Middle: 6,017 yds. Rating: 68.5 Slope: 118
Ladies: 5,365 yds. Rating: 70.8 Slope: 116

Tee Time: 7 days in advance
Price: $10.70 - $14.98

Credit Cards:	■	Restaurant:	■
Driving Range:	■	Lounge:	■
Practice Green:	■	Meeting Rooms:	■
Locker Room:	■	Tennis:	■
Rental Clubs:	■	Swimming:	■
Walkers:	■	Jogging Trails:	■
Snack Bar:	■	Boating:	■

COURSE DESCRIPTION

This is a great course to play if you've never played a links-styled course before.

You won't find any trees on this course so play will be subject to the unpredictability of the wind. That is without question the hardest part of playing here. You'll be doing yourself a great favor if you teach yourself how to play the ball under the wind. It's the only way you'll ever shoot a good score on a course of this design. Another factor to look for is the deep and sometimes hidden hazards and bunkers. Be careful in your pre-stroke preparations for best results.

DIRECTIONS

Exit Hwy. 319 south from I-10 and go south to Hwy. 27. Go west to Blairstone Rd. and south to the course.

SCHALAMAR CREEK GOLF & COUNTRY CLUB
45 U.S. 92 E. #1028, Lakeland, FL 33801 / (961) 666-1623

BASIC INFORMATION

Course Type: Semi-private
Year Built: 1987
Architect: R. Garl
Local Pro: Mark Wickman

Course: N/A
Holes: 18 / Par 72

Back: 6,488 yds. Rating: 70.3 Slope: 127
Middle: 5,850 yds. Rating: 67.3 Slope: 121
Ladies: 4,517 yds. Rating: 65.2 Slope: 112

Tee Time: 2 days in advance
Price: $20 - $30

Credit Cards:	■	Restaurant:	■
Driving Range:	■	Lounge:	■
Practice Green:	■	Meeting Rooms:	■
Locker Room:		Tennis:	
Rental Clubs:	■	Swimming:	
Walkers:	■	Jogging Trails:	
Snack Bar:	■	Boating:	

COURSE DESCRIPTION

Schalamar Creek Golf & Country Club was built in the middle of a wetlands state park. The great variety of birds that can be spotted here is astonishing.

You'll find this course to be quite an enjoyable experience. The playing ground is flat and the course features many trees throughout.

One of the toughest holes on this course is the 15th. It is a par-3 that measures a full 224 yards from the back tees. You'll find a lake on your left and trees with O.B. to your right. To be competitive and post a low score, you'll have to play a consistently accurate game.

DIRECTIONS

Take I-4 and Exit Hwy. 98 south. Go east on Hwy. 92 and the course will be about five miles on your left.

SKYVIEW GOLF & COUNTRY CLUB

1100 Skyview Blvd., Lakeland, FL 33801 / (961) 665-4008

BASIC INFORMATION

Course Type: Public
Year Built: 1967
Architect: J. Jackson
Local Pro: N/A

Course: N/A
Holes: 18 / Par 71

Back: 5,548 yds. Rating: N/A Slope: N/A
Middle: 5,250 yds. Rating: N/A Slope: N/A
Ladies: 4,890 yds. Rating: N/A Slope: N/A

Tee Time: 3 days in advance
Price: $12.50 - $18

Credit Cards:		Restaurant:	
Driving Range:	■	Lounge:	■
Practice Green:	■	Meeting Rooms:	■
Locker Room:		Tennis:	
Rental Clubs:	■	Swimming:	
Walkers:	■	Jogging Trails:	
Snack Bar:	■	Boating:	

COURSE DESCRIPTION

New players, and anyone who is interested in working on their short game, will love this course.

You'll have many occasions when you'll have to play a wedge shot to the greens that are mostly elevated and subtly contoured. The course also features five holes that will allow you to play a bump-and-run shot through the opening in front of their greens.

Despite the fact that the course is short, you'll find many interesting holes that require extra planning in your playing approach. You'll often have to drive your ball accurately to set yourself up for a good approach to the green.

DIRECTIONS

Go south on Hwy. 98 and north on Combee Rd. Make a right on Skyview Dr. to the course.

SUN AIR COUNTRY CLUB

50 Sun Air Blvd. E., Haines City, FL 33844 / (961) 439-4958

BASIC INFORMATION

Course Type: Semi-private
Year Built: 1972
Architect: R. Garl
Local Pro: John Wright

Course: N/A
Holes: 18 / Par 71

Back: 6,717 yds. Rating: 73.4 Slope: 131
Middle: 6,070 yds. Rating: 70.7 Slope: 125
Ladies: 4,919 yds. Rating: 69.0 Slope: 118

Tee Time: 3 days in advance
Price: $15 - $40

Credit Cards:	■	Restaurant:	■
Driving Range:	■	Lounge:	■
Practice Green:	■	Meeting Rooms:	
Locker Room:		Tennis:	
Rental Clubs:		Swimming:	
Walkers:		Jogging Trails:	
Snack Bar:	■	Boating:	

COURSE DESCRIPTION

This course takes you through all the motions that the game of golf has to offer.

You really have to concentrate on every hole to score well. Your tee shots will have to be played long and accurate to gain good postion for your approach shots. The fairways feature rolling terrain that can sometimes set your ball on an uneven lie. Get to the driving-range early and practice the art of hitting golf balls above and below your feet. That will give you the confidence you'll need when you approach this course.

The greens are gently curved and the course features 12 holes that play into water.

DIRECTIONS

Take Hwy. 27 south to Haines City and east to Hwy. 542. The course will be about nine miles further.

WEDGEWOOD GOLF & COUNTRY CLUB

401 Carpenter Way, Lakeland, FL 33809 / (961) 858-4451

BASIC INFORMATION

Course Type: Semi-private
Year Built: 1982
Architect: R. Garl
Local Pro: Jamie Hollingsworth

Course: N/A
Holes: 18 / Par 72

Back: 6,402 yds. Rating: 69.1 Slope: 115
Middle: 5,959 yds. Rating: 66.5 Slope: 110
Ladies: 4,885 yds. Rating: 68.6 Slope: 114

Tee Time: 2 days in advance
Price: $19

Credit Cards:	■	Restaurant:	
Driving Range:	■	Lounge:	■
Practice Green:	■	Meeting Rooms:	■
Locker Room:		Tennis:	■
Rental Clubs:		Swimming:	■
Walkers:		Jogging Trails:	
Snack Bar:	■	Boating:	

COURSE DESCRIPTION

The *Wedgewood Golf & Country Club* is a nicely balanced course with many interesting holes that will challenge golfers of all abilities and playing styles.

Most of the course features fairways that are very tight, with high rough in the summer and low rough in the winter. That will force you to play accurately off the tee towards well-defined landing areas. You'll find this course to be a real shotmakers' type of course. It will have you playing every club in your bag by the time the round is finished. If you have the ability to finesse your shots around the greens, you'll end up scoring a good number. Water comes into play on seven holes.

DIRECTIONS

Take Exit 18 off I-4 to Hwy. 98 and go north to Wedgewood Estate Blvd. Go south on Carpenters Way to the course.

WILLOWBROOK GOLF COURSE

4200 Hwy 544 N., Winter Haven, FL 33881 / (961) 299-7889

BASIC INFORMATION

Course Type: Municipal
Year Built: 1966
Architect: N/A
Local Pro: Tony Brabiner

Course: N/A
Holes: 18 / Par 72

Back: 6,450 yds. Rating: 70.5 Slope: 118
Middle: 6,106 yds. Rating: N/A Slope: 115
Ladies: 5,364 yds. Rating: N/A Slope: N/A

Tee Time: 6 days in advance
Price: $15 - $24

Credit Cards:	■	Restaurant:	■
Driving Range:	■	Lounge:	■
Practice Green:	■	Meeting Rooms:	
Locker Room:	■	Tennis:	
Rental Clubs:	■	Swimming:	
Walkers:	■	Jogging Trails:	
Snack Bar:	■	Boating:	

COURSE DESCRIPTION

Willowbrook Golf Course offers many opportunities to score well. It's an open design with wide fairways that are just waiting for your best possible drives. The action really begins from about 150 yards into the hole. You'll have to play your approach shots accurately, high with lots of back-spin to grab onto the small greens without much of a roll. Many times you'll end up having to chip and one putt for your par.

The par-5's are reachable in two and that is where you should pick up your best numbers. Beware of the 9th and 11th holes. They are both monster par-4's that make par a very difficult number.

DIRECTIONS

Take Hwy. 27 south to Hwy. 544 and go west to the course. It will be on your left.

CASSELBERRY GOLF CLUB

300 South Lake Triplett Dr., Casselberry, FL 32707 / (407) 699-9310

BASIC INFORMATION

Course Type: Semi-private
Year Built: Early 60's
Architect: Unknown
Local Pro: Chris Koon

Course: N/A
Holes: 18 / Par 72

Back: 5,550 yds. Rating: 65.6 Slope: 111
Middle: 4,925 yds. Rating: 63.9 Slope: 107
Ladies: 4,555 yds. Rating: 66.4 Slope: 115

Tee Time: 2 days in advance
Price: $14.95 - $20.56

Credit Cards:		Restaurant:	
Driving Range:	■	Lounge:	■
Practice Green:	■	Meeting Rooms:	
Locker Room:		Tennis:	
Rental Clubs:	■	Swimming:	
Walkers:	■	Jogging Trails:	
Snack Bar:	■	Boating:	

COURSE DESCRIPTION

Cassleberry Golf Club is a short and tight golf course for players of all calibers. The front nine is the shorter of the two with a mentionable difference. It features no par-5's and three tough par-3's.

You'll find a lot of people taking advantage of the inexpensive afternoon walking rates. These people like to play the front because it doesn't take much time and it still offers a good game. The back nine is the more standard of the two. At par-36 it is quite longer than the front and features considerably more water and woods coming into play.

This is a terrific course to practice your short game.

DIRECTIONS

From I-4 go east to SR 436 (Altamonte Springs Exit) three miles to Oxford Rd, left to Overbrook and right to the course.

DEER RUN COUNTRY CLUB

300 Daneswood Way, Casselberry, FL 32707 / (407) 699-9592

BASIC INFORMATION

Course Type: Semi-private
Year Built: 1976
Architect: L. Clifton
Local Pro: Joe "Little Cat" Williams

Course: N/A
Holes: 18 / Par 71

Back: 6,555 yds. Rating: 70.9 Slope: 122
Middle: 6,190 yds. Rating: 69.2 Slope: 118
Ladies: 5,329 yds. Rating: 71.3 Slope: 124

Tee Time: 7 days in advance
Price: $18 - $35

Credit Cards:	■	Restaurant:	■
Driving Range:	■	Lounge:	■
Practice Green:	■	Meeting Rooms:	■
Locker Room:		Tennis:	■
Rental Clubs:	■	Swimming:	■
Walkers:		Jogging Trails:	
Snack Bar:	■	Boating:	

COURSE DESCRIPTION

Deer Run Country Club is a professional caliber course with a fantastic and very competitive layout. Many PGA and LPGA players come here to tune up their games before hitting the Tours' leading tournaments.

The course is a spectacular test of play for golfers of all abilities. This shotmakers course will force you to hit accurate drives onto the narrow landing area and finesse approach shots to the small and often elevated greens. The course is well-bunkered and 15 of the holes feature water coming into play.

DIRECTIONS

Take the East/West Expressway to Rt. 436 West. Go north on Red Bug Rd. and turn left onto Eagle Circle. Get onto Eagle Circle S. and look for the Deer Run Country Club entrance on your right.

EKANA GOLF & COUNTRY CLUB
2100 Ekana Dr., Oviedo, FL 32765 / (407) 366-1201

BASIC INFORMATION

Course Type: Semi-private
Year Built: 1988
Architect: J. Lee
Local Pro: Mark Bootin

Course: N/A
Holes: 18 / Par 72

Back: 6,683 yds. Rating: 72.0 Slope: 130
Middle: 6,279 yds. Rating: 70.1 Slope: 126
Ladies: 5,544 yds. Rating: 72.1 Slope: 128

Tee Time: 4 days in advance
Price: $29.50 - $39

Credit Cards: ■	Restaurant:
Driving Range: ■	Lounge:
Practice Green: ■	Meeting Rooms:
Locker Room: ■	Tennis:
Rental Clubs: ■	Swimming:
Walkers:	Jogging Trails:
Snack Bar: ■	Boating:

COURSE DESCRIPTION

Ekana is an absolutely beautiful course that is nestled between two rivers: the Econlockhatchee and Little Econ. Due to the fact that the front nine is an environmentally protected area that has not been spoiled by home sites, it's not uncommon to see a good variety of wildlife such as deer, alligators, hawks, rabbits, wild boars, foxes, and more.

Joe Lee designed this 18 hole course with 15 lakes and an outstanding number 7, par-3, signature island green hole.

An Augusta styled clubhouse was built in late 1993.

DIRECTIONS

Go north on the East-West Expressway and Exit on Aloma/SR 426. Go three miles to Mitchell Hammock and then go right to the dead-end. Make a right on Lockwood. The course will be one mile on your left.

MAYFAIR COUNTRY CLUB
Hwy. 46A, Lake Mary, FL 32746 / (407) 322-2531

BASIC INFORMATION

Course Type: Semi-private
Year Built: 1919
Architect: D. Ross / W. Hagen
Local Pro: Joe Shurtz

Course: N/A
Holes: 18 / Par 72

Back: 6,375 yds. Rating: 70.3 Slope: 119
Middle: 6,007 yds. Rating: 68.5 Slope: 115
Ladies: 5,188 yds. Rating: 69.3 Slope: 115

Tee Time: 7 days in advance
Price: $16 - $26

Credit Cards: ■	Restaurant: ■
Driving Range: ■	Lounge: ■
Practice Green: ■	Meeting Rooms:
Locker Room: ■	Tennis:
Rental Clubs: ■	Swimming:
Walkers: ■	Jogging Trails:
Snack Bar: ■	Boating:

COURSE DESCRIPTION

This is a wonderful course with many challenging holes. In 1950, Julius Boris, Arnold Palmer, Jack Nicklaus, and Lee Trevino all came here to compete in the PGA Open, an event that lasted up to a decade.

At 6,375 yards the course is very much smaller than the courses used on the PGA Tour today. It wasn't meant to be a long course. You'll have to lay deadly accurate off the tee and finesse your approach shots to the small greens. This is a strategic course built specifically to challenge the best shot-maker rather than the longest.

It makes for a very fair and challenging game of golf.

DIRECTIONS

Take the Lake/Heathrow Exit from I-4 and go east to Rinehart Rd. north to Hwy. 46A and east to the course.

SABLE POINT COUNTRY CLUB

2662 Sabel Club Way, Longwood, FL 32779 / (407) 869-4622

BASIC INFORMATION

Course Type: Semi-private
Year Built: 1974
Architect: W. Northrup
Local Pro: Ronnie Bicknel

Course: N/A
Holes: 18 / Par 72

Back: 6,603 yds. Rating: 71.6 Slope: 126
Middle: 6,107 yds. Rating: 69.4 Slope: 121
Ladies: 5,278 yds. Rating: 70.0 Slope: 119

Tee Time: 2 days in advance
Price: $25 - $50

Credit Cards:	■	Restaurant:	■
Driving Range:	■	Lounge:	■
Practice Green:	■	Meeting Rooms:	■
Locker Room:	■	Tennis:	■
Rental Clubs:	■	Swimming:	■
Walkers:		Jogging Trails:	■
Snack Bar:	■	Boating:	■

COURSE DESCRIPTION

This lush course is bordered by a 3,500 acre nature preserve, sharing its tranquility with various types of water fowl and wildlife. Each hole is uniquely separated by a dense forest featuring towering trees that hug each beautiful fairway. You'll find a well-balanced variety of doglegs and 13 exciting water holes.

The 13th signature hole (par 3 / 195 yards) is an impressively scenic carry over water that partially encircles the front and left side of the green. Pin placement includes two well-positioned bunkers and possible swirling winds which can easily become a one or two club difference, making this long iron blast quite interesting!

DIRECTIONS

I-4 to Exit 49 (Longwood). Go west on SR 434 to Wekira Springs Rd. Make a right to the entrance.

TIMACUAN GOLF & COUNTRY CLUB

550 Timacuan Blvd., Lake Mary, FL 32746 / (407) 321-0010

BASIC INFORMATION

Course Type: Semi-private
Year Built: 1987
Architect: R. Garl
Local Pro: David Armoore

Course: N/A
Holes: 18 / Par 72

Back: 7,019 yds. Rating: 73.5 Slope: 137
Middle: 6,582 yds. Rating: 71.5 Slope: 133
Ladies: 5,401 yds. Rating: 72.1 Slope: 123

Tee Time: 3 days in advance
Price: $35 - $58

Credit Cards:	■	Restaurant:	■
Driving Range:	■	Lounge:	■
Practice Green:	■	Meeting Rooms:	■
Locker Room:	■	Tennis:	■
Rental Clubs:	■	Swimming:	
Walkers:		Jogging Trails:	
Snack Bar:	■	Boating:	

COURSE DESCRIPTION

You'll find a tremendous challenge from all of the tees. The Golf Writers Association has ranked *Timacuan* 14th in the state.

The course plays like two courses in one. The front nine is constructed like a links-style course with open fairways and deep bunkers. It lends itself to the wind and that is when it plays the hardest. A low boring shot is what you'll need to play well. The back nine is filled with pine trees giving it a real mountain course feel. Both sides feature rolling terrain that often places your ball on an uneven lie.

When you're finally done with your game you'll enjoy dining at the Tamacuan Bar & Grill.

DIRECTIONS

Take Exit 50 from I-4 and go east to the third light and left on Rinehart.

WEKIVA GOLF CLUB

200 Hunt Club Rd., Longwood, FL 32779 / (407) 826-5113

BASIC INFORMATION

Course Type: Semi-private
Year Built: 1977
Architect: N/A
Local Pro: Francis Bowman

Course: N/A
Holes: 18 / Par 72

Back: 6,640 yds. Rating: 71.9 Slope: 123
Middle: 6,300 yds. Rating: 70.9 Slope: 121
Ladies: 5,745 yds. Rating: 73.2 Slope: 126

Tee Time: 6 days in advance
Price: $25 - $35

Credit Cards:	■	Restaurant:	
Driving Range:		Lounge:	■
Practice Green:	■	Meeting Rooms:	
Locker Room:	■	Tennis:	
Rental Clubs:	■	Swimming:	
Walkers:		Jogging Trails:	
Snack Bar:	■	Boating:	

COURSE DESCRIPTION

You'll need to have a solid all-around game to perform well here. The narrow fairways make driving the ball one of the most important aspects of the game. If you can't set yourself up for a good approach, you'll have a lot of difficulty getting your pars. Try to stay clear of the harsh rough.

From the fairway, you'll often be facing a two-tiered green with slight undulations. Try to play the ball to the proper side of the green to avoid a hard two putt for par. The course is lined with trees and water comes into the play of action on only three holes.

Consider the middle tees if the course seems too difficult for you.

DIRECTIONS

Exit onto Hwy 436 from I-4 and go west to Hunt Club Blvd. Head north and the course will be on your left.

ZELLWOOD STATION GOLF & COUNTRY CLUB

2728 Cayman Circle, Zellwood, FL 32798 / (407) 886-3303

BASIC INFORMATION

Course Type: Semi-private
Year Built: 1980
Architect: N/A
Local Pro: Tony Gans

Course: N/A
Holes: 18 / Par 72

Back: 6,375 yds. Rating: 70.5 Slope: 122
Middle: 6,005 yds. Rating: 68.6 Slope: 119
Ladies: 5,377 yds. Rating: 71.1 Slope: 122

Tee Time: 2 days in advance
Price: $20 - $40

Credit Cards:		Restaurant:	■
Driving Range:	■	Lounge:	■
Practice Green:	■	Meeting Rooms:	■
Locker Room:		Tennis:	
Rental Clubs:	■	Swimming:	
Walkers:		Jogging Trails:	
Snack Bar:	■	Boating:	

COURSE DESCRIPTION

This scenic course offers a good test of golf with some very demanding holes.

The fairways are wide and allow you to play the ball from both sides. You'll need to keep the ball on target to stay away from the rough. The rough is mostly made up of soft sand and that makes it terribly hard to hit the ball a far distance.

The course places a lot of emphasis on your putting game. The greens are curved and rolling and need to be read carefully if you're going to be successful.

One of the greatest pleasures on this course is the scenery. Many tropical birds and animals can be found wandering on a lucky day.

DIRECTIONS

Go north of Apopka on 441 to Zellwood and look for the sign to the course. It will be on your right.

WINTER SPRINGS GOLF CLUB

900 W. SR 434, Winter Springs, FL 32708 / (407) 699-1833

BASIC INFORMATION

Course Type: Semi-private
Year Built: 1971
Architect: Devlin / Von Hagge
Local Pro: Rob Reed

Course: N/A
Holes: 18 / Par 72

Back: 6,559 yds. Rating: N/A Slope: N/A
Middle: 6,088 yds. Rating: N/A Slope: N/A
Ladies: 5,133 yds. Rating: N/A Slope: N/A

Tee Time: 2 days in advance
Price: $20.50 - $32

Credit Cards: ■	Restaurant: ■
Driving Range: ■	Lounge: ■
Practice Green: ■	Meeting Rooms:
Locker Room:	Tennis:
Rental Clubs: ■	Swimming:
Walkers: ■	Jogging Trails:
Snack Bar: ■	Boating:

COURSE DESCRIPTION

Winter Springs Golf Club is both beautiful and serene with no two holes alike. It is carved through a nature preserve with big cypress trees. The terrain is mostly flat with gentle fairway mounds. You'll need to drive the ball straight to be successful on this course. The front nine is longer and slightly tougher, but features less water. The course also features a nice mixture of tree-lined holes and more open holes framed by beautiful lakes and ponds.

This is really a fun and enjoyable place to play golf. The course has a nice feel from hole to hole with many good opportunities to score well.

DIRECTIONS

Take I-4 to Exit 49. Go east on SR 434 and the course will be four miles on your left side. Look for the sign.

HIGHLANDS

Crystal Lake Club
(813) 385-4104
810 E. Canfield St., Avon Park
Local Pro: N/A
Reciprocal Play: No

On Top Of The World
(904) 854-8430
8700 S.W. 99th St., Ocala
Local Pro: Tommy Bryant
Reciprocal Play: No

LAKE

Harbor Hills Golf & Country Club
(904) 753-7711
6538 Lake Griffin Rd., Lady Lake
Local Pro: Alan Sels
Reciprocal Play: No

Pine Meadows Golf & Country Club
(904) 357-3233
17110 Pine Meadows Dr., Eustis
Local Pro: Tom Lineberger
Reciprocal Play: No

Plantation at Leesburg Country Club
(904) 326-3626
25200 Hwy. 27, Leesburg
Local Pro: Dennis Vercher
Reciprocal Play: Yes

Silver Lake Country Club
(904) 787-3443
9435 Silver Lake Dr., Leesburg
Local Pro: Bill Sowerwine
Reciprocal Play: No

MARION

Golden Hill Golf & Turf Club
(904) 629-7980
4782 N.W. 80th Ave., Ocala
Local Pro: Bill Girard
Reciprocal Play: Yes (Summer)

ORANGE

Country Club of Orlando
(407) 425-2319
1601 Country Club Dr., Orlando
Local Pro: Bill Sellers
Reciprocal Play: No

Errol Contry Club
(407) 886-5000
13355 Errol Pkwy., Apopka
Local Pro: Ron Givens
Reciprocal Play: Yes

Fairways Country Club
(407) 282-7535
14205 E. Colonial Dr., Orlando
Local Pro: Mike Schumaker
Reciprocal Play: No

Interlachen Country Club, The
(407) 657-0850
2245 Interlachen Ct., Winter Park
Local Pro: Michael "Jay" Kennedy
Reciprocal Play: No

Islesworth Country Club
(407) 876-3411
6100 Deacon Dr., Windermere
Local Pro: David O'Conner
Reciprocal Play: No

Lake Nona Club
(407) 851-9091
9011 Chiltern Dr., Orlando
Local Pro: Gregor Jamison
Reciprocal Play: No

ORANGE

Orange Tree Country Club
(407) 351-2521
7540 Woodgreen Dr., Orlando
Local Pro: Heidi Greer
Reciprocal Play: No

Rio Pinar Country Club
(407) 277-5520
8600 El Prado Dr., Orlando
Local Pro: Tommy Giles
Reciprocal Play: Yes

West Orange Country Club
(407) 656-1914
3300 W. Orange C.C. Dr., Winter Garden
Local Pro: Pat Neil
Reciprocal Play: Yes

OSCEOLA

Buenaventura Lakes Country Club
(407) 348-2395
301 Buenaventura Blvd., Kissimmee
Local Pro: N/A
Reciprocal Play: No

POLK

Angler's Green
(961) 425-4551
Lakeview Dr. (Hwy 37), Mulberry
Local Pro: N/A
Reciprocal Play: No

Carefree RV Country Club
(961) 324-3892
9705 Lake Bess Rd., Winter Haven
Local Pro: N/A
Reciprocal Play: No

Cypresswood Golf & Country Club
(961) 324-6174
1099 Clubhouse Rd., Winter Haven
Local Pro: Bob Schade
Reciprocal Play: Yes

Grasslands Golf Course
(961) 680-1600
1600 Grasslands Blvd., Lakeland
Local Pro: Joe Terry
Reciprocal Play: Yes

Highland Fairways
(961) 858-0947
2101 West Griffin Rd., Lakeland
Local Pro: N/A
Reciprocal Play: No

Imperial Lakes Country Club
(961) 425-1154
6 Country Club Ln., Mulberry
Local Pro: Gill Fouschee
Reciprocal Play: Yes

Lake Henry Golf Course
(961) 299-2683
Lucerne Park Rd., Winter Haven
Local Pro:
Reciprocal Play:

Lake Region Yacht & Country Club
(961) 324-4579
4200 Country Club Rd., Winter Haven
Local Pro: Tom Murphy
Reciprocal Play: Yes

Lake Wales Country Club
(961) 676-6519
2925 SR. 60 E., Lake Wales
Local Pro: Bob Lee
Reciprocal Play: No

Lone Palm Golf Course
(961) 499-5481
800 Lone Palm Dr., Lakeland
Local Pro: Joe Hogge
Reciprocal Play: Yes

Mountain Lake Country Club
(961) 676-3494
US 27A N., Lake Wales
Local Pro: N/A
Reciprocal Play: No

SEMINOLE

Alaqua Country Club
(407) 7444-0129
3060 Players Point, Longwood
Local Pro: Wally Kusher
Reciprocal Play: Yes

Heathrow Country Club
(407) 333-1469
1200 Bridgewater Dr., Heathrow
Local Pro: Larry Galloway
Reciprocal Play: Yes

Rolling Hills Golf Course
(407) 831-1312
1749 Art Hagen Pl., Longwood
Local Pro: Pete Osborne
Reciprocal Play: No

Sweetwater Country Club
(407) 889-4666
1000 Wekiva Springs Rd., Longwood
Local Pro: N/A
Reciprocal Play: No

SUMTER

Continental Country Club
(904) 748-3293
SR 44, Wildwood
Local Pro: Steve Girard
Reciprocal Play: Yes

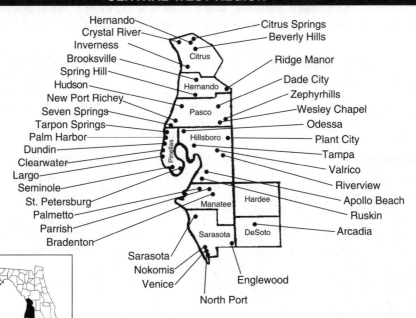

Hernando
Crystal River
Inverness
Brooksville
Spring Hill
Hudson
New Port Richey
Seven Springs
Tarpon Springs
Palm Harbor
Dundin
Clearwater
Largo
Seminole
St. Petersburg
Palmetto
Parrish
Bradenton

Citrus Springs
Beverly Hills
Ridge Manor
Dade City
Zephyrhills
Wesley Chapel
Odessa
Plant City
Tampa
Valrico
Riverview
Apollo Beach
Ruskin
Arcadia

Citrus
Hernando
Pasco
Hillsboro
Pinellas
Manatee
Hardee
Sarasota
DeSoto

Sarasota
Nokomis
Venice
Englewood
North Port

Gulf of Mexico

TOP TEN

Bardmoor North Course
(Pinellas County)

Bloomingdale Golfers Club
(Hillsboro County)

Buffalo Creek Golf Course
(Manatee County)

Cypress Creek
(Hillsboro County)

Eagles Golf Club, The
(Pinellas County)

Hunters Green Country Club
(Pinellas County)

Innisbrook Resort & Golf C.
(Pinellas County)

Northdale Golf & T. Club
(Hillsboro County)

Plantation Golf Resort
(Citrus County)

Saddlebrook Golf Club
(Pasco County)

The **Central-West** features a wide variety of choices for your golfing pleasure.

Make sure you stop at the <u>Plantation Golf Resort</u>. You'll find 27 holes of golf that are both challenging and fun to play. The largest state open of it's kind, *The Florida Woman's Open*, is hosted here annually.

If you're going to be staying in Pasco County, play a round at the <u>Saddlebrook Golf Club</u>. This Arnold Palmer-designed links-styled course is one of the most sought after in the area. It's a great challenge from beginning to end. Some of the finest courses in the region can be found in both Hillsboro and Pinellas. You'll be astonished by the wide variety of choices, which is one reason why so many golfers make this region their golfing destination.

Searching for a new and exciting challenge can be difficult at times. The natural beauty and originality of each architectural design in Central-West section of Florida makes it easy to find the course you've been waiting for. Enjoy!

Average Temperatures (Fahrenheit)

Between **January** and **March** you'll find the low at **50** and the high up to **75**. Between **April** and **June** the low goes down to **64** and the high goes up to **87**. Between **July** and **September** the low goes down to **74** and the high goes up to **93**. And finally, between the months of **October** and **December**, the low goes down to **56** and the high goes up to **78**.

CITRUS HILLS GOLF & COUNTRY CLUB

500 E. Hartford St., Hernando FL 32642 / (352) 746-4425

BASIC INFORMATION

Course Type: Semi-private
Year Built: 1983
Architect: P. Friel
Local Pro: Pete Summers

Course: The Oaks (18 / Par 72)
Holes: 36

Back: 6,323 yds. Rating: 69.7 Slope: 120
Middle: 5,863 yds. Rating: 67.8 Slope: 116
Ladies: 4,647 yds. Rating: 67.0 Slope: 114

Tee Time: 1 day in advance
Price: $24 yearly

Credit Cards:	■	Restaurant:	■
Driving Range:	■	Lounge:	■
Practice Green:	■	Meeting Rooms:	■
Locker Room:	■	Tennis:	■
Rental Clubs:	■	Swimming:	■
Walkers:	■	Jogging Trails:	
Snack Bar:	■	Boating:	■

COURSE DESCRIPTION

Citrus Hills Golf & Country Club demands accuracy over distance on almost every hole. The fairways are narrow, the rough is rather low, and trees do come into play on stray shots.

The 14th hole is the number 1 handicap hole on the course. It is a par-4 that measures 340 yards in length. With a lake sitting in the middle of the fairway, an Eagle attempt becomes far too risky. Most golfers will have to lay-up and face the intimidating lake on their approach shot to the green.

You'll find this course both challenging and fun to play.

DIRECTIONS

Take I-75 north to Hwy. 44. On Country Rd. 486 go south. You'll find the course on the right side of the road.

CITRUS SPRINGS COUNTRY CLUB

8690 N. Golfview Dr., Citrus Springs, FL 32630 / (352) 489-5045

BASIC INFORMATION

Course Type: Semi-private
Year Built: 1977
Architect: N/A
Local Pro: Henry Bono

Course: N/A
Holes: 18 / Par 72

Back: 6,664 yds. Rating: 72.0 Slope: 129
Middle: 6,242 yds. Rating: 70.1 Slope: 125
Ladies: 5,501 yds. Rating: 71.3 Slope: 118

Tee Time: 2 days in advance
Price: $17 - $24

Credit Cards:	■	Restaurant:	■
Driving Range:	■	Lounge:	
Practice Green:	■	Meeting Rooms:	
Locker Room:		Tennis:	
Rental Clubs:	■	Swimming:	
Walkers:		Jogging Trails:	
Snack Bar:	■	Boating:	■

COURSE DESCRIPTION

Citrus Hills Country Club, a multi-elevated course filled with trees, poses a great challenge to golfers who are used to playing on a level field. It would be wise for you to practice shots both above and below your feet before playing this course.

The dogleg left, number 2 hole is the hardest hole on the course. It is a par-4 measuring 402 yards in length. The tee sits deep below the hole making the hole play about another 50 yards longer. To clear the dogleg, you will have to hit your tee shot straight up the hill, on the right side of the fairway, into a landing area about 240 yards out.

DIRECTIONS

Take Hwy. 41 south past the Citrus Hills main entrance. Proceed west on Country Club Blvd. to the course.

LAKESIDE COUNTRY CLUB

P.O. Box 97, Inverness, FL 32651 / (352) 726-1461

BASIC INFORMATION

Course Type: Semi-private
Year Built: 1979
Architect: L, Connell / B. Campbell
Local Pro: John Gilliam

Course: N/A
Holes: 18 / Par 72

Back: 6,475 yds. Rating: 70.4 Slope: 116
Middle: 6,151 yds. Rating: 79.0 Slope: 114
Ladies: 5,439 yds. Rating: 71.3 Slope: 117

Tee Time: 3 days in advance
Price: $15 - $18

Credit Cards:	■	Restaurant:	■
Driving Range:	■	Lounge:	■
Practice Green:	■	Meeting Rooms:	■
Locker Room:	■	Tennis:	
Rental Clubs:	■	Swimming:	
Walkers:		Jogging Trails:	
Snack Bar:	■	Boating:	■

COURSE DESCRIPTION

Lakeside Country Club is a fun-filled course with a good combination of holes.

You'll find many birdie opportunities in the course of a game. The fairways are generous and the rough is set low.

The hardest hole on this course is the 17th hole which is a par-4 measuring 470 yards in length. It's a straight hole with trees lining up the left side. The approach shot is rather simple to a green that is both long and wide.

This may be your "scratch" course of a life-time.

DIRECTIONS

Take I-75 north to the Wildwood Inverness Exit (Hwy. 44) and go west to Hwy. 41. Head north on Hwy. 41 to Inverness and the course will be on your right side.

PINE RIDGE GOLF COURSE

1005 Elkcam Blvd., Beverly Hills, FL 32665 / (352) 746-6177

BASIC INFORMATION

Course Type: Public
Year Built: 1982
Architect: C. Almony Jr. / Chuck Almony Sr.
Local Pro: Brian Almony

Course:N/A
Holes: 18 / Par 72

Back: 6,166 yds. Rating: 68.0 Slope: 116
Middle: 5,624 yds. Rating: 66.3 Slope: 116
Ladies: 5,036 yds. Rating: 68.6 Slope: 120

Tee Time: 3 days in advance
Price: $10 - $22

Credit Cards:	■	Restaurant:	■
Driving Range:	■	Lounge:	■
Practice Green:	■	Meeting Rooms:	
Locker Room:		Tennis:	
Rental Clubs:	■	Swimming:	
Walkers:	■	Jogging Trails:	
Snack Bar:	■	Boating:	■

COURSE DESCRIPTION

Pine Ridge Golf Course is a short and simple layout that is fun for the average player. If you happen to be a 90's player, you'll love the opportunity of scoring par or better on every hole.

Although the course is short, the fairways are tight and hilly. Good course management combined with well-placed tee shots are the two keys to scoring par or better.

On many occasions, you'll find your ball sitting on an uneven lie. If you're not used to playing the ball below or above your stance, take the time to practice these shots on the driving range before you go out and play this course.

DIRECTIONS

Take Hwy. 44 to Hwy. 491 north at Lecanto about four miles. Proceed west to the golf course through Pine Ridge homes.

PLANTATION INN & GOLF RESORT

P.O. Box 1115, Crystal River, FL 32623 / (352) 795-7211

BASIC INFORMATION

Course Type: Resort
Year Built: 1955
Architect: M. Mahannah
Local Pro: Jim Brennan

Course: Championship (18 / Par 72)
Holes: 27

Back: 6,503 yds. Rating: 71.6 Slope: 126
Middle: 6,502 yds. Rating: 70.1 Slope: 123
Ladies: 5,395 yds. Rating: 71.1 Slope: 122

Tee Time: 7 days in advance
Price: $29 - $40

Credit Cards:	■	Restaurant:	■
Driving Range:	■	Lounge:	■
Practice Green:	■	Meeting Rooms:	■
Locker Room:	■	Tennis:	■
Rental Clubs:	■	Swimming:	■
Walkers:	■	Jogging Trails:	■
Snack Bar:	■	Boating:	■

COURSE DESCRIPTION

Plantation Inn & Golf Resort is an old type Florida golf course. You'll find large greens nestled among a great variety of trees throughout the course. Water comes into play on 12 holes.

The Florida Women's Open, the largest state open in the country, is held here annually.

The dogleg right 11th hole is the hardest rated on the course. Water comes into play twice on this hole; once off the tee and secondly on the first approach shot to the well-bunkered green.

The natural wildlife that lives and grows around this course is incredible.

DIRECTIONS

Take Hwy. 19 at South Crystal River. Go west on Fort Island Tr. and the course will be three blocks on the left.

TWISTED OAKS GOLF CLUB

4545 Forest Blvd., Beverly Hills, FL 32665 / (352) 746-6257

BASIC INFORMATION

Course Type: Semi-private
Year Built: 1990
Architect: Karl Litton
Local Pro: Vic Conigliaro

Course:N/A
Holes: 18 / Par 72

Back: 6,876 yds. Rating: 71.8 Slope: 122
Middle: 6,410 yds. Rating: 69.7 Slope: 118
Ladies: 5,241 yds. Rating: 68.5 Slope: 111

Tee Time: 3 days in advance
Price: $10 - $24

Credit Cards:	■	Restaurant:	■
Driving Range:	■	Lounge:	
Practice Green:	■	Meeting Rooms:	
Locker Room:	■	Tennis:	
Rental Clubs:	■	Swimming:	
Walkers:		Jogging Trails:	
Snack Bar:	■	Boating:	

COURSE DESCRIPTION

Twisted Oaks Golf Club is a well-maintained course with plenty of challenging holes.

Most of the holes will allow you to take one of two routes. The first is the "hero" route that may gain you a possible eagle or birdie opportunity if you can pull off the shot. The second is the safe route to a par or possible bogey.

The hardest hole on this course is number 10, which is a par-4 measuring 434 yards in length. From the tee you'll be playing downhill to an undulating fairway that continues to a split-level plateau.

DIRECTIONS

Take Hwy. 44 to Hwy. 491 and head north. Go east on Forest Ridge Dr. and the course will be on your left.

SUNNYBREEZE PALMS GOLF COURSE

Rt. 3, Box 573B, Arcadia, FL 33821 / (352) 494-2521

BASIC INFORMATION

Course Type: Semi-private
Year Built: 1971
Architect: B. Baker
Local Pro: Andrea Knox

Course: The Oaks (18 / Par 71)
Holes: 27

Back: 6,007 yds. Rating: 66.6 Slope: 114
Middle: 5,526 yds. Rating: 66.4 Slope: 111
Ladies: 5,009 yds. Rating: 68.8 Slope: 114

Tee Time: 7 days in advance
Price: $15 - $32

Credit Cards:	■	Restaurant:	■
Driving Range:	■	Lounge:	
Practice Green:	■	Meeting Rooms:	
Locker Room:		Tennis:	
Rental Clubs:	■	Swimming:	
Walkers:	■	Jogging Trails:	
Snack Bar:	■	Boating:	■

COURSE DESCRIPTION

Sunnybreeze Palms Golf Course is the type of course you normally find up north.

Playing golf in this type of a layout is always a lot more fun than playing on a course that features homes and condos peering out of every corner.

One of the most challenging holes on the Oaks course is the number 5 hole. It is a straight par-5 hole that measures a full 560 yards from the back tees. You'll be hitting your drive straight onto a sloping left-to-right fairway between trees on both sides. Trees come into play on the left and a huge waste bunker will be waiting for your ball on the right as you hit your approach. The green is well-guarded and small.

DIRECTIONS

Take Exit 29 off I-75 and go north on Hwy. 17 for about nine miles. Look for the course sign.

LINKS GOLF CLUB, THE

8706 Pavillion Dr., Hudson, FL 34667 / (352) 868-1091

BASIC INFORMATION

Course Type: Semi-private
Year Built: 1989
Architect: S. Smyers
Local Pro: Steve Didik

Course: N/A
Holes: 18 / Par 71

Back: 6,209 yds. Rating: 70.1 Slope: 117
Middle: 5,654 yds. Rating: 66.7 Slope: 107
Ladies: 4,797 yds. Rating: 66.9 Slope: 108

Tee Time: 2 days in advance
Price: $8 - $20

Credit Cards:	■	Restaurant:	■
Driving Range:	■	Lounge:	
Practice Green:	■	Meeting Rooms:	
Locker Room:		Tennis:	■
Rental Clubs:	■	Swimming:	■
Walkers:		Jogging Trails:	
Snack Bar:	■	Boating:	■

COURSE DESCRIPTION

Playing a links-type course demands a different strategy than most of the courses that you will find throughout the US.

With virtually no trees to block the wind and deep bunkers set in hidden view from the tee box, most golfers will fare much better taking the time to learn how to play the "knock down" shot. This shot allows you to hit the ball on a lower trajectory, on line, and below the high winds.

Adding this shot to your repertoire will gain you many advantages on any course with high winds.

DIRECTIONS

Take I-75 North to Hwy. 52. Go right on Little Rd. to a blinking traffic light (Hudson Ave.) 1/2 mile east. Go left at Hudson Ave. and the second entrance on the left will lead you to the clubhouse.

OAK HILL GOLF COURSE

10059 Northcliff Blvd., Spring Hill, FL 34608 / (352) 683-6830

BASIC INFORMATION

Course Type: Public
Year Built: 1981
Architect: N/A
Local Pro: Chuck Almony

Course:N/A
Holes: 18 / Par 72

Back: 6,774 yds. Rating: 72.2 Slope: 123
Middle: 6,331 yds. Rating: 70.3 Slope: 120
Ladies: 5,578 yds. Rating: 71.1 Slope: 119

Tee Time: 7 days in advance
Price: $18 - $25

Credit Cards:	■	Restaurant:	
Driving Range:	■	Lounge:	
Practice Green:	■	Meeting Rooms:	
Locker Room:		Tennis:	
Rental Clubs:		Swimming:	
Walkers:	■	Jogging Trails:	
Snack Bar:	■	Boating:	■

COURSE DESCRIPTION

The Oak Hills Golf Course is a beautifully kept course that plays equally fair to all types of players.

The front nine holes are set on a flat terrain while the back nine are set on a hilly surface. It's like playing two courses for the price of one.

The great PGA professional Raymond Floyd is one of the current owners of this course.

The dogleg left, 14th hole measures 426 yards in length, and is the hardest hole on the course. From the tee you're hitting down a hill that goes up and finally comes back down on the other side of the dogleg. Your approach shot will be to an elevated green.

DIRECTIONS

Take Hwy. 19 to Hwy. 50 and go south for one mile. Go east on Northcliff Blvd.

QUAIL RIDGE GOLF & COUNTRY CLUB

1600 Shady Hills Rd., Spring Hill, FL 34610 / (352) 996-2630

BASIC INFORMATION

Course Type: Semi-private
Year Built: 1983
Architect: N/A
Local Pro: Jane Johnson

Course: N/A
Holes: 18 / Par 71

Back: 5,550 yds. Rating: 66.3 Slope: 117
Middle: 5,155 yds. Rating: 6404 Slope: 112
Ladies: 4,378 yds. Rating: 65.3 Slope: 110

Tee Time: 2 days in advance
Price: $16 - $23

Credit Cards:	■	Restaurant:	■
Driving Range:	■	Lounge:	■
Practice Green:	■	Meeting Rooms:	
Locker Room:		Tennis:	■
Rental Clubs:	■	Swimming:	■
Walkers:	■	Jogging Trails:	
Snack Bar:	■	Boating:	

COURSE DESCRIPTION

Quail Ridge Golf & Country Club is a tight course that demands accurate tee shots. Water comes into play on 13 holes.

The double-dogleg 15th hole is the hardest hole on the course. It is a par-5 that measures 516 yards in length. From the tee, trees come into play on the left side. You'll be out-of-bounds if you hit into them. Having a good approach shot to the tee means having to cut the dogleg right on your second shot over water to set up your approach shot across the dogleg left. The green on this hole is small with bunkers coming into play left and left-center.

DIRECTIONS

Take Hwy. 19 to Hwy. 52 and go east. Stay on this road for about ten miles. Go north into the Shady Hills subdivision.

SEVEN HILLS GOLFERS CLUB

10599 Fairchild Rd., Spring Hill, FL 34608 / (352) 688-8888

BASIC INFORMATION

Course Type: Semi-private
Year Built: 1989
Architect: Dennis Griffith
Local Pro: N/A

Course:N/A
Holes: 18 / Par 72

Back: 6,715 yds. Rating: 70.5 Slope: 126
Middle: 6,302 yds. Rating: 66.8 Slope: 112
Ladies: 4,902 yds. Rating: 66.5 Slope: 109

Tee Time: 7 days in advance
Price: $18.50 - $26.50

Credit Cards:		Restaurant:	
Driving Range:	■	Lounge:	■
Practice Green:	■	Meeting Rooms:	
Locker Room:		Tennis:	
Rental Clubs:	■	Swimming:	
Walkers:		Jogging Trails:	
Snack Bar:	■	Boating:	■

COURSE DESCRIPTION

The Seven Hills Golfers Club is a well-manicured course featuring rolling hills, lots of trees, and very little water.

The fairways are of average size, the rough is kept low, bunkers don't come into play much, and only one hole features water as a hazard.

This is definitely a good place to bring out your driver on almost every hole. If you can keep your tee shots relatively straight, you'll be setting yourself up for many birdie opportunities.

This is a great course for a golfer to take chances and grow as a player.

DIRECTIONS

Take Hwy. 19 south of Spring Hill, go east on Hwy. 578 (County Line Rd.) for six miles and go north on Mariner. The course will be about one mile on your left.

SEVILLE GOLF & COUNTRY CLUB

18200 Seville Clubhouse Dr., Brooksville, FL 34614 / (352) 596-7888

BASIC INFORMATION

Course Type: Public
Year Built: 1988
Architect: A. Hills
Local Pro: N/A

Course: N / A
Holes: 18 / Par 72

Back: 6,653 yds. Rating: 72.7 Slope: 134
Middle: 6,165 yds. Rating: 70.5 Slope: 131
Ladies: 5,236 yds. Rating: 70.8 Slope: 126

Tee Time: 7 days in advance
Price: $15 - $25

Credit Cards:	■	Restaurant:	
Driving Range:	■	Lounge:	
Practice Green:	■	Meeting Rooms:	
Locker Room:	■	Tennis:	
Rental Clubs:	■	Swimming:	
Walkers:		Jogging Trails:	
Snack Bar:	■	Boating:	■

COURSE DESCRIPTION

Seville Golf & Country Club is a links-type golf course with many swales, mounds, and bunkers coming into play.

With a slope rating of 134 from the back tees, you better teach yourself the art of hitting balls from various types of lies.

This course is a tremendous challenge from each of the various tees. Your drives have to be long and accurate and your approach shots have to land softly to stay close to the pins. Most of the greens are undulated and thus will challenge your putting skills often.

DIRECTIONS

Take Hwy. 19 approximately eight miles south of Homosassa Springs. Go east at the sign and the clubhouse will be two miles further.

SPRING HILL GOLF & COUNTRY CLUB
12079 Coronado Dr., Spring Hill, FL 33526 / (352) 683-2261

BASIC INFORMATION

Course Type: Semi-private
Year Built: 1969
Architect: N /A
Local Pro: N /A

Course:N/A
Holes: 18 / Par 72

Back: 6,917 yds. Rating: 73.0 Slope: 133
Middle: 6,245 yds. Rating: 69.9 Slope: 128
Ladies: 5,588 yds. Rating: 71.8 Slope: 117

Tee Time: 7 days in advance
Price: $17.50 - $24.50

Credit Cards:		Restaurant:	■
Driving Range:	■	Lounge:	■
Practice Green:	■	Meeting Rooms:	
Locker Room:	■	Tennis:	
Rental Clubs:	■	Swimming:	
Walkers:	■	Jogging Trails:	
Snack Bar:	■	Boating:	■

COURSE DESCRIPTION
Spring Hill Golf & Country Club will challenge golfers of all abilities. The course is rather long with narrow fairways. Playing well on this course means having the ability to hit the ball both long and accurate on every hole. If you're not a low handicap player, do yourself a favor and play the white tees only.

The dogleg 14th hole is the hardest hole on the course. It's a par-4 that measures 434 yards from the back tees. You'll be standing on a high elevated tee looking down at a narrow fairway that slopes heavily towards the right side. It's crucial for your tee shot to land on the left side of the fairway.

DIRECTIONS
Take Hwy. 19 north to Spring Hill Dr. Go east about eight miles and the course will be on your left side on Coronado Rd.

WHISPERING OAKS COUNTRY CLUB
34450 Whispering Oaks Blvd., Ridge Manor, FL 33525 / (352) 583-4233

BASIC INFORMATION

Course Type: Semi-private
Year Built: 1955
Architect: Buck Chutz
Local Pro: Craig Conway

Course: N/A
Holes: 18 / par 72

Back: 6,313 yds. Rating: 70.0 Slope: 123
Middle: 6,055 yds. Rating: 68.4 Slope: 119
Ladies: 5,162 yds. Rating: 69.8 Slope: 117

Tee Time: 2 days in advance
Price: $10 - $23

Credit Cards:	■	■
Driving Range:	■	
Practice Green:	■	
Locker Room:		■
Rental Clubs:	■	
Walkers:	■	■
Snack Bar:	■	■

COURSE DESCRIPTION
Whispering Oaks demands accuracy over distance on almost every hole. The fairways are narrow, the rough is low, and trees come into play often.

You really have to play your iron shots well to post a good score. You'll find a good combination of hole designs that allow several options on your approach shots. Study the scorecard and work on a game plan that will complement your playing style. If you can stick to a game plan and manage it throughout the course without getting overly emotional about a poorly played shot, you'll have a great time playing this course.

DIRECTIONS
Take exit 61 off I-75 and go east on Hwy. 50. Go north on Hwy. 301 and follow the signs to the course.

BABE ZAHARIS GOLF COURSE
11412 Forest Hills Dr., Tampa, FL 33179 / (352) 932-8932

BASIC INFORMATION

Course Type: Public
Year Built: 1928 / 1973
Architect: R. Garl (1973)
Local Pro: Gary Jones

Course: N/A
Holes: 18 / Par 70

Back: 6,163 yds. Rating: 68.9 Slope: 121
Middle: N/A   Rating: N/A Slope: N/A
Ladies: 5,236 yds. Rating: 68.9 Slope: 118

Tee Time: 1 day in advance
Price: $13.75 - $23.50

Credit Cards:	■	Restaurant:	
Driving Range:		Lounge:	
Practice Green:	■	Meeting Rooms:	
Locker Room:		Tennis:	
Rental Clubs:	■	Swimming:	
Walkers:	■	Jogging Trails:	
Snack Bar:	■	Boating:	

COURSE DESCRIPTION
The Babe Zaharis Golf Course will be best enjoyed by average golfers who are looking for low scores and fun golf. You'll find many opportunities for birdies if you play a well-managed game.

The dogleg right 16th hole is the hardest on the course. It is a par-4 that measures 453 yards in length. The dogleg can only be taken out of play with a 240 yard fade that has to carry the left side of the fairway (which is tree-lined) before landing right.

You'll find eight holes that have water coming into play.

DIRECTIONS
Take Hwy. 275 north to exit Fowler Ave. west. Look for the course two miles further on your left side.

BLOOMINGDALE GOLFER'S CLUB
1802 Natures Way Blvd., Valrico, FL 33594 / (352) 685-4105

BASIC INFORMATION

Course Type: Semi-private
Year Built: 1983
Architect: R.Garl
Local Pro: Tim Fenell

Course:N/A
Holes: 18 / Par 72

Back: 7,165 yds. Rating: 74.4 Slope: 137
Middle: 6,651 yds. Rating: 72.1 Slope: 129
Ladies: 5,506 yds. Rating: 71.6 Slope: 129

Tee Time: 7 days in advance
Price: $39 - $55

Credit Cards:	■	Restaurant:	■
Driving Range:	■	Lounge:	■
Practice Green:	■	Meeting Rooms:	
Locker Room:	■	Tennis:	
Rental Clubs:	■	Swimming:	
Walkers:	■	Jogging Trails:	
Snack Bar:	■	Boating:	

COURSE DESCRIPTION
Bloomingdale Golfer's Club is an excellent layout that is kept in perfect shape all year long. The course plays long and is very demanding. You won't find many options to bail out on this course.

Ron Garl must have been in a Pete Dye state of mind when he designed this course. Most of the holes are shaped in a manner that dictates which way you'll have to play the hole. If you choose to stay back and not heed the call, you'll often end up on the green with only a single putt left for par.

DIRECTIONS
Take I-75 to exit 49 south to the first light. Go east on Bloomingdale Ave for about six miles until you get to Bell Shoals Rd. Go right on Bell Shoals and make a left on Glenhaven. Go right on Natures Way Blvd. and the course will be on your left.

CYPRESS CREEK GOLF CLUB

880 Cypress Village Blvd., Ruskin, FL 33573 / (352) 634-8888

BASIC INFORMATION

Course Type: Semi-private
Year Built: 1988
Architect: S. Smyers
Local Pro: Dennis Buch

Course: Champion (18 / Par 72)
Holes: 36

Back: 6,839 yds. Rating: 74.0 Slope: 133
Middle: 6,369 yds. Rating: 71.7 Slope: 128
Ladies: 4,640 yds. Rating: 66.6 Slope: 114

Tee Time: 4 days in advance
Price: $9 - $45

Credit Cards:	■	Restaurant:	■
Driving Range:	■	Lounge:	■
Practice Green:	■	Meeting Rooms:	■
Locker Room:	■	Tennis:	■
Rental Clubs:	■	Swimming:	
Walkers:		Jogging Trails:	
Snack Bar:	■	Boating:	■

COURSE DESCRIPTION

Cypress Creek Golf Club is both fair to the novice and challenging to the experienced golfer.

This links-styled course features deep bunkers and subtle contours on the fairways that lead up to undulating greens. The course can wreak havoc on a golfer when the wind is in force. This type of situation demands low soaring shots that remain under the wind for both distance and accuracy.

Ask your local pro to teach you the knockdown-shot. You'll find it an invaluable tool when playing this course.

DIRECTIONS

Exit 46B off of I-75 and go about a quarter mile east to the course. You 'll see signs as you get there.

GOLF & SEA CLUB

801 Golf & Sea Blvd., Apollo Beach, FL 33572 / (352) 645-6212

BASIC INFORMATION

Course Type: Public
Year Built: 1965
Architect: R. Trent Jones
Local Pro: Tom Doozan

Course: N/A
Holes: 18 / Par 72

Back: 7,026 yds. Rating: 73.9 Slope: 130
Middle: 6,408 yds. Rating: 70.6 Slope: 123
Ladies: 5,237 yds. Rating: 71.1 Slope: 116

Tee Time: 7 days in advance
Price: $22.50 - $28.00

Credit Cards:	■	Restaurant:	■
Driving Range:	■	Lounge:	■
Practice Green:	■	Meeting Rooms:	
Locker Room:	■	Tennis:	
Rental Clubs:	■	Swimming:	
Walkers:		Jogging Trails:	
Snack Bar:	■	Boating:	■

COURSE DESCRIPTION

The *Golf & Sea Club* is truly an exciting course with spectacular holes.

The dogleg right number 5 hole is notoriously known as the hardest hole in Hillsborough County. This par-5 measures 447 yards in length from tee to green. Both water and trees come into play on the right side. You'll have to hit an accurate drive to stay away from the five fairway bunkers and out-of-bounds on the left.

You'll also have to hit your ball over the bay on holes 13 & 14. The entire course plays into water.

DIRECTIONS

Take I-75 and exit 47. Go west on Big Bend Rd. to Hwy. 41 and south to Miller Mac Rd. Make a right on Golf & Sea Blvd. The course will be on your right.

DIAMOND HILL GOLF & COUNTRY CLUB

P.O. Box 309, Valrico, FL 33594 / (352) 689-7219

BASIC INFORMATION

Course Type: Semi-private
Year Built: 1968
Architect: N/A
Local Pro: Chuck Peters

Course: N/A
Holes: 18 / Par 72

Back: 6,920 yds. Rating: 71.9 Slope: 120
Middle: 6,306 yds. Rating: 69.0 Slope: 114
Ladies: 5,647 yds. Rating: 69.8 Slope: 115

Tee Time: 3 days in advance
Price: $20 - $25

Credit Cards:	■	Restaurant:	■
Driving Range:	■	Lounge:	■
Practice Green:	■	Meeting Rooms:	■
Locker Room:	■	Tennis:	
Rental Clubs:		Swimming:	
Walkers:	■	Jogging Trails:	
Snack Bar:	■	Boating:	

COURSE DESCRIPTION

Diamond Hill Golf & Country Club is a well-balanced course with many interesting holes that are both challenging and unique.

The course is hilly and demanding. It isn't often that you'll find your ball sitting on a level lie. That can get frustrating if you haven't taken the time to learn how to hit a ball from above and beneath your stance.

The dogleg left 13th hole is the hardest hole on the course. It's a par-5 that measures 567 yards from tee to green; a very challenging hole. You'll also find water coming into play on eight holes.

DIRECTIONS

Take I-75 North to Hwy. 60. Go East to Valrico Rd. and North on Sydney Rd. The course will be about 1 1/2 miles on your right.

EAGLES GOLF CLUB, THE

16101 Nine Eagles Dr., Odessa, FL 33556 / (352) 920-6681

BASIC INFORMATION

Course Type: Public
Year Built: 1974
Architect: R. Garl
Local Pro: Bill Keller

Course:Forest / Lakes (18 / Par 72)
Holes: 27

Back: 7,134 yds. Rating: 73.0 Slope: 130
Middle: 6,695 yds. Rating: 71.2 Slope: 120
Ladies: 6,129 yds. Rating: 68.5 Slope: 116

Tee Time: 3 days in advance
Price: $33 - $39

Credit Cards:	■	Restaurant:	■
Driving Range:	■	Lounge:	■
Practice Green:	■	Meeting Rooms:	
Locker Room:		Tennis:	■
Rental Clubs:	■	Swimming:	
Walkers:	■	Jogging Trails:	
Snack Bar:	■	Boating:	

COURSE DESCRIPTION

The *Eagles Golf Club* is a tremendous fusion of 3 nine-hole courses that all play well and are in meticulous shape.

The layout is very modern with 17 holes playing into water. This course, like the majority of courses built today, forces the golfer to keep the ball high and land it soft. If you can control your fade shot, you'll have an edge over your fellow competitors.

The 14th hole (par 4 / 435 yards) is the hardest hole on the Forest / Lakes combination. You'll be hitting your drive onto a tight fairway with a big lake that comes into play in the middle of the fairway. Bombs away! Have fun placing this one.

DIRECTIONS

Take I-275 south to Dale Maydry Rd. north to Hillsborough Ave. west to Racetrack Rd. The course will be two miles on your left.

HALL OF FAME GOLF CLUB
2222 N. Westshore Blvd., Tampa, FL 33607 / (352) 876-4913

BASIC INFORMATION

Course Type: Public
Year Built: N/A
Architect: N/A
Local Pro: Don Grunwaldt

Course:N/A
Holes: 18 / Par 72

Back: 6,946 yds. Rating: 71.5 Slope: 121
Middle: 6,263 yds. Rating: 69.3 Slope: 116
Ladies: 5,286 yds. Rating: 60.0 Slope: N/A

Tee Time: 7 days in advance
Price: $10 - $25

Credit Cards: ■   Restaurant:
Driving Range: ■   Lounge:
Practice Green: ■   Meeting Rooms:
Locker Room: Tennis:
Rental Clubs: ■   Swimming:
Walkers: ■   Jogging Trails:
Snack Bar: Boating:

COURSE DESCRIPTION

The *Hall of Fame Golf Club* is a simple course that is straightforward and fun to play.

Although the course seems to play rather long, the layout does allow a wide margin of error with its wide fairways and large greens.

The number 5 hole is the hardest hole on the course. It is a par-4 that measures 408 yards in length. You'll find both water and tress coming into play on your left and right. A good tee shot to the middle of the fairway is crucial to setting up a good approach shot. The green is long and narrow and can be very difficult to play. A well-executed fade shot will do you wonders!

DIRECTIONS

Take I-275 and exit onto Westshore Blvd. Go one mile further and you'll see the course on your right side (next to airport).

HUNTERS GREEN COUNTRY CLUB
18101 Longwater Run, Tampa, FL 33647 / (352) 973-1700

BASIC INFORMATION

Course Type: Semi-private
Year Built: 1989
Architect: T. Fazio
Local Pro: Jim Tipps / Tom Parsons

Course: N/A
Holes: 18 / Par 72

Back: 6,979 yds. Rating: 73.4 Slope: 126
Middle: 6,504 yds. Rating: 70.9 Slope: 122
Ladies: 5,096 yds. Rating: 70.1 Slope: 113

Tee Time: 4 days in advance
Price: $45 - $60

Credit Cards: ■   Restaurant: ■
Driving Range: ■   Lounge: ■
Practice Green: ■   Meeting Rooms: ■
Locker Room: ■   Tennis: ■
Rental Clubs: ■   Swimming: ■
Walkers: Jogging Trails:
Snack Bar: Boating:

COURSE DESCRIPTION

Modern golf course architecture has taken a quantum "construction leap" over the last decade. More courses are being built today than ever before, but only a handful of people are innovative enough to be considered original and respected by other professionals in their field.

I haven't met a golfer that hasn't enjoyed a Tom Fazio design. He has a gift of building courses that play well to all types of players. *Hunters Green Country Club* is no exception. This is the type of course that golfers tend to talk about with their friends. Don't pass through Tampa without playing it. It's a wonderful tribute to the area.

DIRECTIONS

Take 1-275 to Bears Ave. exit. Go east to Bruce B. Downs Blvd. and the course will be five miles on your right.

NORTHDALE GOLF & TENNIS CLUB
4417 Northdale Blvd., Tampa, FL 33178 / (352) 962-0428

BASIC INFORMATION

Course Type: Semi-private
Year Built: 1978
Architect: R. Garl
Local Pro: Mitchell Joannes

Course:N/A
Holes: 18 / Par 72

Back: 6,791 yds. Rating: 72.1 Slope: 119
Middle: 6,230 yds. Rating: 69.6 Slope: 115
Ladies: 5,397 yds. Rating: 71.0 Slope: 113

Tee Time: 3 days in advance
Price: $15 - $32

Credit Cards:	■	Restaurant:	■
Driving Range:		Lounge:	■
Practice Green:	■	Meeting Rooms:	■
Locker Room:		Tennis:	
Rental Clubs:	■	Swimming:	
Walkers:		Jogging Trails:	
Snack Bar:	■	Boating:	

COURSE DESCRIPTION

Northdale Golf & Tennis Club is a well-rounded course with a solid design that will post a challenge to many golfers.

The fairways are of average size and the rough is kept relatively low in the winter and high in the summer. You'll have many opportunities to bring out your driver and let it rip. Try to be cautious, although the course is set up for low numbers; nine holes do have water coming into play. You may want to bring out your 3-wood for accuracy.

The 16th hole is a par-5 double dogleg that features water from the tee and in front of the green. It is a very challenging hole that will test your course management skills.

DIRECTIONS

Take Rt. 275 to Bears Ave. and go west. Make a right onto Dal Madry Hwy. and a left onto Northdale Blvd. The course will be right.

PEBBLE CREEK GOLF & COUNTRY CLUB
10550 Regents Park Dr., Tampa, FL 33647 / (352) 973-3870

BASIC INFORMATION

Course Type: Semi-private
Year Built: 1968
Architect: N/A
Local Pro: Anthony Greising

Course: N/A
Holes: 18 / Par 71

Back: 6,410 yds. Rating: 71.1 Slope: 127
Middle: 6,023 yds. Rating: 69.1 Slope: 122
Ladies: 5,280 yds. Rating: 70.3 Slope: 120

Tee Time: 3 days in advance
Price: $24 - $34

Credit Cards:	■	Restaurant:	■
Driving Range:	■	Lounge:	■
Practice Green:	■	Meeting Rooms:	■
Locker Room:	■	Tennis:	■
Rental Clubs:	■	Swimming:	■
Walkers:	■	Jogging Trails:	
Snack Bar:	■	Boating:	

COURSE DESCRIPTION

Pebble Creek Golf & Country Club is a beautiful course with many scenic holes.

The challenge unfolds between water, woods, heavy bunkers, and elevated greens with subtle undulations.

If the back tee slope rating of 127 is too much course for you, play the middle tees and have a more enjoyable day.

The par-4 number 5 hole plays to a distance of 365 yards and is considered the hardest hole on the course. You have to hit your tee shot over water and your approach shot to a high elevated green.

DIRECTIONS

Take I-75 North to Exit 56. Make a right and and then a left three miles down the road. Once you see the sign to the course you 'll have to to take the third entrance in.

PLANT CITY GOLF & COUNTRY CLUB

3102 Coronet Rd., Plant City, FL 33178 / (352) 752-1524

BASIC INFORMATION

Course Type: Semi-private
Year Built: 1928 / 1973
Architect: Consolidated Mineral Inc. (CMI)
Local Pro: Chris Aylers

Course:N/A
Holes: 18 / Par 72

Back: 6,479 yds. Rating: 70.4 Slope: 118
Middle: 5,663 yds. Rating: 66.4 Slope: 109
Ladies: 4,929 yds. Rating: 67.3 Slope: 109

Tee Time: 2 days in advance
Price: $12 - $23.50

Credit Cards:	■	Restaurant:	
Driving Range:	■	Lounge:	
Practice Green:	■	Meeting Rooms:	
Locker Room:		Tennis:	
Rental Clubs:	■	Swimming:	
Walkers:	■	Jogging Trails:	
Snack Bar:	■	Boating:	

COURSE DESCRIPTION

Plant City Golf & Country Club is one of Florida's hidden treasures. It was originally built in 1928 by a mineral company and later modified in 1973.

It's interesting to look at this layout and imagine golf being played here with hickory shafted clubs during the emergence of the Wound Rubber Ball (circa 1900). This ball changed the game forever. It allowed the golfer maximum spin and control.

The hardest hole on this course is the straight number 2 that measures 400 yards from tee to green. If you can set yourself up to play your second shot as a soft fade to the green, you may walk off with a bird.

DIRECTIONS

Take I-4 to exit 14 (Park Rd.). Go south to Coronet Rd. and make a left. The course will be two miles on your left.

RIVER HILLS COUNTRY CLUB

3943 New River Hills Pkwy., Valrico, FL 33594 / (352) 653-3323

BASIC INFORMATION

Course Type: Semi-private
Year Built: 1981
Architect: J.Lee
Local Pro: Bob Swezey

Course: N/A
Holes: 18 / Par 72

Back: 7,004 yds. Rating: 73.5 Slope: 134
Middle: 6,502 yds. Rating: 71.1 Slope: 122
Ladies: 5,292 yds. Rating: 70.7 Slope: 124

Tee Time: 2 days in advance
Price: $40 all year round.

Credit Cards:	■	Restaurant:	■
Driving Range:	■	Lounge:	■
Practice Green:	■	Meeting Rooms:	■
Locker Room:	■	Tennis:	■
Rental Clubs:	■	Swimming:	■
Walkers:	■	Jogging Trails:	
Snack Bar:	■	Boating:	

COURSE DESCRIPTION

River Hills Country Club is a monster of a course from the championship tees. 7,004 yards of real estate have to be considered en route to par.

Bob Swezey made it mandatory for you to play good golf. The course is filled with mounds and fast slopes. Water comes into play on 15 holes.

If the 135 Slope Rating is too much for you, play the course from the middle tees. This is truly a professional caliber course.

Look out for the challenging par-3 14th hole. You'll have to carry the ball 200 yards over marshland from the back tees.

DIRECTIONS

Take the Turnpike exit to Kendell Dr. west. Go left on 133rd Ave. and left again at the upcoming fork. That will take you to 130th Ave.

ROCKY POINT GOLF COURSE

4151 Dana Shores Dr., Tampa, FL 33614 / (352) 884-5141

BASIC INFORMATION

Course Type: Public
Year Built: 1918
Architect: N/A
Local Pro: Bob Arnot

Course:N/A
Holes: 18 / Par 71

Back: 6,489 yds. Rating: 710. Slope: 122
Middle: 5,986 yds. Rating: 68.7 Slope: 117
Ladies: 4,910 yds. Rating: 65.7 Slope: 111

Tee Time: 3 days in advance
Price: $22.25 -$23.50

Credit Cards:	■	Restaurant:	
Driving Range:	■	Lounge:	
Practice Green:	■	Meeting Rooms:	
Locker Room:	■	Tennis:	
Rental Clubs:	■	Swimming:	
Walkers:	■	Jogging Trails:	
Snack Bar:	■	Boating:	

COURSE DESCRIPTION

Picturing the past as you stand on the first tee of an unspoiled landmark is a rare treat. *Rocky Point Golf Course* is another eclectic antique, just one of many hidden treasures in the Sunshine State.

The club, to this day, holds a trophy that dates back to 1922. It is also interesting to note that this course was used as an Army base during World War II.

Consider entering the "Horses For The Handicap" competition if you're scheduled to be in town around August. Your money will go to helping people who are diagnosed with Spinabifida, the deterioration of the spinal column.

DIRECTIONS

Take I-275 south to Airport exit. Eisenhower Blvd. Left to Independance Pkwy. At Memorial, make a left to course.

RODGERS PARK GOLF COURSE

7910 N. 30th St., Tampa, FL 33610 / (352) 234-1911

BASIC INFORMATION

Course Type: Public
Year Built: 1979
Architect: M. Garl
Local Pro: Burt Stump

Course: N/A
Holes: 18 / Par 72

Back: 6,845 yds. Rating: 72.3 Slope: 125
Middle: 6,583 yds. Rating: 71.1 Slope: 122
Ladies: 5,456 yds. Rating: 70.7 Slope: 119

Tee Time: 7 days in advance
Price: $13.75 - $23.50

Credit Cards:	■	Restaurant:	
Driving Range:	■	Lounge:	■
Practice Green:	■	Meeting Rooms:	
Locker Room:		Tennis:	
Rental Clubs:	■	Swimming:	
Walkers:	■	Jogging Trails:	
Snack Bar:	■	Boating:	■

COURSE DESCRIPTION

Rodgers Park Golf Course is yet another Ron Garl design. He is without question the most infamous Architect in the Central-West Florida area.

This course plays nicely to all types of players. If a handicap player between 10 -15 is in their comfort zone, birdie opportunities will come frequently.

Water comes into play on seven holes. The par-3 12th hole is rated the hardest. You have to hit the ball between two giant pines that are only 15 yards apart. The putting green is both undulating and small. The pin can easily be hidden behind one of the trees.

DIRECTIONS

Take I-275 south to Sligh Ave. Go east to 30th St. The course will be on the north side. Once you enter, follow the road straight in.

SUMMERFIELD GOLF CLUB

13050 Summerfied Blvd., Riverview, FL 33569 / (352) 671-3311

BASIC INFORMATION

Course Type: Semi-private
Year Built: 1986
Architect: R. Garl
Local Pro: John Bauer

Course:N/A
Holes: 18 / Par 71

Back: 6,883 yds. Rating: 73.0 Slope: 125
Middle: 6,375 yds. Rating: 70.0 Slope: 121
Ladies: 5,139 yds. Rating: 69.6 Slope: 114

Tee Time: 5 days in advance
Price: $18 - $25

Credit Cards:	■	Restaurant:	■
Driving Range:	■	Lounge:	■
Practice Green:	■	Meeting Rooms:	
Locker Room:		Tennis:	
Rental Clubs:	■	Swimming:	
Walkers:		Jogging Trails:	
Snack Bar:	■	Boating:	

COURSE DESCRIPTION

Summerfield Golf Course is a links type of golf course with deep bunkers and many hidden lies. The wind often swirls at a rate of 10-15 miles.

If you want to walk out of this course with a good score posted, practice a three-quarter swing into the wind. You'll often have to use a less lofted club to gain back the yardage that you will lose. The swing is designed to keep the ball on a low trajectory below the wind with maximum accuracy. Watch for Paul Azinger, the next time you're viewing professional golf; he is the master of this type of swing. Book an appointment with your local professional for a lesson.

DIRECTIONS

Take I-75 to Exit 47 and then go east two miles on Big Bend Rd. The course will be on your right side.

UNIVERSITY OF SOUTH FLORIDA GOLF COURSE

4202 Fowler Ave., Tampa, FL 33620 / (853) 974-2071

BASIC INFORMATION

Course Type: Public
Year Built: 1967
Architect: B. Mitchell
Local Pro: Chuck Winship

Course: N/A
Holes: 18 / Par 72

Back: 6,971 yds. Rating: 73.9 Slope: 132
Middle: 6,532 yds. Rating: 69.9 Slope: 121
Ladies: 5,831 yds. Rating: N/A Slope: N/A

Tee Time: 5 days in advance
Price: $11 - $30

Credit Cards:	■	Restaurant:	■
Driving Range:		Lounge:	
Practice Green:	■	Meeting Rooms:	
Locker Room:	■	Tennis:	
Rental Clubs:	■	Swimming:	
Walkers:	■	Jogging Trails:	
Snack Bar:	■	Boating:	

COURSE DESCRIPTION

The *University of South Florida Golf Course* is an exceptional design for golfers of differing abilities. If you're not an above average golfer, play the course from the middle tees. With a course rating of 73.9 and a slope rating of 132, the back tees can be severely damaging to a 10-15 handicapper and above.

This course is beautifully laid out in a manner that blends well with its natural surroundings. Once on the course, not many homes come into view. If you enjoy playing golf in a peaceful forest setting, this is the course you've been searching for.

DIRECTIONS

Take I-275 exit to Fletcher Ave. Go east for three miles until you get to 46th St. The course will be on your left side.

BUFFALO CREEK GOLF COURSE

8100 Erie Rd., Palmetto, FL 34221 / (352) 776-2611

BASIC INFORMATION

Course Type: Municipal
Year Built: 1988
Architect: R. Garl
Local Pro: Becky Ross

Course: N/A
Holes: 18 / Par 72

Back: 7,005 yds. Rating: 73.1 Slope: 125
Middle: 6,450 yds. Rating: 70.5 Slope: 118
Ladies: 5,261 yds. Rating: 69.7 Slope: 114

Tee Time: 2 days in advance
Price: $7 - $30

Credit Cards:	■	Restaurant:	
Driving Range:	■	Lounge:	■
Practice Green:	■	Meeting Rooms:	
Locker Room:		Tennis:	
Rental Clubs:	■	Swimming:	
Walkers:	■	Jogging Trails:	
Snack Bar:	■	Boating:	■

COURSE DESCRIPTION

This beautiful links style course will satisfy both the novice and the expert golfer. The playing field features rolling mounds, love grass, big waste areas, and wide open fairways. Like all true links courses cut out of the fabric of Scottish past, this one can get awfully hard to tame when the wind decides to make an uninvited grand entrance. Work on your low ball and you'll fare well.

The beautiful landscaping around the course is spectacular. There isn't a house to be found in sight. All of this adds up to playing golf in a pleasurable atmosphere without a single distraction to irritate you.

DIRECTIONS

Take I-75 to Exit 43 and go east for several miles until you reach Erie Rd. Go north to course.

IMPERIAL LAKES GOLF CLUB

6807 Buffalo Rd., Palmetto, FL 34221 / (352) 747-2829

BASIC INFORMATION

Course Type: Semi-private
Year Built: 1986
Architect: T. McAnlis
Local Pro: Pat Walsh

Course: N/A
Holes: 18 / Par 72

Back: 6,658 yds. Rating: 71.5 Slope: 123
Middle: 6,036 yds. Rating: 68.7 Slope: 117
Ladies: 5,270 yds. Rating: 69.7 Slope: 117

Tee Time: 2 days in advance
Price: $10 - $35

Credit Cards:	■	Restaurant:	
Driving Range:	■	Lounge:	
Practice Green:	■	Meeting Rooms:	
Locker Room:		Tennis:	
Rental Clubs:	■	Swimming:	
Walkers:	■	Jogging Trails:	
Snack Bar:	■	Boating:	

COURSE DESCRIPTION

The *Imperial Lakes Golf Course* has a long history of good reviews by some of the most prominent magazines in golf.

What you will find is a good combination of holes that are evenly balanced. You'll have to keep your drives long and accurate to get the type of setup needed to score well on your approach shots.

If you shoot above a 15 handicap, play the course from the white tees for maximum fun. The challenge is still there for you to conquer minus the extreme distance off the tee.

This is a terrific course for all types of players to enjoy.

DIRECTIONS

Take Exit 45 off I-75 and go east for about a mile straight to the course.

MANATEE COUNTY GOLF COURSE
5290 66th St. West, Bradenton, FL 32642 / (352) 792-6773

BASIC INFORMATION

Course Type: Municipal
Year Built: 1977
Architect: L. Marshall
Local Pro: Penny Porter

Course: N/A
Holes: 18 / Par 72

Back: 6,747 yds. Rating: 71.6 Slope: 122
Middle: 6,216 yds. Rating: 69.0 Slope: 118
Ladies: 5,619 yds. Rating: 71.6 Slope: 117

Tee Time: 2 days in advance
Price: $8 - $29

Credit Cards: ■
Driving Range: ■
Practice Green: ■
Locker Room:
Rental Clubs: ■
Walkers: ■
Snack Bar: ■
Restaurant:
Lounge:
Meeting Rooms:
Tennis:
Swimming:
Jogging Trails:
Boating: ■

COURSE DESCRIPTION

This public course is one of the finest in Manatee County. The shape of the course is amazingly good considering it plays to 80,000 rounds of golf per year.

The most difficult hole on the course is the 10th hole. This par-4 measures 443 yards from tee to green. You'll be hitting onto an undulating fairway that slopes left-to-right off the tee. If you can grab the left side of the fairway on your landing area, the ball should set up well for your approach to the green. You'll find huge bunkers on both sides of the green with a narrow opening to its huge platform. The wind often makes this hole longer than it appears.

DIRECTIONS

Take I-75 north to Hwy. 44. On Country Rd. 486 you'll have to go south and the course will be on your right.

PALMA SOLA GOLF CLUB
3807 75th St. West, Bradenton, FL 32630 / (352) 792-7476

BASIC INFORMATION

Course Type: Public
Year Built: 1968
Architect: A. Anderson
Local Pro: Robert Skelton

Course: N/A
Holes: 18 / Par 72

Back: 6,464 yds. Rating: 68.4 Slope: 118
Middle: 5,920 yds. Rating: 68.2 Slope: 115
Ladies: 5,311 yds. Rating: 69.7 Slope: 114

Tee Time: 2 days in advance
Price: $15-$34

Credit Cards:
Driving Range:
Practice Green: ■
Locker Room: ■
Rental Clubs:
Walkers: ■
Snack Bar: ■
Restaurant: ■
Lounge:
Meeting Rooms:
Tennis:
Swimming:
Jogging Trails:
Boating: ■

COURSE DESCRIPTION

The closest Public course from the beach in Bradenton county is the *Palma Sola Golf Club*. The course plays flat with an interesting combination of holes that will test your ability to shape your shots. With most greens waiting for a soft landing high ball, those of you who can shape your shots from left to right (fade) will have a slight advantage over your draw counterparts (people who shape their shots from right to left).

The course is an admirable challenge from both the blue and white tees. If you can drive the ball well, many birdie opportunities will be coming your way.

DIRECTIONS

Take Hwy. 41 and go west on Cortez Rd. Continue on with this course until you get to 75th St. West.

PALMETTO PINES GOLF COURSE

14355 Golf Course Rd., Parrish, FL 34219 / (352) 776-1375

BASIC INFORMATION

Course Type: Semi-private
Year Built: 1970
Architect: F. Myers
Local Pro: Tommy Smith

Course: White / Blue (18 / Par 72)
Holes: 36

Back: 5,358 yds. Rating: 65.8 Slope: 107
Middle: N/A.   Rating: N/A   Slope: N/A
Ladies: N/A   Rating: N/A   Slope: N/A

Tee Time: 1 day in advance
Price: $5 - $9

Credit Cards:		Restaurant:	
Driving Range:	■	Lounge:	
Practice Green:	■	Meeting Rooms:	
Locker Room:	■	Tennis:	
Rental Clubs:	■	Swimming:	
Walkers:	■	Jogging Trails:	
Snack Bar:	■	Boating:	■

COURSE DESCRIPTION

Before I even talk about the character of this course, take a minute to look over the prices. I wouldn't think it would be possible to have a bad day regardless of your performance.

Obviously, this is a course that will be best enjoyed by beginners and senior citizens. It is a very short layout and all you really have to worry about is how you'll perform with your iron shots. The course has no sand traps and only five holes feature water coming into the play of action.

The course has a healthy variety of wildlife hidden amongst dense trees.

DIRECTIONS

Take Hwy. 70 several miles west of Hwy. 41. The course will be on your right.

RIVER CLUB, THE

6600 River Club Rd., Bradenton, FL 34202 / (352) 751-4211

BASIC INFORMATION

Course Type: Semi-private
Year Built: 1988
Architect: Ron Garl
Local Pro: Talbot Griffin

Course: N/A
Holes: 18 / Par 72

Back: 7,004 yds. Rating: 73.6 Slope: 133
Middle: 6,600 yds. Rating: 71.6 Slope: 129
Ladies: 5,252 yds. Rating: 70.1 Slope: 122

Tee Time: 1 day in advance
Price: $16 - $40

Credit Cards:	■	Restaurant:	■
Driving Range:	■	Lounge:	■
Practice Green:	■	Meeting Rooms:	■
Locker Room:	■	Tennis:	■
Rental Clubs:	■	Swimming:	■
Walkers:	■	Jogging Trails:	
Snack Bar:	■	Boating:	■

COURSE DESCRIPTION

The *River Club* is yet another beautifully designed course by Ron Garl. When it first made its debut in 1988, Golf Digest magazine named it one of the top new courses in the country.

You'll find the course a tremendous challenge from the back tees at 7,004 yards. If you're not a single digit handicap player, do yourself a favor and play the course from the white tee. You'll need the extra 22 yards off the tee to get yourself in good position off the tee.

The 16th (Par-4 / 416 yards) signature hole plays to an island green. It is by far the most dramatic hole.

DIRECTIONS

Take I-75 to exit 41. When you reach Hwy. 70 go east. You'll see signs that will lead you to the course about a mile further.

RIVER RUN GOLF LINKS

1801 27th St. E., Bradenton, FL 34208 / (352) 747-6331

BASIC INFORMATION

Course Type: Public
Year Built: 1987
Architect: W. Northrup
Local Pro: David Beauchamp

Course: N/A
Holes: 18 / Par 70

Back: 5,900 yds. Rating: 67.9 Slope: 115
Middle: 5,460 yds. Rating: 65.9 Slope: 111
Ladies: 4,811 yds. Rating: 66.5 Slope: 110

Tee Time: 2 days in advance
Price: $10 - $23

Credit Cards:		Restaurant:	
Driving Range:		Lounge:	
Practice Green:	■	Meeting Rooms:	
Locker Room:		Tennis:	
Rental Clubs:	■	Swimming:	
Walkers:	■	Jogging Trails:	
Snack Bar:	■	Boating:	■

COURSE DESCRIPTION

You can't judge this course entirely by its rating and slope. For many, the challenge seems much more demanding than the numbers posted.

You'll find demanding fairways that will only hold onto the most accurate tee shots and bunkers scattered strategically to post an even greater challenge. If that isn't enough to rattle your game, maybe the 16 holes that play into water will.

The dogleg right (par-5 /470 yards) 5th hole is the most demanding on the course. You'll find both water and trees on both sides of the hole.

DIRECTIONS

Take Hwy. 41 and go east on Manatee Ave. East. Go south on 27th St. and that will lead you directly to the course.

TARA GOLF & COUNTRY CLUB

6602 Drewry's Bluff., Bradenton, FL 34203 / (352) 758-7961

BASIC INFORMATION

Course Type: Semi-private
Year Built: 1988
Architect: T. McAnlis
Local Pro: Suzanne Pace

Course: N/A
Holes: 18 / Par 72

Back: 6,934 yds. Rating: 75.6 Slope: 130
Middle: 6,378 yds. Rating: 70.1 Slope: 126
Ladies: 5,391 yds. Rating: 70.8 Slope: 116

Tee Time: 3 days in advance
Price: $26 - $40

Credit Cards:	■	Restaurant:	■
Driving Range:	■	Lounge:	■
Practice Green:	■	Meeting Rooms:	■
Locker Room:		Tennis:	■
Rental Clubs:	■	Swimming:	■
Walkers:	■	Jogging Trails:	
Snack Bar:	■	Boating:	■

COURSE DESCRIPTION

This is an exciting course with many challenging holes of various sizes.

Having a great time here means hitting your drives long and accurate on most of the holes. If you can position yourself for a good approach shot, make sure you aim for the flags. The greens are very undulating and if you don't get the ball up close, you may end up three-putting a few of the holes.

The 14th (par-4 /405 yards) hole is the hardest rated on the course. Your tee shot has to be accurate to avoid the big waste bunker that comes into play. The green is both well-bunkered and undulating.

DIRECTIONS

Take I-75 to Exit 41 (Hwy. 70) and go West to the course. It will be on your left.

LINKS OF LAKE BERNADETTE

5430 Links Lane, Zephyrhills, FL 33541 / (352) 788-4653

BASIC INFORMATION

Course Type: Semi-private
Year Built: 1985
Architect: D. Refram
Local Pro: David Bishop

Course: N/A
Holes: 18 / Par 71

Back: 6,392 yds. Rating: 70.0 Slope: 117
Middle: 6,044 yds. Rating: 69.1 Slope: 113
Ladies: 5,031 yds. Rating: 68.0 Slope: 118

Tee Time: 3 days in advance
Price: $20 - $30

Credit Cards: ■	Restaurant: ■
Driving Range:	Lounge: ■
Practice Green: ■	Meeting Rooms:
Locker Room:	Tennis:
Rental Clubs: ■	Swimming:
Walkers:	Jogging Trails:
Snack Bar: ■	Boating:

COURSE DESCRIPTION

The *Links of Lake Bernadette* is a beautiful layout that features lots of trees and wildlife.

You'll find water coming into play on eight holes. This Scottish links-style course is set up to allow the average golfer a good score. At only 6,392 yards from the back tee, your main objective will be to get your tee shots on the fairway. This is yet another example of a course that favors accuracy over distance.

The hardest hole on this course is the 14th. It is a par-4 measuring 417 yards. It's a challenging dogleg left with both trees and water coming into play.

DIRECTIONS

Take I-75 to Exit 58 (SR. 54) and make a right. The course will be eight miles down on your left side.

MAGNOLIA VALLEY GOLF & COUNTRY CLUB

7223 Massachusetts Ave., New Port Richey, FL 34653 / (352) 847-2342

BASIC INFORMATION

Course Type: Semi-private
Year Built: 1962
Architect:
Local Pro: Dave Cahoun

Course: Championship (18 / 71)
Holes: 27

Back: 6,106 yds. Rating: 69.4 Slope: 122
Middle: 5,533 yds. Rating: 66.7 Slope: 117
Ladies: 4,869 yds. Rating: 68.1 Slope: 118

Tee Time: 2 days in advance
Price: $17 - $22

Credit Cards: ■	Restaurant: ■
Driving Range: ■	Lounge: ■
Practice Green: ■	Meeting Rooms: ■
Locker Room:	Tennis:
Rental Clubs: ■	Swimming:
Walkers: ■	Jogging Trails:
Snack Bar: ■	Boating:

COURSE DESCRIPTION

Magnolia Valley Golf & Country Club is a simple course that holds no surprises.

If you're a mid-to-high handicapper, this course will work wonders for your ego. You'll find many chances throughout the course for a birdie or an occasional eagle.

Let's look at the 12th hole. This par-4 measuring 402 yards from the back tees demands an accurate tee shot down the very center of the fairway. You have trees on both sides of the fairway and around the small undulating green. The green slopes from back-to-front. The best shot to play is a high-flying fade.

DIRECTIONS

Take Hwy. 19 to Hwy. 54 east to Hwy. 77. Go north to Massachusetts Ave. and turn right. The course will be 200 yards on your left.

MEADOW OAKS GOLF & COUNTRY CLUB
13114 Wynn Ranch Rd., Hudson, FL 34669 / (352) 856-2878

BASIC INFORMATION

Course Type: Semi-private
Year Built: 1985
Architect: Bill Amick
Local Pro: Ron Johnston

Course: N/A
Holes: 18 / Par 70

Back: 6,010 yds. Rating: 64.5 Slope: 107
Middle: 5,005 yds. Rating: 64.5 Slope: 106
Ladies: 4,140 yds. Rating: 59.4 Slope: 92

Tee Time: 7 days in advance
Price: $15 - $22

Credit Cards:	■	Restaurant:	■
Driving Range:	■	Lounge:	■
Practice Green:	■	Meeting Rooms:	
Locker Room:	■	Tennis:	
Rental Clubs:	■	Swimming:	
Walkers:	■	Jogging Trails:	
Snack Bar:	■	Boating:	■

COURSE DESCRIPTION

Meadow Oaks Golf & Country Club is the type of forgiving course every new player should play in the beginning stages of their development.

Most of the holes are straightforward without any surprises. If you can get your iron play off to a good start and keep it gong throughout the game, you'll end up shooting a respectable score.

If you play golf in the mid-to-high 80's on courses rated above 70, this may be the first course that you'll shoot par or better on.

This scenic course features lots of trees and eight holes that play into water. The course is well-designed and fun to play.

DIRECTIONS

Take Hwy. 19 south until you get to Hwy. 52 and go east. The course will be ten miles further down.

QUAIL HOLLOW GOLF & COUNTRY CLUB
100 Pasco Rd., Zephyrhills, FL 34249 / (352) 973-0097

BASIC INFORMATION

Course Type: Semi-private
Year Built: 1964
Architect: N/A
Local Pro: Mike Moore

Course:N/A
Holes: 18 / Par 72

Back: 6,761 yds. Rating: 71.1 Slope: 122
Middle: 6,161 yds. Rating: 68.5 Slope: 117
Ladies: 5,521 yds. Rating: 71.2 Slope: 118

Tee Time: 3 days in advance
Price: $19 - $26

Credit Cards:	■	Restaurant:	■
Driving Range:	■	Lounge:	■
Practice Green:	■	Meeting Rooms:	■
Locker Room:	■	Tennis:	■
Rental Clubs:	■	Swimming:	■
Walkers:		Jogging Trails:	
Snack Bar:	■	Boating:	

COURSE DESCRIPTION

Quail Hollow Golf & Country Club is a perfect course for average golfers. The course features a nice layout with plenty of trees and seven holes that feature water.

With the out-of-bounds line playing on the left side of the front nine, players who tend to play a natural fade (left-to-right ball flight) will find this side easier. The back nine is the exact opposite with more trees coming into play.

The dogleg left number 7 hole is the hardest on the course. This par-4 hole measures 415 yards from tee to green. The challenge on this hole is having to hit the ball over trees and water. Good luck!

DIRECTIONS

Take I-75 exit 58. Go west on Hwy. 54 and North on Pasco Rd. for one mile.

SADDLEBROOK GOLF & TENNIS RESORT

5700 Saddlebrook Way, Wesley Chapel, FL 33543 / (352) 973-1111

BASIC INFORMATION

Course Type: Resort
Year Built: 1985
Architect: A. Palmer
Local Pro: Neal Postlethwait

Course: Palmer / Saddlebrook (18 / Par 71)
Holes: 36

Back: 6,469 yds. Rating: 71.0 Slope: 126
Middle: 6,044 yds. Rating: 69.0 Slope: 122
Ladies: 5,212 yds. Rating: 70.2 Slope: 121

Tee Time: 2 days in advance
Price: $35 - $95

Credit Cards:	■	Restaurant:	■
Driving Range:	■	Lounge:	■
Practice Green:	■	Meeting Rooms:	■
Locker Room:		Tennis:	■
Rental Clubs:	■	Swimming:	■
Walkers:		Jogging Trails:	■
Snack Bar:	■	Boating:	

COURSE DESCRIPTION

Saddlebrook Golf & Tennis Resort is a finely crafted golf course with many beautiful, challenging holes.

If your attraction happens to be for links-type golf, you'll undoubtedly want to play here for a good 36 holes. This beautiful Arnold Palmer- designed course features all of the elements that make for a fine links course: rolling hills, big mounds, heavy bunkering and, most importantly, small greens.

The open architecture of a links course lends itself naturally to the forces of the wind. Playing in these types of conditions can often become difficult because of the winds' unpredictability.

DIRECTIONS

Take 1-75 north to exit 58 (St. Rd. 54). Go one mile east - the course will be on your right.

SEVEN SPRINGS GOLF & COUNTRY CLUB

7000 Country Club Blvd., Seven Springs, FL 33553 / (352) 376-0035

BASIC INFORMATION

Course Type: Semi-private
Year Built: 1971
Architect: R. Garl
Local Pro: Steve Purviance

Course:Champion (18 / Par 72)
Holes: 36

Back: 6,566 yds. Rating: 71.1 Slope: 123
Middle: 6,120 yds. Rating: 69.2 Slope: 120
Ladies: 5,250 yds. Rating: 70.4 Slope: 112

Tee Time: 2 days in advance
Price: $31 - $45

Credit Cards:	■	Restaurant:	■
Driving Range:	■	Lounge:	■
Practice Green:	■	Meeting Rooms:	■
Locker Room:	■	Tennis:	
Rental Clubs:	■	Swimming:	
Walkers:		Jogging Trails:	
Snack Bar:	■	Boating:	

COURSE DESCRIPTION

A heavy amount of weight is placed on both your accuracy and distance off the tee. Huge Cypress trees fill the course in their natural splendor only to be outdone by the presence of water on every hole. Most of the fairways slope to water over low rough. If this description frightens you, play from the white tees! The average golfer will find the course much more calm and fun from this point.

The 14th hole (par-3 / 192 yards) is the hardest hole on the course. From the elevated tee, you'll be facing a creek on your left. Your approach shot will be to a small green with a big bunker on the front-right.

DIRECTIONS

Take I-75 north to St. Rd. 54. Head west for 21 miles. Course will be on your right.

SILVER OAKS GOLF & COUNTRY CLUB

33841 Clubhouse Dr., Zephyrhills, FL 33541 / (352) 788-1225

BASIC INFORMATION

Course Type: Public
Year Built: 1987
Architect: R. Simmons
Local Pro: Joseph Alfieri

Course: N/A
Holes: 18 / Par 72

Back: 6,609yds. Rating: 71.1 Slope: 120
Middle: 6,105 yds. Rating: 68.6 Slope: 116
Ladies: 5,147 yds. Rating: 68.8 Slope: 109

Tee Time: 7 days in advance
Price: $12 - $29

Credit Cards:	■	Restaurant:	■
Driving Range:	■	Lounge:	■
Practice Green:	■	Meeting Rooms:	
Locker Room:		Tennis:	
Rental Clubs:	■	Swimming:	
Walkers:		Jogging Trails:	
Snack Bar:	■	Boating:	

COURSE DESCRIPTION

Silver Oaks Golf & Country Club is a very playable course for many different types of players. The front nine will gently warm you up with its big fairways. The generous size of the fairways allows you to get the most wood from your driver. If you're going to experiment with your swing, do it on the front nine. You'll find the back nine a much more demanding architectural layout. The fairways are tighter and the course is played through big shaded oak trees.

This is a wonderful course at an affordable price.

DIRECTIONS

Take 1-275 to Bears Ave. exit. Go east to Bruce B. Downs Blvd. and the course will be five-and- a-half miles on your right.

SUNDANCE GOLF & COUNTRY CLUB

4600 Hwy 301 South, Zephyrhills, FL 33525 / (352) 567-7600

BASIC INFORMATION

Course Type: Public
Year Built: 1988
Architect: W. Rinaldo
Local Pro: William Rinaldo

Course:N/A
Holes: 18 / Par 72

Back: 6,611 yds. Rating: 70.9 Slope: 118
Middle: 5,897 yds. Rating: 68.0 Slope: 112
Ladies: 4,855 yds. Rating: 69.8 Slope: 111

Tee Time: 2 days in advance
Price: $10 - $25

Credit Cards:	■	Restaurant:	
Driving Range:		Lounge:	■
Practice Green:	■	Meeting Rooms:	■
Locker Room:		Tennis:	
Rental Clubs:	■	Swimming:	
Walkers:		Jogging Trails:	
Snack Bar:	■	Boating:	■

COURSE DESCRIPTION

The *Sundance Golf & Country Club* is a hilly links-styled course with many undulating greens. It is the type of course that allows you to take chances for high rewards. If you can keep your ball on the fairway off the tee, you'll often find yourself in good position to score par or better throughout the day.

The course is unpredictable at times, especially when the wind comes into play. Learn to keep your ball sailing on a low trajectory. That is the weapon of choice for the best golfers in the world whenever they play a links-styled course.

You'll find a good combination of hole designs that are both challenging and fun to play.

DIRECTIONS

Take Hwy. 301 south of Dade City and then go east on Wire Road .

TOWN & COUNTRY RV & GOLF CLUB
3005 N. Hwy. 301, Dade City, FL 33525 / (352) 567-6622

BASIC INFORMATION

Course Type: Pulic
Year Built: 1986
Architect: Jerry Marcum
Local Pro: Ray Smith

Course: A & C (18 / Par 71)
Holes: 27

Back: 5,575 yds. Rating: 67.3 Slope: 113
Middle: 5,263 yds. Rating: 66.5 Slope: 113
Ladies: 4,910 yds. Rating: 68.2 Slope: 113

Tee Time: 2 days in advance
Price: $8.50 - $10

Credit Cards:	Restaurant:
Driving Range: ■	Lounge:
Practice Green: ■	Meeting Rooms:
Locker Room:	Tennis:
Rental Clubs: ■	Swimming: ■
Walkers: ■	Jogging Trails:
Snack Bar: ■	Boating: ■

COURSE DESCRIPTION

Town & Country RV & Golf Club is an easy layout designed solely for the purpose of fun. You shouldn't have much trouble winding your way around this course.

The price is right and the course is forgiving. You'll be playing through many scenic holes that feature a great variety of wildlife. The course gets hilly at times and that's when it posts the greatest challenge of all.

You need the ability to hit the ball below and above your feet to score well. Some of the holes feature beautiful oak trees just waiting to deflect your drives. You'll find water coming into play on six holes.

DIRECTIONS
Take Hwy. 301 north of Dade City and the course will be on your left.

ZEPHYRHILLS GOLF & COUNTRY CLUB
39248 B Ave., Zephyrhills, FL 33540 / (352) 782-0714

BASIC INFORMATION

Course Type: Public
Year Built: N/A
Architect: N/A
Local Pro: N/A

Course:N/A
Holes: 18 / Par 68

Back: N/A yds. Rating: N/A Slope: N/A
Middle: N/A yds. Rating: N/A Slope: N/A
Ladies: N/A yds. Rating: N/A Slope: N/A

Tee Time: 7 days in advance
Price: $12 all year long.

Credit Cards:	Restaurant:
Driving Range:	Lounge: ■
Practice Green: ■	Meeting Rooms: ■
Locker Room: ■	Tennis:
Rental Clubs: ■	Swimming:
Walkers: ■	Jogging Trails:
Snack Bar: ■	Boating:

COURSE DESCRIPTION

Zephyrhills Golf & Country Club is an open-structured golf course that lends itself to low scores by the nature of its short distance. You'll find many trees that hide and shade the natural wildlife that is abundant around the course. The course is open for many pars and birdies. You can attack many of the holes aggressively. If by chance your shot is not what you had envisaged, the course is set up to at least give you a chance at a one-putt par.

If you enjoy a less demanding layout with many opportunities for low scores, this course will certainly treat you right. If you're an above average player think of this course as a possible par-59.

DIRECTIONS
Take I-75 south to Hwy. 54. Go south on 20th and east on South Ave. The course will be on your right.

AIRCO GOLF COURSE

3650 Roosevelt Blvd., Clearwater, FL 34622 / (352) 573-4653

BASIC INFORMATION

Course Type: Public
Year Built: 1961
Architect: C. Adams
Local Pro: N/A

Course: N/A
Holes: 18 / Par 72

Back: 6,635 yds. Rating: 70.1 Slope: 114
Middle: 6,088 yds. Rating: 67.6 Slope: 109
Ladies: 4,773 yds. Rating: 61.6 Slope: 97

Tee Time: 6 days in advance
Price: $20 - $33

Credit Cards:	■	Restaurant:	■
Driving Range:	■	Lounge:	■
Practice Green:	■	Meeting Rooms:	■
Locker Room:		Tennis:	
Rental Clubs:	■	Swimming:	
Walkers:	■	Jogging Trails:	
Snack Bar:	■	Boating:	

COURSE DESCRIPTION

Airco Golf Course is a simple course attuned to high handicap golfers.

If you haven't played a round of golf in the last six months and you're seriously thinking about getting back to it, use this course as a warm-up session until you finally get your game back. A good round of golf is always memorable, no matter how hard a particular course may be, and serves well as an ego booster for courses to come.

The 17th hole (par-3 / 225 yards) plays the toughest on the course. On one of those rare but brutal occasions, you'll find the pin hidden behind both a tree and a large-mouth bunker just waiting to apprehend your ball in flight.

DIRECTIONS

Take Hwy. 19 to Hwy. 688 (Ulmerton Rd.) and go east. The course is adjacent to the St. Pete-Clearwater Airport.

BARDMOOR NORTH COURSE

7919 Bardmoor Blvd., Largo, FL 34647 / (352) 397-0483

BASIC INFORMATION

Course Type: Public
Year Built: N/A
Architect: N/A
Local Pro: Tom West

Course:N/A
Holes: 18 / Par 68

Back: 6,960 yds. Rating: N/A Slope: N/A
Middle: 6,484 yds. Rating: N/A Slope: N/A
Ladies: 5,569 yds. Rating: N/A Slope: N/A

Tee Time: 4 days in advance
Price: $25 - $55

Credit Cards:	■	Restaurant:	■
Driving Range:	■	Lounge:	■
Practice Green:	■	Meeting Rooms:	
Locker Room:		Tennis:	■
Rental Clubs:	■	Swimming:	■
Walkers:		Jogging Trails:	
Snack Bar:	■	Boating:	

COURSE DESCRIPTION

The Bardmoor North Course is a challenging course for all golfers. The back tees are long and the middle tees are just perfect for a 10-15 handicapper.

The course features a new clubhouse and restaurant, a new practice range, daily clinics, and much more.

You'll find ten holes with water that come into play. The 6th hole (par-5 /545 yards) is the most challenging hole on the course. Water comes into play on the right and trees line up both sides of the fairway.

This is really a well-kept course that is fun to play. The course hosts many Tournaments that allow outside play. Please call to verify.

DIRECTIONS

Take I-275 south to SR 688 and go west to Starkey Rd. Go south to Bardmoor and look for the course on your right.

BELLEVIEW MIDO COUNTRY CLUB
1501 Indian Rocks Rd., Clearwater, FL 34616 / (352) 581-5498

BASIC INFORMATION

Course Type: Semi-private
Year Built: 1925
Architect: D. Ross
Local Pro: Neil Richards

Course: N/A
Holes: 18 / Par 72

Back:　6,550 yds. Rating: 70.7　Slope: 118
Middle: 6,221 yds. Rating: 61.1　Slope: 115
Ladies: 5,001 yds. Rating: 72.1　Slope: 119

Tee Time: 1 day in advance
Price: $25 - $55

Credit Cards:	■	Restaurant:	■
Driving Range:	■	Lounge:	■
Practice Green:	■	Meeting Rooms:	
Locker Room:	■	Tennis:	
Rental Clubs:	■	Swimming:	
Walkers:	■	Jogging Trails:	
Snack Bar:	■	Boating:	

COURSE DESCRIPTION

Belleview Mido Country Club is a thoughtfully planned golf course with many challenging holes that can be played from various angles. The great Donald Ross put his signature on this course in 1925. His architectural genius is still admired and studied to this very day. Ross had a gift for building holes with options that would allow both the scratch player and the average player separate routes to the pin. The first would be the harder route with maximum rewards (birdie or eagle) and the easier second would play to a par or bogey.

Each one of his courses is unique in style and form. You won't be disappointed.

DIRECTIONS
Take East Bay Dr. west to Indian Rocks Rd. Go north and the course will be two miles further on your right.

CLEARWATER COUNTRY CLUB
525 N. Betty Lane., Clearwater, FL 34615 / (352) 443-5078

BASIC INFORMATION

Course Type: Semi-private
Year Built: 1920 / 1930
Architect: D. Ross redesign (1930's)
Local Pro: Greg McClimans

Course:N/A
Holes: 18 / Par 72

Back:　6,300　yds. Rating: 69.5 Slope: 125
Middle: 6,000　yds. Rating: 68.0 Slope: 120
Ladies: 5,500　yds. Rating: 67.5 Slope: 118

Tee Time: 2 days in advance
Price: $22 -$30

Credit Cards:	■	Restaurant:	■
Driving Range:	■	Lounge:	■
Practice Green:	■	Meeting Rooms:	■
Locker Room:	■	Tennis:	
Rental Clubs:	■	Swimming:	
Walkers:	■	Jogging Trails:	
Snack Bar:	■	Boating:	

COURSE DESCRIPTION

Clearwater Country Club is another Florida jewel designed by Donald Ross. You'll find an abundance of opportunities for birdies and pars if you can hit your approach shots high and soft to the greens.

Most of the greens do have openings in the middle front for a bump-and-run type of shot. The number 2 hole is the hardest hole on the course. It is a par-3 that plays 210 yards in length. You'll be playing into an elevated green that is both undulating and well-bunkered.

This course stands as another historical link to the many Donald Ross courses throughout the State of Florida.

DIRECTIONS
Take Hwy. 19 south to Drew St. Go west to Clearwater Beach and follow the signs. The course will be on the north side.

COVE CAY COUNTRY CLUB
2612 Cove Cay Dr., Clearwater, FL 34624 / (352) 788-1225

BASIC INFORMATION

Course Type: Semi-private
Year Built: 1975
Architect: N/A
Local Pro: Steve Bagely

Course: N/A
Holes: 18 / Par 70

Back: 5,985 yds. Rating: 66.8 Slope: 118
Middle: 5,693 yds. Rating: 66.0 Slope: N/A
Ladies: 5,322 yds. Rating: 67.6 Slope: N/A

Tee Time: 2 days in advance
Price: $22.50 between May 1 - Oct. 31

Credit Cards:		Restaurant:	■
Driving Range:	■	Lounge:	■
Practice Green:	■	Meeting Rooms:	■
Locker Room:	■	Tennis:	
Rental Clubs:	■	Swimming:	■
Walkers:		Jogging Trails:	
Snack Bar:	■	Boating:	■

COURSE DESCRIPTION

This course has a tremendous amount of character. It gets more and more interesting as you play it. The front nine plays straight and tight and favors accuracy over length, but on the opposite end the very scenic back nine is more relaxing and forgiving.

At only 5,985 yards from the back tees, you'll want to hit your 3-wood for accuracy and dependability.

On almost every hole, a well-placed tee shot will set you up for a birdie opportunity.

The 10th hole (par-4 /425 yards) is the hardest on the course. You'll be hitting your tee shot onto a narrow fairway with water on the left, sand on the right, and trees on both sides of the fairway.

DIRECTIONS

Take Hwy. 19 one mile north of east Bay Dr.

CRESCENT OAKS COUNTRY CLUB
3300 Cresent Oaks Blvd., Tarpon Springs, FL 34689 / (352) 942-6182

BASIC INFORMATION

Course Type: Semi-private
Year Built: 1990
Architect: S. Smyers / J. Colbert
Local Pro: Steve Leslie

Course:N/A
Holes: 18 / Par 72

Back: 6,882 yds. Rating: 73.4 Slope: 133
Middle: 6,420 yds. Rating: N/A   Slope: N/A
Ladies: 5,204 yds. Rating: 70.4 Slope: 120

Tee Time: 2 days in advance
Price: $25 -$35

Credit Cards:	■	Restaurant:	■
Driving Range:	■	Lounge:	■
Practice Green:	■	Meeting Rooms:	
Locker Room:	■	Tennis:	■
Rental Clubs:	■	Swimming:	■
Walkers:		Jogging Trails:	
Snack Bar:	■	Boating:	■

COURSE DESCRIPTION

Crescent Oaks Country Club plays long and demanding. You'll have to "stripe" your tee shots right down the middle of the pencil width fairways to post a good score. Smyers and Colbert (the course architects) must have had an affinity for bunkers: they're everywhere!

The 133 slope rating from the back tees is a good indication of how severe this course plays. If your average game score is above 80, play the course from the white tees and leave your ego at home. The 18th (par-4 / 470 yards) plays tough with water on the left from tee to green. Your approach shot will be to a well- bunkered small green.

DIRECTIONS

Take Hwy. 19 north to Tarpon Ave. Go east to Lake Rd. and make a left. The course will be half a mile further on your right.

DUNEDIN COUNTRY CLUB
1050 Palm Blvd., Dunedin, FL 34698 / (352) 733-7836

BASIC INFORMATION

Course Type: Semi-private
Year Built: 1926
Architect: D. Ross
Local Pro: Van Tanner

Course: N/A
Holes: 18 / Par 72

Back: 6,565 yds. Rating: 71.5 Slope: 125
Middle: 6,245 yds. Rating: 69.9 Slope: 121
Ladies: 5,726 yds. Rating: 66.6 Slope: 115

Tee Time: 2 days in advance
Price: $31 - $38

Credit Cards:		Restaurant:	■
Driving Range:	■	Lounge:	■
Practice Green:	■	Meeting Rooms:	■
Locker Room:	■	Tennis:	
Rental Clubs:	■	Swimming:	
Walkers:	■	Jogging Trails:	
Snack Bar:	■	Boating:	

COURSE DESCRIPTION

Dunedin Country Club is a fine example of a classic course with all of the right elements falling in place with effortless ease.

Once again, Donald Ross's signature shines through on every hole. Opportunities are open for both the scratch player and beginner. Donald had a keen sense for making his golf courses fun to play, regardless of individual abilities.

The 2nd hole (par-4 /439 yards) is the hardest hole on the course. It is a dogleg left that plays uphill from the tee onto an average size fairway. Your approach shot will be to a small green with a big oak tree coming into play on the left side.

DIRECTIONS

Take Hwy. 19 west on Curlew Rd. Go south on Alt. 19 to Palm Blvd. and make a left. Look for the course on your left.

EAST BAY GOLF CLUB
702 Country Club Dr., Largo, FL 34641 / (352) 581-3333

BASIC INFORMATION

Course Type: Semi-private
Year Built: 1961
Architect: N/A
Local Pro: Ken Bladen

Course: N/A
Holes: 18 / Par 72

Back: 6,755 yds. Rating: 72.2 Slope: 119
Middle: 6,272 yds. Rating: 70.0 Slope: 115
Ladies: 5,445 yds. Rating: 71.5 Slope: 112

Tee Time: 2 days in advance
Price: $20 - $28

Credit Cards:	■	Restaurant:	■
Driving Range:	■	Lounge:	■
Practice Green:	■	Meeting Rooms:	■
Locker Room:	■	Tennis:	
Rental Clubs:	■	Swimming:	
Walkers:		Jogging Trails:	
Snack Bar:	■	Boating:	■

COURSE DESCRIPTION

East Bay Golf Club plays fair and true. Although the course plays long from the back tees (6,755 yards) the course rating and slope is on the friendly side, indicating that the course leaves many opportunities for low numbers.

The fairways are of average size, leaving a good amount of room for your tee shots to land on. If you're not careful, the course will slap you across the face. You really do have to pay attention to the landscape. Bunkers are plenty and at times severe. The rough, when left on the high side, makes this course play hard and demanding. Accuracy prevails over distance.

DIRECTIONS

Take 1-75 south to the Howard Franklin Bridge and Exit Hwy. 686 (East Bay Dr.) going west. The course will be on your left.

INNISBROOK RESORT & GOLF COURSE

P.O. Drawer 1088, Tarpon Springs, FL 34688 / (352) 942-2000

BASIC INFORMATION

Course Type: Resort
Year Built: 1970
Architect: L. Packard
Local Pro: Jay Oberton

Course: Copperhead (18 / Par 71)
Holes: 63

Back: 7,087 yds. Rating: 74.4 Slope: 140
Middle: 6,536 yds. Rating: 71.9 Slope: 132
Ladies: 5,506 yds. Rating: 72.0 Slope: 128

Tee Time: 1 day in advance
Price: $75 - $140

Credit Cards:	■	Restaurant:	■
Driving Range:	■	Lounge:	■
Practice Green:	■	Meeting Rooms:	■
Locker Room:	■	Tennis:	■
Rental Clubs:	■	Swimming:	■
Walkers:		Jogging Trails:	■
Snack Bar:	■	Boating:	■

COURSE DESCRIPTION

Innisbrook Resort & Golf Course is worth every penny of play. Each one of the 63 holes is lushly landscaped and well cared for. Golfweek magazine has rated *Innisbrook* their number one Florida course for the past seven years. The J.C. Penney Mixed Team Classic is played here every year. This tournament pairs an LPGA player with a PGA player in team competition.

The Copperhead course is an incredible trip around rolling terrain and tall pine trees. The 14th hole is the signature hole on this course. You'll be teeing off from the infamous flowerbed platform onto an uphill fairway leading to a small well-contoured green.

DIRECTIONS

Take US 19 north and continue five miles north of Clearwater. Follow signs.

LANSBROOK GOLF CLUB

2500 Village Center Dr., Palm Harbor, FL 34685 / (352) 785-7501

BASIC INFORMATION

Course Type: Semi-private
Year Built: 1975
Architect: R. Garl
Local Pro: Greg Gagliardi

Course: N/A
Holes: 18 / Par 72

Back: 6,630 yds. Rating: 71.6 Slope: 126
Middle: 6,018 yds. Rating: 68.4 Slope: 118
Ladies: 5,180 yds. Rating: 69.3 Slope: 119

Tee Time: 4 days in advance
Price: $18 - $40

Credit Cards:	■	Restaurant:	■
Driving Range:	■	Lounge:	■
Practice Green:	■	Meeting Rooms:	■
Locker Room:	■	Tennis:	
Rental Clubs:	■	Swimming:	■
Walkers:	■	Jogging Trails:	■
Snack Bar:	■	Boating:	■

COURSE DESCRIPTION

Lansbrook Golf Club is a special golfing experience. The course features tight fairways with many bunkers and lakes. Water comes into play on 15 holes.

If you're like the majority of golfers, you've probably dreamt about playing in the Masters at Augusta National (Georgia) at least once. The 11th hole green on this course is a replica of the notorious number 16th at Augusta. It's a par-3 that measures 186 yards from the back tees.

The 4th hole (Par-4 /365 yards) is the number 1 handicap hole on the course. You'll find the fairway narrow and tight leading to the small undulating green.

DIRECTIONS

Take Hwy. 19 north on Tampa Rd. Go left at east Lake Rd. North three miles to Village Center Drive. Course will be on your right.

MANGROVE BAY GOLF COURSE

3875 N.E. 62nd Ave., St. Petersburg, FL 33702 / (352) 893-7797

BASIC INFORMATION

Course Type: Municipal
Year Built: 1978
Architect: B. Amick
Local Pro: Jeff Hollis

Course: N/A
Holes: 18 / Par 68

Back: 6,779 yds. Rating: 71.5 Slope: 120
Middle: 6,113 yds. Rating: 68.4 Slope: 113
Ladies: 5,172 yds. Rating: 68.5 Slope: 112

Tee Time: 7 days in advance
Price: $19 - $29

Credit Cards:	■	Restaurant:	■
Driving Range:	■	Lounge:	
Practice Green:	■	Meeting Rooms:	
Locker Room:	■	Tennis:	
Rental Clubs:	■	Swimming:	
Walkers:	■	Jogging Trails:	
Snack Bar:	■	Boating:	

COURSE DESCRIPTION

Mangrove Bay Golf Course is a great design that features open fairways and large greens. Although the course is set up for low scores, it will catch up to you sooner or later.

The dogleg left 12th hole is a great example of what I mean. It is a par-4 that measures 465 yards from tee to green.

The distance in itself would seem enough for most of us, but this hole takes the distance with added pressure. Most of the time the hole plays against the wind, making it harder and tougher to play. To add to the difficulty, your approach shot will have to be played over the water that comes into play in front of the green. Five holes feature water.

DIRECTIONS

Take Hwy. 19 south to 62nd Ave. and go east. Drive past 4th St. and the course will be a one mile further on your right.

SILVER DOLLAR GOLF & TRAP CLUB

17000 Patterson Rd., Odessa, FL 33556 / (352) 920-3884

BASIC INFORMATION

Course Type: Public
Year Built: 1985
Architect: D. Maddox
Local Pro: Bob Capobianco

Course: Gator / Panther (18 / Par 72)
Holes: 27

Back: 6,481yds. Rating: N/A Slope: 120
Middle: 6,055 yds. Rating: N/A Slope: N/A
Ladies: 5,080 yds. Rating: N/A Slope: N/A

Tee Time: 7 days in advance
Price: $15 - $30

Credit Cards:		Restaurant:	
Driving Range:	■	Lounge:	■
Practice Green:	■	Meeting Rooms:	
Locker Room:		Tennis:	
Rental Clubs:	■	Swimming:	
Walkers:	■	Jogging Trails:	
Snack Bar:	■	Boating:	

COURSE DESCRIPTION

The *Silver Dollar Golf & Trap Club* will please many golfers with 27 holes of golf to choose from.

You'll find many birdie opportunities on this course. The fairways are open, the rough is of average height, and bunkers mostly come into play around the greens.

Most of the greens are elevated and are in great shape. The people that I spoke to at the pro shop felt that the course is in the best shape that it has ever been.

If you enjoy a straight game of golf without much punishment from the course, you'll have a great time playing this one.

DIRECTIONS

Take Hwy. 19 south to Tarpon Ave. and go east to Patterson Rd. Go south on Patterson and the course will be two-and-a-half miles on your right.

TARPON SPRINGS GOLF CLUB

1310 S. Pinellas Ave., Tarpon Springs, FL 34689 / (352) 937-6906

BASIC INFORMATION

Course Type: Public
Year Built: 1961
Architect: C. Adams
Local Pro: N/A

Course: N/A
Holes: 18 / Par 72

Back: 6,099 yds. Rating: 68.9 Slope: 112
Middle: 5,819 yds. Rating: 71.5 Slope: 110
Ladies: 5,338 yds. Rating: N/A Slope: N/A

Tee Time: 2 days in advance
Price: $17 - $23

Credit Cards:	Restaurant:	■
Driving Range:	Lounge:	■
Practice Green: ■	Meeting Rooms:	
Locker Room:	Tennis:	
Rental Clubs: ■	Swimming:	
Walkers: ■	Jogging Trails:	
Snack Bar: ■	Boating:	

COURSE DESCRIPTION

Tarpon Springs Golf Club plays short and sweet. The overall design is sound with many interesting holes.

Most of the course has remained in its original form since the day that it was first built in 1908. That in itself should be enough to lure you into playing here. History has a special way of reminding us how quickly the game has changed in such a short time span.

You'll find interesting doglegs with subtle elevation changes throughout the course. Despite the short distance of every hole, you'll surely enjoy the fact that this course doesn't have a single house to be found around it! Water comes into play on three holes.

DIRECTIONS

Take Alt. Hwy. 19 and go one mile north of Klosterman. Look for the sign.

TARPON WOODS GOLF & COUNTRY CLUB

1100 Tarpon Woods Blvd. / Palm Harbor, FL. 34685 / (352) 784-7606

BASIC INFORMATION

Course Type: Semi-private
Year Built: 1974
Architect: N/A
Local Pro: Scott Swangl

Course: N/A
Holes: 18 / Par 72

Back: 6,692 yds. Rating: 71.2 Slope: 128
Middle: 6,265 yds. Rating: 69.1 Slope: 120
Ladies: 5,406 yds. Rating: 65.5 Slope: 115

Tee Time: 2 days in advance
Price: $15 - $40

Credit Cards: ■	Restaurant:	■
Driving Range: ■	Lounge:	■
Practice Green: ■	Meeting Rooms:	
Locker Room:	Tennis:	■
Rental Clubs: ■	Swimming:	■
Walkers: ■	Jogging Trails:	
Snack Bar: ■	Boating:	■

COURSE DESCRIPTION

Tarpon Woods Golf & Country Club is a challenging course that winds through tall pines and flowing water.

It's a fun course loaded with options!

In my opinion, this is how every course should be constructed. If you can hit your drive 270 yards over fairway water and then follow up with an eight iron approach shot, bravo! I'll hit mine 255 yards and play my approach shot with a 7-iron.

I like having the option of choosing when to be aggressive rather than having to be aggressive without choice. This course will challenge your ability to manage your game at all times. You don't have to be long, but you do have to be accurate.

DIRECTIONS

Take Hwy. 275 south to Hillsborough Ave. Go west to east Lake Rd. Make a right at Tarpon Woods Blvd. and follow the signs.

TIDES COUNTRY CLUB

11832 66th Ave., Seminole, FL 34642 / (352) 393-8483

BASIC INFORMATION

Course Type: Semi-private
Year Built: 1973
Architect: N/A
Local Pro: Gallen Hearth

Course:N/A
Holes: 18 / Par 72

Back: 6,329 yds. Rating: 70.5 Slope: 118
Middle: 6,013 yds. Rating: 69.0 Slope: 114
Ladies: 5,698 yds. Rating: 72.5 Slope: 120

Tee Time: 3 days in advance
Price: $25 - $31

Credit Cards:	■	Restaurant:	■
Driving Range:		Lounge:	■
Practice Green:	■	Meeting Rooms:	
Locker Room:	■	Tennis:	
Rental Clubs:	■	Swimming:	
Walkers:	■	Jogging Trails:	
Snack Bar:	■	Boating:	

COURSE DESCRIPTION

The *Tides Country Club* is a straight-forward course that is fun to play.

The front nine is the easiest half of the course. Play for the pins and get your birdies quickly. The back nine is much harder and more demanding!

A good example is the 13th hole. This dogleg right /par-4 measures 415 yards from tee to green. You'll be hitting your tee shot from a shoot onto a narrow fairway with trees coming into play both left and right. You'll have to follow your drive with a soft landing fade to get into good position on the green. The game here is fun and pleasurable.

DIRECTIONS

Take Hwy. 19 South to Park Blvd. Go west to 113th Ave. and south to 66th Ave. The course will be on your left.

BOBBY JONES GOLF CLUB

1000 Azinger Way, Sarasota, FL 34232 / (352) 955-8097

BASIC INFORMATION

Course Type: Municipal
Year Built: 1926
Architect: D. Ross
Local Pro: N/A

Course: British (18 / Par 72)
Holes: 45

Back: 6,468 yds. Rating: 70.0 Slope: 111
Middle: 6,284 yds. Rating: 69.2 Slope: 110
Ladies: 5,695 yds. Rating: 72.3 Slope: 116

Tee Time: 3 days in advance
Price: $16 - $24

Credit Cards:	■	Restaurant:	■
Driving Range:	■	Lounge:	■
Practice Green:	■	Meeting Rooms:	■
Locker Room:		Tennis:	■
Rental Clubs:	■	Swimming:	
Walkers:	■	Jogging Trails:	
Snack Bar:	■	Boating:	■

COURSE DESCRIPTION

If you haven't had the pleasure of playing a traditional Scottish-type links course, the *Bobby Jones Golf Course* should be on your "must" list for the New Year (Bobby Jones personally opened the course on Feb. 26th, 1927).

The natural terrain of the land is of great importance to the overall design. If the winds rise from the surface, the course can get quite uncomfortable fore those golfers without the ability to hit a low boring shot beneath gushing winds.

You'll love the variety of golf that this establishment has to offer.

DIRECTIONS

Take I-75 north to Hwy. 44.On Country Rd. 486 you'll have to go south and the course will be on your right.

CALUSA LAKES GOLF CLUB

1195 Calusa Lakes Blvd., Nakomis, FL 32630 / (352) 484-8995

BASIC INFORMATION

Course Type: Semi-private
Year Built: 1991
Architect: T. McAnlis
Local Pro: Jay Hosey

Course: N/A
Holes: 18 / Par 72

Back: 6,760 yds. Rating: 72.4 Slope: 124
Middle: 6,176 yds. Rating: 69.5 Slope: 118
Ladies: 5,969 yds. Rating: 68.4 Slope: 115

Tee Time: 2 days in advance
Price: $20 - $33

Credit Cards:	■	Restaurant:	■
Driving Range:	■	Lounge:	■
Practice Green:	■	Meeting Rooms:	
Locker Room:		Tennis:	■
Rental Clubs:	■	Swimming:	
Walkers:	■	Jogging Trails:	
Snack Bar:	■	Boating:	■

COURSE DESCRIPTION

If you enjoy walking through nature preserves and watching beautiful Florida wildlife all around you, you'll undoubtedly love playing golf at *Calusa Lakes Golf Club*.

Lush landscaping can be found throughout in a complementary fashion to its natural surroundings. The few homes that can be spotted on the course are all set back enough to retain the "North Carolina" appeal of this course.

The course is challenging and fun to play.

DIRECTIONS

Take I-75 to Exit 36 (Hwy 68) and go west to Hwy. 41. Go south to Laurel Rd., east to Mission Valley Blvd., and east on Calusa Lakes Blvd.

CAPRI ISLE GOLF CLUB

849 Capri Isles Blvd., Venice, FL 34292 / (352) 485-3371

BASIC INFORMATION

Course Type: Semi-private
Year Built: 1972
Architect: A. Anderson
Local Pro: Gary Dennis

Course: N/A
Holes: 18 / Par 72

Back: 6,472 yds. Rating: 70.0 Slope: 123
Middle: 6,051 yds. Rating: 68.0 Slope: 119
Ladies: 5,480 yds. Rating: 69.8 Slope: 113

Tee Time: 3 days in advance
Price: $18 - $32

Credit Cards:	■	Restaurant:	■
Driving Range:	■	Lounge:	■
Practice Green:	■	Meeting Rooms:	
Locker Room:		Tennis:	
Rental Clubs:	■	Swimming:	
Walkers:	■	Jogging Trails:	
Snack Bar:	■	Boating:	■

COURSE DESCRIPTION

At only 6,472 yards from the back tees, you'll have an opportunity to feel the excitement that happens on the PGA Tour all week. If you're a 10-15 handicapper, this course will play into your hands if you can place your shots accurately.

Play the course to your advantage. There is no need to hit a ripping drive for a good approach setup. Take out your 3-wood for accuracy and pick a landing area that will give you the most advantageous shot to the green. Most of your approach shots will be played with highly-lofted clubs, making this course an excellent place to sharpen your short game. Water comes into play on thirteen holes.

DIRECTIONS

Take I-75 north to Hwy. 44. On Country Rd. 486 you'll have to go south and the course will be on your right.

COUNTRY CLUB AT JACARANDA WEST, THE

601 Jacaranda Blvd., Venice, FL 33595 / (352) 493-2664

BASIC INFORMATION

Course Type: Semi-private
Year Built: 1974
Architect: M. Mahannah
Local Pro: Rich Whalen

Course: N/A
Holes: 18 / Par 72

Back: 6,602 yds. Rating: 71.9 Slope: 126
Middle: 6,301 yds. Rating: 69.0 Slope: 120
Ladies: 5,321 yds. Rating: 70.7 Slope: 120

Tee Time: 2 days in advance
Price: $20 - $40

Credit Cards:	■	Restaurant:	■
Driving Range:	■	Lounge:	■
Practice Green:	■	Meeting Rooms:	■
Locker Room:	■	Tennis:	■
Rental Clubs:	■	Swimming:	
Walkers:		Jogging Trails:	
Snack Bar:	■	Boating:	■

COURSE DESCRIPTION

This course is the perfect test of golf for the above average golfer from the back tees. At 6,602 yards, the course is in a niche of its own. Somehow that yardage is neither short nor long. The course design moves beautifully from hole to hole. You'll find a good amount of dogleg holes mixed in a challenging manner.

The staff prides itself on keeping the course in top shape all year long. The rough is at its lowest during the winter and at its highest during the summer. The fairways are average width, with 84 bunkers strategically placed to swallow your ball. Water comes into play on eighteen holes. This is a very scenic course with wonderful wildlife.

DIRECTIONS

Take Hwy. 41 to Jacaranda Blvd. and go north for about one mile to the course.

FOREST LAKES COUNTRY CLUB

2401 Beneva Rd., Sarasota, FL 34232 / (352) 922-1312

BASIC INFORMATION

Course Type: Semi-private
Year Built: 1964
Architect: A. Anderson
Local Pro: Jay Nash

Course: N/A
Holes: 18 / Par 71

Back: 6,450 yds. Rating: 70.8 Slope: 124
Middle: 6,024 yds. Rating: 68.5 Slope: 119
Ladies: 5,445 yds. Rating: 71.3 Slope: 117

Tee Time: 3 days in advance
Price: $18 - $32

Credit Cards:	■	Restaurant:	■
Driving Range:	■	Lounge:	■
Practice Green:	■	Meeting Rooms:	■
Locker Room:	■	Tennis:	■
Rental Clubs:	■	Swimming:	■
Walkers:	■	Jogging Trails:	
Snack Bar:	■	Boating:	

COURSE DESCRIPTION

Forest Lakes Country Club features lushly landscaped holes beautifully attuned to their surroundings. The course does a wonderful job of filling the gap that can be found between different caliber players. The various tees will attest to that.

It's a shot players' course in every sense of the word. Every swing of the club has to be calculated in perfect rhythm.

The number 8 hole is unquestionably the hardest hole on the course. It is a par-4 hole that measures 463 yards from the tips. You'll have to hit a perfect drive to a landing area 250 yards out with trees both left and right of the fairway.

DIRECTIONS

Exit 39 off I-75 and go west to Beneva Rd. On Beneva Rd. go south to the course.

FOXFIRE GOLF CLUB
7200 Proctor Rd., Sarasota, FL 34232 / (352) 921-7757

BASIC INFORMATION

Course Type: Semi-private
Year Built: 1977
Architect: A. Anderson
Local Pro: George Ritch

Course: Palm / Oak (Par 72)
Holes: 27

Back: 6,280 yds. Rating: 71.1 Slope: 121
Middle: 5,903 yds. Rating: 69.4 Slope: 117
Ladies: 5,524 yds. Rating: 74.9 Slope: 117

Tee Time: 3 days in advance
Price: $25 - $35

Credit Cards:	■	Restaurant:	■
Driving Range:	■	Lounge:	■
Practice Green:	■	Meeting Rooms:	■
Locker Room:		Tennis:	
Rental Clubs:	■	Swimming:	
Walkers:	■	Jogging Trails:	
Snack Bar:	■	Boating:	■

COURSE DESCRIPTION

The tranquil forest setting of this course makes it easy to concentrate on your golf game and perform at your peak level. It is both aesthetically appealing and fun to play.

The course wraps around a beautiful forest that is naturally landscaped with exotic flowers, birds, and animals. If you love the look of Mother Nature in her most profound and dignified posture, this course will serve your needs well.

The 6th hole (Par 4 /372 yards) on the Oaks course is one of the most exciting. You have to drive your ball onto a narrow fairway and follow that with an approach shot across a trench ravine.

DIRECTIONS

Take I-75 to Exit 37 (Clark Rd.). Go east to Proctor Rd. and north to the club. It will be on your left.

GOLF CLUB AT OAK FORD
1552 Palm View Rd., Sarasota, FL 34240 / (352) 371-3680

BASIC INFORMATION

Course Type: Semi-private
Year Built: 1990
Architect: R. Garl
Local Pro: Marty Dickerson

Course: Myrtle / Palms (18 / Par 72)
Holes: 27

Back: 6,753 yds. Rating: 72.7 Slope: 131
Middle: 6,321 yds. Rating: 70.6 Slope: 126
Ladies: 5,051 yds. Rating: 69.0 Slope: 118

Tee Time: 4 days in advance
Price: $16 - $35

Credit Cards:	■	Restaurant:	■
Driving Range:	■	Lounge:	
Practice Green:	■	Meeting Rooms:	
Locker Room:		Tennis:	
Rental Clubs:	■	Swimming:	
Walkers:	■	Jogging Trails:	
Snack Bar:	■	Boating:	■

COURSE DESCRIPTION

This is yet another local attraction that is well worth the price of admission. I love the feeling that comes with playing golf in a natural forest without a house or condominium in sight. Nothing can beat the feeling of playing golf in an enclosed forest with only shimmering morning dew highlighting the course that you're about to play.

Playing golf at the *Golf Club at Oak Ford* is a special and wonderful experience. The wildlife is abundant and the golf is spectacular.

This is another fine accomplishment by golf course designer Ron Garl.

DIRECTIONS

Take I-75 to Exit 39 (Fruitville Rd.) and go east. The course will be about nine miles further. Follow the signs to the entrance.

LAKE VENICE GOLF CLUB
Harbor Drive South, Venice, FL 33595 / (352) 488-3948

BASIC INFORMATION

Course Type: Resort
Year Built: 1977
Architect: G. Wilson
Local Pro: Ed Causey

Course: N/A
Holes: 18 / Par 72

Back: 6,664 yds. Rating: 72.0 Slope: 129
Middle: 6,242 yds. Rating: 70.1 Slope: 125
Ladies: 5,501 yds. Rating: 71.3 Slope: 118

Tee Time: 2 days in advance
Price: $17 - $24

Credit Cards:	■	Restaurant:	■
Driving Range:	■	Lounge:	■
Practice Green:	■	Meeting Rooms:	■
Locker Room:	■	Tennis:	■
Rental Clubs:	■	Swimming:	■
Walkers:	■	Jogging Trails:	■
Snack Bar:	■	Boating:	■

COURSE DESCRIPTION

This is the type of course you won't mind playing at any time of the day, even between the hours of 10:00 am - 2:00 pm when the sun is at its hottest. The close proximity to the ocean welcomes the cool breezes that make their way around the course.

The 14th hole is an indication of what you will be up against. It's a par-4 that measures 447 yards from the back tees. From that point, you'll be hitting your drive to a generous size fairway with a large tree in the middle of it. Your approach will have to sail over water before landing on the green.

The wildlife here is spectacular. It's a beautiful place to enjoy some great golf.

DIRECTIONS

Take Hwy. 41 south past the Citrus Hills main entrance, proceed west on Country Club Blvd. to the course.

MYAKKA PINES GOLF CLUB
P.O. Box 126, Englewood, FL 34295 / (352) 474-3296

BASIC INFORMATION

Course Type: Semi-private
Year Built: 1976
Architect: L. Marshall
Local Pro: Frank Perilli

Course: Red / White (18 / Par 72)
Holes: 27

Back: 6,311 yds. Rating: 70.3 Slope: 127
Middle: 6,285 yds. Rating: 68.6 Slope: 122
Ladies: 5,538 yds. Rating: 71.7 Slope: 123

Tee Time: 2 days in advance
Price: $10 - $35

Credit Cards:		Restaurant:	■
Driving Range:	■	Lounge:	
Practice Green:	■	Meeting Rooms:	■
Locker Room:	■	Tennis:	
Rental Clubs:	■	Swimming:	
Walkers:	■	Jogging Trails:	
Snack Bar:	■	Boating:	■

COURSE DESCRIPTION

Myakka Pines Golf Club has a wonderful feel to it. The overall course design is well-planned for a surprisingly demanding test of golf. Many of the holes will challenge you to think about your next shot.

Having the ability to work the ball from a distance of about 150 yards will help you out tremendously. If you're a 20 handicapper and over, you'll often be chipping to the green for a 1 putt for par. Do yourself a favor and bring an alternate wedge.

Many of the holes feature 2-tier greens with many subtle undulations that can play games with your sight. Stay focused and concentrate on your line. The course won't disappoint you.

DIRECTIONS

Take Hwy. 41 to south River Rd., and look for the course on your right.

NORTH PORT COUNTRY CLUB
701 Greenwood Ave., North Port, FL 34287 / (352) 426-2804

BASIC INFORMATION

Course Type: Public
Year Built: 1971
Architect: C. Ankrum
Local Pro: Jim Kelly

Course: N/A
Holes: 18 / Par 72

Back: 6,681 yds. Rating: 70.9 Slope: 122
Middle: 6,250 yds. Rating: 68.8 Slope: 117
Ladies: 5,504 yds. Rating: 70.8 Slope: 119

Tee Time: 5 days in advance
Price: $22 - $38

Credit Cards: ■		Restaurant: ■
Driving Range: ■		Lounge: ■
Practice Green: ■		Meeting Rooms: ■
Locker Room: ■		Tennis:
Rental Clubs: ■		Swimming: ■
Walkers:		Jogging Trails:
Snack Bar: ■		Boating: ■

COURSE DESCRIPTION

The smart layout on this scenic course is exhilarating. It features wide open fairways and low rough. At first sight, the course leads you to believe that you can hit your drives as hard as possible with a minimum of punishment if you were to hit a bad one. Wrong!

With water coming into play on 14 holes, you'll have to play a smarter game of golf. From the back tees, the course only measures in at 6,681 yards. If you're a 10-15 handicapper, the distance shouldn't cause you much trouble. Bring out your 3-wood for accuracy and distance to set yourself up for your approach shot. If you're above a 15 handicapper, play from the middle tees.

DIRECTIONS

Take Hwy. 41 to North Port and go east on Sumpter Blvd. Look for the course sign.

PLANTATION GOLF & COUNTRY CLUB
500 Rockley Blvd., Venice, FL 34293 / (352) 493-2000

BASIC INFORMATION

Course Type: Semi-private
Year Built: 1987
Architect: R. Garl
Local Pro: Keith Struble

Course: Panther (18 / Par 72)
Holes: 36

Back: 6,307 yds. Rating: 71.6 Slope: 101
Middle: 5,910 yds. Rating: 68.9 Slope: 118
Ladies: 5,001 yds. Rating: 70.1 Slope: 122

Tee Time: 1 day in advance
Price: $24 yearly

Credit Cards: ■		Restaurant: ■
Driving Range: ■		Lounge: ■
Practice Green: ■		Meeting Rooms: ■
Locker Room: ■		Tennis: ■
Rental Clubs: ■		Swimming: ■
Walkers: ■		Jogging Trails: ■
Snack Bar: ■		Boating: ■

COURSE DESCRIPTION

This uniquely designed links course will make your golfing experience a pleasure. It isn't terribly hard, but it does bring about a good challenge in its undulating fairways. For those of you who have mostly played golf on level fairways, this course will be quite an education. Hitting the ball from either below or above your feet is a technique that takes many hours of practice.

The biggest challenge in playing golf on a links-styled course is the wind factor. If you have the ability to hit low boring shots that stay under the wind, you'll be very competitive on this course.

Water comes into play on 15 holes.

DIRECTIONS

Take Hwy. 41 south of Venice and look for the course four miles further on your left.

ROLLING GREEN GOLF CLUB
4501 N. Tuttle Ave., Sarasota, FL 34234 / (352) 355-6620

BASIC INFORMATION

Course Type: Public
Year Built: 1968
Architect: A. Anderson
Local Pro: Joe Mann

Course: N/A
Holes: 18 / par 72

Back: 6,495 yds. Rating: 70.3 Slope: 113
Middle: 6,441 yds. Rating: 68.3 Slope: 109
Ladies: 5,387 yds. Rating: 70.7 Slope: 113

Tee Time: 2 days in advance
Price: $20 - $30

Credit Cards: ■	Restaurant: ■
Driving Range: ■	Lounge: ■
Practice Green: ■	Meeting Rooms:
Locker Room: ■	Tennis:
Rental Clubs: ■	Swimming:
Walkers:	Jogging Trails:
Snack Bar: ■	Boating: ■

COURSE DESCRIPTION

This wonderfully designed course is kept in good condition all year long. It is a friendly course that demands a well-balanced game from all of its tees.

The staff is proud of the fact that the course is kept in excellent condition all year long. Like many other courses in Florida, this one has been built on the most challenging format of all: a flat area of land.

Joe Mann did an artful job of designing holes that test the nature of both the professional and the duffer. Your particular playing style can easily be catered to from one of the several tees. This is a most enjoyable course.

DIRECTIONS

On Hwy. 301 go east on Desota Rd. Go south to Tuttle and follow the signs to the course.

SARASOTA GOLF COURSE
7280 N. Leewyn Dr., Sarasota, FL 34240 / (352) 371-2431

BASIC INFORMATION

Course Type: Semi-private
Year Built: 1958
Architect: W. Treadway
Local Pro: David Tyree

Course: N/A
Holes: 18 / Par 72

Back: 7,080 yds. Rating: 73.5 Slope: 117
Middle: 6,231 yds. Rating: 79.4 Slope: 112
Ladies: 5,592 yds. Rating: 72.1 Slope: 116

Tee Time: 3 days in advance
Price: $18 - $28

Credit Cards: ■	Restaurant: ■
Driving Range: ■	Lounge:
Practice Green: ■	Meeting Rooms:
Locker Room: ■	Tennis:
Rental Clubs: ■	Swimming:
Walkers: ■	Jogging Trails:
Snack Bar: ■	Boating: ■

COURSE DESCRIPTION

The *Sarasota Golf Club* is a popular attraction among the many locals that play it. You would think that a course of this length (back tees: 7,080 yards) would post a much higher Rating and Slope.

Get ready for the time of your life. The fairways are large enough for a T-Rex to dash around in and the rough is cut at about average height. All this adds up to a grip and rip approach with your favorite driver.

Average players will find the course much more playable from the middle tees with 849 yards of real estate taken out of play. This may be the course to boost your golfing ego.

DIRECTIONS

Take I-75 to Exit 38 and go east on Bee Ridge Rd. to Sarasota Golf Club Blvd. Go north to the course and follow the signs.

SERENOA GOLF CLUB
6773 Serenoa Dr., Sarasota, FL 34241 / (352) 925-2755

BASIC INFORMATION

Course Type: Public
Year Built: 1990
Architect: M. Alden
Local Pro: Jim Owen

Course: N/A
Holes: 18 / Par 72

Back: 6,270 yds. Rating: 70.0 Slope: 120
Middle: 6,028 yds. Rating: 67.9 Slope: 114
Ladies: 5,201 yds. Rating: 64.5 Slope: 106

Tee Time: 3 days in advance
Price: $30 - $40

Credit Cards:		Restaurant:	■
Driving Range:	■	Lounge:	■
Practice Green:	■	Meeting Rooms:	
Locker Room:	■	Tennis:	■
Rental Clubs:	■	Swimming:	
Walkers:	■	Jogging Trails:	
Snack Bar:	■	Boating:	■

COURSE DESCRIPTION

Serenoa Golf Club has quickly become a local favorite for its thoughtful design. It isn't a long course by any means, but it is a wonderful challenge.

Oddly enough, the course is wide open off the tee. If you can hit your drives with dead- aim accuracy, go ahead; you'll gain a tremendous edge on your competitor. But if you're prone to hitting a bad fade or slice without warning, you'll have to think twice, because water comes into play on every single hole.

The challenge here is to keep your composure intact and not to be frightened by the many intimidating water view holes. It really is a wonderful course.

DIRECTIONS

Take I-75 to Exit 37 (Clark Rd.) and go east to Ibis and south to the course. Follow the signs to the course.

SUNRISE COUNTRY CLUB
5710 Draw Ln., Sarasota, FL 34238 / (352) 924-1402

BASIC INFORMATION

Course Type: Semi-private
Year Built: 1962
Architect: A. Anderson
Local Pro: Tom Zellers

Course: N/A
Holes: 18 / Par 72

Back: 6,529 yds. Rating: 70.6 Slope: 122
Middle: 6,100 yds. Rating: 69.0. Slope: 118
Ladies: 5,299 yds. Rating: 69.3 Slope: 117

Tee Time: 3 days in advance
Price: $13 - $34

Credit Cards:	■	Restaurant:	■
Driving Range:	■	Lounge:	■
Practice Green:	■	Meeting Rooms:	
Locker Room:	■	Tennis:	
Rental Clubs:	■	Swimming:	
Walkers:	■	Jogging Trails:	
Snack Bar:	■	Boating:	■

COURSE DESCRIPTION

Sunrise Country Club will challenge you from the tips of the 1st tee all the way down to the 18th hole. The course in not an overpowering design. Most of the 12 holes that feature water allow you several options to the hole. The course is set up in a friendly matter. You won't have to carry much water on your way to a par.

The greens are very well-kept and designed creatively to allow more than just one type of shot to their surface. You can choose to play your shots high and soft without much roll on contact, or play a bump-and-run approach to the front portion of the green and roll the ball to the hole. Donald Ross would have been proud of this one.

DIRECTIONS

Take I-75 to Exit 37 (Clark Rd.). On Clark go west and watch for the course.

TATUM RIDGE GOLF LINKS

421 N. Tatum Rd., Sarasota, FL 34240 / (352) 378-4211

BASIC INFORMATION

Course Type: Semi-private
Year Built: 1988
Architect: T. McAnlis
Local Pro: Bob Keller

Course: N/A
Holes: 18 / 72

Back: 6,657 yds. Rating: 71.9 Slope: 124
Middle: 6,190 yds. Rating: 69.2 Slope: 117
Ladies: 5,149 yds. Rating: 68.9 Slope: 114

Tee Time: 3 days in advance
Price: $12 - $32

Credit Cards:	■	Restaurant:	■
Driving Range:	■	Lounge:	■
Practice Green:	■	Meeting Rooms:	
Locker Room:		Tennis:	
Rental Clubs:	■	Swimming:	
Walkers:		Jogging Trails:	
Snack Bar:	■	Boating:	■

COURSE DESCRIPTION

The *Tatum Ridge Golf Links* is an extraordinary example of the richly engrossing trend that Sarasota County seems to pass along to the great variety of architects that have worked there. Somehow, through the magic of osmosis, the great majority of these architects have designed courses that blend beautifully with their natural surroundings in a meaningful, seamless, and perfect fashion.

This links styled course is no exception. It plays well to golfers of all abilities. Much excitement has been incorporated into the design of the course. With multiple tees to choose from, make sure you pick the tees that will offer you the most enjoyment for your particular game.

DIRECTIONS

Take I-75 to Exit 39 (Fruitville Rd.) and go east to the course.

WATERFORD GOLF CLUB

1454 Gleneagles Dr., Venice, FL 34292 / (352) 484-6621

BASIC INFORMATION

Course Type: Semi-private
Year Built: 1989
Architect: T. McAnlis
Local Pro: Jack McFaul

Course: N/A
Holes: 18 / Par 72

Back: 6,601 yds. Rating: 71.6 Slope: 124
Middle: 6,068 yds. Rating: 68.8 Slope: 118
Ladies: 5,242 yds. Rating: 69.7 Slope: 116

Tee Time: 2 days in advance
Price: $20 - $35

Credit Cards:	■	Restaurant:	■
Driving Range:	■	Lounge:	■
Practice Green:	■	Meeting Rooms:	
Locker Room:	■	Tennis:	
Rental Clubs:	■	Swimming:	
Walkers:	■	Jogging Trails:	
Snack Bar:	■	Boating:	■

COURSE DESCRIPTION

Waterford Golf Club is a viable challenge to all. Think of it as a U.S. Open course for the average-to-above-average golfer. With the fairways as narrow as they are, you'll need to think about which club to hit off the tee for the greatest of accuracy. Although the rough is kept low during season, you'll have to watch out for the many strategically placed bunkers that often come into play.

Combine the water with the undulating fairways and greens and you'll quickly come to the conclusion that this is a true shotmakers course: a challenging test demanding your very best.

DIRECTIONS

Go three miles west on Venice Ave. and make a right on Capri Isles Blvd.

182

CENTRAL WEST - THE PRIVATE COURSES

HILLSBOROUGH

Golden Lakes Golf Course
(352) 752-6010
478 Falcon Crest Rd., Plant City
Local Pro: N/A
Reciprocal Play: No

Palma Ceia Golf & Country Club
(352) 253-3061
1601 S. MacDill Ave., Tampa
Local Pro: Gill Gonsalvez
Reciprocal Play: No

Sun City Center Golf Courses
(352) 634-3377
1000 Kings Blvd., Sun City Center
Local Pro: Jack Hodgskin
Reciprocal Play: No

Tampa Palms Golf & Country Club
(352) 972-1991
5811 Tampa Plams Blvd., Tampa
Local Pro: Steve Rainney
Reciprocal Play: Yes

Temple Terrace Golf & Country Club
(352) 988-2601
200 Inverness Ave., Temple Terrace
Local Pro: Carl James
Reciprocal Play: No

TPC of Tampa Bay
(352) 949-0090
5100 Terrain DeGolf Dr., Lutz
Local Pro: Jerry Couzunse
Reciprocal Play: Yes

MANATEE

Bradenton Country Club
(352) 792-4159
4646 9th Ave. W., Bradenton
Local Pro: Jim Dargis
Reciprocal Play: Yes (Local)

El Conquistador Country Club
(352) 758-1464
4350 El Conquistador Pkwy, Bradenton
Local Pro: Mel Baranek
Reciprocal Play: Yes (Local)

Key Royale Club Inc.
(352) 778-3055
700 Key Royale Dr., Homes Beach
Local Pro: Al Chase
Reciprocal Play: No

River Isles Golf Course
(352) 746-8650
4300 Hwy. 64 E., Bradenton
Local Pro: N/A
Reciprocal Play: No

River Wilderness Yacht & Country Club
(352) 776-2602
1 Wilderness Blvd., Parrish
Local Pro: Jeff Wood
Reciprocal Play: Yes

Sarah Bay Country Club
(352) 355-6544
7011 Willow St., Sarasota
Local Pro: Steve Dietz
Reciprocal Play: Yes (Local)

PASCO

Beacon Woods Golf Course
(352) 868-9528
12507 Clocktower Pkwy., Bayonet Point
Local Pro: Alan Senior
Reciprocal Play: No

Silver Oaks Golf & Country Club
(352) 788-1225
36841 Clubhouse Dr., Zephyrhills
Local Pro: Joe Alfieri
Reciprocal Play: Yes

PASCO

Timber Oaks Golf Course
(352) 863-1072
8575 Ponderosa Ave., Port Richey
Local Pro: Butch White
Reciprocal Play: Yes

PINELLAS

Bayou Club, The
(352) 399-1000
8000 Bardmoor Blvd., Largo
Local Pro: N/A
Reciprocal Play: Yes

Belleaire Country Club, The
(352) 461-7171
1 Country Club Ln., Belleaire
Local Pro: Bill Conway
Reciprocal Play: Yes

Belleview Mido Country Club
(352) 581-5498
1501 Indian Rocks Rd., Belleaire
Local Pro: Neil Richards
Reciprocal Play: Yes

Countryside Country Club
(352) 796-1135
3001 Country SIde Blvd., Clearwater
Local Pro: Donald Prigmore
Reciprocal Play: Yes

Cypress Run Golf Club
(352) 938-3774
2669 St. Andrews Blvd., Tarpon Springs
Local Pro: Drew Johnston
Reciprocal Play: No

East Lake Woodlands Golf & C.C.
(352) 784-7270
301 Lake Woodlands Pkwy., Palm
Harbor
Local Pro: Tom Roener
Reciprocal Play: Yes

Fairway Village Golf Course
(352) 531-3524
1100 Belcher Rd., Largo
Local Pro: N/A
Reciprocal Play: No

Feather Sound Country Club
(352) 572-6677
2222 Feather Sound Dr., Clearwater
Local Pro: Paul Coe
Reciprocal Play: No

Highland Lakes Golf Course
(352) 785-9818
3300 Mc.Gregor Dr., Palm Harbor
Local Pro: N/A
Reciprocal Play: No

Isla Del Sol Yacht & Country Club
(352) 864-2417
6000 Sun Blvd., St. Petersburg
Local Pro: Fred Curtis
Reciprocal Play: Yes

On Top Of The World Golf Course
(352) 796-9773
2069 World Pkwy. Blvd., Clearwater
Local Pro: Don Tipton
Reciprocal Play: Yes

Seminole Lake Country Club
(352) 391-6255
6100 Augusta Blvd., Seminole
Local Pro: Bruce Chaleff
Reciprocal Play: No

Wentworth Golf Course
(352) 938-0692
2990 Wentworth Way, Tarpon Springs
Local Pro: Dave Stokeley
Reciprocal Play: No

SARASOTA

Bent Tree Country Club
(352) 371-8200
4700 Bent Tree Blvd., Sarasota
Local Pro: Bob Forgea
Reciprocal Play: Yes

Gator Creek Golf Course
(352) 924-1111
9000 Gator Creek Rd., Sarasota
Local Pro: Will be announced.
Reciprocal Play: No

Longboat Key Club
(352) 383-8821
301 Gulf of Mexico Dr., Longboat Key
Local Pro: Ed Causey
Reciprocal Play: No

Meadows Country Club, The
(352) 378-6000 (Ext. 242)
3101 Long Meadow, Sarasota
Local Pro: Glen Vito
Reciprocal Play: Yes

Mission Valley Country Club
(352) 488-7747
1851 Mission Valley Blvd., Laurel
Local Pro: Jim Duval
Reciprocal Play: Yes (Local)

Misty Creek Country Club
(352) 921-5258
8954 Misty Creek Dr., Sarasota
Local Pro: Steven Johnson
Reciprocal Play: Yes

Oaks Club, The
(352) 966-2191
650 Tamiami Trail, Osprey
Local Pro: Jimmy Wright
Reciprocal Play: Yes (Local)

Palm Air Country Club Sarasota
(800) 336-2108
5601 Country Way, Sarasota
Local Pro: Tom Malone
Reciprocal Play: Yes

TPC at Prestancia
(352) 922-7488
4409 TPC Blvd., Sarasota
Local Pro: Bob Radunz
Reciprocal Play: Yes

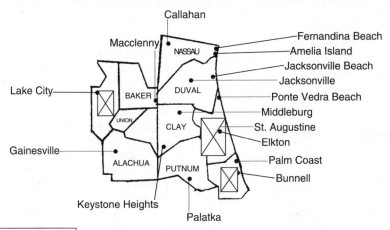

Gulf of Mexico

TOP TEN

Amelia Island Plantation
(Nassau County)

Matanzas Woods Golf C.
(Flager County)

Mill Cove Golf Course
(Duval County)

**Oaks Bridge Club at
Sawgr.**
(St. John's County)

Pine Lakes Country Club
(Flager County)

Pineview Golf & C. C.
(Baker County)

Ponce de Leon Resort
(St. John's County)

Ponte Vedra Inn & Club
(St John's County)

Ravines Golf & C.C.
(Columbia County)

St. John's County G.C.
(St. John's County)

The **Northeast** region has a style all its own.

From the moment you step onto the links at Amelia Island in Nassau County, you'll be taken aback by the natural beauty of the surroundings. Two of the games most notable architects, Tom Fazio and Pete Dye, have designed courses here. Their accomplishments are phenomenal.

If you're visiting Duval county, you'll want to play the Mills Cove Golf Course. This Arnold Palmer-designed layout has a wonderful mixture of holes that are fun and challenging for all types of players.

If you're searching for a course with a rich history, the Ponce de Leon Resort should fit the bill. This Donald Ross-designed course was completed in 1916. Another sensational historical golf course can be found at the Ponte Vedra Inn & Club. This Robert Trent Jones Sr.-designed course was built in 1927. It features a strategic layout with many exciting and challenging holes.

Whether you prefer strategic, penal, or heroic courses, this region will fulfill your greatest expectations.

Average Temperatures (Fahrenheit)

Between **January** and **March** you'll find the lowat **47** and the high up to **70**. Between **April** and **June** the low goes down to **64** and the high goes up to **86**. Between **July** and **September** the low goes down to **72** and the high goes up to **91**. And finally, between the months of **October** and **December**, the low goes down to **50** and the high goes up to **74**.

IRONWOOD GOLF CLUB

2100 N.E. 39th Ave., Gainesville, FL 32609 / (904) 334-3120

BASIC INFORMATION

Course Type: Public
Year Built: 1969
Architect: N/A
Local Pro: Bill Iwinski

Course: N/A
Holes: 18 / Par 72

Back: 6,465 yds. Rating: 71.3 Slope: 122
Middle: 6,088 yds. Rating: 70.4 Slope: 118
Ladies: 5,270 yds. Rating: 70.1 Slope: 115

Tee Time: 7 days in advance
Price: $9.54 - $12.72

Credit Cards:
Driving Range: ■   Restaurant:
Practice Green: ■   Lounge:
Locker Room: ■   Meeting Rooms:
Rental Clubs: ■   Tennis:
Walkers: ■   Swimming:
Snack Bar: ■   Jogging Trails:
                         Boating:

COURSE DESCRIPTION

Ironwood Golf Club is one of the most charismatic courses in Alachua county. If the famous French Impressionist painter Claude Monet (1840-1926) were alive today, he would undoubtedly take the time to paint one of the many beautiful scenes that a golfer will run into while playing this course.

The wildlife here ranges from graceful flying osprey birds, high jumping deer, to the slow-paced Florida Alligator!

The soothing nature of this course works in a therapeutic manner, allowing your mind to sink into your "playing zone."

DIRECTIONS

Take I-75 to Exit 77 and go east on Hwy. 222 (39th Ave.). Look for the course nine miles further down on your left.

MEADOWBROOK GOLF CLUB

10401 N.W. 37th Place, Gainesville, FL 32606 / (904) 332-0577

BASIC INFORMATION

Course Type: Semi-private
Year Built: 1987
Architect: S. Smyers
Local Pro: Ric Nolwd

Course: N/A
Holes: 18 / Par 72

Back: 6,306 yds. Rating: 69.9 Slope: 119
Middle: 5,594 yds. Rating: 66.5 Slope: 110
Ladies: 4,720 yds. Rating: 66.7 Slope: 117

Tee Time: 2 days in advance
Price: $17 - $20

Credit Cards: ■   Restaurant:
Driving Range: Lounge: ■
Practice Green: ■   Meeting Rooms:
Locker Room: ■   Tennis:
Rental Clubs: ■   Swimming:
Walkers: ■   Jogging Trails:
Snack Bar: ■   Boating:

COURSE DESCRIPTION

The **Meadowbrook Golf Club** is a well structured series of golf holes that wind around a compelling design. The rolling hills and undulating greens post a great challenge to the double-digit handicapper.

The 5th hole (Par-4 / 435 yards) is the one to be prepared for. You'll be hitting your drive onto a narrow fairway with a small defined area to land onto safely. If you have a good lie on your landing area, you'll be in prime position to play the tough approach shot to the small two-tiered green. A birdie opportunity is possible with a well-played soft-landing fade shot.

DIRECTIONS

Take I-75 to Exit 77 and go west for about one mile. Look for the course on your left side.

PINEVIEW GOLF & COUNTRY CLUB
P.O. Drawer 504, Macclenny, FL 32063 / (904) 259-3447

BASIC INFORMATION

Course Type: Public
Year Built: 1968
Architect: W. Amick
Local Pro: Ray Odom

Course: N/A
Holes: 18 / Par 72

Back: 6,540yds.   Rating: 70.3   Slope: 115
Middle: 6,372 yds.   Rating: 69.1   Slope: 112
Ladies: 5,738 yds.   Rating: 71.1   Slope: 116

Tee Time: 2 days in advance
Price: $14 - $20

Credit Cards:		Restaurant:	■
Driving Range:	■	Lounge:	■
Practice Green:	■	Meeting Rooms:	■
Locker Room:	■	Tennis:	
Rental Clubs:	■	Swimming:	
Walkers:	■	Jogging Trails:	
Snack Bar:	■	Boating:	

COURSE DESCRIPTION

This beautiful course is another prized gem out of the many fabulous courses that William W. Amick has designed. It has a wonderful feel to it with many interesting holes that are designed to challenge both the professional and the amateur.

The putting greens on this course are tremendous. The roll is always true to the line of the stroke. The fairways play wide with many good opportunities to let you "rip" at your drives. The rough is cut low and most of the bunkers on the course can be found around the greens just waiting to eat up your ball. Water comes into the play of action on five holes.

DIRECTIONS
Exit Hwy. 228 off I-10 and go north to Hwy. 90. Go west to Hwy. 23A and go north to the course. Look for the sign on your left.

KEYSTONE HEIGHTS GOLF & COUNTRY CLUB
P.O. Box 245, Keystone Heights, FL 32656 / (904) 473-4540

BASIC INFORMATION

Course Type: Semi-private
Year Built: 1959
Architect: N/A
Local Pro: D. Haines

Course: N/A
Holes: 18 / Par 71

Back: 6,684 yds.   Rating: 68.5   Slope: 113
Middle: N/A   Rating: N/A   Slope: N/A
Ladies: 5,580 yds.   Rating: 71.3   Slope: 114

Tee Time: First come basis.
Price: $12 - $14

Credit Cards:		Restaurant:	
Driving Range:	■	Lounge:	■
Practice Green:	■	Meeting Rooms:	
Locker Room:		Tennis:	
Rental Clubs:	■	Swimming:	
Walkers:	■	Jogging Trails:	
Snack Bar:	■	Boating:	■

COURSE DESCRIPTION
Keystone Heights Golf & Country Club is a great challenge for the weekend golfer.

The tree-lined narrow fairways will test your ability to hit the ball straight and accurate. If you're driving the ball well, the rest of the course should not be too difficult.

Consider using your 3-wood off the tee. Length isn't particularly important here. You'll often find yourself in a birdie position with a short approach shot to the green. Play for the pin as often as you can. With a well-placed shot, you'll be one putt away from a birdie.

DIRECTIONS
Take Hwy. 100 south to Keystone Heights and go west on Hwy. 21. The course will be on your right.

RAVINES COUNTRY CLUB
2932 Ravines Rd., Middleburg, FL 32068 / (904) 282-7888

BASIC INFORMATION

Course Type: Semi-private
Year Built: 1979
Architect: M. McCumber / R. Garl
Local Pro: Mike Cooney

Course: N/A
Holes: 18 / Par 72

Back: 6,733 yds. Rating: 72.4 Slope: 133
Middle: 6,214 yds. Rating: 70.0 Slope: 128
Ladies: 4,817 yds. Rating: 67.4 Slope: 120

Tee Time: 7 days in advance
Price: $26 - $48

Credit Cards: ■	Restaurant: ■
Driving Range: ■	Lounge: ■
Practice Green: ■	Meeting Rooms: ■
Locker Room: ■	Tennis: ■
Rental Clubs: ■	Swimming: ■
Walkers:	Jogging Trails: ■
Snack Bar: ■	Boating: ■

COURSE DESCRIPTION

Be prepared for something special. Mark McCumber and Ron Garl have done an astonishing job designing this course.

It rolls through hilly terrain with many trees and strategically-placed hazards. You'll also find many ravines that snake their way around the course and into the play of action on 11 holes.

This is really a thinking man's golf course. With many of the holes playing dramatically different from each other, the course does get difficult at times. Consider playing from the middle tees if your handicap is above a 10. This aesthetically beautiful course is a great place to play golf.

DIRECTIONS

Take I-295 and go south on Hwy. 21 to Middleburg. Go east on Hwy. 218 and follow the signs to the course.

LAKE CITY COUNTRY CLUB
Rt.13, Box 436, Lake City, FL 32055 / (904) 752-2266

BASIC INFORMATION

Course Type: Semi-private
Year Built: 1969
Architect: W. Byrd
Local Pro: Jim Custer

Course: N/A
Holes: 18 / Par 72

Back: 6,777 yds. Rating: 72.1 Slope: 123
Middle: 6,364 yds. Rating: 70.2 Slope: 118
Ladies: 5,097 yds. Rating: 68.6 Slope: 117

Tee Time: 7 days in advance
Price: $26.50 - $31.80

Credit Cards: ■	Restaurant: ■
Driving Range: ■	Lounge: ■
Practice Green: ■	Meeting Rooms: ■
Locker Room: ■	Tennis:
Rental Clubs:	Swimming:
Walkers:	Jogging Trails:
Snack Bar: ■	Boating:

COURSE DESCRIPTION

This wonderful course has played to some of the greatest upcoming players in the world. Both the past Hogan Tour and the present Nike Tour have used this location as a qualifying stop for their competitions. You'll find many interesting holes with subtle undulations both on the fairways and greens.

You'll have to drive your ball dead straight to keep it in play on the many narrow fairways throughout the course. Many of the holes go through elevation changes and feature water coming into play. You'll need to hit many of your shots on uneven lies both above and below your setup. This is a tremendous place to play golf.

DIRECTIONS

Exit onto Hwy. 90 from I-75 and go east on the service road to course.

DEERFIELD LAKE GOLF & COUNTRY CLUB

P.O. Box 18330, Jacksonville, FL 32229 / (904) 879-1210

BASIC INFORMATION

Course Type: Public
Year Built: 1968
Architect: D. Klein
Local Pro: Mike Mollis

Course: N/A
Holes: 18 / Par 72

Back: 6,856 yds. Rating: 70.2 Slope: 114
Middle: 6,196 yds. Rating: 68.2 Slope: 110
Ladies: 5,266 yds. Rating: 69.0 Slope: 102

Tee Time: 2 days in advance
Price: $15 - $30

Credit Cards:	■	Restaurant:	■
Driving Range:	■	Lounge:	■
Practice Green:	■	Meeting Rooms:	■
Locker Room:	■	Tennis:	
Rental Clubs:	■	Swimming:	
Walkers:	■	Jogging Trails:	
Snack Bar:	■	Boating:	

COURSE DESCRIPTION

Deerfield Lake Golf & Country Club is a well-conditioned, reasonably priced golf course that plays well for beginning golfers and senior citizens.

This is a good place to experiment with your game by attempting things that you wouldn't normally try on harder courses. If you make a mistake here and shoot a bogey, you'll have plenty of opportunities to bounce back with a birdie. Playing aggresive golf takes courage and determination. When you finally feel comfortable with it, your confidence level will take your game to a new plateau. With control and confidence at your side, you'll be scoring much lower numbers.

DIRECTIONS

Take I-295 to Lem Turner Rd. and drive north for about seven miles. Follow the signs to the course.

DUNES GOLF CLUB

P.O. Box 18330, Jacksonville, FL 32225 / (904) 641-8444

BASIC INFORMATION

Course Type: Public
Year Built: 1966
Architect: N/A
Local Pro: Eddie Davis

Course: N/A
Holes: 18 / Par 72

Back: 6,696 yds. Rating: 71.3 Slope: 109
Middle: 6,160 yds. Rating: 69.2 Slope: 103
Ladies: 5,729 yds. Rating: 73.1 Slope: 110

Tee Time: 7 days in advance
Price: $12 - $25

Credit Cards:	■	Restaurant:	
Driving Range:		Lounge:	■
Practice Green:	■	Meeting Rooms:	
Locker Room:	■	Tennis:	
Rental Clubs:	■	Swimming:	
Walkers:	■	Jogging Trails:	
Snack Bar:	■	Boating:	

COURSE DESCRIPTION

This is yet another course that is easy to play and master quickly. But if you're higher than a 10 handicap, don't take the course for granted. Some of the fairways play narrow and long. On these occasions, you'll have to hit your tee shot long and accurate to get into good position for your second shot.

Although the slope rating is below average (109), the overall design of the holes make for interesting golf. You'll find many holes that are set up to allow you more than one required approach to the green. That, above all else, is the most attractive part of the Dunes Golf Club.

Water comes into play on three holes.

DIRECTIONS

From Alt. 90 and Hwy. 113, the course is four and a half miles north of Regency Square.

GOLF CLUB OF JACKSONVILLE

10440 Tournament Lane, Jacksonville, FL 32222 / (904) 249-8600

BASIC INFORMATION

Course Type: Public
Year Built: 1964
Architect: N/A
Local Pro: N/A

Course: N/A
Holes: 18 / Par 72

Back: 6,510 yds. Rating: 70.5 Slope: 119
Middle: 6,181 yds. Rating: 68.9 Slope: 115
Ladies: 5,245 yds. Rating: 69.2 Slope: 114

Tee Time: 7 days in advance
Price: $23.50 - $25.90

Credit Cards:		Restaurant:	■
Driving Range:	■	Lounge:	■
Practice Green:	■	Meeting Rooms:	
Locker Room:		Tennis:	
Rental Clubs:	■	Swimming:	
Walkers:	■	Jogging Trails:	
Snack Bar:	■	Boating:	■

COURSE DESCRIPTION

The *Golf Club of Jacksonville* is set on a flat terrain with nine holes featuring water hazards.

The course is set up for relatively easy play. If you manage your game well, you should find yourself shooting for birdie quite often. Try to get them as early as possible, preferably on the front nine. The back nine, overall, is a harder test of golf.

The hardest hole on the course is the slight dogleg left 18th. It measures 430 yards in length. The hole really becomes difficult when you have to play against the prevailing winds that seem to move through ol' number 18 90% of the time!

DIRECTIONS

Exit 103rd St. from I-295 and go west. Follow the signs to the course.

HYDE PARK GOLF & COUNTRY CLUB

6939 Hyde Grove Ave., Jacksonville, FL 32210 / (904) 786-5410

BASIC INFORMATION

Course Type: Public
Year Built: 1925
Architect: D. Ross
Local Pro: Billy Maxwell

Course: N/A
Holes: 18 / Par 72

Back: 6,468 yds. Rating: 70.3 Slope: 120
Middle: 6,153 yds. Rating: 68.8 Slope: 117
Ladies: 5,558 yds. Rating: 71.0 Slope: 122

Tee Time: 5 days in advance
Price: $16 - $27

Credit Cards:		Restaurant:	
Driving Range:	■	Lounge:	■
Practice Green:	■	Meeting Rooms:	
Locker Room:		Tennis:	
Rental Clubs:	■	Swimming:	
Walkers:	■	Jogging Trails:	
Snack Bar:	■	Boating:	■

COURSE DESCRIPTION

Hyde Park Golf & Country Club is a fun course for all types of players.

If you can get your game together quickly, preferably on the front nine, you'll have a greater chance of achieving a low score. The terrain here is mostly flat. You should find your ball lying nicely on most occasions on your second shot. In contrast, the back nine is much more hilly; dramatically reducing your chances of getting an even lie. On many occasions, you'll have to shape your shots from uneven lies.

Learn to play the ball from above and below your feet. This course demands it! Water comes into play on eight holes.

DIRECTIONS

Exit Lane Ave. off of I-10 and go south to Hyde Grove Ave.

MILL COVE GOLF CLUB
1700 Monument Rd., Jacksonville, FL 32225 / (904) 646-4653

BASIC INFORMATION

Course Type: Public
Year Built: 1990
Architect: A. Palmer
Local Pro: John Vickers

Course: N/A
Holes: 18/ Par 71

Back: 6,622 yds. Rating: 71.3 Slope: 124
Middle: 5,950 yds. Rating: 67.9 Slope: 118
Ladies: 4,719 yds. Rating: 66.3 Slope: 112

Tee Time: 3 days in advance
Price: $25 - $34

Credit Cards:	■	Restaurant:	■
Driving Range:	■	Lounge:	■
Practice Green:	■	Meeting Rooms:	
Locker Room:	■	Tennis:	
Rental Clubs:	■	Swimming:	
Walkers:		Jogging Trails:	
Snack Bar:	■	Boating:	■

COURSE DESCRIPTION

Arnold Palmer has outdone himself on this course. You'll have to be mentally prepared to play a good round. Proper course management is essential.

The variety of hole designs is unique at the *Mill Cove Golf Club.* Arnold Palmer in his peak always played an aggressive game of golf and his "go for the pin whenever you can" attitude gained him the greatest following ("Arnie's Army") in the history of golf.

The surprise at this course is that you'll find many holes that will allow you to get par or better without having to play aggressively. This is a wonderful golf challenge.

DIRECTIONS

Take Hwy. 10 to Monument Rd. and go north to St. Johns Bluff. Follow the signs to the course.

PINE LAKES GOLF COURSE
153 Norhside Dr. S., Jacksonville, FL 32218 / (904) 757-0318

BASIC INFORMATION

Course Type: Semi-private
Year Built: 1965
Architect: Pat Schwab
Local Pro: Mitch Linton

Course: N/A
Holes: 18 / Par 72

Back: 6,604 yds. Rating: 71.1 Slope: 127
Middle: 6,208 yds. Rating: 69.3 Slope: 124
Ladies: 5,264 yds. Rating: 69.8 Slope: 121

Tee Time: 14 days in advance
Price: $16 - $24

Credit Cards:	■	Restaurant:	■
Driving Range:	■	Lounge:	■
Practice Green:	■	Meeting Rooms:	
Locker Room:	■	Tennis:	
Rental Clubs:	■	Swimming:	
Walkers:	■	Jogging Trails:	
Snack Bar:	■	Boating:	■

COURSE DESCRIPTION

Pine Lakes Golf Course is a joy to play. The course is well manicured and the design, from hole to hole, seems to flow with perfect ease. The terrain is mostly flat with only nine holes playing into water.

The greens here are great. The roll never leaves its line towards the cup. That's a comforting feeling when you have to make a ten-footer for birdie.

This course is a good test of golf for both beginner and professional. You really have to think about each hole carefully and decide which route will be best for your particular type of game. Good course management is the key to scoring well here.

DIRECTIONS

Take I-95 north to Pecan Park Rd. and onward to Hwy. 17. Continue going north for less than a mile. Look for the course sign.

UNIVERSITY GOLF CLUB

P.O. Box 8723, Jacksonville, FL 32211 / (904) 744-2124

BASIC INFORMATION

Course Type: Semi-private
Year Built: 1966
Architect: L. Sanders / B. Toski
Local Pro: John Milam

Course: N/A
Holes: 18 / Par 72

Back: 6,489 yds. Rating: 70.5 Slope: 122
Middle: 6,234 yds. Rating: 69.2 Slope: 120
Ladies: 5,587 yds. Rating: 72.1 Slope: 120

Tee Time: 7 days in advance
Price: $21 - $27

Credit Cards:	■	Restaurant:	■
Driving Range:		Lounge:	■
Practice Green:	■	Meeting Rooms:	■
Locker Room:	■	Tennis:	■
Rental Clubs:	■	Swimming:	■
Walkers:	■	Jogging Trails:	
Snack Bar:	■	Boating:	■

COURSE DESCRIPTION

You'll find this course a daring attraction that will have you playing your best shots from tee to green.

Distance isn't half as important as the accuracy of your game and your overall ability to manage your way around the course. The fairways play very tight and demanding. On most of the par-4's, you really have to place your ball in the proper landing area to be in a good position for your approach shot to the green.

Most of the greens are well-bunkered and small.

Despite the length of the course, this really is a shotmakers' course.

DIRECTIONS

Take Hwy. 90A across the Mathews Bridge and go north on Hwy. 109 (University Blvd.) to the course.

WEST MEADOWS GOLF CLUB

11400 W. Meadows Dr., Jacksonville, FL 32221 / (904) 781-4834

BASIC INFORMATION

Course Type: Public
Year Built: N/A
Architect: N/A
Local Pro: Chris Caruso

Course: N/A
Holes: 18 / Par 72

Back: 6,197 yds. Rating: 68.7 Slope: 110
Middle: 6,061 yds. Rating: 68.1 Slope: 109
Ladies: 5,648 yds. Rating: 71.1 Slope: 115

Tee Time: N/A
Price: $13 - $20

Credit Cards:		Restaurant:	
Driving Range:	■	Lounge:	■
Practice Green:	■	Meeting Rooms:	
Locker Room:		Tennis:	
Rental Clubs:	■	Swimming:	
Walkers:	■	Jogging Trails:	
Snack Bar:	■	Boating:	

COURSE DESCRIPTION

This is a great course for the many new golfers that have recently taken up the game. This straightforward, no surprise, simple layout is a local favorite among the senior citizens in the area.

The terrain is mostly flat and comfortable to play. The hardest part of playing this course begins at the tee. Most of the fairways are narrow and demand a straight tee shot. Don't panic! All you have to do is use a more lofted club for control. Remember, distance is only relative to the individual; most golfers will have no problem getting into good position for their approach shots to the green.

DIRECTIONS

Take I-10 to Exit 51 and go over the bypass. Go south on Chaffee Rd. and the course will be about two miles further on your right.

WILLOW LAKES GOLF CLUB
7300 Blanding Blvd., Jacksonville, FL 32244 / (904) 771-6656

BASIC INFORMATION

Course Type: Public
Year Built: 1970
Architect: N/A
Local Pro: Tim Hodes

Course: Troon (18 / Par 72)
Holes: 27

Back: 6,543 yds. Rating: 70.6 Slope: 123
Middle: 6,275 yds. Rating: 69.1 Slope: 119
Ladies: 5,496 yds. Rating: 70.7 Slope: 114

Tee Time: 3 days in advance
Price: $17.50 - $26.50

Credit Cards:	■	Restaurant:	■
Driving Range:	■	Lounge:	■
Practice Green:	■	Meeting Rooms:	■
Locker Room:	■	Tennis:	
Rental Clubs:	■	Swimming:	
Walkers:		Jogging Trails:	
Snack Bar:	■	Boating:	

COURSE DESCRIPTION
This links course dares you to take chances from beginning to end. With all of its subtle contours and deep hidden hazards, you'll often think that the shot you're about to play should post no trouble, only to find your ball in a deep trap hidden from view.

This Scottish links course allows the natural surroundings to grow untouched. The only element that you find manicured is the greens.

The wind factor on this course can be brutal at times. Look here to play a low boring shot below the wind.

DIRECTIONS
Take I-295 and exit onto Blanding Blvd. and go north to the course. It will be one mile past Collins Rd. on your left side.

CYPRESS KNOLL GOLF COURSE
East Hampton Blvd., Palm Coast, FL 32137 / (904) 437-5804

BASIC INFORMATION

Course Type: Semi-private
Year Built: 1990
Architect: G. Player
Local Pro: Joe Gutterman

Course: N/A
Holes: 18 / Par 72

Back: 6,591 yds. Rating: 71.6 Slope: 130
Middle: 6,261 yds. Rating: 70.0 Slope: 127
Ladies: 5,386 yds. Rating: 69.3 Slope: 117

Tee Time: 6 days in advance
Price: $36 - $47

Credit Cards:	■	Restaurant:	■
Driving Range:	■	Lounge:	■
Practice Green:	■	Meeting Rooms:	■
Locker Room:	■	Tennis:	
Rental Clubs:	■	Swimming:	
Walkers:		Jogging Trails:	■
Snack Bar:	■	Boating:	■

COURSE DESCRIPTION
This beautiful scenic course is reminiscent of the pine and hardwood forests that can be found in North Carolina.

Cypress Knoll is both challenging and interesting from tee to green. The course features narrow fairways that wind through marshlands and trees. Small pot bunkers are placed in inconspicuous places just waiting to get a piece of your ball. Abundant "love grass" is left to grow naturally along the fields, adjacent to some of the fairways and the many surrounding trees. Water comes into play on 15 holes.

Play the course from the middle tees if your handicap is above 10.

DIRECTIONS
Take I-95 to the 91C exit and go west on Palm Coast Pkwy., south on Belle Terre Pkwy., and west on East Hampton Blvd.

MATANZAS WOODS GOLF COURSE
398 Lakeview Blvd., Palm Coast, FL 32151 / (904) 446-6330

BASIC INFORMATION

Course Type: Semi-private
Year Built: 1985
Architect: A. Palmer / E. Seay
Local Pro: Ed Crowell

Course: N/A
Holes: 18 / Par 72

Back: 6,985 yds. Rating: 73.2 Slope: 126
Middle: 6,514 yds. Rating: 71.0 Slope: 121
Ladies: 5,407 yds. Rating: 70.6 Slope: 118

Tee Time: 6 days in advance
Price: $36 - $46

Credit Cards:	■	Restaurant:	■
Driving Range:	■	Lounge:	■
Practice Green:	■	Meeting Rooms:	
Locker Room:		Tennis:	
Rental Clubs:	■	Swimming:	
Walkers:		Jogging Trails:	
Snack Bar:	■	Boating:	■

COURSE DESCRIPTION
This interesting course features a splendid layout with many inviting features that will have you smiling from cheek-to-cheek throughout the day.

The hardest hole on the course is the slight dogleg left number 4 hole. This par-5 measures 589 yards in length. To set yourself up in good position for your first of two approach shots, carry your ball right and hook it around the dogleg. Play your second shot straight and to the left of the green. Water comes into play on the right side of the fairway. You'll have to play your approach shot from about 150 yards out over water to the green.

DIRECTIONS
Exit 91C off of I-95 and go west on Palm Coast Pkwy. Go north on Belle Terre to the dead end. Go left on Matanzas Woods Pkwy., and right on Lakeview Blvd.

PALM HARBOR GOLF COURSE
Casper Lane Ext., Palm Coast, FL 32137 / (904) 445-0845

BASIC INFORMATION

Course Type: Semi-private
Year Built: 1977
Architect: N/A
Local Pro: Henry Bono

Course: N/A
Holes: 18 / Par 72

Back: 6,664 yds. Rating: 72.0 Slope: 129
Middle: 6,242 yds. Rating: 70.1 Slope: 125
Ladies: 5,501 yds. Rating: 71.3 Slope: 118

Tee Time: 2 days in advance
Price: $17 - $36

Credit Cards:	■	Restaurant:	■
Driving Range:	■	Lounge:	■
Practice Green:	■	Meeting Rooms:	■
Locker Room:	■	Tennis:	■
Rental Clubs:	■	Swimming:	■
Walkers:	■	Jogging Trails:	■
Snack Bar:	■	Boating:	■

COURSE DESCRIPTION
This is an exciting layout with many options off the tee.

The best feature of this course is that it allows you a second shot at par by keeping the rough low. Water only comes into play on three holes.

If you can keep your ball straight off the tee and maneuver it around the trees and the dogleg-shaped holes, you'll be in prime position to come in with a very low score.

The number 5 hole (Par 4 / 434 yards) is the hardest hole on the course. On most occasions you'll be hitting your drive straight into the wind. Your approach shot will be to an average size green with a small trap front right.

DIRECTIONS
Exit 91C from I-95 and go east at Palm Coast Pkwy., and left on Palm Harbor Dr.

PINE LAKES COUNTRY CLUB
400 Pine Lakes Pkwy., Plam Coast, FL 32151 / (904) 445-0852

BASIC INFORMATION

Course Type: Semi-private
Year Built: 1981
Architect: A. Palmer / E. Seay
Local Pro: Ken Van Leuven

Course: N/A
Holes: 18 / Par 72

Back: 7,074 yds. Rating: 73.5 Slope: 126
Middle: 6,122 yds. Rating: 70.6 Slope: 121
Ladies: 5,166 yds. Rating: 71.4 Slope: 124

Tee Time: 6 days in advance
Price: $44 - $51

Credit Cards:	■	Restaurant:	■
Driving Range:	■	Lounge:	■
Practice Green:	■	Meeting Rooms:	
Locker Room:	■	Tennis:	■
Rental Clubs:	■	Swimming:	■
Walkers:		Jogging Trails:	
Snack Bar:	■	Boating:	■

COURSE DESCRIPTION

If you're ready for a challenge you'll never forget, this is the place. At 7,074 yards from the back tees, *Pine Lakes Country Club* is the longest course in Palm Coast County.

Most of us mere mortals will have to settle on playing the middle tees (6,122) with a reduction of 952 yards of real estate. That is an average of 53 yards off of every drive.

The fairways are wide with lots of trees. Many sand traps and hazards come into play. *Pine Lakes* has hosted the PGA Qualifying School in the past. It is really an exceptional course.

DIRECTIONS

Exit 91C from I-95 and go west on Palm Coast Pkwy. Go south on Belle Terre Pkwy., right on Pine Lakes Pkwy., and the course will be about a mile further on your right.

AMELIA ISLAND PLANTATION
P.O. Box 3000, Amelia Island, FL 32034 / (904) 277-5907

BASIC INFORMATION

Course Type: Resort
Year Built: 1986
Architect: T. Fazio
Local Pro: John Andrew

Course: Long Point (18 / Par 72)
Holes: 45

Back: 6,775 yds. Rating: 72.5 Slope: 127
Middle: 6,068 yds. Rating: 69.5 Slope: 121
Ladies: 4,927 yds. Rating: 69.1 Slope: 121

Tee Time: 2 days in advance
Price: $75 - $95

Credit Cards:		Restaurant:	■
Driving Range:	■	Lounge:	■
Practice Green:	■	Meeting Rooms:	■
Locker Room:		Tennis:	■
Rental Clubs:	■	Swimming:	■
Walkers:		Jogging Trails:	■
Snack Bar:	■	Boating:	■

COURSE DESCRIPTION

If you're looking for a place that will totally take you out of your everyday routine and into the reality of some distant golf dream, welcome to Oz. At the *Amelia Island Plantation,* you will be taken on a magical trip around 45 of the most stunning golf holes in the world. These holes make their way around marsh lands, trees, and ocean water.

I can't begin to explain the feeling you'll get when you hit your first shot over the ocean and onto a green. Consider this place the Pebble Beach of the East Coast.

This particular course has two par-3's over the ocean and six holes along the intracoastal. It is worth every penny of admission.

DIRECTIONS

Take I-95 to Exit A1A into Fernando Beach. That will lead you to Amelia Pkwy. Go south for about five miles to the course.

FERNANDINA BEACH MUNICIPAL GOLF COURSE

2800 Bill Melton Rd., Fernandina Beach, FL 32034 / (904) 277-7370

BASIC INFORMATION

Course Type: Municipal
Year Built: N/A
Architect: E. Mattison
Local Pro: N/A

Course: West & South (18 / Par 73)
Holes: 27

Back: 7,027 yds. Rating: 72.6 Slope: 123
Middle: 6,551 yds. Rating: 70.3 Slope: 119
Ladies: 5,308 yds. Rating: 69.5 Slope: 120

Tee Time: 3 days in advance
Price: $22.50 - $25.50

Credit Cards:		Restaurant:	■
Driving Range:	■	Lounge:	■
Practice Green:	■	Meeting Rooms:	■
Locker Room:		Tennis:	
Rental Clubs:	■	Swimming:	
Walkers:	■	Jogging Trails:	
Snack Bar:	■	Boating:	■

COURSE DESCRIPTION

Wow! 7,027 yards from the back tees: is there another Municipal golf course as long as this one on our planet? If the yardage from the back tees is too much for you, play the middle tees at 6,551 yards. That will give you a gain of 26 yards on every hole.

I like the combination of these two nine hole courses. The West plays longer but does allow a greater margin of error off the tee.

The South is a little more demanding because of its narrow fairways. You'll need to drive the ball well to set yourself up for your following shot.

You'll need a good all-around game to post a good score.

DIRECTIONS

Go north on A1A off of I-95 and follow the signs on the west side of the beach to the course.

PALATKA MUNICIPAL GOLF COURSE

1715 Moseley Ave., Palatka, FL 32177 / (904) 329-0141

BASIC INFORMATION

Course Type: Municipal
Year Built: 1926
Architect: D. Ross
Local Pro: Greg Bacon

Course: N/A
Holes: 18 / Par 70

Back: 5,942 yds. Rating: 67.1 Slope: 115
Middle: 5,700 yds. Rating: 66.0 Slope: 119
Ladies: 5,217 yds. Rating: 70.3 Slope: 118

Tee Time: 1 day in advance
Price: $15.90 - $24.83

Credit Cards:	■	Restaurant:	■
Driving Range:	■	Lounge:	■
Practice Green:	■	Meeting Rooms:	
Locker Room:	■	Tennis:	
Rental Clubs:	■	Swimming:	
Walkers:	■	Jogging Trails:	
Snack Bar:	■	Boating:	■

COURSE DESCRIPTION

This course doesn't hold much of a challenge to the accomplished single digit handicap player. But if you're a beginner or a senior citizen, you'll find it a pleasure to play from beginning to end.

With no holes playing into water, you'll have all the room in the world to experiment with your game - most especially your drives. Get out the 3-wood and hit it for both distance and accuracy.

Keep in mind that this is first and foremost a Donald Ross-designed course, one of the most influential designers in the history of the game. Playing any one of his courses is an education into the game of golf.

DIRECTIONS

Take Hwy. 17 to Moseley Ave. and turn south. Follow the signs to the course.

OAKS BRIDGE CLUB AT SAWGRASS
P.O. Box 1677, Ponte Vedra Beach, FL 32082 / (904) 285-0204

BASIC INFORMATION

Course Type: Semi-private
Year Built: 1973
Architect: E. Seay
Local Pro: Chip Dutton

Course: N/A
Holes: 18 / Par 70

Back: 6,383 yds. Rating: 70.3 Slope: 126
Middle: 6,031 yds. Rating: 68.8 Slope: 123
Ladies: 5,504 yds. Rating: 67.8 Slope: 116

Tee Time: 7 days in advance
Price: $50 - $85

Credit Cards:	■	Restaurant:	■
Driving Range:	■	Lounge:	■
Practice Green:	■	Meeting Rooms:	■
Locker Room:	■	Tennis:	■
Rental Clubs:	■	Swimming:	■
Walkers:	■	Jogging Trails:	■
Snack Bar:	■	Boating:	■

COURSE DESCRIPTION
You'll have to dig deep inside yourself to play well on this exciting course. Although the total yardage from the back tees is only 6,383 yards, you'll find out-of-bounds and other demanding hazards coming into play on every hole. You'll also be confronting six par-3 holes rather than the average of four that are found on most golf courses.

The fairways on this course are mostly narrow and demand a well-controlled drive to place the ball in the right landing area.

If you don't feel totally comfortable in your iron play, you should play from the middle tees for maximum fun.

This is truly a great design!

DIRECTIONS
Take the A1A south of Butler Blvd. (Hwy. 202). Follow the signs to the course.

PONCE DE LEON RESORT & CONVENTION CENTER
P.O. Box 1677, St. Augustine, FL 32082 / (904) 829-5314

BASIC INFORMATION

Course Type: Resort
Year Built: 1916
Architect: D. Ross
Local Pro: Mary Hafeman

Course: N/A
Holes: 18 / Par 71

Back: 6,878 yds. Rating: 72.9 Slope: 131
Middle: 6,472 yds. Rating: 71.1 Slope: 127
Ladies: 5,315 yds. Rating: 73.2 Slope: 125

Tee Time: 1 day in advance
Price: $48 - $58

Credit Cards:	■	Restaurant:	■
Driving Range:	■	Lounge:	■
Practice Green:	■	Meeting Rooms:	■
Locker Room:	■	Tennis:	■
Rental Clubs:	■	Swimming:	■
Walkers:	■	Jogging Trails:	■
Snack Bar:	■	Boating:	■

COURSE DESCRIPTION
This incredible course was built in 1916 by one of golf's greatest designers: Donald Ross. *Ponce de Leon* feels like two courses in one. The front nine is more lush and more refined. You'll have to hit your drives accurately on this side because of the mature oak trees that come into play on some of the holes. The back nine, which opens up to the Intracoastal Waterway, is the complete opposite of the front nine. Playing into the wind can often be difficult and unpredictable.

Consider playing from the middle tees if you're above a single digit handicap.

DIRECTIONS
Take Hwy. 1 three miles North of St. Augustine. Follow signs to the course.

PONTE VEDRA INN & COUNTRY CLUB
200 Ponte Vedra Blvd., Ponte Vedra Beach, FL 32082 / (904) 285-2044

BASIC INFORMATION

Course Type: Resort
Year Built: 1927
Architect: R. Trent Jones Sr.
Local Pro: Jim Howard

Course: Ocean (18 / Par 72)
Holes: 36

Back: 6,573 yds. Rating: 71.3 Slope: 120
Middle: 6,055 yds. Rating: 68.9 Slope: 115
Ladies: 5,237 yds. Rating: 69.6 Slope: 119

Tee Time: 1 day in advance
Price: $50 - $60

Credit Cards: Restaurant: ■
Driving Range: ■   Lounge: ■
Practice Green: ■   Meeting Rooms: ■
Locker Room: ■   Tennis: ■
Rental Clubs: ■   Swimming: ■
Walkers: ■   Jogging Trails: ■
Snack Bar: ■   Boating: ■

COURSE DESCRIPTION
Ponte Vedra Inn & Country Club is a well-designed course with many clever hole designs that will have you thinking throughout the game.

If you can manage your game correctly, the course will open up to you and allow you many good chances at a birdie.

The number 5 hole (Par-5 / 516 yards) is the hardest hole on the course. You'll be hitting your drive across water and towards several facing bunkers. The second shot is a blind attempt over a hill with a bunker that comes into play on the far side. Your approach shot will be to a high elevated green that favors a soft landing fade.

DIRECTIONS
Take the A1A to Butler Blvd. and turn right. When you get to the second stop sign, turn right again and follow the road to the course.

ST. AUGUSTINE SHORES COUNTRY CLUB
707 Shores Blvd., St. Augustine, FL 32086 / (904) 794-0303

BASIC INFORMATION

Course Type: Public
Year Built: 1974
Architect: C. Almony
Local Pro: Brandon Fluman

Course: N/A
Holes: 18 / Par 70

Back: 5,367 yds. Rating: 64.6 Slope: 102
Middle: 5,091 yds. Rating: 63.7 Slope: 100
Ladies: 4,365 yds. Rating: 64.2 Slope: 116

Tee Time: 5 days in advance
Price: $14 - $23

Credit Cards: ■   Restaurant: ■
Driving Range: ■   Lounge: ■
Practice Green: ■   Meeting Rooms:
Locker Room: ■   Tennis:
Rental Clubs: ■   Swimming:
Walkers: ■   Jogging Trails:
Snack Bar: ■   Boating: ■

COURSE DESCRIPTION
This beautiful little course is a nice challenge for high handicap players and senior citizens looking for a course that plays short and forgiving.

Anyone below a 15 handicap will have a chance at birdie on almost every hole. The fairways are wide with low-cut grass and the rough is kept low for maximum playability. You don't have to pull out the driver here on every hole. If you play for position by using a 3 or 4-wood off the tee, you'll increase your chances of achieving a very low score.

You won't mind the length of the course if you're an average golfer. If you ever wondered what it would be like to play like John Daly, this is definitely the course to play.

DIRECTIONS
Take Hwy. 1 about 10 miles south of St. Augustine.

ST. JOHN'S COUNTY GOLF COURSE

4900 Cpress Links Blvd., Elkton, FL 32033 / (904) 825-4900

BASIC INFORMATION

Course Type: Public
Year Built: 1989
Architect: R. Walker
Local Pro: Wes Tucker

Course: N/A
Holes: 18 / Par 72

Back: 6,926 yds. Rating: 72.9 Slope: 130
Middle: 6,510 yds. Rating: 71.2 Slope: 126
Ladies: 5,173 yds. Rating: 68.8 Slope: 117

Tee Time: 7 days in advance
Price: $25

Credit Cards:	■	Restaurant:	■
Driving Range:	■	Lounge:	■
Practice Green:	■	Meeting Rooms:	
Locker Room:	■	Tennis:	
Rental Clubs:	■	Swimming:	
Walkers:	■	Jogging Trails:	
Snack Bar:	■	Boating:	

COURSE DESCRIPTION

St. John's County Golf Course is a scenic course built around a natural habitat. As a modern day golf club, the shape of the course is unique. Each half of the course is set up in a circle of its own. Parallel holes that run along each other do not exist. It's a layout that makes for a faster game of golf and will allow you the luxury of staying in your playing zone undisturbed.

The number 7 hole (Par 4 / 433 yards) is considered the hardest on the course. From the tee you'll be hitting between trees to an undulating fairway with a left-to-right kick. Your next shot on most occasions will be a blind shot to a huge green that measures roughly 10,000 sq. ft.

DIRECTIONS

Exit onto Hwy. 207 from I-95 and go west to the course. It will be on your left.

HALIFAX PLANTATION

2990 S. Atlantic Ave., Ormond Beach, FL 32118 / (904) 676-9600

BASIC INFORMATION

Course Type: Semi-private
Year Built: 1992
Architect: B. Amick
Local Pro: Dan Caverly

Course: N/A
Holes: 18 / Par 72

Back: 7,128 yds. Rating: 73.9 Slope: 129
Middle: 6,711 yds. Rating: 71.9 Slope: 124
Ladies: 5,656 yds. Rating: 71.8 Slope: 121

Tee Time: 2 days in advance
Price: $25 - $34

Credit Cards:	■	Restaurant:	
Driving Range:	■	Lounge:	
Practice Green:	■	Meeting Rooms:	
Locker Room:	■	Tennis:	
Rental Clubs:	■	Swimming:	
Walkers:	■	Jogging Trails:	
Snack Bar:	■	Boating:	■

COURSE DESCRIPTION

This is another brilliant course by golf architect Bill Amick.

All of the notable challenges of golf can be found throughout this course. It plays fair to both the professional and the beginner. Whichever tee you choose to play from, you'll be in for a wonderful game.

The course is set on a high rolling terrain with beautiful views that compliment the overall area. A great amount of attention was put into preserving the natural surroundings and wildlife around the course.

This is an outstanding golf course that gives you a feeling of seclusion from the rest of the busy world. You're going to love playing here!

DIRECTIONS

Take Exit 90 off I-95 and go east on Old Dixie Hwy. The course will be about two miles on your right.

ALACHUA

Gainsville Golf & Country Club
(904) 372-0961
Gainsville
Local Pro: Chuck Brasington
Reciprocal Play: Yes

Turkey Creek Golf & RC
(904) 462-4655
3500 Turkey Creek Blvd., Alachua
Local Pro: Ray Hunter
Reciprocal Play: Yes

CLAY

Magnolia Point Golf & Country Club
(904) 269-9315
3616 Magnolia Point. Blvd.
Green Cove Springs
Local Pro: Jeff Harris
Reciprocal Play: Yes

Penney Retirement Country Club
(904) 284-8200
101 Hoffman St., Penney Farms
Local Pro: N/A
Reciprocal Play: No

DUVAL

Deercreek Country Club
(904) 363-1604
7816 Mc.Laurin Rd., Jacksonville
Local Pro: Mark Blakewood
Reciprocal Play: No

Deerwood Club
(904) 642-5917
10239 Golf Club Dr., Jacksonville
Local Pro: Jeff Wagner
Reciprocal Play: Yes (Local)

Hidden Hills Golf Course
(904) 641-7544
3901 Monument Rd., Jacksonville
Local Pro: Ted Hopkins
Reciprocal Play: No

FLAGLER

Hammock Dunes Links Course
(904) 446-6222
301 Camino Del Mar, Palm Coast
Local Pro: Dan Malizia
Reciprocal Play: No

ST. JOHNS

Cimarrone at Cart Wheel Bay
(904) 287-2000
2690 Cimarrone Blvd., Jacksonville
Local Pro: Mike Linch
Reciprocal Play: Yes (Local)

Marsh Creek Country Club
(904) 461-1145
88 Marshside Dr., St. Augustine
Local Pro: Hugh McCracken
Reciprocal Play: No

Marsh Landing Country Club
(904) 285-6459
25655 Marsh Landing Pkwy., Pt. Vendra Bch.
Local Pro: Jimmy Upton
Reciprocal Play: Yes

Plantation at Ponte Vendra, The
(904) 285-0002
220 Plantation Cr., Ponte Vendra Beach
Local Pro:
Reciprocal Play:

Sawgrass Country Club
(904) 273-3720
A1A Bypass, Ponte Vendra Beach
Local Pro: Joe Burch
Reciprocal Play: Yes

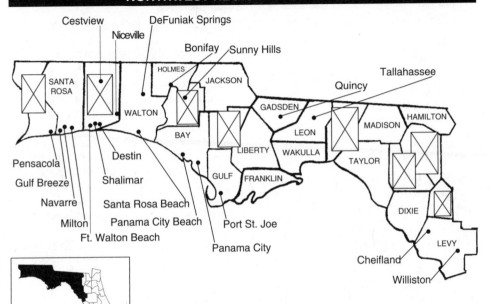

TOP TEN

Bay Point Yacht & C.C.
(Bay County)

Bluewater Bay Resort
(Okaloosa County)

Club at Hidden Creek, The
(Okaloosa County)

Killearn C. C. & Inn
(Leon County)

Perdido Bay Resort
(Escambia County)

St. Joseph's Bay C.C.
(Calhoun County)

Sandestin Golf Club
(Okaloosa County)

Seminole Golf Course & C.
(Leon County)

Shalimar Pointe G. & C.C.
(Okaloosa County)

Tiger Point C.C.
(Santa Rosa County)

As you enter the **Northwest** region of Florida, you'll be minutes away from some of the most exciting golfing venues in the game today.

Imagine the exhilarating feeling of golfing on a playing field you've only experienced in your dreams. No homes, no traffic, just your best friends and the bounty of nature. The magical qualities of playing golf in a secluded area are readily available throughout this region.

The Northwest is a rich and exciting place to explore. The great variety of golf courses that can be found here are spectacular. The architecture is superb. Some of golf's greatest architects have come here to reshape the many different land structures found throughout the region. Collectively, their work stands as a monument to the advancement of course design.

Average Temperatures

Between **January** and **March** you'll find the low at **45** and the high up to **68**. Between **April** and **June** the low goes down to **62** and the high goes up to **87**. Between **July** and **September** the low goes down to **72** and the high goes up to **90**. And finally, between the months of **October** and **December**, the low goes down to **49** and the high goes up to **75**.

HOLIDAY GOLF CLUB

100 Fairway Blvd, Panama City Beach, FL 32407 / (904) 234-1800

BASIC INFORMATION

Course Type: Semi-private
Year Built: 1968
Architect: J. Duckelery
Local Pro: Pat Lanetot

Course: N/A
Holes: 18 / Par 72

Back: 6,790 yds. Rating: 72.2 Slope: 118
Middle: 6,340 yds. Rating: 70.1 Slope: 114
Ladies: 5,803 yds. Rating: 70.1 Slope: 112

Tee Time: 5 days in advance
Price: $27.95 - $34.95

Credit Cards:	■	Restaurant:	■
Driving Range:	■	Lounge:	■
Practice Green:	■	Meeting Rooms:	
Locker Room:		Tennis:	■
Rental Clubs:	■	Swimming:	
Walkers:	■	Jogging Trails:	
Snack Bar:	■	Boating:	■

COURSE DESCRIPTION

Holiday Golf Club is a nice course that plays long from both the back and middle tees. If you feel most confident with a driver in your hand, you'll love the fact that this course will allow you to rip at the ball on most occasions off the tee. The low rough makes it easy to hit a good approach to the green.

Most of the dogleg holes can be shortened quite considerably with a good cutting drive across the corner of the dogleg. If you play these holes smart, they will allow you many oppurtunities for birdie.

The number 9 hole (par-4 / 433 yards), a dogleg right, is the hardest hole on the course.

DIRECTIONS

Take Hwy. 98 three-quarter miles east of Hwy 79.

HOMBRE GOLF CLUB

120 Coyote Pass, Panama City Beach, FL 32407 / (904) 234-3673

BASIC INFORMATION

Course Type: Semi-private
Year Built: 1989
Architect: W. Burnham
Local Pro: Steve Childree

Course: N/A
Holes: 18 / Par 72

Back: 6,820 yds. Rating: 73.4 Slope: 136
Middle: 6,063 yds. Rating: 70.3 Slope: 130
Ladies: 4,793 yds. Rating: 68.4 Slope: 119

Tee Time: 2 days in advance
Price: $49.50 for all seasons.

Credit Cards:	■	Restaurant:	■
Driving Range:	■	Lounge:	■
Practice Green:	■	Meeting Rooms:	
Locker Room:	■	Tennis:	
Rental Clubs:	■	Swimming:	
Walkers:	■	Jogging Trails:	
Snack Bar:	■	Boating:	

COURSE DESCRIPTION

The *Hombre Golf Club* is a superb course that is perfectly cared for all year long.

The dogleg right number 2 hole on this course is without question the hardest on the course. This par-4 measures an incredible 457 yards in length from tee to green. Both water and trees come into play on the right-hand side. You really have to hit an awesome drive to be in good position for the long approach shot. This hole was ranked the hardest by the players during the 1991-1992 Hogan Tour.

This course has also been used for the second stage of the PGA Tour school.

DIRECTIONS

Take Hwy. 98 over the Hathaway Bridge and stay on the right side of the Hwy. as it splits. The course will be two miles on your left.

MARRIOTT'S BAY POINT RESORT

100 Dellwood Beach Rd., Panama City, FL 32407 / (904) 234-3307

BASIC INFORMATION

Course Type: Resort
Year Built: 1986
Architect: Von Hagge / Devlin
Local Pro: Tom Weaver

Course: Legend (18 / Par 72)
Holes: 36

Back: 6,885 yds. Rating: 75.3 Slope: 152
Middle: 6,421 yds. Rating: 73.0 Slope: 148
Ladies: 4,942 yds. Rating: 69.8 Slope: 127

Tee Time: Call to confirm.
Price: $45 - $70

Credit Cards:	■	Restaurant:	■
Driving Range:	■	Lounge:	
Practice Green:	■	Meeting Rooms:	■
Locker Room:	■	Tennis:	■
Rental Clubs:	■	Swimming:	■
Walkers:		Jogging Trails:	
Snack Bar:	■	Boating:	■

COURSE DESCRIPTION

If you ever wanted to experience what it would be like to play on the PGA Tour, this course will certainly give you a taste of it.

Take a look at the slope rating from the back tees. Astonishing, isn't it? It's the second highest rating in the State of Florida. If your main concern is having a good time, play from the middle tees if your handicap is above a five.

This is an incredible layout with many brilliantly designed holes. You'll need to carry your drives long and straight for a good approach shot to the green on many of them. Good course management is the key to posting a respectable score.

DIRECTIONS

Take Hwy. 98 west of the Hathaway Bridge and go left on Thomas Dr. Make a left at Magnolia Beach and follow the signs.

CREEKSIDE GOLF CLUB

2355 W. Michigan Ave., Pensacola, FL 32506 / (904) 944-7969

BASIC INFORMATION

Course Type: Public
Year Built: 1968
Architect: N/A
Local Pro: N/A

Course: N/A
Holes: 18 / Par 72

Back: 6,130 yds. Rating: 67.8 Slope: 111
Middle: 5,655 yds. Rating: 66.1 Slope: 107
Ladies: 4,766 yds. Rating: 68.4 Slope: 115

Tee Time: 1 day in advance
Price: $11 - $14

Credit Cards:	■	Restaurant:	
Driving Range:		Lounge:	
Practice Green:	■	Meeting Rooms:	
Locker Room:		Tennis:	
Rental Clubs:	■	Swimming:	
Walkers:	■	Jogging Trails:	
Snack Bar:	■	Boating:	

COURSE DESCRIPTION

Creekside Golf Club is a good place for mid-to-high handicap players.

The course plays short at 6,130 yards from the back tees. Most of the fairways are on the wide side with minimal rough. It will take a severe hook or slice to place your ball entirely out of play.

Many birdie opportunities will come your way if you play the course aggressively. Hit your drives long and land your approach shots soft.

The dogleg right 16th hole is a Par 5 that measures 475 yards from tee to green. Water comes into play on three holes.

DIRECTIONS

Take the I-10 Exit 5 to Brent Lane west and continue on that road for four miles. Follow the signs to the course.

MARCUS POINTE GOLF CLUB

2500 Oak Pointe Dr., Pensacola, FL 32505 / (904) 484-9770

BASIC INFORMATION

Course Type: Public
Year Built: 1990
Architect: E. Stone
Local Pro: Jim Wright

Course: N/A
Holes: 18 / Par 72

Back: 6,737 yds. Rating: 72.3 Slope: 129
Middle: 6,095 yds. Rating: 69.9 Slope: 125
Ladies: 5,252 yds. Rating: 69.6 Slope: 120

Tee Time: 3 days in advance
Price: $33 - $37

Credit Cards:	■	Restaurant:	■
Driving Range:	■	Lounge:	■
Practice Green:	■	Meeting Rooms:	
Locker Room:	■	Tennis:	
Rental Clubs:	■	Swimming:	
Walkers:	■	Jogging Trails:	
Snack Bar:	■	Boating:	■

COURSE DESCRIPTION

This course is a fair challenge to a wide spectrum of golfers of differing abilities. You have to play a good solid game of golf to score well from the back tees. Most of us would be much more at home playing from the middle tees. With an average of 36 yards taken off of every hole, you can bring out your 3-wood for accuracy.

The course does allow a good margin of error off the teeing ground with its wide fairways. The rough is kept at average height.

You won't find any water on this course and most of the greens are big enough for a yardage variance of two club lengths.

DIRECTIONS

Take the I-10 Exit 3 south on Hwy. 29 for one and a half miles. Follow the signs to the course.

OSCEOLA MUNICIPAL GOLF COURSE

300 Tonawanda Dr., Pensacola, FL 32506 / (904) 456-2761

BASIC INFORMATION

Course Type: Semi-private
Year Built: 1928
Architect: N/A
Local Pro: N/A

Course: N/A
Holes: 18 / Par 72

Back: 6,498 yds. Rating: 70.0 Slope: 114
Middle: 6,284 yds. Rating: 68.6 Slope: 111
Ladies: 5,530 yds. Rating: 71.1 Slope: 115

Tee Time: 1 day in advance
Price: $13

Credit Cards:		Restaurant:	■
Driving Range:		Lounge:	■
Practice Green:	■	Meeting Rooms:	
Locker Room:	■	Tennis:	
Rental Clubs:	■	Swimming:	
Walkers:	■	Jogging Trails:	
Snack Bar:	■	Boating:	

COURSE DESCRIPTION

Osceola Municipal Golf Course is a well-balanced course with a good variety of dogleg and straight holes.

With a length of only 6,498 yards from the back tees, most average golfers should have the ability to post a good score.

The course is very playable. You'll find many trees surrounding the course and only one hole featuring water.

The 3rd hole (Par 4 / 400) is rated the hardest on the course. You have to hit your tee shot through a narrow shoot of trees onto a very narrow landing area with a lateral hazard guarding the left side. Have fun!

DIRECTIONS

Take Hwy. 90 to Fairfeild St. and go two blocks west. Follow the signs.

PERDIDO BAY RESORT

1 Doug Ford Dr., Pensacola, FL 32507 / (904) 492-1223

BASIC INFORMATION

Course Type: Resort
Year Built: 1962
Architect: Bill Amick
Local Pro: Bud Cooper

Course: N/A
Holes: 18 / Par 72

Back: 7,154 yds. Rating: 73.8 Slope: 125
Middle: 6,496 yds. Rating: 70.9 Slope: 119
Ladies: 5,476 yds. Rating: 71.4 Slope: 121

Tee Time: 2 days in advance
Price: $25 - $45

Credit Cards: ■   Restaurant:
Driving Range: ■   Lounge: ■
Practice Green: ■   Meeting Rooms: ■
Locker Room: ■   Tennis:
Rental Clubs: ■   Swimming:
Walkers: Jogging Trails:
Snack Bar: ■   Boating:

COURSE DESCRIPTION

The *Perdido Bay Resort* will delight and entertain you from the moment you step onto it.

The Pensacola Open was once a featured PGA Tour event that took place here. In fact, Curtis Strange (the two time, back-to-back, US Open winner) won his first "Tour" game here.

The 10th hole (Par-4 / 447 yards) plays the hardest on the course. You'll be facing a water hazard on your right with trees on both sides of the fairway. Try to hit your tee-shot 230 yards down the middle of the fairway. Anything further may end up in water.

DIRECTIONS

Take I-10 to exit 29 and go south on Hwy. 110. Go west on Brent Ln. and south on Hwy. 292 to Doug Ford Dr. Follow the signs to the course.

GADSDEN COUNTRY CLUB

P.O. Box 1078, Quincy, FL 32351 / (904) 627-8386

BASIC INFORMATION

Course Type: Semi-private
Year Built: 1968
Architect: J. Lee
Local Pro: John Mc.Donald

Course: N/A
Holes: 18 / Par 72

Back: 6,642 yds. Rating: 70.4 Slope: 121
Middle: 6,289 yds. Rating: 69.8 Slope: 117
Ladies: 5,398 yds. Rating: 68.9 Slope: 117

Tee Time: 7 days in advance
Price: $12 - $14

Credit Cards: ■   Restaurant: ■
Driving Range: ■   Lounge: ■
Practice Green: ■   Meeting Rooms: ■
Locker Room: ■   Tennis: ■
Rental Clubs: ■   Swimming: ■
Walkers: ■   Jogging Trails:
Snack Bar: ■   Boating:

COURSE DESCRIPTION

This is a fun and challenging course with many scenic holes. It was built on hilly terrain that features many trees bordering the wide fairways and low rough. It makes for a good driving course that will allow you many chances at birdie.

Shot placement is important because of the undulating fairways and greens. Make it your objective to play each ball to a chosen landing area. You need to set yourself up well for your approach shots to score a low number here.

The course is a wonderful challenge from all of the tees. Play from the set that will give you the hardest challenge with the most amount of fun. You won't be disappointed.

DIRECTIONS

Take Exit 26 off I-10 and go straight to the course. You'll find it on your left.

ST. JOSEPH'S BAY COUNTRY CLUB

Rt. C-30 South, Port St. Joe, FL 32456 / (904) 227-1751

BASIC INFORMATION

Course Type: Semi-private
Year Built: 1972
Architect: C. W. Roberts
Local Pro: Leonard "Bubba" Patrick

Course: N/A
Holes: 18 / Par 72

Back: 6,673 yds. Rating: N/A Slope: 119
Middle: 6,473 yds. Rating: N/A Slope: 116
Ladies: 5,234 yds. Rating: N/A Slope: 117

Tee Time: 1 day in advance
Price: $28.70

Credit Cards:	Restaurant: ■
Driving Range: ■	Lounge: ■
Practice Green: ■	Meeting Rooms:
Locker Room:	Tennis: ■
Rental Clubs: ■	Swimming: ■
Walkers:	Jogging Trails:
Snack Bar: ■	Boating: ■

COURSE DESCRIPTION

St. Joseph's Bay Country Club is a hidden gem of a golf course.

The well-balanced design makes it a pleasure to play for both low and high handicappers. Most of the locals that I have talked to emphasized the natural beauty of the course and the many different varieties of animals that have made the course their home, including hawks, eagles, deer, alligators, water birds, egrets, etc.

If you'll be playing this course during the first week of October, you can enter the Tapper Tournament. It is a three day event that benefits the Gulf Coast Jr. College in Panama City. They will be looking forward to your support.

DIRECTIONS

Take Hwy. 98 West for about six miles to Hwy. C-30. Stay left and follow the signs to the course which will be on your right side.

DOGWOODS, THE

Rt. 3, Box 954, Bonifay, FL 32425 / (904) 547-9381

BASIC INFORMATION

Course Type: Public
Year Built: N/A
Architect: N/A
Local Pro: Andy Langeley

Course: N/A
Holes: 18 / Par 72

Back: 7,042 yds. Rating: 73.5 Slope: N/A
Middle: 6,583 yds. Rating: 71.4 Slope: N/A
Ladies: 5,580 yds. Rating: 70.1 Slope: N/A

Tee Time: 1 day in advance
Price: $16 yearly

Credit Cards: ■	Restaurant:
Driving Range: ■	Lounge:
Practice Green: ■	Meeting Rooms:
Locker Room: ■	Tennis:
Rental Clubs:	Swimming:
Walkers: ■	Jogging Trails:
Snack Bar: ■	Boating:

COURSE DESCRIPTION

This course has just been recently purchased and is being renovated back to tip-top shape.

All of the tees are an inviting challenge well worth the effort. It is a long and tough challenge from the back tees. If you play golf above a 10 handicap, consider playing from the middle tees for the most amount of fun.

The fairways are of average width and the rough is kept low to allow for aggressive play off the tee. You need not be long if you can keep the ball on a straight path. That is, of course, if the fluctuating weather patterns permit. The course is in great shape!

DIRECTIONS

Take I-10 Exit 17 to Bonifay. The course will be about six miles northwest of Bonifay on Hwy. 117. Follow the signs to the course.

HILAMAN PARK MUNICIPAL GOLF COURSE

2737 Blairstone Rd., Tallahassee, FL 32301 / (904) 891-3935

BASIC INFORMATION

Course Type: Public
Year Built: 1974
Architect: E. Packard
Local Pro: Bill Zimmer

Course: N/A
Holes: 18 / Par 72

Back: 6,364 yds. Rating: 70.1 Slope: 121
Middle: 6,017 yds. Rating: 68.5 Slope: 118
Ladies: 5,365 yds. Rating: 70.8 Slope: 116

Tee Time: 7 days in advance
Price: $10.70 - $14.98

Credit Cards:	■	Restaurant:	■
Driving Range:	■	Lounge:	■
Practice Green:	■	Meeting Rooms:	
Locker Room:	■	Tennis:	■
Rental Clubs:	■	Swimming:	■
Walkers:	■	Jogging Trails:	
Snack Bar:	■	Boating:	■

COURSE DESCRIPTION

Hilaman Park Municipal Golf Course is a local favorite in Leon County. You have to play a good game with your iron shots to post a low number.

One of the most challenging holes on the course is the number 2. It is a par-4 that measures 410 yards from the back tees and doglegs to the left. From the tee, you'll have to hit your drive onto a landing area about 230 yards out, on the left side of the left-to-right sloping fairway. Your approach shot will be played to a huge green that measures approximately 15,000 sq. ft. If you don't get the ball close to the pin, you'll have a long two-putt to complete the hole.

DIRECTIONS

Exit Hwy. 319 South from I-10 and go south to Hwy. 27. Go west to Blairstone Rd. and south to the course.

KILLEARN COUNTRY CLUB & INN

100 Tyron Circle, Tallahassee, FL 32308 / (904) 893-2186

BASIC INFORMATION

Course Type: Semi-Private/Private
Year Built: 1967
Architect: B. Amick
Local Pro: Kevin Gabard

Course: South & East (18 / Par 72)
Holes: 27

Back: 7,025 yds. Rating: 73.9 Slope: 133
Middle: 6,412 yds. Rating: 71.0 Slope: 126
Ladies: 5,661 yds. Rating: 73.0 Slope: 123

Tee Time: 7 days in advance
Price: $30-35

Credit Cards:	■	Restaurant:	■
Driving Range:	■	Lounge:	■
Practice Green:	■	Meeting Rooms:	■
Locker Room:	■	Tennis:	■
Rental Clubs:	■	Swimming:	■
Walkers:	■	Jogging Trails:	
Snack Bar:	■	Boating:	

COURSE DESCRIPTION

The Sprint Classic, one of the most exciting tournaments on the PGA Tour, is played here each year. The back tees are an awesome challenge at 7,025 yards. Play from the white tees if you're above a single digit handicapper. You'll need the reduced yardage to place your drives in good position for your approach shots to the greens.

This scenic course features some of the most beautiful holes you'll ever see. The layout is one that needs to be studied in advance to play well. The total make-up of the course will drive you to play the best that you can. You'll love the type of golf that this place has to offer.

DIRECTIONS

Exit Hwy. 319 off I-10 and go north to Killearney Way and east to Shamrock. Go west and follow the signs to the course.

SEMINOLE GOLF COURSE & CLUB

2550 Pottsdamer Rd., Tallahassee, FL 32304 / (904) 644-2582

BASIC INFORMATION

Course Type: Public
Year Built: 1960
Architect: B. Amick
Local Pro: Kent Smith

Course: N/A
Holes: 18 / Par 72

Back: 7,035 yds. Rating: 73.4 Slope: 129
Middle: 6,500 yds. Rating: 71.0 Slope: 125
Ladies: 5,930 yds. Rating: 73.0 Slope: 111

Tee Time: 7 days in advance
Price: $20 - $25

Credit Cards:	■	Restaurant:	■
Driving Range:	■	Lounge:	■
Practice Green:	■	Meeting Rooms:	
Locker Room:	■	Tennis:	
Rental Clubs:	■	Swimming:	
Walkers:	■	Jogging Trails:	
Snack Bar:	■	Boating:	■

COURSE DESCRIPTION

This is just one of many brilliantly designed courses by William W. Amick. He has a special way of building his courses so that they are fun and challenging for both the amateur and the professional caliber player.

The **Seminole Golf Course & Club** is set on the highest point of Tallahassee. Unpredictable winds are often a factor that you'll have to deal with. Keep the ball on a low trajectory when the wind is playing towards you and from side-to-side. Take advantage of the wind when it is blowing behind you - you'll gain a considerable amount of distance. Water only comes into play on two holes.

DIRECTIONS

Exit Airport - Capital Circle off I-10 and go south. The road will turn into Lake Bradford Rd. Look for it on your left.

WILLISTON HIGHLANDS COUNTRY CLUB

Rt. 2, Box 1590, Williston, FL 32696 / (352) 528-2520

BASIC INFORMATION

Course Type: Semi-private
Year Built: 1969
Architect: N/A
Manager: Joanne Stuart

Course: N/A
Holes: 18 / Par 72

Back: 6,695 yds. Rating: 70.7 Slope: 120
Middle: 6,298 yds. Rating: 69.3 Slope: 121
Ladies: 5,572 yds. Rating: 71.0 Slope: 118

Tee Time: 1 day in advance
Price: $16 - $22

Credit Cards:		Restaurant:	
Driving Range:	■	Lounge:	■
Practice Green:	■	Meeting Rooms:	■
Locker Room:	■	Tennis:	■
Rental Clubs:	■	Swimming:	■
Walkers:	■	Jogging Trails:	
Snack Bar:	■	Boating:	■

COURSE DESCRIPTION

Williston Highlands Country Club is a scenic course with a healthy variety of wildlife. The course is a fair challenge to all. It makes for a great place to play aggressive golf with minimum punishment. If you're not accustomed to this type of play, you'll have to take chances on the course to post a low number. It makes for a great way to learn how to play golf aggressively.

Try to focus on the layout of each of the holes in advance and ask yourself how you should go about playing them. Stick to your game plan and learn from your results.

The course is void of water but is waiting for you to take some chances.

DIRECTIONS

Exit Hwy. 121 off I-75 and go west for about six miles. The course will be on your right.

BLUEWATER BAY

P.O. Box 247, Niceville, FL 32578 / (904) 897-3241

BASIC INFORMATION

Course Type: Resort
Year Built: 1981
Architect: T. Fazio / J. Pate
Local Pro: David Trimm

Course: Marsh / Magnolia (18 / Par 72)
Holes: 36

Back: 6,622 yds. Rating: 73.0 Slope: 140
Middle: 6,311 yds. Rating: 70.0 Slope: 134
Ladies: 5,778 yds. Rating: 70.6 Slope: 124

Tee Time: 5 days in advance
Price: $35

Credit Cards:	■	Restaurant:	■
Driving Range:	■	Lounge:	■
Practice Green:	■	Meeting Rooms:	■
Locker Room:	■	Tennis:	■
Rental Clubs:	■	Swimming:	■
Walkers:	■	Jogging Trails:	■
Snack Bar:	■	Boating:	■

COURSE DESCRIPTION

Bluewater Bay is home to 36 holes of pure golfing pleasure. All three (9-hole) courses are fine examples of modern golf architecture.

The Marsh / Magnolia combination is a phenomenal challenge that should only be played by single digit handicap players for the ultimate test. The 140 slope rating is far too much for the average golfer. Please play from the middle tees if your handicap is above 10. The slope rating from here at 134 is still very high.

Tom Fazio and Steve Pate have laid their signatures to some of the finest holes that this country has to offer.

DIRECTIONS

Take Hwy. 85 to Niceville and go east at Hwy. 20 for about three-and-a-half miles. Follow the signs to the course.

FOXWOOD COUNTRY CLUB

4927 Antioch Rd., Crestview, FL 32536 / (904) 682-2012

BASIC INFORMATION

Course Type: Semi-private
Year Built: 1954
Architect: N/A
Local Pro: N/A

Course: N/A
Holes: 72

Back: 6,210 yds. Rating: N/A Slope: N/A
Middle: 6,000 yds. Rating: N/A Slope: N/A
Ladies: 5,125 yds. Rating: N/A Slope: N/A

Tee Time: 1 day in advance
Price: $22 yearly

Credit Cards:	■	Restaurant:	
Driving Range:	■	Lounge:	■
Practice Green:	■	Meeting Rooms:	■
Locker Room:	■	Tennis:	■
Rental Clubs:	■	Swimming:	■
Walkers:	■	Jogging Trails:	■
Snack Bar:	■	Boating:	

COURSE DESCRIPTION

Foxwood Country Club is a straightforward course that would be most enjoyed by the average weekend golfer rather than the scratch player who plays the game on a day-to-day basis.

The number one rated handicap hole on this course is the 15th hole. It's a par-4 that measures 390 yards from the back tees to the green. From the tee you'll be facing water on your right with trees coming into play on both sides of the fairway. You'll also have to watch out for the fairway bunker on the right. Water comes into play on eight holes.

DIRECTIONS

Take the I-10 Exit Hwy. 85 south and make a west on PJ Adams Pkwy. Rd. The course will be four miles on your right.

FT. WALTON BEACH MUNICIPAL GOLF COURSE
P.O. Box 4009, Ft. Walton Beach, FL 32549 / (904) 862-3314

BASIC INFORMATION

Course Type: Municipal
Year Built: 1962
Architect: B. Amick
Local Pro: David Smith

Course: The Pines (18 / Par 72)
Holes: 36

Back: 6,583 yds. Rating: 69.9 Slope: 110
Middle: 6,083 yds. Rating: 67.7 Slope: 105
Ladies: 5,300 yds. Rating: 64.1 Slope: 98

Tee Time: 1 day in advance
Price: $15

Credit Cards:		Restaurant:	
Driving Range:	■	Lounge:	
Practice Green:	■	Meeting Rooms:	■
Locker Room:		Tennis:	
Rental Clubs:	■	Swimming:	
Walkers:	■	Jogging Trails:	
Snack Bar:	■	Boating:	■

COURSE DESCRIPTION

The *Ft. Walton Beach Municipal Golf Course* has been kept in great shape. It is an exceptionally challenging design that will keep you on your toes.

The fairways are wide and allow a good amount of roll. The rough is cut low in the winter months and a little higher during the summer. You'll find bunkers coming into play on every hole and water coming into play on four.

The slight dogleg right 4th hole is the number one handicap hole on the course. It is a par-4 that measures 416 yards from tee to green. Watch for the out-of-bounds that comes into play on the right side.

DIRECTIONS

Take Hwy. 98 and go north on Hwy. 189 (Louis Turner Blvd.). Follow the road and you'll see the course on your right side.

INDIAN BAYOU GOLF & COUNTRY CLUB
P.O. Box 306, Destin, FL 32541 / (904) 837-6191

BASIC INFORMATION

Course Type: Semi-private
Year Built: 1978
Architect: E. Stone
Local Pro: Jim Carpenter

Course: Seminole / Creek (18 / Par 72)
Holes: 27

Back: 7,016 yds. Rating: 73.7 Slope: 128
Middle: 6,286 yds. Rating: 69.1 Slope: 117
Ladies: 5,081 yds. Rating: 69.2 Slope: 115

Tee Time: 30 days in advance
Price: $32 - $42

Credit Cards:	■	Restaurant:	■
Driving Range:	■	Lounge:	■
Practice Green:	■	Meeting Rooms:	■
Locker Room:	■	Tennis:	
Rental Clubs:	■	Swimming:	
Walkers:	■	Jogging Trails:	
Snack Bar:	■	Boating:	■

COURSE DESCRIPTION

This is a challenging and diverse course. The Seminole / Creek combination is the course of choice among the better players. It is a long layout with open fairways and large undulating greens.

Although the course places a great amount of emphasis on hitting the ball long and accurate off the tee, your putting game will surely be put to the test too. With the greens being as large as they are, you'll often be faced with a long two putt for par.

This is a unique course that is kept in meticulous shape.

DIRECTIONS

Take Hwy. 98 east and go north on Airport Rd. You'll see a sign about 75 yards away on your right. Follow it to the course.

SANDESTIN BEACH RESORT

Emerald Coast Pkwy., Destin, FL 32541 / (904) 267-8144

BASIC INFORMATION

Course Type: Resort
Year Built: 1989
Architect: T. Jackson
Local Pro: Bruce Gerlander

Course: Troon & Dunes (18 / Par 72)
Holes: 45

Back: 7,196 yds. Rating: 73.9 Slope: 126
Middle: 6,544 yds. Rating: 71.7 Slope: 121
Ladies: 5,158 yds. Rating: 69.1 Slope: 115

Tee Time: 2 days in advance
Price: $35 - $70

Credit Cards:	■	Restaurant:	■
Driving Range:	■	Lounge:	■
Practice Green:	■	Meeting Rooms:	■
Locker Room:		Tennis:	■
Rental Clubs:	■	Swimming:	■
Walkers:		Jogging Trails:	■
Snack Bar:	■	Boating:	■

COURSE DESCRIPTION

The golfing here is spectacular. I like the way Tom Jackson designed this course to be playable for both the beginner and the professional.

One would think that a course of this length from the back tees would post a much higher slope rating. The reason for this is simple. Most of the fairways are wide and open with the rough cut low. This allows golfers to play aggressively from the tee with a chance to save par even from the rough. The course definitely favors long hitters.

The *Sandestin Beach Resort* plays host to the Ladies Florida Amateurs.

DIRECTIONS

Take Hwy. 98 and go east of Destin approximately six miles. Follow the signs to the course.

SEASCAPE RESORT

100 Seascape Dr. / Destin, Fl. 32541 / (904) 654-7888

BASIC INFORMATION

Course Type: Resort
Year Built: 1972
Architect: J. Lee
Local Pro: Mark Zachery

Course: N/A
Holes: 18 / Par 72

Back: 6,500 yds. Rating: 71.5 Slope: 120
Middle: 6,090 yds. Rating: 69.7 Slope: 116
Ladies: 5,379 yds. Rating: 70.3 Slope: 113

Tee Time: 1 day in advance
Price: $32 - $52

Credit Cards:	■	Restaurant:	
Driving Range:	■	Lounge:	
Practice Green:	■	Meeting Rooms:	■
Locker Room:		Tennis:	■
Rental Clubs:	■	Swimming:	■
Walkers:	■	Jogging Trails:	
Snack Bar:	■	Boating:	■

COURSE DESCRIPTION

Don't forget to bring your life-jacket to the *Seascape Resort.* With water coming into play on every hole, accuracy is at a premium.

The course does play a lot differently from the middle tees. With 410 yards taken off in distance, your chances of getting a birdie will vastly improve.

Your course management skills will play an important part in scoring low numbers. Think of each hole individually and how you would like to play them. Many holes will be better played with a 3-wood off the tee rather than a driver. Play the course with your mind rather than your ego.

DIRECTIONS

Take Hwy. 98 east and follow the signs to the course.

SHALIMAR POINTE GOLF & COUNTRY CLUB

2 Country Club Rd., Shalimar, FL 32579 / (904) 651-1416

BASIC INFORMATION

Course Type: Semi-private
Year Built: 1986
Architect: J. Finger & Associates
Local Pro: Craig Champlain

Course: N/A
Holes: 18 / Par 72

Back: 6,765 yds. Rating: 72.9 Slope: 125
Middle: 6,470 yds. Rating: 71.6 Slope: 122
Ladies: 5,427 yds. Rating: 70.7 Slope: 115

Tee Time: 2 days in advance
Price: $20 - $35

Credit Cards:	■	Restaurant:	
Driving Range:	■	Lounge:	■
Practice Green:	■	Meeting Rooms:	
Locker Room:	■	Tennis:	■
Rental Clubs:	■	Swimming:	■
Walkers:		Jogging Trails:	
Snack Bar:	■	Boating:	■

COURSE DESCRIPTION

Shalimar Pointe Golf & Country Club has hosted events such as the U.S. Amateur Qualifiers and the Emerald Coast Tour.

This is a quality course at an unbelievable price. It is well-rounded, and allows you to approach each hole from more than just one obligatory way. Many modern course designs force you to play each hole in one particular path or suffer the consequences.

It's nice to know that some designers are conscious of that fact and decide not to follow those patterns in their layouts. The golf here is very enjoyable and the people are truly friendly.

DIRECTIONS

Go north on Hwy. 85 over the Shalimar Bridge. Go right at the second light and right at Old Ferry Rd. Make a left at Meigs St. and follow the signs to the course

SHOAL RIVER GOLF & COUNTRY CLUB

Rt. 2, Box 325, Crestview, FL 32536 / (904) 689-1111

BASIC INFORMATION

Course Type: Semi-private
Year Built: 1986
Architect: D. Benett
Local Pro: Darren Stubbs

Course: N/A
Holes: 18 / Par 72

Back: 6,782 yds. Rating: 73.5 Slope: 136
Middle: 6,237 yds. Rating: 70.4 Slope: 126
Ladies: 5,183 yds. Rating: 70.3 Slope: 124

Tee Time: 3 days in advance
Price: $30

Credit Cards:	■	Restaurant:	■
Driving Range:		Lounge:	■
Practice Green:	■	Meeting Rooms:	■
Locker Room:	■	Tennis:	■
Rental Clubs:	■	Swimming:	■
Walkers:	■	Jogging Trails:	
Snack Bar:	■	Boating:	■

COURSE DESCRIPTION

Shoal River Golf & Country Club plays hard and accurate from the back tees.

The 10th hole is the number one rated handicap hole on the course. This double dogleg hole measures 532 yards from tee to green. Water comes into play in front of the tee and you'll find the out-of-bounds area on your left inside of the trees.

You'll have to hit your tee shot at least 175 yards to a landing area on the left side of the fairway. This allows you a good angle to bite off the second dogleg (right) and set yourself up for your approach shot to the middle of the green.

DIRECTIONS

Take the I-10 exit to Hwy. 85 and go south for approximately one mile. Make a left at Live Oak Church Rd. The course will be on your right.

FRANK W. DAHLINGER GOLF COURSE

NAS Whiting Field, Milton, FL 32570 / (904) 623-7348

BASIC INFORMATION

Course Type: Semi-private
Year Built: N/A
Architect: N/A
Local Pro: Henry Bono

Course: N/A
Holes: 18 / Par 72

Back: 7,035 yds. Rating: 72.0 Slope: 124
Middle: 6,625 yds. Rating: N/A Slope: N/A
Ladies: 5,245 yds. Rating: N/A Slope: N/A

Tee Time: 1 day in advance
Price: $8 - $15

Credit Cards:	■	Restaurant:	■
Driving Range:	■	Lounge:	■
Practice Green:	■	Meeting Rooms:	
Locker Room:	■	Tennis:	
Rental Clubs:	■	Swimming:	
Walkers:	■	Jogging Trails:	
Snack Bar:	■	Boating:	

COURSE DESCRIPTION

Playing golf at the *Frank W. Dahlinger Golf Course* is both challenging and fun.

The course plays long and demanding from the back tees. The solid layout does give you the opportunity to play the ball long off the tee with minimal worry. The fairways are on the wide side and the rough is cut low.

The middle tees are a great challenge for handicaps above 15. With the length of the course shortened 410 yards, players will have a greater chance of making birdie and posting a good 18 hole score.

The 16th hole (Par 5 / 605 yards) is the hardest rated hole on the course. Look out for the hills on both sides of the fairway.

DIRECTIONS

Take Hwy. 90 to Hwy. 87 and go north until you see the NAS Whiting Field sign. Follow the signs to the course.

HIDDEN CREEK, THE CLUB AT

3070 PGA Blvd., Navarre, FL 32566 / (904) 939-4604

BASIC INFORMATION

Course Type: Semi-private
Year Built: 1988
Architect: R. Garl
Local Pro: John Childs

Course: N/A
Holes: 18 / Par 72

Back: 6,862 yds. Rating: 73.2 Slope: 139
Middle: 6,287 yds. Rating: 70.6 Slope: 133
Ladies: 5,213 yds. Rating: 70.1 Slope: 124

Tee Time: 3 days in advance
Price: $25 - $41.50

Credit Cards:	■	Restaurant:	■
Driving Range:	■	Lounge:	■
Practice Green:	■	Meeting Rooms:	■
Locker Room:	■	Tennis:	
Rental Clubs:	■	Swimming:	
Walkers:		Jogging Trails:	
Snack Bar:	■	Boating:	■

COURSE DESCRIPTION

This course is a tremendous challenge from both the back and middle tees.

The fairways are on the narrow side and only the most accurate drives will stay in the middle of the landing area. You'll find this description to be true on most of the course. Posting a good score means having to drive the ball long and accurate throughout the day. Practice hitting your 3-wood and 1-4 irons. Many of the approach shots will force you to play one of these clubs from a long distance.

Many events, including the U.S. Open qualifier, have been played here.

DIRECTIONS

Take Hwy. 98 to the main entrance at Holly-By-Sea. Follow the signs to the course.

TANGLEWOOD GOLF & COUNTRY CLUB
P.O. Box 725, Milton, FL 32572 / (904) 623-6176

BASIC INFORMATION

Course Type: Semi-private
Year Built: 1965
Architect: N/A
Local Pro: Terry Gandy

Course: N/A
Holes: 18 / Par 72

Back: 6,311 yds. Rating: 70.0 Slope: 115
Middle: 6,414 yds. Rating: 68.6 Slope: 112
Ladies: 5,269 yds. Rating: 69.9 Slope: 118

Tee Time: 7 days in advance
Price: $15 - $18

Credit Cards:	■	Restaurant:	
Driving Range:	■	Lounge:	■
Practice Green:	■	Meeting Rooms:	■
Locker Room:	■	Tennis:	■
Rental Clubs:	■	Swimming:	■
Walkers:	■	Jogging Trails:	
Snack Bar:	■	Boating:	

COURSE DESCRIPTION

Tanglewood Golf & Country Club is a well-rounded golf course with many competitive holes.

If your game has faltered and you need to work on your basics to build your confidence back up, this may be the course to change your game around.

The main challenge on this course is to keep the ball in play off the tee. If you can master that, you'll often find yourself in good position for a mid-to-low iron shot to the green. These situations can often lead you into a birdie with a good solid shot from the fairway.

DIRECTIONS

Take I-10 to Hwy. 87 and go north to Milton. Go west on Hwy. 191 and the course will be about two miles further.

TIGER POINT GOLF & COUNTRY CLUB
1255 Country Club Rd., Gulf Breeze, FL 32561 / (904) 932-1333

BASIC INFORMATION

Course Type: Semi-private
Year Built: 1983
Architect: J. Pate
Local Pro: T. J. Young

Course: East (18 / Par 72)
Holes: 36

Back: 7,033 yds. Rating: 73.9 Slope: 145
Middle: 6,621 yds. Rating: 72.0 Slope: 141
Ladies: 5,209 yds. Rating: 70.3 Slope: 132

Tee Time: 4 days in advance
Price: $38 - $45

Credit Cards:	■	Restaurant:	■
Driving Range:	■	Lounge:	■
Practice Green:	■	Meeting Rooms:	■
Locker Room:	■	Tennis:	■
Rental Clubs:	■	Swimming:	■
Walkers:	■	Jogging Trails:	
Snack Bar:	■	Boating:	■

COURSE DESCRIPTION

If you're looking for an ultimate challenge that will rival any course on the PGA Tour, *Tiger Point East* is it.

With an awesome slope rating of 145, you'd better have all of the elements of your game in top form.

Here is an example of what you can look forward to. The number 6 hole (Par-4 / 470 yards) is one of the hardest holes on the course. You'll often be playing the hole into prevailing winds that gust out of the intracoastal and the Gulf. Water comes into play on both sides of the fairway. The green is small and demands a soft landing fade.

The 1988 Pensacola Open was played here.

DIRECTIONS

Take Hwy. 98 east of Gulf Breeze and follow the signs to the course.

SANTA ROSA GOLF & BEACH CLUB
Rt. 1, Box 450, Santa Rosa Beach, FL 32459 / (904) 267-2229

BASIC INFORMATION

Course Type: Semi-private
Year Built: 1971
Architect: T. Jackson
Local Pro: Vicki Mc.Clurg

Course: N/A
Holes: 18 (Par 72)

Back: 6,439 yds. Rating: 70.7 Slope: 127
Middle: 6,058 yds. Rating: 68.6 Slope: 113
Ladies: 4,904 yds. Rating: 67.4 Slope: 110

Tee Time: 3 days in advance
Price: $30 - $43

Credit Cards:	■	Restaurant:	■
Driving Range:	■	Lounge:	■
Practice Green:	■	Meeting Rooms:	■
Locker Room:	■	Tennis:	■
Rental Clubs:	■	Swimming:	
Walkers:	■	Jogging Trails:	
Snack Bar:	■	Boating:	■

COURSE DESCRIPTION

This challenging design plays beautifully from beginning to end.

Part of the attraction on this course is the northern type feel that you get as you play through the wide expanse of trees. Three holes in particular (3,4, & 5) capture stunning views of the Gulf.

You'll love the way the course flows through its natural surroundings without a home or condo in sight.

If you've been searching for an interesting, exciting course, this is the one for you.

DIRECTIONS

Take Hwy. 98 south to Hwy. 393 and make a right on Hwy. 30A. You can follow the signs from this point to the course.

SUNNY HILLS COUNTRY CLUB
1150 Country Club Blvd., Sunny Hills, FL 32428 / (904) 773-3619

BASIC INFORMATION

Course Type: Public
Year Built: 1974
Architect: Denton & Associates
Local Pro: J. Sayers / K. Venturi

Course: N/A
Holes: 18 / Par 72

Back: 7,250 yds. Rating: 71.6 Slope: 113
Middle: 6,821 yds. Rating: 70.3 Slope: 111
Ladies: 5,755 yds. Rating: 76.2 Slope: 123

Tee Time: 7 days in advance
Price: $15 - $22

Credit Cards:	■	Restaurant:	■
Driving Range:	■	Lounge:	
Practice Green:	■	Meeting Rooms:	
Locker Room:	■	Tennis:	■
Rental Clubs:	■	Swimming:	
Walkers:	■	Jogging Trails:	
Snack Bar:	■	Boating:	■

COURSE DESCRIPTION

Sunny Hills Country Club plays long and true. At 7,250 yards from the championship tees, a lot of pressure will be placed on the length of your tee shots.

I find it quite interesting that a course of this length could post such a friendly slope rating of 113.

How could that be possible? Everything on this course appears larger than life. The fairways are wide with minimal rough and most of the greens are large enough for a 3 to 4 iron variance. Get into your zone and play this course aggressively from beginning to end. You'll have the time of your life.

DIRECTIONS

Take I-10 to Hwy. 77 and go south. The course will be about 20 miles further down the road.

BAY

Edgewater Beach Resort Golf Course
(904) 2354044
11212 Front Beach Rd., Panama City
Local Pro: N/A
Reciprocal Play: No

Panama City Country Club
(904) 265-2911
100 Country Club Dr., Lynn Haven
Local Pro: Doug Quilling
Reciprocal Play: No

ESCAMBIA

Monsanto Golf Course
(904) 968-8406
2365 Chemstrand Rd., Gonzalez
Green Cove Springs
Local Pro: Tom Werner
Reciprocal Play: No

Pensacola Country Club
(904) 455-1488
1500 Bayshore Dr., Pansacola
Local Pro: Charles Hendley
Reciprocal Play: Yes

LEON

Capital City Country Club
(904) 224-1815
1601 Golf Terrace Dr., Tallahassee
Local Pro: John Berry
Reciprocal Play: Yes

Golden Eagle Country Club
(904) 668-1071
3700 Golden Eagle Dr., Tallahassee
Local Pro: Tim Lawson
Reciprocal Play: Yes (Local)

Killearn Country Club & Inn
(904) 893-2144
100 Tyron Circle, Tallahassee
Local Pro: Keven Gabbard
Reciprocal Play: Yes

MADISON

Madison Country Club
(904) 973-6701
Country Club Rd., Madison
Local Pro: Lee Posack
Reciprocal Play: Yes

OKALOOSA

Rocky Bayou Golf & Country Club
(904) 678-3217
Country Club Dr., Niceville
Local Pro: N/A
Reciprocal Play: No

INDEX
(Private Courses appear in *italics*)

FROM THE AUTHOR

You know my Top Ten picks for each of Florida's seven regions, but I'd like to hear your opinion. Please send me your top three Florida golf choices, or more if you're so inclined, so I can see which courses you enjoy the most. Your input will help make future editions the best they can be. And if you disagree with one of my selections, I'd be interested in hearing that too.

FROM THE PUBLISHER

Our goal is to provide you with a guide book that is second to none. Please bear in mind, however, that things change: phone numbers, prices, addresses, etc. Should you come across any new information, we'd appreciate hearing from you. No item is too small for us, so if you have any recommendations or suggested changes, please write. The address is:

Jimmy Shacky
c/o Open Road Publishing
P.O. Box 20226
Columbus Circle Station
New York, NY 10023